Benchmark Papers
in Animal Behavior

Series Editor: Martin W. Schein
West Virginia University

PUBLISHED VOLUMES

HORMONES AND SEXUAL BEHAVIOR
Carol Sue Carter
TERRITORY
Allen W. Stokes
SOCIAL HIERARCHY AND DOMINANCE
Martin W. Schein
EXTERNAL CONSTRUCTION BY ANIMALS
Nicholas E. Collias and Elsie C. Collias
PSYCHOPHYSIOLOGY
Stephen W. Porges and Michael G. H. Coles
SOUND RECEPTION IN FISHES
William N. Tavolga

VOLUMES IN PREPARATION

IMPRINTING
E. H. Hess
PLAY
Dietland Müller-Schwarze
PARENTAL BEHAVIOR IN BIRDS
Rae Silver
VERTEBRATE SOCIAL ORGANIZATION
Edwin M. Banks
THERMOREGULATION
Evelyn Satinoff

Benchmark Papers
in Animal Behavior / 7

A BENCHMARK® Books Series

SOUND RECEPTION
IN FISHES

Edited by

WILLIAM N. TAVOLGA
City University of New York
and
American Museum of Natural History

Dowden, Hutchinson
& Ross, Inc.

STROUDSBURG, PENNSYLVANIA

Distributed by

HALSTED
PRESS

A Division of
John Wiley & Sons, Inc.

LIBRARY OF CONGRESS CATALOGING IN PUBLICATION DATA
Main entry under title:
Sound reception in fishes
   (Benchmark papers in animal behavior/7)
   Includes references and indexes.
   1. Hearing.   2. Sense-organs—Fishes. I. Tavolga, William N., 1922–
QL639.1.S66   597'.01'82508   76-13525
ISBN 0-87933-239-5

Exclusive Distributor: **Halsted Press**
A Division of John Wiley & Sons, Inc.
ISBN: 0-470-98907-6

PERMISSIONS

The following papers have been reprinted or translated with permission of the authors and copyright holders.

ACADEMIC PRESS, INC.—*Fish Physiology*
   Sound Production and Detection

ACOUSTICAL SOCIETY OF AMERICA—*Journal of the Acoustical Society of America*
   Evidence That the Lateral-Line Organ Responds to Near-Field Displacements of Sound
      Sources in Water
   Sound Detection and Processing by Teleost Fishes

AMERICAN MUSEUM OF NATURAL HISTORY—*Bulletin of the American Museum of Natural
      History*
   Auditory Capacities in Fishes: Pure Tone Thresholds in Nine Species of Marine Teleosts

BIRKHAUSER VERLAG—*Experientia*
   Über die Reizung des Ferntastsinnes bei Fischen und Amphibien

W. JUNK—*Physiologia Comparata et Oecologia*
   Untersuchungen über die Funktionen des Ohrlabyrinths bei Meeresfischen

MACMILLAN (JOURNALS) LTD.—*Nature*
   The Sense of Hearing in Fish

SPRINGER-VERLAG—*Zeitschrift fuer Vergleichende Physiologie*
   Die absoluten Hörschwellen des Zwergwelses (*Amiurus nebulosus*) und Beiträge zur Physik
      des Weberschen Apparates der Ostariophysen
   Können Fische die Schallrichtung wahrnehmen?
   Neue Versuche über das Tonunterscheidungsvermögen der Elritze

VEB GEORG THIEME—*Biologisches Zentralblatt*
   Ein Zwergwels, der kommt, wenn man ihm pfeift

SERIES EDITOR'S FOREWORD

Not many years ago virtually all research publications dealing with animal behavior could be housed within the covers of a few hardbound volumes that were easily accessible to the few workers in the field. Times have changed. Present-day students of animal behavior have all they can do to keep abreast of developments within their own area of special interest, let alone in the field as a whole.

It was even fewer years ago that those who taught animal behavior courses could easily choose a suitable textbook from among the few available; all "covered" the field, according to the bias of the author. Students working on a special project used *the* text and *the* journal as reference sources, and for the most part successfully covered their assigned topics. Times have indeed changed. Today's teacher of animal behavior is confronted with a bewildering array of books to choose among, some purporting to be all-encompassing, others confessing to strictly delimited coverage, and still others professing to be collections of recent and important writings.

In response to the problem of the steadily increasing and overwhelming volume of information in the area, the Benchmark Papers in Animal Behavior was launched as a series of single topic volumes designed to be some things to some people. Each volume contains a collection of what an expert considers to be the significant research papers in a given topic area. Each volume serves several purposes. For teachers, a Benchmark volume serves as a supplement to other written materials assigned to students; it permits in-depth consideration of a particular topic while confronting students (often for the first time) with original research papers of outstanding quality. For researchers, a Benchmark volume saves countless hours of digging through the various journals to find the basic articles in their area of interest; often the journals are not easily available. For students, a Benchmark volume provides a readily accessible set of original papers on the topic in question, a set that forms the core of the more extensive bibliography that they are likely to compile; it also permits them to see at first hand what an "expert" thinks is important in the area and to react accordingly. Finally, for librarians, a Benchmark volume represents a collection of important papers from many diverse sources that makes readily available materials that might otherwise not be economically possible to obtain or physically possible to keep in stock.

The choice of topics to be covered in this series is no small matter. Each of us could come up with a long list of possible topics and then search for potential volume editors. Alternatively, we could draw up long lists of recognized and prominent scholars and try to persuade them to do a volume on a topic of their choice. For the most part, I have followed a mix of both approaches: match a distinguished researcher with a desired topic, and the results should be outstanding. And so it is with the present volume.

Dr. Tavolga was one of the early workers in the area of acoustics and behavior in fishes and is still actively engaged in such studies. His extensive research and publications over the years have earned for him an international reputation in the field of behavior. Few persons would have been as qualified to undertake a Benchmark project on acoustics in fishes. He has wisely elected to cover this topic in two volumes: the present one on sound reception and a companion volume on sound production in fish. Taken singly or together, these volumes admirably reflect the basic philosophy underlying the Benchmark Series, that of tracing the development of ideas through a confrontation with the original literature.

MARTIN W. SCHEIN

PREFACE

The notion that fish, or any aquatic animal, could hear sounds seemed to be impossible to accept through much of the history of biology. The superb exercise in functional anatomy by Ernst Weber in 1820 failed to convince many biologists, and even a century later, unequivocal conclusions were still drawn that fish were quite deaf. This was in spite of the work of such eminent scientists as G. H. Parker and Karl von Frisch. The acoustic function of the ossicles that bear Weber's name was still being argued a hundred years after his elegant illustrations were published.

Currently, the problems under investigation are far beyond those of the 1920s and 1930s in focussing upon the aspects of fish audition that are uniquely adapted to the water medium. Directional hearing and frequency discrimination are among the auditory properties considered. How is it possible to accomplish frequency analysis without a cochlea and basilar membrane? How is directional hearing accomplished? By the lateral line? The inner ear? The swim bladder?

In keeping with the concept of the Benchmark Series, examples were chosen that represent major advances in the study of fish audition, beginning with the classic Weber work of 1820, and ending with the interdisciplinary report by Harris and van Bergeijk of 1962, through which many aquatic biologists first began to appreciate the science of acoustics.

I am indebted to Dr. Lester R. Aronson, Department of Animal Behavior, American Museum of Natural History, for making available the translations of several of the articles reprinted here. The translations of the von Frisch papers were all done under the direction of G. K. Noble, who founded the department and established the concept of experimental research as being appropriate in a museum. In addition, he managed to use the work force made available to him under the WPA (of depression days) to its maximum productivity, finding personnel with foreign language skills to translate hundreds of papers of importance in animal behavior and natural history in general. It is unfortunate that the names of the translators were not included, and the work must remain anonymous.

The later translations included here were done by my former assistant and secretary, Mrs. Brigitte Cappelli, and by Dr. Helmut E. Adler, of the American Museum and Yeshiva University.

Preface

    Mr. G. Robert Adlington, of the Department of Invertebrates, American Museum, made the photographic reproductions of the figures from Weber's 1820 book. This volume, one of the few still in existence, had undergone some water damage, and through skillful retouching, Mr. Adlington managed to restore the original clarity to these beautifully precise drawings. This volume, along with other services, was made available through the cooperation of the library at the American Museum—certainly one of the finest of its kind in the world.

    I am also grateful to Miss Donna Johnson, of the Mote Marine Laboratory, Sarasota, Florida, for her careful typing of the translations reproduced here, and also to Dr. Perry W. Gilbert, Director of the Mote Marine Laboratory, for the loan of the reprints of papers by G. H. Parker.

WILLIAM N. TAVOLGA

CONTENTS

Contents

PART IV: HEARING MECHANISMS AND PSYCHOPHYSICS

PART V: DIRECTIONAL HEARING AND THE LATERAL LINE

CONTENTS BY AUTHOR

Part I
REVIEW AND RECENT ADVANCES

Editor's Comments
on Papers 1 and 2

Paper 1, reprinted here through the courtesy of Academic Press, Inc., is from a review that appeared in 1971 in Volume 5 of *Fish Physiology* (edited by W. S. Hoar and D. J. Randall). Paper 2 is a review written especially for this volume of significant research in the field during the period 1971–1975. Together, the two papers are intended to serve as an introduction to this volume, as well as a survey of the literature.

1

Reprinted from *Fish Physiology*, W. S. Hoar and D. J. Randall, eds., Academic Press, Inc., New York, 1971, pp. 135–136, 138–142, 162–182, 192–205

SOUND PRODUCTION AND DETECTION

WILLIAM N. TAVOLGA

I. INTRODUCTION

The field of aquatic bioacoustics has grown rapidly in many directions, involving many allied areas of research. Major recent reviews of the subject include those by Moulton (1963), Protasov (1965), and Tavolga (1965). Three international symposia on aquatic bioacoustics have been held and their proceedings published (Cahn, 1967; Tavolga, 1964a, 1967a).

Sound is probably the most effective channel for long-range communication under water, and it has become clear over the past 20 years that many fishes utilize this channel. The mechanisms of sound production and the sounds themselves have formed an active area of research, aided by recent technical developments in underwater acoustics. Although sound production may be restricted to some as yet unknown fraction of all fish species, it is apparent that all fishes must be capable of receiving acoustic stimuli. Sound detection in an aquatic medium presents certain problems not normally encountered by terrestrial organisms, e.g., the separation of pressure from displacement detection seems to be characteristic of aquatic animals.

[*Editor's Note:* Material has been omitted at this point.]

3

B. Underwater Acoustics

Any study of sound production or sound detection in fishes necessitates an understanding of the acoustic properties of water as a medium. Since water is much denser than air, the velocity of sound in water is almost 1500 meters/sec while in air it is about 330 meters/sec. In air, sound velocity is affected slightly by humidity, temperature, and barometric pressure. In water, temperature and pressure are independent variables in shallow areas, while at greater depths pressure affects the temperature. The curves that relate sound velocity to depth, therefore, become quite complex (Albers, 1965; Tschiegg and Hays, 1959; MacKenzie, 1960) (Fig. 1). Salinity increases sound velocity, and in the oceans sound velocity may attain 1540 meters/sec.

As a corollary to this almost fivefold difference in sound velocity, c, between air and water, the wavelengths, λ, of underwater sounds are almost five times the length of those in air for the same frequency, f, i.e., $\lambda = c/f$.

Since water is about a thousand times denser than air, more input energy is required to initiate the propagation of sound in water. However, once the sound is propagated, the acoustic energy will be transmitted faster in water. This transmission is further enhanced by the reflection of sound from the water surface (up to 99.9% is reflected back), from the sea bottom, and from interfaces that are formed by layers of water at different temperatures (Vigoreux, 1960; Albers, 1965).

If we measure the sound level under ideal conditions, that is, with

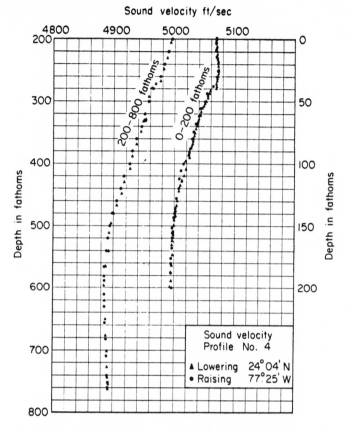

Fig. 1. Velocity of sound in the sea. The two series of determinations show that velocity varies from about 5070 ft/sec (1546 meters/sec) at the surface, to about 4800 ft/sec (1464 meters/sec) at depths below 500 fathoms (915 meters). After Tschiegg and Hays (1959).

the sea at dead calm and with no vessels or sound-producing animals about, there is still an ambient noise whose pressure is about 0.18 to 0.20 dyne/cm². This is usually expressed in terms of decibels (dB) with respect to a reference level of 1 dyne/cm² [= 1 μb (microbar)], and, in this case, the noise level would be about 15 dB below this reference level. In air, the reference level is usually taken to be 0.0002 μb, since this is the standard threshold of human hearing for a frequency of 1000 cps (Hz). This reference level has little objective meaning in underwater acoustics. Thus the 1-μb level is now almost universally used as the reference level in water and all the sound pressure values given in this report will be in decibels re 1 μb (abbreviated to dB μb) (Table I).

Table I

Comparative Chart of Approximate Acoustic Pressure Levels of Common
Sounds in Air and in Water[a]

Sounds in air	Acoustic pressure (dB)	Sounds in water
Jet aircraft takeoff (at 75 meters)	60	Underwater dynamite explosion (at 100 meters)
Threshold for human aural discomfort (discomfort at 1000 Hz)	50	25 hp outboard motor (at 15 meters)
Loud auto horn (at 1 meter)	40	Toadfish boat-whistle sound (at 1 meter)
Small propeller aircraft (at 5 meters)	30	Rough sea (state 6)
New York subway train (at 10 meters)	20	Large chorus of marine catfish
Noisy business office	10	Noise of ships in busy harbor
Home high fidelity set	0	Large chorus of snapping shrimp (at 100 meters)
Average conversation (at 1 meter)	−10	Calm sea (state 0)
Private business office	−20	Squirrelfish hearing threshold (at 800 Hz)
Average residence	−30	
	−40	Threshold of hearing of ostario-physine fishes
Quiet country residence	−50	
Quiet whisper	−60	
Human hearing threshold (at 1000 Hz)	−70	
	−80	

[a] The reference point is set at 0 dB = 1 μb (= 1 dyne/cm^2). To convert to a reference point of 0.0002 μb add 74 dB.

Ambient noise in the sea normally includes the sounds produced by wave motion on the surface, friction of moving water currents against the bottom and against each other, the noise of shipping traffic, and, superimposed on all that, the noises of marine animals (Wenz, 1962, 1964) (Fig. 2). The average level of ambient sea noise is about 10 or 15 dB μb.

In air, sound is usually defined as a more or less periodic form of compression waves that can be detected by the human ear. The frequency range, again with reference to human hearing, is normally considered to be from 20 to 20,0000 Hz. At 20 Hz, the sound is "felt" rather than heard, and most people cannot detect sounds above about 16,000 Hz (= 16 kHz). This is a subjective and anthropomorphic definition of sound and does not apply to acoustic energy in water. Since water is highly resistant to compression, the propagation of sound in water usually involves particle displacement as well as compression. This displacement is partic-

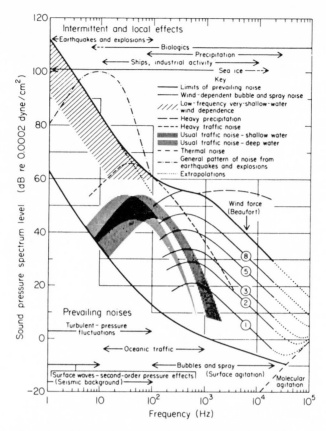

Fig. 2. Typical ambient noise spectra in the sea. Horizontal bars show approximate band of influence of various sources. Sound pressure level on the ordinate is given in decibels with reference to 0.0002 dyne/cm²; to convert to reference level used in this paper subtract 74 dB from all values. After Wenz (1964), with permission of Pergamon Press.

ularly evident at close range to the sound source, and the phenomenon has been termed the "near-field" effect, as opposed to the "far-field" compression waves. The relationship between these two forms of acoustic energy has been discussed extensively by van Bergeijk (1964, 1967a), Harris (1964), and Harris and van Bergeijk (1962). Under most conditions in the field and in aquarium tanks, both near- and far-field energy occur together and are difficult to separate with standard equipment, since a hydrophone is basically a pressure transducer and will respond to compression produced at its surface as a result of particle displacement, i.e., to near-field energy as well as to far-field energy. The energy propagated by the fins of a fish, the flow of water along the body of a moving fish, and even the currents of water flow in rivers and seas are essentially acoustic phenomena, and a line of demarcation between such energy and that of a distinctly audible hoot of a toadfish is difficult to draw. Some investigators have referred to these extremely low frequency or steady state displacements and pressures as "unsound" or "pseudo-sound" (Parvulescu, 1964, 1967; Ffowcs-Williams, 1967).

It is apparent, therefore, that in water the usual definitions of sound are not entirely applicable, and the distinction between rheotaxis and hearing is not clear. As evidenced by the problems and discussions at a recent conference on the lateral line of fishes (Cahn, 1967), the concern over underwater bioacoustics has extended far below what is ordinarily considered the audiofrequency range.

[*Editor's Note:* Material has been omitted at this point.]

III. SOUND DETECTION

A. Historical Background

Since fish have been known, from early times, to be capable of sound production, it was logically assumed that they could also hear. The earliest study of significance in this field was the classic report by Weber (1820) in which he not only described the morphology of the fish ear but also postulated the function of the small ossicles that in the Ostariophysi connect the swim bladder with the inner ear. He compared these structures, since known as the Weberian ossicles, to the middle ear bones of mammals and concluded that they functioned in a similar fashion, i.e., to conduct sound from the swim bladder to the fluids of the inner ear.

It was not until after the turn of the century that the ability of fish to hear was finally established. Several experimenters, notably Kreidl (1895), had concluded that fish were deaf or, at best, could receive some vibrations through a cutaneous sense. However, the investigations of Bigelow (1904), Parker (1902, 1910a,b, 1918), and Parker and van Heusen (1917) proved conclusively that fish receive sound stimuli both through the inner ear and the lateral line. Numerous reports confirming Parker's conclusions followed, in which many other species of fish were shown to possess the ability to detect water-borne sound. The significant studies and reviews of the time included those by Bull (1928, 1929, 1930), Evans (1935), von Frisch (1923, 1936, 1938a), Froloff (1925), Lafite-Dupont (1907), McDonald (1922), Marage (1906), Moorhouse (1933), and Warner (1932).

The first attempts at any quantitative study of fish hearing consisted of determinations of the highest frequency to which fish would respond. In a summary of the results of most of these studies, it is clear that the upper frequency limits of members of the Ostariophysi are significantly higher than representatives of other orders (cf. Tables in Lowenstein, 1957, and Moulton, 1963).

In most of the listed reports, little or no data were given on the intensities of the signals used, and, indeed, in many cases the sound stimuli were poorly controlled, e.g., whistles, plucked strings, and other crude sound makers. Stetter (1929) was the first to control stimulus intensity and attempt to measure it.

The relation of the inner ear to sound reception was demonstrated by means of extirpation techniques. Manning (1924) and von Frisch and Stetter (1932) localized the main sound detection sense in the sacculus and lagena, and von Frisch (1938b) further demonstrated the importance of the Weberian ossicles in transmitting the sound from the swim bladder to the sacculus.

The morphology of the inner ear and swim bladder of fishes has been extensively studied, beginning with the report of Weber (1820) and detailed works by Bridge and Haddon (1893, 1889) on the Weberian apparatus of siluroid fishes. The 1930 decade seemed to be one of the most productive periods, with many major anatomical contributions (de Burlet, 1934; Farkas, 1938a,b; Froese, 1938; Tomaschek, 1936, 1937; Wohlfahrt, 1938). The report by Froese (1938) covered 68 species in 42 families and stressed the various types of connections existing between the swim bladder and the inner ear. This connection and its possible function in clupeid fishes was explored by Wohlfahrt (1936, 1938) and in mormyrids by Stipetić (1939). The course of the VIIIth nerve and its connections with the inner ear in fishes was described by Pearson (1936), including data on the connection of Mauthner's cells and the swim bladder. By means of electrophysiological techniques, the microphonic response of the fish labyrinth and action potentials in the VIIIth nerve were demonstrated (Adrian, 1938).

Controversy as to the function of the lateral line system has existed for a long time. Parker (1902, 1905) theorized that the lateral line system is capable of detecting only shock waves, currents, and possibly low frequency sounds. Whether these periodic and nonperiodic phenomena can be called sound, and their detection hearing, depends upon one's definitions of sound and hearing. This question is related to the distinction between near-field and far-field acoustics and is taken up elsewhere in this chapter.

Several investigators confirmed Parker's contention that the lateral line is a low frequency sound (*sensu latu*) detector (Rode, 1929; Schriever, 1936). This property of the lateral line appeared to be associated with the ability of a fish to orient itself with respect to obstacles and sources of water currents. Although Reinhardt (1935) denied that fish were capable of localizing sound sources, Dijkgraaf (1934) and von Frisch and Dijkgraaf (1935) demonstrated clearly that fish could orient with respect to obstacles, nearby sources of water movements, and nearby low frequency sound sources. Some sort of cutaneous sensory system was postulated, and the lateral line system was considered a strong possibility in such orientations (Sand, 1937).

The innervation of the lateral line system including head canals, indicates strongly that its function must be in some way related to that of the ear, i.e., in some form of vibration detection. Pearson (1936) traced out the course of the VIIIth nerve and showed that the peripheral sensory supply to the lateral line system was derived from the acoustic nerve VIII. In spite of this report, and the earlier descriptions of Herrick (1898), some recent textbooks and manuals of comparative anatomy still give the innervation of the lateral line and head canals as the facial (VII), glossopharyngeal (IX), and vagus (X) nerves, based upon gross anatomical observations. This error has been pointed out most recently by van Bergeijk (1967a).

B. Mechanisms of Sound Detection

1. Inner Ear

The morphological aspects of sound detection in fishes will be treated briefly here. The structure of the labyrinth, including the inner ear, has been reviewed in some detail by Grassé (1958) and Moulton (1963), and will be covered by Lowenstein in another chapter in this volume. The pars superior consists of the semicircular canals and associated ampullae, and the pars inferior consists of the sacculus and lagena, each of which contain an otolith (Fig. 16).

The earliest studies in which sound detection function in fishes was localized to the labyrinth were the extirpation experiments of Manning (1924) and von Frisch and Stetter (1932). Pearson (1936) described the central connections of nerves from the inner ear and postulated that the coarse fibers from the saccular root transmit sonic stimuli. Von Frisch (1938b) described the connection of the Weberian ossicles in *Phoxinus* as transmitting vibrations from the swim bladder to the saccular otolith (sagitta) (Fig. 17). He also stated that the lagenar otolith can receive sonic stimuli by way of bone conduction. In *Lebistes*, which lacks a Weberian apparatus, Farkas (1938a,b) reported that the sagitta is the

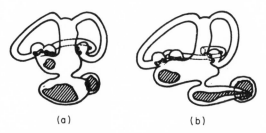

(a)   (b)

Fig. 16. Simplified diagrams of inner ears of fishes: (a) the "typical" form and (b) the ostariophysine form. Redrawn from von Frisch (1936), after Tavolga (1965), with permission of the U. S. Naval Training Device Center.

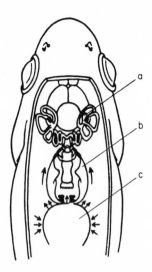

Fig. 17. Members of the order Ostariophysi are characterized by the presence of the Weberian apparatus. The swim bladder (c) serves as the primary transducer and vibrates (see arrows) in response to an impinging pressure wave; the vibration is transmitted to the largest of the Weberian ossicles, the tripus (b); the tripus is coupled to the fluids of the inner ear (a) through three additional ossicles (intercalarium, scaphium, and claustrum). Redrawn from von Frisch (1938b), after Tavolga (1965), with permission of the U. S. Naval Training Device Center.

otolith that receives vibrations through the fenestra sacculi. The most definitive work was that of Dijkgraaf (1949, 1952a) who demonstrated that the auditory function of the inner ear resides in the sacculus and lagena, although the contribution of the lagena to sound detection is as yet not clear. Electrophysiological techniques were used by Zotterman (1943) to locate auditory reception in the macula sacculi. Similar results were obtained by Lowenstein and Roberts (1951) in elasmobranchs, but in addition they were able to detect response potentials from the utriculus. The electrical activity of single sensory nerve fibers of the acoustic nerve of the sculpin, *Cottus scorpius*, was detected and analyzed, and at least four types of neurons were identified on the basis of electrical activity in response to sound (Enger, 1963).

The most recent neurophysiological studies on the inner ear of fishes have confirmed the preeminence of the sacculus as the acoustic detector. In the goldfish, saccular hair cells were found to be divided into a dorsal and a ventral group, with the kinocilia of the hair cells oriented at 180° in the two groups (Flock and Wersäll, 1962). Two groups of afferent nerve fibers are present, one from the anterior and the other from the posterior sections of the sacculus, and the associated hair cells, including those of the lagena, were shown to respond to both vibratory and static bending (Furukawa and Ishii, 1967a,b). Using neurophysiological techniques, some determinations of hearing capacities have been made in herring, *Clupea,* codfish, *Gadus,* and sculpin, *Cottus,* by Enger (1963, 1967a) and Enger and Andersen (1967). The connections between acoustic nerve fibers and Mauthner's neurons were reviewed by Moulton and Dixon (1967), together with extensive discussion and evidence for the relation of these connections to directional responses to sound in fishes.

2. Swim Bladder and Hearing

According to Griffin (1950, 1955) and Pumphrey (1950), a fish is essentially transparent to water-borne sound and its only acoustic discontinuity is the swim bladder (or other air chamber). Sound reception under water requires the presence of a transducer constructed of material very different in acoustic properties and density from the surrounding medium. Air bubbles are known to be excellent reflectors and resonators (Horton, 1959; Meyer, 1957) and certainly the swim bladder can serve efficiently as a transducer. Jones and Pearce (1958), N. B. Marshall (1951), and Midttun and Hoff (1962) have shown that fish swim bladders are effective sonic reflectors and that 50% or more of impinging sound energy is returned by the bladder, while a smaller percentage is reflected by the rest of the fish's body. Kleerekoper and Roggenkamp (1959) demonstrated that damage to the swim bladder in the catfish, *Ictalurus,* raised thresholds by 20 dB or more. It is quite probable, however, that some portions of the fish, such as the skull, may also serve as acoustic discontinuities and thus permit sound reception by bone conduction, although the swim bladder still appears to be the most obvious and efficient sonic transducer that the fish possesses.

If the above is correct, then fishes with swim bladders should have better hearing than those without. Furthermore, those species in which the swim bladder is acoustically coupled to the inner ear should have the highest auditory sensitivity and broadest range.

It appears that the Ostariophysi possess the lowest auditory thresholds and highest upper frequency limits. This is undoubtedly a function of the Weberian apparatus which couples the auditory signal received by the swim bladder to the inner ear in a manner analogous to the operation of the middle ear ossicles in mammals. Other air chambers can serve in similar fashion, as, for example, the branchial cavity in the labyrinthine fishes (Schneider, 1941).

Among nonostariophysines, there are a number of forms in which the swim bladder has anterior extensions which are either coupled directly to the perilymphatic fluid (as in many clupeids) or attached to the occipital region of the neurocranium (Froese, 1938; Grassé, 1958; Tracy, 1920). Wohlfahrt (1936, 1938) described long, thin anterior extensions of the swim bladder in clupeids. These terminate in gas-filled capsules enclosed in bone and coupled to the perilymph through an elastic fenestra. Although auditory thresholds using psychophysical methods are not yet available for any clupeid fishes, Enger (1967a) obtained action potentials generated in the medulla in response to acoustic stimuli in the herring, *Clupea harengus*. The tentative audiogram so generated showed a rather flat frequency response over a range of 30–1200 Hz with a threshold of −20 to −25 dB μb, and a sharp increase to +35 dB μb at 4000 Hz.

In contrast to the neurophysiological technique used by Enger (1967a), a number of workers have resorted to conditioning techniques in which the fish are trained to make some behavioral response in the presence of the test sound. By means of avoidance conditioning, Tavolga and Wodinsky (1963) showed that the squirrelfish, *Holocentrus ascensionis*, has a low threshold and broad frequency response spectrum. It is probable that this is related to the contiguity of the anterior end of the swim bladder to the skull, as described by E. M. Nelson (1955).

Species with reduced or absent swim bladders should have poor hearing, but the evidence for this is sparse. Bull (1928) was unable to condition a blenny, *Blennius*, to respond to sound. In *Gobius*, Dijkgraaf (1949, 1952b) showed an upper frequency limit of only 800 Hz, and he postulated that most sound reception in this species took place through lateral line or cutaneous tactile senses.

On this basis, sharks and other elasmobranchs should be virtually deaf, yet the studies of Kritzler and Wood (1961) and D. R. Nelson (1967a) and the electrophysiological work of Lowenstein and Roberts (1951) show this is not true. The validity of the statement that the fish is acoustically transparent needs to be reexamined, and the possibilities that the skull, vertebral column, and other portions of the body can act as acoustic discontinuities should be investigated. Furthermore the contribution of the lateral line to hearing needs clarification.

3. LATERAL LINE AND HEARING

Fish possess two sensory modalities for the detection of underwater vibrations. In addition to the inner ear, they possess a series of integumentary sense organs collectively known as the lateral line system (Fig. 18). This system will be covered in detail by Flock in Chapter 8 of this volume. Most of the anatomical studies on the lateral line in fishes

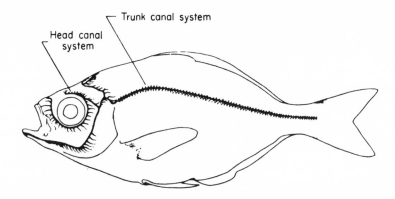

Fig. 18. Lateral line system of the surfperch, *Hyperprosopon*. After Walker (1967). Reprinted from "Lateral Line Detectors" edited by Phyllis Cahn, copyright © 1967 by Indiana University Press. Reprinted by permission.

have been summarized by Disler (1960), and the microscopic anatomy of the individual receptors was described by Dijkgraaf (1952a), Cahn and Shaw (1962), and many other authors (cf. Cahn, 1967) (Figs. 19 and 20). As reviewed by Dijkgraaf (1963a), some of the early literature

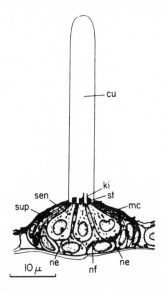

Fig. 19. Schematic of a neuromast unit of the lateral line system. Key: cu, cupula; ki, kinocilium; mc, mantle cell; ne, nerve ending; nf, nerve fiber; sen, sensory cell; st, stereocilium; and sup, supporting cell. After Iwai (1967). Reprinted from "Lateral Line Detectors" edited by Phyllis Cahn, copyright © 1967 by Indiana University Press. Reprinted by permission.

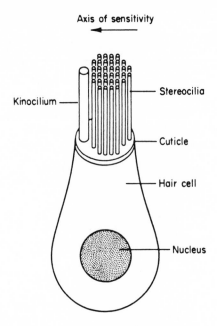

Fig. 20. Idealized cell of the acoustico-lateralis system. The position of the kinocilium determines the axis of sensitivity of the cell, and displacement in the direction of the arrow results in action potentials in connecting nerve fibers. After van Bergeijk (1967a), with permission of Academic Press.

on the function of the lateral line was contradictory, but strong indications were that it responds to minute water currents and to frequencies below 500 Hz (Kleerekoper and Roggenkamp, 1959). Electrophysiological studies by Suckling and Suckling (1950), Suckling (1962), Harris and van Bergeijk (1962), Jielof *et al.* (1952), and Kuiper (1956) have established the fact that the lateral line functions as a tactile receptor specialized for the detection of water displacements. Dijkgraaf (1947b, 1967) developed the idea that the lateral line could function as a sort of low frequency sonar system to detect the presence of nearby obstacles.

Acoustic energy is present in two forms: a pressure wave and a displacement. The pressure wave (far-field) is usually measured by a hydrophone, and its intensity drops off as the square of the distance from the source. Displacement (near-field) is detectable only close to the sound source since its intensity drops off as the cube of the distance. Harris and van Bergeijk (1962) demonstrated the importance of the near field in acoustic detection by fishes. They showed that the lateral line is strictly a near-field receptor, and operates only at low frequencies. An effective near field would exist at distances of about one-sixth of a wavelength, as calculated by van Bergeijk (1964).

It is clear from the neurophysiological studies of Kuiper (1956), Jielof *et al.* (1952), Suckling and Suckling (1950, 1964), and others that the lateral line organ is a displacement detector, with a threshold in the order of magnitude of about 20 Å (Harris and van Bergeijk, 1962). Based on additional behavioral studies, Dijkgraaf (1963a, 1964, 1967) concluded that these structures primarily respond to "current-like water disturbances." He also made the point that the lateral line organs are not acoustic detectors, i.e., they do not respond to a propagated pressure wave. Many behavioral studies, however, have referred to the lateral line as responding to "sound." As pointed out by van Bergeijk (1967c), Dijkgraaf's original contention (1934) that the lateral line organ can only detect water motion is perfectly correct. However, the near-field effect is an inseparable component of acoustic energy, and the entire lateral line system acts as a near-field acoustic detector. The functional similarity of the inner ear and the lateral line can be illustrated by the following: (1) Both inner ear hair cells and lateral line organs have a fundamental structural similarity, even to the polarity of response and arrangement of kino- and stereocilia (Fig. 20); (2) both inner ear and lateral line are supplied by branches of the acoustic nerve; (3) both are essentially displacement detectors (van Bergeijk, 1967a). The lateral line system remained a near-field detector, while the inner ear, by virtue of the proximity of the swim bladder, became a far-field detector (van Bergeijk, 1967a). Both can be considered as acoustic sense organs.

C. Hearing Capacities

1. PSYCHOPHYSICAL STUDIES

In the majority of studies on teleostean auditory capacities, the objective was to determine the upper frequency limits to which the animals could respond. Attempts have been made in only a few studies to measure absolute intensity thresholds (Autrum and Poggendorf, 1951; Diesselhorst, 1938; Kritzler and Wood, 1961; Maliukina, 1960; Poggendorf, 1952; Stetter, 1929; von Boutteville, 1935). In most of these reports, only one or a few selected frequencies were actually tested. With the exception of the work of Griffin (1950), the intensity measurements were only approximations. Griffin's determinations were based upon measurements taken with calibrated hydrophones, amplifiers, and decibel meters.

For most of the ostariophysine fishes tested, the auditory thresholds were low, in the order of −40 to −60 dB μb, and the most sensitive frequency range was about 100–1500 Hz (Stetter, 1929; Diesselhorst, 1938; von Boutteville, 1935; Dorai Raj, 1960b; Autrum and Poggendorf, 1951;

Kleerekoper and Roggenkamp, 1959). Upper frequency limits for these fishes were given as over 7000 Hz (Farkas, 1936; Kleerekoper and Chagnon, 1954; von Boutteville, 1935; von Frisch, 1938b).

The first attempt to determine a complete audiogram for a fish was done with the bullhead, *Ictalurus nebulosus*, by Poggendorf (1952) (Fig. 21). In recent years, audiograms for two additional ostariophysine species have been reported: the goldfish, *Carassius auratus*, by Enger (1966, 1967b), Jacobs and Tavolga (1967), and Weiss (1967, 1969); and the Mexican blind characin, *Astyanax mexicanus*, by Popper (1970).

A comparison of the three audiograms obtained for the goldfish shows some interesting results of different techniques. Enger (1967b) used a positive reward conditioning (Fig. 22), while Jacobs and Tavolga (1967) (Fig. 21) and Weiss (1967) (Fig. 23) used different forms of avoidance conditioning. Enger used a loudspeaker in the water and also in air; Jacobs and Tavolga used a loudspeaker in air, but in an enclosed chamber such that the backwave of the speaker was damped out; Weiss used a tank with two large speaker surfaces at the ends, with the speakers operating 180° out of phase. The quality of the stimulus in each of these experiments was somewhat different. The Enger underwater-loudspeaker

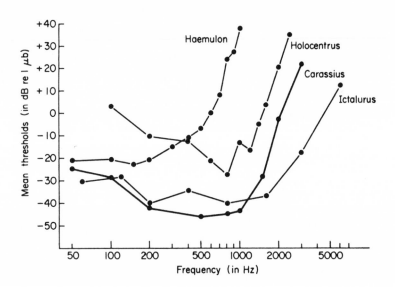

Fig. 21. Comparison of audiograms for four species of teleost fishes. Goldfish, *Carassius auratus*, from Jacobs and Tavolga (1967); brown bullhead, *Ictalurus nebulosus*, from Poggendorf (1952); blue-striped grunt, *Haemulon sciurus*, from Tavolga and Wodinsky (1965); and squirrelfish, *Holocentrus ascensionis*, from Tavolga and Wodinsky (1963).

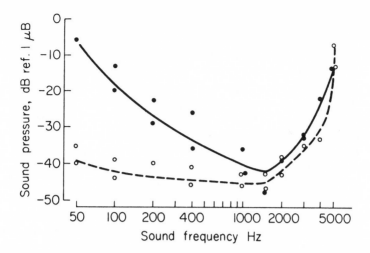

Fig. 22. Audiogram for the goldfish using air and underwater loudspeakers: (●) loudspeaker in air and (○) loudspeaker in water. After Enger (1967b). Reprinted from "Lateral Line Detectors" edited by Phyllis Cahn, copyright © 1967 by Indiana University Press. Reprinted by permission.

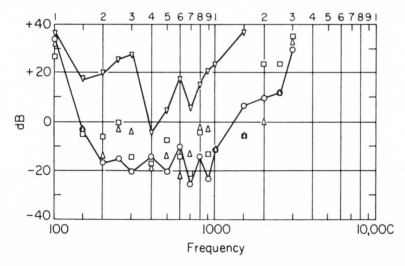

Fig. 23. Audiogram for the goldfish obtained with an essentially near-field stimulus: (▽) subject 2, (△) subject 3, (○) subject 5, and (□) subject 6. After Weiss (1967). Reprinted from "Lateral Line Detectors" edited by Phyllis Cahn, copyright © 1967 by Indiana University Press. Reprinted by permission.

19

system undoubtedly produced a complex of acoustic energy involving both pressure waves and displacement. The Enger air-loudspeaker system was even more complex acoustically, since the speaker was close enough to the water surface to induce near field, and the energy from the back of the speaker was not damped. The Jacobs–Tavolga system was based essentially upon the suggestions of Parvulescu (1964, 1967) and van Bergeijk (1967a), and was an attempt to attain a pure pressure field, although its "purity" could not be measured. The Weiss system produced a push–pull effect in the water and probably approached a pure near-field condition.

Weiss (1967, 1969) described his apparatus as producing a "uniform sound field," but he presented no data to validate this point. If by uniformity he meant equal sound pressure at all points, this would be a remarkable achievement, especially in a small tank. Although he made no measurements of displacement, he claimed to be able to separate inner ear from lateral line reception. By contrast, Cahn et al. (1969) obtained separate pressure and velocity (displacement) measures in a tank similar to Weiss's, and they found variations in the pressure levels at different part of the tank over a range of about 10 dB.

At 1000 Hz, Enger's and Jacobs and Tavolga's data were roughly in agreement, but Weiss' thresholds were about 20 dB higher. All the audiograms were essentially flat over the 200–1000-Hz range, except Enger's air-loudspeaker data, which showed a significant rise in threshold at 200 Hz. Above 1000 Hz, Enger obtained thresholds of about −10 dB μb at 5000 Hz, while the other two audiograms rose abruptly to about +30 dB μb at 3000 Hz.

A factor in threshold studies that must be considered is the level and spectrum of background noise in the experimental tank or chamber. Tavolga (1967b) demonstrated that masking noise effects in fishes are essentially similar to those in human hearing studies (Fletcher and Munson, 1937). In general, if the thresholds are 10 dB or more above the noise level in the region of the test frequency, the probability is high that the threshold values obtained are not masked and are unaffected by the ambient noise. The threshold data obtained by Jacobs and Tavolga (1967) gave values that were at least 10 dB higher than the noise level in the appropriate band, and at least 30 dB higher than the spectrum level (in noise per cycle). Unfortunately, Enger (1967b) and Weiss (1967) gave no data on ambient noise levels.

With so many differences in conditioning techniques, acoustic circumstances, and, above all, the lack of comparable noise level data, it is not possible at this time to bring all the above results into consonance. However, Wodinsky (1969) found that the high thresholds obtained by Weiss resulted from the omission of shock during the testing trials, and extinction of the response took place. It is possible, therefore, that Weiss's data do not represent auditory thresholds at all. Such differences in technique may also explain why thresholds obtained by Weiss *et al.* (1969) on *Ictalurus nebulosus* were 10–20 dB higher than those reported earlier by Poggendorf (1952).

Fishes without a Weberian apparatus have not been tested as extensively as the ostariophysines. However, the mormyrids and labyrinthine fishes possess air chambers directly coupled to the perilymphatic fluid and inner ear. The studies of Diesselhorst (1938), Stipetić (1939), and Schneider (1941) showed upper frequency limits of over 3000 Hz for mormyrids, with a threshold of −50 to −40 dB μb at 258 Hz (Diesselhorst, 1938). Schneider (1941) reported upper frequency limits of 4500 Hz for certain labyrinthines.

Upper frequency limits in most other nonostariophysine species are considerably lower. Table II summarizes the majority of reports.

Complete audiograms obtained for several marine teleosts were reported by Tavolga and Wodinsky (1963, 1965) and Wodinsky and Tavolga (1964) (Fig. 24). Based upon data on nine species from Bahamas waters, the most sensitive range was 200–600 Hz, with average thresholds of about 0 dB μb. The snappers (Lutjanidae), grunts (Pomadasyidae), sea basses, and groupers (Serranidae) tended to show thresholds of +10 to +20 dB μb in the 300–600-Hz range. Above this range, the threshold

Table II

Upper Frequency Limits

Genus and family	Upper frequency limit (Hz)	Reference
Gobius (Gobiidae)	800	Dijkgraaf (1952b)
Corvina (Sciaenidae)	1000	Dijkgraaf (1952b)
Corvina (Sciaenidae)	1500–2000	Maliukina (1960)
Sargus (Sparidae)	1250	Dijkgraaf (1952b)
Anguilla (Anguillidae)	600	Diesselhorst (1938)
Lebistes (Poeciliidae)	435 (640 in young)	Farkas (1935)
Lebistes (Poeciliidae)	2068	Farkas (1936)
Mugil (Mugilidae)	1600–2500	Maliukina (1960)
	Threshold (re 1 μb)	
Anguilla (Anguillidae)	−20 to 0 dB at 250 Hz	Diesselhorst (1938)
Mugil (Mugilidae)	−50 dB at 640 Hz	Maliukina (1960)
Corvina (Sciaenidae)	−45 dB at 320 Hz	Maliukina (1960)
Corvina (Sciaenidae)	−50 dB at 500–600 Hz	Maliukina (1960)
Mullus (Mullidae)	Below −30 dB at 450–900 Hz	Maliukina (1960)
Gaidropsarus (Gadidae)	−30 dB at 750 Hz	Maliukina (1960)
Perca (Percidae)	−14 dB at 100 Hz	Wolff (1967)

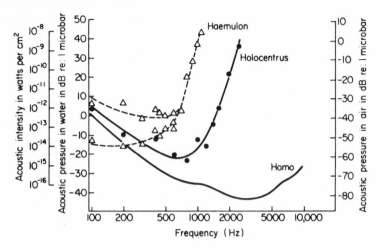

Fig. 24. Comparison of the audiograms of the grunt, *Haemulon,* the squirrel-fish, *Holocentrus,* and the human. All curves are plotted against the extreme left-hand ordinate in terms of acoustic power (W/cm²). The equivalent acoustic pressures in air (against which the human audiogram is plotted) are on the right ordinate. After Wodinsky and Tavolga (1964), with permission of Pergamon Press.

curve rose sharply to +40 or +50 dB μb at 1500–2000 Hz. At frequencies below 300 Hz, these species exhibited high thresholds at first, but after additional training and testing, the thresholds were 0 to +10 dB μb at 100 Hz.

Cohen and Winn (1967) determined the audiogram for the midshipman, *Porichthys notatus,* electrophysiologically, and they based their thresholds on a 20 μV saccular microphonic response. The lowest thresholds were about +7 dB μb at 30 Hz. The curve rose slowly to about +22 dB μb at 120 Hz, then showed a sharp dip to +11 dB μb at 150 Hz. Above 150 Hz, the audiogram rose steeply to +40 dB μb at 240 Hz. Significantly, the dip at 150 Hz corresponded roughly to the average fundamental of the sounds normally produced by this species.

Some species showed higher sensitivities. The squirrelfishes, *Holocentrus,* and a few others were found to have thresholds of −20 dB μb at 600 Hz and could respond to frequencies as high as 2000 Hz. The only data that are presently available on the hearing of pelagic species were reported by Iversen (1967) (Fig. 25). The yellowfin tuna, *Thunnus albacares,* possessed lowest thresholds of −13 dB μb at 300 Hz and −17 dB μb at 500 Hz. The audiogram rose steeply to about +20 dB μb at 1000 Hz and showed a more gradual rise toward the low end to about +20 dB μb at 100 Hz. These pelagic, fast-swimming fish are difficult to maintain under any aquarium conditions. This study is particularly note-

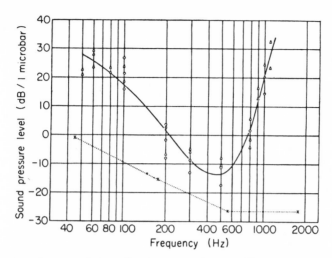

Fig. 25. Audiogram of the yellowfin tuna, *Thunnus albacares:* (○) 50 cm and (△) 60 cm. The lower dotted line indicates the background noise plotted as total noise in a narrow band. After Iversen (1967), with permission of Pergamon Press.

worthy since the fish not only kept in good health for considerable periods of time but were also trained and tested repeatedly. It should be noted that Iversen provided data on ambient noise in his experimental tanks, and it seems clear that his threshold data were unmasked values, i.e., unaffected by the ambient noise.

The shape of the audiogram for the Atlantic cod, *Gadus morhua,* is significantly different from those of other marine fishes tested. Buerkle (1967) showed that at frequencies below 200 Hz, the thresholds (determined by conditioned cardiac rhythm changes) were in the order of 0 to −10 dB μb. The curve rose steeply to about +20 dB μb at 400 Hz, and this frequency probably marks the upper limit of hearing in the species. It is also probable that the lateral line is the primary receptor. Buerkle (1968) also demonstrated the effect of masking noise on these thresholds. The flat portion of the audiogram (35–141 Hz) was most consistently affected by the masking noise, and the signal-to-noise ratio in this range was about 20 dB, using the spectrum level (noise per cycle) as the reference.

In a report of preliminary data, two species of pollack (*Pollachius pollachius* and *P. virens*) were found to have a hearing range similar to that of the cod. The lowest threshold was at about −9 dB μb at 300 Hz, and the audiogram rose sharply above 450 Hz (Parrish *et al.*, 1968).

In a series of studies on fishes of the family Percidae, Wolff (1967,

1968) used avoidance conditioning to demonstrate auditory thresholds. In the common perch, *Perca fluviatilis*, the lowest threshold was about −14 dB μb at 100 Hz, and the curve rose sharply to +35 dB μb at 50 Hz, and almost +45 dB μb at 200 Hz. In the pike perch, *Lucioperca sandra*, thresholds were about 0 to +5 dB μb from 50 to 200 Hz, rising to +60 dB μb at 800 Hz. The audiogram for the stone perch, *Acerina cernua*, was similar in shape to that of the pike perch, but consistently about 10 dB higher. It is possible, as in the case of the cod, that these percids may be primarily sensitive to displacements mediated by the lateral line.

Deserving special mention is the attempt by Kritzler and Wood (1961) to determine a complete audiogram in the bull shark, *Carcharhinus leucas*. Their data, based upon positive reward conditioning, ranged in threshold values from +10 dB μb at 100 Hz, to a low level of about −15 dB μb 400–600 Hz, to over +10 dB μb at 1400 Hz. Considering the fact that the shark has no swim bladder and therefore receives all sounds either through direct conduction to the inner ear or by way of the lateral line system, these low thresholds are quite remarkable. This may serve to indicate that an air chamber need not function as the main transducer in sound reception, and the acoustical difference between the water medium and the bone or cartilage of the neurocranium may be sufficient to permit detection of frequencies up to 1000 Hz.

The above report by Kritzler and Wood (1961) was the first behavioral study of hearing in any elasmobranch fish, although the ability of sharks to detect and respond to acoustic signals has long been known (Parker, 1910a). Interest in the hearing of sharks has, of course, been spurred by practical aspects of dealing with attacks of these animals on human beings. Many of the problems in experimental work on the hearing of sharks have been summarized by Wisby *et al.* (1964), and Backus (1963). In a preliminary report, D. R. Nelson and Gruber (1963) reported that they were able to attract sharks in open sea conditions to a sound source playing back recordings of low frequency pulses, similar to those produced by a struggling, wounded fish.

Davies *et al.* (1963) conditioned four species of sharks to respond to sounds and obtained data on response to both pure tones and octaves of broad-band noise. The results gave a fairly flat audiogram curve (+10 dB μb) from 50 to 7000 Hz. The pressure levels ranged from +5 to +25 dB μb, and the lowest sensitivities of the animals were within a few decibels of the background noise levels at the tested frequencies. The authors concluded that the sharks are capable of determining the location of the sound source but are not capable of any significant frequency discrimination. These results should be considered as highly preliminary and probably do not represent true thresholds or audiograms, since it is quite probable that under conditions of low ambient noise the shape and level of the sensitivity curves would be very different.

In other studies on the hearing of sharks, Wisby *et al.* (1964) and D. R. Nelson (1967b) obtained heart-rate responses to sound pressures of about +30 to +40 dB μb in the lemon shark, *Negaprion brevirostris*, at frequencies up to 1000 Hz. Dijkgraaf (1963b) obtained similar values at 180 Hz in the dogfish, *Scyliorhinus canicula,* using classic conditioning. Neither of these studies showed thresholds as low as those reported by Kritzler and Wood (1961).

Nelson (1967a) also found thresholds in the lemon shark, *Negaprion brevirostris,* that were significantly different from the values reported by Kritzler and Wood (1961). His data gave values of from 0 to —10 dB μb from 10 to 320 Hz, and a sharp rise to about +30 dB μb at 640 Hz (Fig. 26). It is probable that differences in the conditioning techniques and, especially, in the acoustic conditions may account for the differences in threshold values obtained by various investigators.

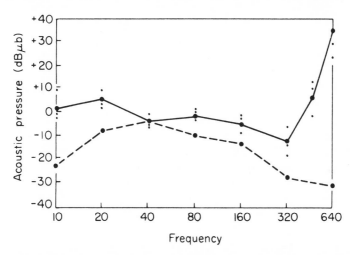

Fig. 26. Audiogram of the lemon shark, *Negaprion brevirostris,* plotted together with the mean filtered ambient noise: (——) mean hearing thresholds and (- - -) mean filtered ambient noise. After Nelson (1967a).

2. Discriminatory Capacities

A further step in the psychophysical study of hearing in fish is the investigation of the ability to discriminate sounds of different intensities and frequencies. It is clear that in contrast to mammalian hearing the frequency range of most fish is significantly narrower. Although in some species thresholds can be obtained at frequencies up to 3 or even 5 kHz, the intensities of the test sounds are in the 20–30 dB μb range, and such acoustic intensities are probably much higher than sounds normally encountered in the fish's environment. The usable frequency range in most fish, therefore, does not extend beyond about 2 kHz (higher in ostariophysines), and the dynamic range covers a span of about 60 dB. By contrast, human hearing has a usable range of at least 10 kHz and over 100 dB.

Within the narrow frequency and dynamic range of fish, the ability for discrimination has been found to be remarkably good. The first reports on intensity discrimination were those of Wohlfahrt (1939), who concluded that this ability was completely lacking in fish, and Dijkgraaf and Verheijen (1950), who were able to show that the minnow, *Phoxinus laevis*, was capable of distinguishing between tones of equal frequency but different intensity. In another ostariophysine, the goldfish, *Carassius auratus*, Jacobs and Tavolga (1967) demonstrated that the "just-noticeable-difference" (*jnd*) was from 3 to 6 dB. This compares to a *jnd* of about 0.5 dB for human hearing (Licklider, 1951).

The ability of fish to discriminate between different frequencies was first studied by Stetter (1929), who found that *Phoxinus* was capable of discriminating between two tones that were about a minor third apart, i.e., about a 20% difference in frequency. For the same species, Wohlfahrt (1939) obtained a *jnd* of about 6% (a half tone). This discriminatory capacity was found to be somewhat temperature dependent (Dudok van Heel, 1956).

Much of the above work was done with poorly controlled intensities and crude sound-producing devices (flutes, tuning forks, etc.). Using more accurate sound generators, Dijkgraaf and Verheijen (1950) reported that *Phoxinus* was capable of discriminating tones with a 3% (one-quarter tone) difference in frequency. Using more accurately calibrated equipment, standard psychophysical techniques, more animals, and a different conditioning procedure, Jacobs and Tavolga (1968) were able to confirm these data for the goldfish. The mean *jnd* at 200 Hz was 9.4 Hz (4.7%), at 500 Hz the *jnd* was 17.4 Hz (3.5%), and at 1000 Hz the *jnd* was 50.1 Hz (5.0%). For comparison human subjects possess a *jnd* of 0.4–0.8% at 100 Hz and 0.2–0.3% at 1000 Hz.

It is significant that species of fish other than Ostariophyi have a much larger *jnd* for frequency. In two species of mormyrids, Stipetić (1939) reported a *jnd* of 12–25%, and Dijkgraaf (1952b) stated that *Gobius, Corvina,* and *Sargus* were capable of discriminating a 9–15% difference in frequency. Even larger values of 50–100% were given for other nonostariophysines: *Umbra* (Westerfield, 1921), *Anguilla* (Diesselhorst, 1938), *Macropodus* (Schneider, 1941), and the lemon shark, *Negaprion* (D. R. Nelson, 1967a). In addition to possessing lower absolute thresholds, the Ostariophysi also appear to have better discriminatory capacities, and the possibility appears that the Weberian apparatus may play a role in frequency analysis.

The mechanism of frequency discrimination in fish was investigated by Enger (1963) by means of neurophysiological techniques. In the sculpin, *Cottus*, he demonstrated the presence of four types of neural units, some of which displayed a following response to the acoustic stimulus. He concluded that frequency discrimination in fishes takes place in part by the following response, and in part by a separation into low and high frequency sensitive units. This volley theory would not, however, explain the fine degree of discrimination demonstrated above (Jacobs and Tavolga, 1968). Furthermore, Enger used extremely high sound levels up to 50 dB μb, and van Bergeijk (1967a) pointed out that such intensities at close range would stimulate inertial receptors as well as acoustic receptors and produce, in effect, a vertigo.

The inadequacies of a volley theory to explain human auditory discrimination led to the classic work of von Békésy (1960), where he demonstrated the applicability of a place theory. The place theory, however, rests on the morphological basis of a cochlea with a basilar membrane that is differentially responsive to different frequencies. Fish do not have a cochlea, or anything apparently analogous to a basilar membrane. The question of the mechanism of frequency analysis by the fish ear remains an intriguing problem.

Much of the support for the place theory in human hearing is derived from psychophysical data on the effects of masking noise and the presence of a critical band (Fletcher and Munson, 1937; J. E. Hawkins and Stevens, 1950; Scharf, 1961, 1966). Some evidence has been presented that a critical band for masking may exist in fish (Tavolga, 1967b), and van Bergeijk (1967a,b) pointed out that a basilar membrane as such is not essential for a place theory to apply. Any structure with some acoustic asymmetry would respond differentially to traveling waves of different frequencies. Even a bongo drum can generate sounds over a range of at least an octave, and van Bergeijk (1967b) presented a most plausible explanation for frequency analysis in the fish's ear. This "bongo drum hypothesis" depends upon the fact that the saccular otolith and its underlying macula behaves as a bounded membrane with sufficient acoustic asymmetry to resonate differentially at different frequencies.

The problem of whether a fish can detect the direction of a sound source has been given little attention until recently. Kleerekoper and

Chagnon (1954) presented strong evidence that *Semotilus* can orient with respect to a sound source, especially if there are standing waves present. Reinhardt (1935) and von Frisch and Dijkgraaf (1935) came to the opposite conclusion, i.e., that fish could not localize a sound. Their data, however, showed that localization took place at close range to the sound source. Van Bergeijk (1964) reviewed the available data with respect to the nature of the acoustic stimulus presented, and he emphasized that the distinction between the two forms of acoustic energy must be made, i.e., between far field (pressure) and near field (displacement). For localization to take place, a minimum of two receptors is necessary (Kuroki, 1967). Fishes have, at best, only a single pressure receptor: one median swim bladder coupled to the two inner ears. Displacement detectors in the form of lateral line organs, however, form a complex array of numerous units. Van Bergeijk's conclusion is, therefore, that fish are not able to localize except within the range of the near field of a sound source (about one-sixth of a wavelength).

Through a combination of neuroanatomical, neurophysiological and behavioral techniques, Moulton and Dixon (1967) demonstrated that certain directional responses in fish consist of rapid tail flips. These are two-neuron reflexes involving a sensory and a Mauthner's neuron and are associated with a rapid escape response, although conditioning can alter this to an approach response. Moulton and Dixon proposed that these were directional resonses to a far-field stimulus, but the intensity of the test sounds was high and the loudspeaker was close to the animal in their experimental conditions. It is probable that a substantial near field was generated (cf. comments by Tavolga and van Bergeijk and p. 232 in Moulton and Dixon, 1967).

Experiments and observations on the movements of carp in a large tank, monitored by means of a matrix of photoconductive cells, showed that orientation in a sound field takes place by a sort of klinotaxis. In response to nodal and antinodal sound pressure variations, the turning angle of the fish is modified, and it is postulated that this response is mediated by Mauthner cells (Kleerekoper and Malar, 1968).

According to the analysis by van Bergeijk (1964), elasmobranchs, lacking a swim bladder, should not be able to detect far-field energy. In field observations, however, D. R. Nelson and Gruber (1963) and Wisby and Nelson (1964) were able to attract sharks with low frequency signals (20–60 Hz). The range over which this attraction took place (about 200 meters) brings up the possibility that the animals were reacting to a far-field pressure wave. However, sensitivity to displacement energy in the lemon shark, *Negaprion brevirostris*, was found to be below 10 Å in some cases (Banner, 1967).

D. Evolution of Hearing

Probably one of the most primitive interactions between an organism and its environment is one that is dependent upon physical contact. On the multicellular level of organization, the specialization of contact receptor cells appears to be one of the earliest to evolve. It is clear that the specialization of an organ for reception of sound should be traceable from primitive touch receptors with displacement-sensitive hairs. The classic approach to the study of this evolutionary sequence is exemplified in the review by Pumphrey (1950). The essentials of the sequence are: free neuromasts that are groups of hair cells; the addition of a gelatinous cupula and the organization of the neuromasts into more or less enclosed lateral line organs; the development of otoconia and, later, otoliths that mass-load the hair cells; and the enclosure of the hair cell groups within the labyrinth. The functional sequence is: simple mechanoreceptors that develop into more sensitive displacement detectors; enclosed mechano-receptors become pressure sensitive as a result of the intervention of an air-filled swim bladder; and in terrestrial vertebrates, the middle ear takes on the coupling function of the swim bladder. According to Pumphrey (1950), the response of the inner ear to gravity is "a by-product of the improvement of hearing."

Based upon a reexamination of the concepts of "sound" and "hearing," van Bergeijk (1966, 1967a) presented an intensive survey of the problem of the evolution of hearing in vertebrates and attempted to trace this evolution in physiological terms. The lateral line organ is essentially a displacement detector and, as a result, a hydrodynamic motion detector. The organization of the lateral line system, however, provides new inputs into the acoustic centers of the central nervous system, and the lateral line system becomes a near-field hearing organ, with the capabilities of localizing sound sources (van Bergeijk, 1964). By contrast with Pumphrey, van Bergeijk (1967a) proposed that the inner ear labyrinth arose as an inertial receptor organ. Only the later development of a swim bladder (a hydrostatic organ) gave the labyrinth the property of hearing. The acoustic discontinuity of a swim bladder in an aquatic organism enables it to respond to pressure waves, i.e., far-field sound, and the bladder therefore generates a local near field that can excite the inner ear. Specializations such as the Weberian apparatus improve the coupling of the swim bladder and the inner ear and enhance far-field hearing. Van Bergeijk carried this evolutionary sequence into the development of hearing in terrestrial vertebrates. His entire argument was brilliantly presented and thoroughly documented, and it deserves recognition as a milestone in the field of biology.

[*Editor's Note:* Material has been omitted at this point.]

REFERENCES

Adrian, E. D. (1938). Potential changes in the ears of reptiles and fish. *Nature* **141**, 553.

Albers, V. M. (1965). "Underwater Acoustics Handbook—II." Penn. State Univ. Press, University Park, Pennsylvania.

Alexander, R. M. (1959a). The physical properties of the swim bladder in intact Cypriniformes. *J. Exptl. Biol.* **36**, 315–332.

Alexander, R. M. (1959b). The physical properties of the swim bladders of fish other than Cypriniformes. *J. Exptl. Biol.* **36**, 347–355.

Autrum, H., and Poggendorf, D. (1951). Messung der absoluten Hörschwelle bei Fischen (*Amiurus nebulosus*). *Naturwissenschaften* **38**, 434–435.

Backus, R. H. (1963). Hearing in elasmobranchs. *In* "Sharks and Survival" (P. W. Gilbert, ed.), pp. 243–254. Heath, Boston, Massachusetts.

Banner, A. (1967). Evidence of sensitivity to acoustic displacements in the lemon shark, *Negaprion brevirostris* (Poey). *In* "Lateral Line Detectors" (P. Cahn, ed.), pp. 265–273. Indiana Univ. Press, Bloomington, Indiana.

Banner, A. (1968). Attraction of young lemon sharks, *Negaprion brevirostris,* by sound. *Copeia* pp. 871–872.

Bigelow, H. B. (1904). The sense of hearing in the goldfish *Carassius auratus* L. *Am. Naturalist* **38**, 275–284.

Bridge, T. W., and Haddon, A. C. (1889). Contribution to the anatomy of fishes. I. The airbladder and Weberian ossicles in the Siluroidea. *Proc. Roy. Soc.* **46**, 309–328.

Bridge, T. W., and Haddon, A. C. (1893). Contributions to the anatomy of fishes. II. The air-bladder and Weberian ossicles in the siluroid fishes. *Phil. Trans. Roy. Soc. London* **B184**, 65–333.

Buerkle, U. (1967). An audiogram of the Atlantic cod, *Gadus morhua* L. *J. Fisheries Res. Board Can.* **24**, 2309–2319.

Buerkle, U. (1968). Relation of pure tone thresholds to background noise level in the Atlantic cod (*Gadus morhua*). *J. Fisheries Res. Board Can.* **25**, 1155–1160.

Bull, H. O. (1928). Studies on conditioned responses in fishes. Part I. *J. Marine Biol. Assoc. U. K.* **15**, 485–533.

Bull, H. O. (1929). Studies on conditioned responses in fishes. Part II. *J. Marine Biol. Assoc. V. K.* **16**, 615–637.

Bull, H. O. (1930). Can fish hear? *Sci. Progr. Twentieth Cent.* **25**, 97–101.

Busnel, R.-G., ed. (1963). "Acoustic Behaviour of Animals." Elsevier, Amsterdam.

Cahn, P. H., ed. (1967). "Lateral Line Detectors." Indiana Univ. Press, Bloomington, Indiana.

Cahn, P. H., and Shaw, E. (1962). The first demonstration of lateral line cupulae in the Mugiliformes. *Copeia* **1962**, 109–114.

Cahn, P. H., Siler, W., and Wodinsky, J. (1969). Acoustico-lateralis system of fishes: tests of pressure and particle-velocity sensitivity in grunts, *Haemulon sciurus* and *Haemulon parrai*. *J. Acoust. Soc. Am.* **46**, 1572–1578.

Cohen, M. J., and Winn, H. E. (1967). Electrophysiological observations on hearing and sound production in the fish, *Porichthys notatus. J. Exptl. Zool.* **165**, 355–370.

Davies, D. H., Lochner, J. P. A., and Smith, E. D. (1963). Preliminary investigations on the hearing of sharks. *Oceanog. Res. Inst., Durban, S. A. Rept.* No. 7, 1–10.

de Burlet, H. M. (1934). Die innere Ohrsphäre. Vergleichende Anatomie des Stato-Akustischen Organs. *Handbuch Vergleich. Anat. Wirbelt.* **2**, 1293–1380.

Delco, E. A., Jr. (1960). Sound discrimination by males of two cyprinid fishes. *Texas J. Sci.* 12, 48–54.

Diesselhorst, G. (1938). Hörversuche an Fischen ohn Weberschen Apparat. *Z. Vergleich. Physiol.* 25, 748–783.

Dijkgraaf, S. (1934). Untersuchungen über die Funktion der Seitenorgane an Fischen. *Z. Vergleich. Physiol.* 20, 162–214.

Dijkgraaf, S. (1947b). Über die Reizung des Ferntastsinnes bei Fischen und Amphibien. *Experientia* 3, 206–216.

Dijkgraaf, S. (1949). Untersuchungen über die Funktionen des Ohrlabyrinths bei Meeresfischen. *Physiol. Comparata Oecolog.* 2, 81–106.

Dijkgraaf, S. (1952a). Bau und Funktionen der Seitenorgane und des Ohrlabyrinths bei Fischen. *Experientia* 8, 205–216.

Dijkgraaf, S. (1952b). Über die Schallwahrnehmung bei Meeresfischen. *Z. Vergleich. Physiol.* 34, 104–122.

Dijkgraaf, S. (1963a). The function and significance of the lateral line organs. *Biol. Rev.* 38, 51–105.

Dijkgraaf, S. (1963b). Sound reception in the dogfish. *Nature* 197, 93–94.

Dijkgraaf, S. (1964). The supposed use of the lateral line as an organ of hearing in fish. *Experientia* 20, 586.

Dijkgraaf, S. (1967). Biological significance of the lateral line organs. *In* "Lateral Line Detectors" (P. Cahn, ed.), pp. 83–95. Indiana Univ. Press, Bloomington, Indiana.

Dijkgraaf, S., and Verheijen, F. J. (1950). Neue Versuche über das Tonuntershceidungsvermögen der Elritze. *Z. Vergleich. Physiol.* 32, 248–256.

Disler, N. N. (1960). "Organs of Sensation in the Lateral Line System and their Significance in the Behavior of Fishes." Akad. Nauk, Moscow.

Dobrin, M. B. (1947). Measurements of underwater noise produced by marine life. *Science* 105, 19–23.

Dorai Raj, B. S. (1960b). The lateral line system and sound perception in catfish. *J. Madras Univ.* B30, 9–19.

Dudok van Heel, W. H. (1956). Pitch discrimination in the minnow (*Phoxinus laevis*) at different temperature levels. *Experientia* 12, 75.

Enger, P. S. (1963). Unit activity on the fish auditory system. *Acta Physiol. Scand.* 59, Suppl. 1–48.

Enger, P. S. (1966). Acoustic threshold in goldfish and its relation to the sound source distance. *Comp. Biochem. Physiol.* 18, 859–868.

Enger, P. S. (1967a). Hearing in herring. *Comp. Biochem. Physiol.* 22, 527–538.

Enger, P. S. (1967b). Effect of the acoustic near field on the sound threshold in fishes. *In* "Lateral Line Detectors" (P. Cahn, ed.), pp. 239–248. Indiana Univ. Press, Bloomington, Indiana.

Enger, P. S., and Andersen, R. (1967). An electrophysiological field study of hearing in fish. *Comp. Biochem. Physiol.* 22, 517–525.

Evans, H. M. (1935). Hearing in fishes. *J. Ipswich Nat. Hist. Soc.* 1, 217–230.

Farkas, B. (1935). Untersuchungen über das Hörvermögen bei Fischen. *Allat. Kozlem.* 32, 19–20.

Farkas, B. (1936). Zur Kenntnis des Hörvermögens und des Gehörorgans der Fische. *Acta Oto-Laryngol.* 23, 499–532.

Farkas, B. (1938a). Über den schalleitenden Apparat der Knochenfische. I. Fenestra Sacculi, Protoperculum und Protocolumella bei *Lebistes reticulatus* Pet. *Z. Morphol. Oekol. Tiere* 34, 367–415.

Farkas, B. (1938b). Zur Kenntnis des Baues und der Funktion des Saccolithen der Knochenfische. *Zool. Anz.* **11**, Suppl., 193–206.

Ffowcs-Williams, J. E. (1967). Flow noise. *In* "Underwater Acoustics" (V. M. Albers, ed.), Vol. 2, pp. 89–102. Plenum Press, New York.

Fletcher, H., and Munson, W. A. (1937). Relation between loudness and masking. *J. Acoust. Soc. Am.* **9**, 1–10.

Flock, Å., and Wersäll, J. (1962). A study of the orientation of the sensory hairs of the receptor cells in the lateral line organ of fish, with special reference to the function of the receptors. *J. Cell Biol.* **15**, 19–27.

Froese, H. (1938). Vergleichend-Anatomische Studien über das Knochenfisch-labyrinth. *Z. Morphol. Oekol. Tiere* **34**, 610–646.

Froloff, J. (1925). Bedingte Reflexe bei Fischen. I. *Arch. Ges. Physiol.* **208**, 216–271.

Furakawa, T., and Ishii, Y. (1967a). Effects of static bending of sensory hairs on sound reception in the goldfish. *Japan. J. Physiol.* **17**, 572–588.

Furakawa, T., and Ishii, Y. (1967b). Neurophysiological studies on hearing in goldfish. *J. Neurophysiol.* **30**, 1377–1403.

Grassé, P.-P. (1958). L'oreille et ses annexes. *In* "Traité de Zoologie" (P.-P. Grassé, ed.), Vol. 13, pp. 1063–1098. Masson, Paris.

Harris, G. G. (1964). Considerations on the physics of sound production by fishes. *In* "Marine Bio-Acoustics" (W. N. Tavolga, ed.), pp. 233–247. Pergamon Press, Oxford.

Harris, G. G., and van Bergeijk, W. A. (1962). Evidence that the lateral-line organ responds to near-field displacements of sound sources in water. *J. Acoust. Soc. Am.* **34**, 1831–1841.

Hawkins, J. E., and Stevens, S. S. (1950). The masking of pure tones and of speech by white noise. *J. Acoust. Soc. Am.* **22**, 6–13.

Herrick, C. J. (1898). The cranial nerves of bony fishes. *J. Comp. Neurol.* **8**, 162–170.

Iversen, R. T. B. (1967). Response of yellowfin tuna (*Thunnus albacares*) to underwater sound. *In* "Marine Bio-Acoustics" (W. N. Tavolga, ed.), Vol. 2, pp. 105–121. Pergamon Press, Oxford.

Iwai, T. (1967). Structure and development of lateral line cupulae in teleost larvae. *In* "Lateral Line Detectors" (P. Cahn, ed.), pp. 27–44. Indiana Univ. Press, Bloomington, Indiana.

Jacobs, D. W., and Tavolga, W. N. (1967). Acoustic intensity limens in the goldfish. *Animal Behaviour* **15**, 324–335.

Jacobs, D. W., and Tavolga, W. N. (1968). Acoustic frequency discrimination in the goldfish. *Animal Behaviour* **16**, 67–71.

Jielof, R., Spoor, A., and de Vries, H. (1952). The microphonic activity of the lateral line. *J. Physiol. (London)* **116**, 137–157.

Kleerekoper, H., and Chagnon, E. C. (1954). Hearing in fish, with special reference to *Semotilus atromaculatus atromaculatus* (Mitchill). *J. Fisheries Res. Board Can.* **11**, 130–152.

Kleerekoper, H., and Malar, T. (1968). Orientation through sound in fishes. *In* "Hearing Mechanisms in Vertebrates" (A. V. S. De Reuck and J. Knight, eds.), pp. 188–206. Little, Brown, Boston, Massachusetts.

Kleerekoper, H., and Roggenkamp, P. A. (1959). An experimental study on the effect of the swimbladder on hearing sensitivity in *Ameiurus nebulosus nebulosus* (Lesueur). *Can. J. Zool.* **37**, 1–8.

Kreidl, A. (1895). Ueber die Perception der Schallwellen bei den Fischen. *Arch. Ges. Physiol.* **61**, 450–464.

Kritzler, H., and Wood, L. (1961). Provisional audiogram for the shark, *Carcharinus leucas*. *Science* **133**, 1480–1482.

Kuiper, J. W. (1956). "The Microphonic Effect of the Lateral Line Organ," Publ. Biophys. Group Natuurk. Lab. Groningen, Netherlands.

Kuroki, T. (1967). Theoretical analysis of the role of the lateral line in directional hearing. *In* "Lateral Line Detectors" (P. Cahn, ed.), pp. 217–237. Indiana Univ. Press, Bloomington, Indiana.

Lafite-Dupont, J. (1907). Recherches sur l'audition des poissons. *Compt. Rend. Soc. Biol.* 63, 710–711.

Licklider, J. C. R. (1951). Basic correlates of the auditory stimulus. *In* "Handbook of Experimental Psychology" (S. S. Stevens, ed.), pp. 985–1039. Wiley, New York.

Lowenstein, O. (1957). The sense organs: The acoustico-lateralis system. *In* "The Physiology of Fishes" (M. E. Brown, ed.), Vol. 2, pp. 155–186. Academic Press, New York.

Lowenstein, O., and Roberts, T. D. M. (1951). The localization and analysis of the responses to vibration from the isolated elasmobranch labyrinth. A contribution to the problem of the evolution of hearing in vertebrates. *J. Physiol. (London)* 114, 471–489.

Mackenzie, K. V. (1960). Formulas for the computation of sound speed in sea water. *J. Acoust. Soc. Am.* 32, 100.

McDonald, H. E. (1922). Ability of *Pimephales notatus* to form associations with sound vibrations. *J. Comp. Psychol.* 2, 191–193.

Maliukina, G. A. (1960). Hearing in certain Black Sea fishes in connection with ecology and particulars in the structure of their hearing apparatus. *Zh. Obschch. Biol.* 21, 198–205.

Maliukina, G. A., and Protasov, V. R. (1960). Hearing, "voice" and reactions of fish to sounds. *Usp. Sovrem. Biol.* 50, 229–242.

Manning, F. B. (1924). Hearing in goldfish in relation to the structure of its ear. *J. Exptl. Zool.* 41, 5–20.

Marage, M. (1906). Contribution à l'étude de l'audition des poissons. *Compt. Rend.* 143, 852–853.

Moorhouse, V. H. K. (1933). Reactions of fish to noise. *Contrib. Can. Biol.* 7, 467–475.

Moulton, J. M., and Dixon, R. H. (1967). Directional hearing in fishes. *In* "Marine Bio-Acoustics" (W. N. Tavolga, ed.), Vol. 2, pp. 187–232. Pergamon Press, Oxford.

Myrberg, A. A., Jr., Banner, A., and Richard, J. D. (1969). Shark attraction using a video-acoustic system. *Marine Biol.* 2, 264–276.

Nelson, D. R. (1967a). Hearing thresholds, frequency discrimination and acoustic orientation in the lemon shark, *Negaprion brevirostris* (Poey). *Bull. Marine Sci.* 17, 741–768.

Nelson, D. R. (1967b). Cardiac responses to sounds in the lemon shark, *Negaprion brevirostris. In* "Sharks, Skates and Rays" (P. W. Gilbert, R. F. Mathewson, and D. P. Rall, eds.), pp. 533–544. Johns Hopkins Press, Baltimore, Maryland.

Nelson, D. R., and Gruber, S. H. (1963). Sharks: Attraction by low-frequency sounds. *Science* 142, 975–977.

Nelson, E. M. (1955). The morphology of the swim bladder and auditory bulla in Holocentridae. *Fieldiana, Zool.* 37, 121–137.

Parker, G. H. (1902). Hearing and allied senses in fishes. *Bull. U. S. Fish. Comm.* 22, 45–64.

Parker, G. H. (1905). The function of the lateral-line organs in fishes. *Bull. U. S. Bur. Fish.* 24, 185–207.

Parker, G. H. (1910a). Influence of the eyes, ears, and other allied sense organs on the movements of the dogfish, *Mustelus canis*. *Bull. U. S. Bur. Fish.* **29**, 43–57.

Parker, G. H. (1910b). Sound as a directing influence in the movements of fishes. *Bull. U. S. Bur. Fish.* **30**, 97–104.

Parker, G. H. (1918). Hearing in fishes. *Copeia* pp. 11–12.

Parker, G. H., and van Heusen, A. P. (1917). The reception of mechanical stimuli by the skin, lateral line organs and ears of fishes, especially in Amiurus. *Am. J. Physiol.* **44**, 463–489.

Parvulescu, A. (1964). Problems of propagation and processing. *In* "Marine Bio-Acoustics" (W. N. Tavolga, ed.), pp. 87–100. Pergamon Press, Oxford.

Parvulescu, A. (1967). Acoustics of small tanks. *In* "Marine Bio-Acoustics" (W. N. Tavolga, ed.), Vol. 2, pp. 7–13. Pergamon Press, Oxford.

Pearson, A. A. (1936). The acoustic-lateral nervous system in fishes. *J. Comp. Neurol.* **64**, 235–273.

Poggendorf, D. (1952). Die absoluten Hörschwellen des Zwergwelses (*Amiurus nebulosus*) und Beiträge zur Physik des Weberschen Apparates der Ostariophysen. *Z. Vergleich. Physiol.* **34**, 222–257.

Popper, A. N. (1970). Auditory capacities of the Mexican blind cavefish (*Astyanax jordani*) and its eyed ancestor (*Astyanax mexicanus*). *Animal Behaviour* **18**, 552–562.

Protasov, V. R. (1965). "Bioakustika Ryb." Akad. Nauk, Moscow.

Reinhardt, F. (1935). Über Richtungswahrnehmung bei Fischen, besonders bei der Elritze (*Phoxinus laevis* L.) und beim Zwergwels (*Amiurus nebulosus* Raf.). *Z. Vergleich. Physiol.* **22**, 570–603.

Rode, P. (1929). Recherches sur l'organe sensorial latéral des téléostéens. *Bull. Biol. France Belg.* **63**, 1–84.

Sand, A. (1937). The mechanism of the lateral sense organs of fishes. *Proc. Roy. Soc.* **B123**, 472–495.

Scharf, B. (1961). Complex sounds and critical bands. *Psychol. Bull.* **58**, 205–217.

Scharf, B. (1966). "Special Report on Critical Bands." Lab. Sensory Commun., Syracuse University, Syracuse, New York.

Schneider, H. (1941). Die Bedeutung der Atemhöhle der Labyrinthfische für ihr Hörvermögen. *Z. Vergleich. Physiol.* **29**, 172–194.

Schriever, H. (1936). Über die Funktion der Seitenorgane der Fische. *Verhandl. Physik.-Med. Ges. Wurzburg* **59**, 67–68.

Stetter, H. (1929). Untersuchungen über den Gehörsinn der Fische, besonders von *Phoxinus laevis* L. und *Amiurus nebulosus* Raf. *Z. Vergleich. Physiol.* **9**, 339–477.

Stipetić, E. (1939). Über das Gehörorgan der Mormyriden. *Z. Vergleich. Physiol.* **26**, 740–752.

Suckling, E. E. (1962). Lateral line in fish—possible mode of action. *J. Acoust. Soc. Am.* **34**, 127.

Suckling, E. E., and Suckling, J. A. (1950). The electrical response of the lateral line system of fish to tone and other stimuli. *J. Gen. Physiol.* **34**, 1–8.

Suckling, E. E., and Suckling, J. A. (1964). Lateral line as a vibration receptor. *J. Acoust. Soc. Am.* **36**, 2214–2216.

Tavolga, W. N., ed. (1964a). "Marine Bio-Acoustics." Pergamon Press, Oxford.

Tavolga, W. N. (1965). "Review of Marine Bio-Acoustics. State of the Art: 1964," Tech. Rept. 1212-1. U. S. Naval Training Device Center, Port Washington, New York.

Tavolga, W. N., ed. (1967a). "Marine Bio-Acoustics," Vol. 2. Pergamon Press, Oxford.

Tavolga, W. N. (1967b). Masked auditory thresholds in teleost fishes. *In* "Marine Bio-Acoustics" (W. N. Tavolga, ed.), Vol. 2, pp. 233–245. Pergamon Press, Oxford.

Tavolga, W. N., and Wodinsky, J. (1963). Auditory capacities in fishes. Pure tone thresholds in nine species of marine teleosts. *Bull. Am. Museum Nat. Hist.* 126, 177–240.

Tavolga, W. N., and Wodinsky, J. (1965). Auditory capacities in fishes: Threshold variability in the blue-striped grunt, *Haemulon sciurus. Animal Behaviour* 13, 301–311.

Tomaschek, H. (1936). Beiträge zur Klärung der Frage über das Hören der Fische. *Zool. Jahrb. Abt. Allgem. Zool. Physiol.* 56, 553–580.

Tomaschek, H. (1937). Histologische Untersuchungen des Gehörorgans von *Trutta fario. Zool. Jahrb. Abt. Allgem. Zool. Physiol.* 57, 159–162.

Tschiegg, C. E., and Hays, E. E. (1959). Transistorized velocimeter for measuring the speed of sound in the sea. *J. Acoust. Soc. Am.* 31, 1038–1039.

van Bergeijk, W. A. (1964). Directional and nondirectional hearing in fish. *In* "Marine Bio-Acoustics" (W. N. Tavolga, ed.), pp. 281–299. Pergamon Press, Oxford.

van Bergeijk, W. A. (1966). Evolution of the sense of hearing in vertebrates. *Am. Zoologist* 6, 371–377.

van Bergeijk, W. A. (1967a). The evolution of vertebrate hearing. *In* "Contributions to Sensory Physiology" (W. D. Neff, ed.), Vol. 2, pp. 1–49. Academic Press, New York.

van Bergeijk, W. A. (1967b). Discussion of critical bands in hearing of fishes. *In* "Marine Bio-Acoustics" (W. N. Tavolga, ed.), Vol. 2, pp. 244–245. Pergamon Press, Oxford.

van Bergeijk, W. A. (1967c). Introductory comments on lateral line function. *In* "Lateral Line Detectors" (P. Cahn, ed.), pp. 73–81. Indiana Univ. Press, Bloomington, Indiana.

Vigoureux, P. (1960). Underwater sound. *Proc. Roy. Soc.* B152, 49–51.

von Békésy, G. (1960). "Experiments in Hearing." McGraw-Hill, New York.

von Boutteville, K. F. (1935). Untersuchungen über den Gehorsinn bei Characiniden und Gymnotiden und den Bau ihres Labyrinthes. *Z. Vergleich. Physiol.* 22, 162–191.

von Frisch, K. (1923). Ein Zwergwels der kommt, wenn man ihm pfeift. *Biol. Zentr.* 43, 439–446.

von Frisch, K. (1936). Über den Gehörsinn der Fische. *Biol. Rev.* 11, 210–246.

von Frisch, K. (1938a). The sense of hearing in fish. *Nature* 141, 8–11.

von Frisch, K. (1938b). Über die Bedeutung des Sacculus und der Lagena für den Gehörsinn der Fische. *Z. Vergleich. Physiol.* 25, 703–747.

von Frisch, K., and Dijkgraaf, S. (1935). Konnen Fische die Schallrichtung wahrnehmen? *Z. Vergleich Physiol.* 22, 641–655.

von Frisch, K., and Stetter, H. (1932). Untersuchungen über den Sitz des Gehörsinnes bei der Elritze. *Z. Vergleich. Physiol.* 17, 686–801.

Walker, T. J. (1967). History, histological methods, and details of the structure of the lateral line of the walleye surfperch. *In* "Lateral Line Detectors" (P. Cahn, ed.), pp. 13–25. Indiana Univ. Press, Bloomington, Indiana.

Warner, L. H. (1932). The sensitivity of fishes to sound and to other mechanical stimulation. *Quart. Rev. Biol.* 7, 326–339.

Wodinsky, J. (1969). The effect of omission of shock during auditory threshold testing with the avoidance method (in manuscript).

Wodinsky, J., and Tavolga, W. N. (1964). Sound detection in teleost fishes. In "Marine Bio-Acoustics" (W. N. Tavolga, ed.), pp. 269–280. Pergamon Press, Oxford.

Wohlfahrt, T. A. (1936). Das Ohrlabyrinth der Sardine (Clupea pilchardus Walb.) und seine Beziehungen zur Schwimmblase und Seitenlinie. Z. Morphol. Öekol. Tiere 31, 371–410.

Wohlfahrt, T. A. (1938). Von den Ohren der Fische. Die Beziehungen des inneren Ohres zur Schwimmblase besonders bei heringsartigen Fischen. Aus der Natur (Leipzig) 15, 82–87.

Wohlfahrt, T. A. (1939). Untersuchungen über das Tonunterscheidungsvermögen der Elritze (Phoxinus laevis Agass.). Z. Vergleich. Physiol. 26, 570–604.

Wolff, D. L. (1966). Akustische Untersuchungen zur Klapperfischerei und verwandter Methoden. Z. Fischerei [N.S.] 14, 277–315.

Wolff, D. L. (1967). Das Hörvermögen des Flussbarsches (Perca fluviatilis L.). Biol. Zentr. 86, 449–460.

Wolff, D. L. (1968). Das Hörvermögen des Kaulbarsches (Acerina cernua L.) und des Zanders (Lucioperca sandra Cuv. und Val.). Z. Vergleich. Physiol. 60, 14–33.

Zotterman, I. (1943). The microphonic effect of teleost labyrinths and biological significance. J. Physiol. (London) 102, 313–318.

2

RECENT ADVANCES IN THE STUDY OF FISH AUDITION

William N. Tavolga

This article was prepared expressly for this Benchmark volume by William N. Tavolga

Since the publication of the review reprinted here, in part, as Paper 1, there have been a number of significant advances in the study of fish audition. As demonstrated by the emphasis in two recent major reviews by Popper and Fay (1973) and Hawkins (1973), the main questions investigated have been in the area of mechanisms of hearing.

PSYCHOPHYSICS

Once it became clearly evident that fishes do hear, the question of what they could hear was the next logical problem; i.e., what is the hearing frequency range? Again in logical sequence, the next question was quantitative; i.e., what are the hearing thresholds? Because there are so many highly different species with diverse adaptations, the collection of audiograms for different species occupied the attention of many workers, and there have been several significant reports on hearing thresholds in the recent literature.

The essentially Pavlovian technique of conditioned heart rate changes was successfully used by several workers, and in particular, Offutt (1971) and Fish and Offutt (1972) determined audiograms for the tautog *(Tautoga onitis)* and the toadfish *(Opsanus tau)*, respectively.* In the latter study, some field experiments were done using playbacks of artificial sounds and of recorded toadfish sounds. Based upon the responses of animals in the vicinity of the playback, the thresholds were estimated to be at least within the same order of magnitude as those measured in the laboratory.

Among the ostariophysine fishes, the goldfish has been the commonly used experimental animal. As a matter of fact, it has become the "wet rat" in psychophysics. As far as audition is concerned, however, it turns out to have an audiogram almost identical with its "wild" ancestor, the carp, *Cyprinus carpio* (Popper, 1972a). Another report (Köhler, 1973) gave thresholds that were at least 15 dB higher, but these data were based upon a very small sample and in a situation with considerable masking noise present. Although Köhler used

---

*The use of mks rather than cgs units for second pressure was proposed, i.e., in newtons/m² rather than dynes/cm² (= microbar, μb), and a reference level of 1 micronewton per square meter. Previously, the reference level of 1 μb was standard, and this value equals 100 dB re 1 μN/m². One advantage of the change would be to eliminate unwieldy negative numbers. The familiar human threshold at 0.0002 μb (= −74 db re 1 μb) now becomes 26 dB re 1 μN/m². Usage prevails, however, and the 1-μb reference level is still widely used.

juveniles, their size should not have made any significant difference (Popper, 1971).

As reviewed by Popper and Fay (1973) and Popper (1972a), the audiograms for the ostariophysines are remarkably similar, but the report by Schade (1971) on the minnow, *Leucaspius delineatus,* appeared to be almost 20 dB higher than in most other species. Curiously, these data matched those of Weiss (1967) on the goldfish. Schade used a technique similar to that of Weiss in that he turned off the shock when the animal appeared to be working close to threshold. As noted earlier (Tavolga, 1971a), this could produce an extinction of the avoidance response, and, therefore, a falsely high threshold value.

Another factor that is evidently critical in producing variability in results is the acoustic condition of the experimental tank. The ambient noise level could act as a masker, and the acoustic reverberant conditions can change the nature of the stimulus under test. The psychophysical technique seems to have little effect. Even such diverse methods as conditioned heart rate, as compared to avoidance and positive instrumental conditioning, gave similar results (Popper and Fay, 1973), and in a specific comparison, conditioned suppression of respiration (classical conditioning) and avoidance conditioning gave identical thresholds for the goldfish (Popper, Chan, and Clarke, 1973).

Additional recent psychophysical studies on the goldfish included a report on the limited ability of goldfish to generalize an acoustic stimulus to stimuli of differing frequencies (Fay, 1970a) and the use of this generalization paradigm to determine the ability of goldfish to detect amplitude modulation (Fay, 1972). Popper (1972b) described an experiment in which he was able to demonstrate that goldfish showed identical thresholds to long- and short-duration (pulsed) pure tones, and he concluded that goldfish do not possess temporal summation capacities.

A major advance in the psychophysics of fish hearing over the past few years has been in the use of open water, i.e., field conditions. Not only are audiograms obtained in this situation probably more relevant to the animals' normal ecology and behavior, but the confounding effects of small-tank acoustics are avoided. The codfish *(Gadus morhua)* was found to have an audiogram from 30 to 470 Hz, with its greatest sensitivity in the 60- to 310-Hz range (−18 to −26 dB re 1 μb). In this study by Chapman and Hawkins (1973), the fish were restrained, and the heart rate conditioning method was used, but all in a large body of water approximating free field conditions.

Comparable results were obtained for the haddock *(Melanogrammus aeglefinus),* the pollack *(Pollachius pollachius),* and the ling *(Molva molva)* by Chapman (1973), and for two species of flatfish (Chapman and Sand, 1974). Additional open-water psychophysics was done on the codfish by Schuijf (1975) and other workers, but these will be discussed in more detail under the heading of directional hearing.

In an attempt to correlate laboratory and field studies, the behavior of free-swimming bonefish *(Albula vulpes)* was compared to laboratory-obtained auditory thresholds (Tavolga, 1974a). The audiogram showed this species to have its highest sensitivity in the region of 300 Hz (−26 db re 1 μb). The bonefish is a well-known game fish, and is easily frightened by man-made noises. It was found that many of these noises have a strong peak at about 300 Hz. This included sounds made by tapping on the boat hull, dropping of bait, outboard-motor noise, and similar disturbances generated during the course of shallow-water fishing. The responsiveness of the fish is not so much dependent on any unusually sensitive hearing but, rather, on the coincidence of many sounds with the fish's most sensitive range and the readiness with which the fright response can be evoked. In other words, the bonefish does not *hear* any better than most; it just *listens* better.

THE ROLE OF THE SWIM BLADDER IN HEARING

According to van Bergeijk's (1964) model of fish audition, the swim bladder plays an essential role as a pressure transducer. Since the body of a fish has a density close to that of water, the swim bladder functions as an acoustical discontinuity (Cushing, 1973) and becomes excited by water-borne pressure waves (far-field). In turn, it generates a near-field of displacement energy, and it is this energy that is received by the inner ear. In the Ostariophysi and a few other groups, the swim bladder is closely coupled to the inner ear, enhancing its sensitivity. The classic and best-known coupling mechanism is the Weberian apparatus.

Confirmation of this model has appeared in several recent reports. In the ostariophysine goldfish, Fay and Popper (1974) showed that the air bladder is an important pressure transducer when they found that saccular microphonics from stimuli above 100 Hz were reduced when the bladder was deflated.

Comparable results were reported in the carp *(Cyprinus carpio)*, in which action potentials in the acoustico-lateral region of the medulla were almost completely eliminated after swim-bladder deflation (Astafyeva and Vaitulevich, 1974).

In another ostariophysine, the bullhead *(Ictalurus)*, the same effect was obtained, but in the cichlid *(Tilapia)*, deflation of the bladder had no effect (Fay and Popper, 1975). The auditory sensitivity in *Tilapia*, however, was extremely poor (Tavolga, 1974b), and it is likely that far-field reception plays a minor role in hearing in this species.

Sand and Enger (1973) found that in the codfish, saccular microphonics were decreased by about 20 dB if the swim bladder were deflated, and they concluded that the swim bladder is necessary not only to enhance acoustic sensitivity, but to increase the total hearing range. Swim-bladder deflation had little effect on sensitivity below 100 Hz. Fay and Popper (1974), however, suggested that the breadth of frequency range was determined by inner-ear properties.

In actual measurements of the acoustical properties of the fish swim bladder, Popper (1974) found that the mechanical properties of the swim bladder and its surrounding tissues in the goldfish were such as to permit an efficient coupling to the surrounding medium, with a minimal loss of energy. The swim bladder is in many ways unlike a comparable theoretical air bubble in water. Although it does have a natural, resonant frequency, the overall frequency response is remarkably flat; i.e., the system is broadly tuned. This was a confirmation of an earlier observation for the toadfish (Tavolga, 1964). The resonant frequency of the swim bladder turns out, upon actual measurement, to be considerably different than that of a theoretical equivalent air bubble. In the codfish *(Gadus morhua),* Sand and Hawkins (1973) found it to be considerably higher—beyond the hearing range of the species. Even compression of the bladder at greater water depths did not reduce the resonant frequency to the hearing range. They theorized that this could be an adaptive mechanism to avoid the possible deleterious effects on hearing sensitivity of a resonating mechanism.

By contrast, Vaitulevich and Ushakov (1974) demonstrated much lower resonant frequencies. Using holographic techniques, they observed the vibration patterns of the swim bladder of the carp *(Cyprinus carpio)* and obtained a resonant frequency of about 300 Hz in an isolated bladder, and 450 Hz in the intact animal. The 300-Hz value corresponds to the theoretical resonant frequency of a 25-cm air bubble.

In a comparable investigation, using laser light-scattering techniques, Clarke, Popper, and Mann (1975) observed the modes of vibration of swim bladders of goldfish. Although their results should be considered preliminary, the effectiveness of the technique was demonstrated. They found a resonant frequency at about 400 Hz in a 3-cm goldfish, and a rapid decrease in response at frequencies above 900 Hz. A significant observation [also noted by Vaitulevich and Ushakov (1974)] was that different parts of the swim-bladder wall showed different frequency responses. In addition, Clarke et al. emphasized the importance of using fresh, living preparations, because the acoustic characteristics of the tissues change rapidly after death.

All previous tests on swim-bladder function included the deflation of the swim bladder as a test procedure. In an elegantly conceived experiment, Chapman and Sand (1974) did the reverse. By placing a small air-filled balloon next to the head of a flatfish, the dab *(Limanda limanda),* they, in effect, provided a swim bladder to a species that normally does not possess one. They obtained almost 10-dB improvement in the hearing sensitivity, demonstrating the importance of the swim bladder and lending support to van Bergeijk's model.

It appears that, indeed, the swim bladder is a necessary and essential transducer for acoustic pressure energy (far-field) and that it transforms the pressure energy, by virtue of its compressibility, to displacement energy to which the inner-ear mechanisms can respond. The closer the acoustic coupling between the swim bladder and the inner-ear fluids, the greater the sensitivity and frequency range of the entire receptor system. This is especially evident in the members of the order Ostariophysi, and, after more than 150 years, Weber's original hypothesis has been confirmed.

SOUND LOCALIZATION AND DIRECTIONAL HEARING

As part of his model for fish audition, van Bergeijk (1964) proposed that the swim bladder-inner ear complex was not adequate for directional hearing. Since this complex is essentially a far-field detector only, it follows that the fish effectively has only one ear. Pressure being a scalar, rather than a vector, form of energy, there is no mechanism for determining the position of a sound source relative to the swim-bladder transducer. Sound localization, therefore, could only take place in the near-field, in which adequate displacement energy was present. This energy has direction (vector), and according to the physics of acoustical phenomena, the range of effective near-field energy was limited to about one-sixth of a wavelength. Obviously, low frequencies would have the greatest near-field range. This range could be extended in situations where the source energy was so high as to generate strong pressure-induced displacements. The mathematics of these phenomena was discussed by Harris (1964).

Van Bergeijk (1964) argued further that the only receptor that was adequately sensitive at low frequencies and specifically adapted for detection of displacement energy was the lateral line system. He visualized the lateral line as an array of minute displacement detectors with their axes of sensitivity in different directions and sufficiently widely distributed over the body of the fish to provide all the directional data necessary for the central nervous system to correlate and to obtain range and bearing information needed.

One of the critics of this model was Dijkgraaf (1964), whose own work was a pioneering effort in contributing to our understanding of fish audition. He pointed out that all the studies on acoustical function of the lateral line were based upon neurophysiological experiments, not behavioral ones, and he expressed strong doubts that the lateral line was an acoustic receptor. The kind of stimuli to which the lateral line responds are slow, relatively massive water displacements, as exemplified in his concept of "distance-touch-sense" (Ferntastsinn) (Dijkgraaf, 1947, and see translation in this volume).

Investigations of lateral-line function have not supported van Bergeijk's model. In the recent literature, only two papers of significance were found. Russell and Roberts (1972) and Roberts and Russell (1972) demonstrated the inhibitory function of efferent nerve stimulation on the activity of the lateral-line sensory output. This might tend to support the notion that the system is strongly buffered and would tend to respond to massive water movements. Such water movements as those generated by swimming fishes could be effective lateral-line stimuli, for example. Cahn (1972) confirmed the earlier work of Breder (1965) on the effect of turbulent volumes of water on schooling fishes. The trail of vortices that a fish generates as it swims serves as a spacing mechanism in maintaining fish-to-fish spacing in a school, and the detection of such hydrodynamic energy is thought to be the main function of the lateral-line system.

Support for the acoustic and directional function of the lateral line can be found in the report by Horch and Salmon (1973) on sound production and reception in squirrelfish. Lateral-line microphonics were observed in response to sounds of 300 and 400 Hz. By using an arrangement in which pressure and displacement amplitudes could be varied independently, the lateral-line response was found to be primarily to the displacement component, as expected. The critical observation was made by shifting sound source position, and the lateral-line microphonics were significantly stronger with the sound source behind the fish than in front.

By contrast, however, there has been an accumulation of recent work to show that the swim bladder-inner ear complex can serve as a directional sound detector. The techniques used in these studies included conditioned heart and respiration rate changes, behavioral changes, and saccular microphonics, and most of the data were obtained from open-water, field conditions.

Part of van Bergeijk's original model has been supported, to the extent that directionalization can only take place in the near-field: Schuijf, Baretta, and Wildschut (1972) on the wrass, *Labrus berggylta;* Popper, Salmon, and Parvulescu (1973) on the squirrelfish *Myripristis;* Chapman and Johnstone (1974) on the codfish and haddock, *Gadus morhua* and *Melanogrammus aeglefinus;* and Schuijf (1975) on the codfish, *Gadus morhua.* The limitations of close range and low frequency still hold.

In the codfish, at least, ablation of the lateral line does not impair directional hearing. Using a surgical technique developed by Dijkgraaf (1973), Schuijf and Siemelink (1974) used behavioral techniques (positive reinforcement) to demonstrate this, and, additionally, showed that unilateral severing of the nerve supply to the pars inferior of the labyrinth abolished a directional response. Schuijf (1975) also found that such unilateral nerve sectioning did not reduce the sensitivity of the animals to sound—only to the direction of the sound source.

Using heart rate conditioning, Chapman and Johnstone (1974) obtained directional thresholds in the order of 10° to 20° as a difference limen in codfish and haddock. In one of few such studies, they also obtained a difference limen in amplitude of 1.3 to 9.5 dB over a range of 50 to 380 Hz (a value in the order of what was reported earlier for the goldfish by Jacobs and Tavolga, 1967). They proposed that the swim bladder is unlikely to play a role in directional hearing, since the vibrations of this structure would affect both inner ears equally. The otoliths, however, are efficient displacement detectors, by virtue of their relative mass and delicate suspension, and direct near-field stimulation of the otoliths could provide directional information.

Van Bergeijk (1964) considered the above notion, but rejected it because he thought that the strong near-field generated by the nearby swim bladder would totally mask any such binaural directional information. It is beginning to appear that this objection is not valid. Enger, Hawkins, Sand, and Chapman (1973); Sand (1974); and Sand and Enger (1974) found that the saccular hair cells were significantly organized in terms of their axes of sensitivity. Groups of cells with their axes of sensitivity (kinocilium position) parallel to the long axis of the fish would enhance the sensitivity to the reradiated signal from the swim bladder. Other cells were found that were relatively insensitive to the highly directional swim-bladder displacements. By contrast, these were vertically sensitive and, consequently could detect externally generated near-fields, unmasked by that of the swim bladder.

A somewhat different model for directional sound detection in the fish sacculus was presented by Schuijf and Buwalda (1975). They considered the entire complex of phase relationships that exist at the receptor: phase differences between the pressure and the displacement energy; how these phase differences are re-radiated by the swim bladder or impinge directly upon the saccular sensors; the distinctions between horizontal–vertical and radial–axial displacements. They concluded that phase differences would enable the discrimination of direct near-field from swim bladder re-radiated information. The fact that fishes are capable of phase discrimination has been demonstrated by Piddington (1972), so this model becomes more plausible in the light of new data.

In general, this is probably the most trenchant of the research areas currently under way in fish acoustics. We are discovering that the fish ear is capable of much finer and more complex discriminations than was conceived only a few years ago. The fact that echolocation is possible in a fish no longer seems remarkable. The low-frequency sounds produced by a species of marine catfish *(Arius felis)* appear to enable the animal to detect nearby obstacles (Tavolga, 1971b, 1976), and the directional mechanisms of hearing such as modeled above would be essential for the effectiveness of such acoustic orientation.

FREQUENCY DISCRIMINATION AND THE CRITICAL BAND

As compared to mammals, the auditory spectrum in fishes is narrow, both in frequency and dynamic range. Few species have been found capable of detecting sounds above 2000 Hz in frequency or below -45 db re 1 μb in amplitude. In terms of frequency discrimination, difference limens have been obtained in only a few species, and the capacities in fish are inferior to those of most tetrapods. However, the fact that fishes are capable of any degree of frequency discrimination is of interest, since fishes do not possess any cochlear structure for frequency analysis. In mammals and other terrestrial vertebrates, the elongated cochlea and its basilar membrane account for the capacity to discriminate one frequency from another. Furthermore, the place theory of hearing is strongly supported by the concept of the "critical band." The classic notion of a critical masking band was originally proposed by Fletcher (1940) and defined as the narrow band of frequencies above and below a specified signal tone that are effective in masking the tone. At complete masking, the power of the masking band is equal to or greater than that of the signal. One approach, therefore, to looking for explanations and mechanisms in fish audition has been to explore frequency discrimination and the effects of masking noise.

In the first quantitative and controlled study of this sort, Dijkgraaf and Verheijen (1950; Paper 8) obtained difference limens in the minnow *(Phoxinus)* of about one-quarter tone (about 3 percent frequency difference). In another ostariophysine, the goldfish, Jacobs and Tavolga (1968) and Fay (1970b) reported comparable values, based on more subjects and different pscyhophysical methods. The data showed remarkable agreement, in that Fay's determinations (using conditioned suppression of respiration) and those of Jacobs and Tavolga (using avoidance conditioning), were almost identical. Among nonostariophysines, however, frequency discrimination is not nearly as good, ranging from 10 to 100 percent (Popper and Fay, 1973; Fay, 1975).

The effects of masking noise in fishes was first described for the squirrel fish (Tavolga, 1967) and, later, in other species (Buerkle, 1968, 1969; Chapman and Hawkins, 1973). Initially, the concern over masking noise was over the possibility that ambient noise could be producing artificially high thresholds in determinations of audiograms for various species. The use of masking noise as a way of elucidating auditory mechanisms, however, was not developed until very recently. Here again, Fay and myself, working independently, obtained almost identical results. In the goldfish, Fay (1974) reported a signal/noise ratio (critical ratio) of about 20 dB, and my data (Tavolga, 1974b) gave a mean value of 22.8 dB. These values are certainly not significantly different, in spite of many differences in the techniques used. Such a signal/noise ratio is in the same range as that of many mammals.

The signal/noise ratio, or critical ratio, can be converted into an estimation of the critical band (Hawkins and Stevens, 1950; Scharf, 1970), but this depends upon whether one accepts the notion of a place principle as it applies to fish audition. Van Bergeijk (1967) pointed out that a basilar membrane as such is not necessary for a place-theory model to operate. Any structure with sufficient acoustical asymmetry would respond differentially to traveling waves of different frequencies. He provided the analogy of a bongo drum, saying that even such a primitive sound generator can emit different frequencies over a span of at least an octave by virtue of its being a bounded membrane with some asymmetry in tension. According to this "bongo drum hypothesis," the otolith, delicately suspended in the sacculus, could develop a variety of modes or axes of vibration that correspond to different impinging frequencies. In addition, the studies on saccular microphonics by Enger et al. (1973), Sand (1974), and Sand and Enger (1974) (all cited earlier) have shown that there are areas of the sacculus where axes of sensitivity of the hair cells are arranged along different vectors. The place for a place theory may exist in the fish's ear after all.

We must, however, always keep in mind the caution that fish are not ancestral to mammals, and their sensory and central nervous system organization is not only quantitatively but qualitatively different from that of tetrapods. In addition, the tremendous adaptive radiation among fishes makes comparison among orders, families, and even genera a practice to be approached carefully. The evidence from auditory activity in the brain of the goldfish, for example, shows that masking effects are centrally correlated (Enger, 1973). It may well be that the site of the place theory may be central.

All the above, however, has been primarily confined to members of the Ostariophysi, and the evidence shows that frequency discrimination in other fishes is much poorer or may not exist at all. What discrimination there is can probably be attributed to differences in intensity sensitivity within a narrow dynamic range, and masking noise data in such species do not support the existence of any critical bands (Tavolga, 1974b).

However, Fay (1974) presented several arguments against the place model in the fish sacculus. The alternative model is based on the familiar volley principle (Wever, 1949). Wever (1969) proposed that the inertial mass of the otolith is the crucial factor. With an impinging acoustic signal, the sensory hairs of the macula are stimulated by their relative movement against the massive otolith. Frequency analysis would be a central function. Given the fact that the frequency range in fishes is considerably narrower than in most tetrapods, the volley principle becomes even more plausible. Fay (1974) noted that, in contrast to mammalian hair cells, saccular hair cells in fishes may have their axes of sensitivity as much as 180° out of phase. This could account for the ability of the goldfish to discriminate between compressions and rarefactions of the same acoustic stimulus (Piddington, 1972), and would provide the fish ear with more detailed information that would then be centrally processed.

A rather novel theory of the function of the otoliths was proposed by Offutt (1970). Otoliths are densely organized crystals that contain materials such as aragonite, and may exhibit a piezoelectric effect like that of Rochelle salt, a common component of hydrophones. Unfortunately, no evidence to support such a notion is available, and the idea must remain as a highly improbable theory.

As in the field of directional hearing, the mechanisms by which fish can discriminate frequencies are still subject to controversy, and this is what makes the research area exciting and stimulating.

AUDITION IN ELASMOBRANCHS

Hearing in elasmobranchs, especially sharks, has been a special area of interest ever since the report by Nelson and Gruber (1963) that sharks can be attracted to the source of a low-frequency sound. Such low-frequency sounds can be generated by wounded or disabled fishes, other feeding sharks, and even human swimmers thrashing about (Myrberg, Banner, and Richard, 1969). Two recent reports have added to our knowledge of the specific parameters of a sound that make it attractive to predatory sharks. Nelson and Johnson (1972), observing reef sharks in the Marshall Islands, and Myrberg, Ha, Walewski, and Banbury (1972), on pelagic sharks in the Florida straits, found that the most effective signals were in the 25- 50-Hz range, and if they were projected in short, irregular pulses.

The distance over which sharks can be attracted is of interest, since some information about their hearing mechanisms may be deduced thereby. In earlier accounts, distances of several kilometers have been claimed, and assumptions were made that sharks, even with no swim bladder, could detect and localize sound sources on the basis of far-field (pressure) energy alone. The main objection to such field tests was that there was no way to establish if the shark that was sighted a kilometer or more away was indeed the same specimen that was later observed close to the sound source. In the report by Myrberg et al. (1972) it was claimed that sharks could be attracted from a distance of at least 200 m. Swimming directions and "unhurried" movements of sharks were observed at two separated points. However, the presence of several sharks in the vicinity of the main vessel and a distant skiff was noted even in the absence of sound signals. A careful reading of the paper still leaves one unconvinced that sharks were actually attracted by a sound over that great a distance. However, this simply illustrates the difficulties in obtaining anything approaching psychophysical data under field conditions with unrestrained subjects.

The use of acoustics by predatory sharks hitherto has been based on indirect, deductive evidence, but Banner (1972) has been able to confirm this by a correlation of stomach-content analysis, behavioral observations, and playback experiments in the field. He concluded that audition was useful in sharks in locating prey, locating sites of other predator activity, compensating for limitations of vision, and generally responding to acoustic and hydrodynamic disturbances in an investigatory fashion.

One of the main difficulties in interpreting the acoustic responses of sharks has been a basic lack of understanding on the mechanisms of transduction of an acoustic stimulus from the water into the inner ear. Sharks lack any swim bladder, and their otoliths are not the massive bony aggregates that teleosts possess. Tester, Kendall, and Milisen (1972) described the anatomical and histological details of the inner ear of *Carcharinus* and made a special point of describing the relationship between the highly sensitive *macula neglecta* and nearby chondrocranial fenestrae that could possible function as vibration detectors. In a further study, Fay, Kendall, Popper, and Tester (1974) were able to provide physiological evidence that, in fact, the parietal fossa and fenestra do form a direct vibrational pathway to the *macula neglecta*. With this evidence in hand, it should now be possible, for the first time, to hypothesize a model for acoustic energy (displacement, primarily) transduction to the shark's inner ear, and perhaps our understanding of how a shark can locate sound sources will be enhanced.

SUMMARY

Advances in the study of hearing in fishes from 1971 to date (August 1975) have been primarily in the analysis of hearing mechanisms. The major research efforts have been:

1. The use of open-water, i.e., field conditions, in the study of auditory responses in fish.

2. The analysis of the role of the swim bladder as a pressure-to-displacement transducer in teleost audition.

3. The accumulation of evidence, behavioral and neurophysiological, that the teleost inner ear, rather than the lateral line, is capable of detecting the position of a sound source.

4. The search for an understanding of the mechanism of frequency discrimination and signal/noise separation in the teleost ear.

5. The discoveries of reception mechanisms in elasmobranch fishes.

LITERATURE CITED

Note: The entries marked * are also included in the bibliography for Tavolga (1971a), reprinted in this volume.

Astafyeva, S. N., and Vaitulevich, S. F. (1974). On the role of the swim bladder in acoustic function in the carp, *Cyprinus carpio.* [In Russian] *Biofizika, 19,* 420–423.
Banner, A. (1972). Use of sound in predation by young lemon sharks, *Negaprion brevirostris* (Poey). *Bull. Marine Sci., 22,* 251–283.

Breder, C. M., Jr. (1965). Vortices and fish schools. *Zoologica, 50,* 97–114.

*Buerkle, U. (1968). Relation of pure tone thresholds to background noise level in the Atlantic cod *(Gadus morhua). J. Fisheries Res. Board Canada, 25,* 1155–1160.

Buerkle, U. (1969). Auditory masking and the critical band in Atlantic cod *(Gadus morhua). J. Fisheries Res. Board Canada, 26,* 1113–1119.

Cahn, P. (1972). Sensory factors in the side-to-side spacing and positional orientation of the tuna, *Euthynnus affinis,* during schooling, *Fishery Bull., 70,* 197–204.

Chapman, C. J. (1973). Field studies of hearing in teleost fish. *Helgoländer Wiss. Meeresunters., 24,* 371–390.

Chapman, C. J., and Hawkins, A. D. (1973). A field study of hearing in the cod, *Gadus morhua* L. *J. Comp. Physiol., 85,* 147–167.

Chapman, C. J., and Johnstone, A. D. F. (1974). Some auditory discrimination experiments on marine fish. *J. Exp. Biol., 61,* 521–528.

Chapman, C. J., and Sand, O. (1974). Field studies of hearing in two species of flatfish, *Pleuronectes platessa* (L.) and *Limanda limanda* (L.) *Comp. Biochem. Physiol., 47A,* 371–385.

Clarke, N. L., Popper, A. N., and Mann, J. A., Jr. (1975). Laser light-scattering investigations of the teleost swim bladder response to acoustic stimuli. *Biophysical J., 15,* 307–318.

Cushing, D. H. (1973). *The Detection of Fish.* Pergamon Press: Oxford.

*Dijkgraaf, S. (1947). Über die Reizung des Ferntastsinnes bei Fischen und Amphibien. *Experientia, 3,* 206–216.

*Dijkgraaf, S. (1964). The supposed use of the lateral line as an organ of hearing in fish. *Experientia, 20,* 586.

Dijkgraaf, S. (1973). A method for complete and selective surgical elimination of the lateral-line system on codfish, *Gadus morhua. Experientia, 29,* 737–738.

*Dijkgraaf, S., and Verheijen, F. J. (1950). Neue Versuche über das Tonunterscheidungsvermögen der Elritze. *Ztschr. Vergleich. Physiol., 32,* 248–256.

Enger, P. S. (1973). Masking of auditory responses in the medulla oblongata of goldfish. *J. Exp. Biol., 59,* 415–424.

Enger, P. S., Hawkins, A. D., Sand, O., and Chapman, C. J. (1973). Directional sensitivity of saccular microphonic potentials in the haddock. *J. Exp. Biol., 59,* 425–433.

Fay, R. R. (1970a). Auditory frequency generalization in the goldfish *(Carassius auratus). J. Exper. Anal. Behav., 14,* 353–360.

Fay, R. R. (1970b). Auditory frequency discrimination in the goldfish *(Carassius auratus). J. Comp. Physiol. Psychol., 73,* 175–180.

Fay, R. R. (1972). Perception of amplitude-modulated auditory signals by the goldfish. *J. Acoust, Soc. Amer., 52,,* 660–666.

Fay, R. R. (1974). Masking of tones by noise for the goldfish *(Carassius auratus). J. Comp. Physiol. Psychol.,* in press.

Fay, R. R. (1975). Frequency discrimination in vertebrates. *J. Acoust. Soc. Amer.,* in press.

Fay, R. R., Kendall, J. I., Popper, A. N., and Tester, A. L. (1974). Vibration detection by the macula neglecta of sharks. *Comp. Biochem. Physiol., 47A,* 1235–1240.

Fay, R. R., and Popper, A. N. (1974). Acoustic stimulation of the ear of the goldfish *(Carassius auratus). J. Exp. Biol., 61,* 243–260.

Fay, R. R., and Popper, A. N. (1975). Modes of stimulation of the teleost ear. *J. Exp. Biol., 62,* 379–388.

Fish, J. F., and Offutt, G. C. (1972). Hearing thresholds from toadfish, *Opsanus tau,* measured in the laboratory and field. *J. Acoust. Soc. Amer., 51,* 1318–1321.

Fletcher, H. (1940). Auditory patterns. *Rev. Mod. Physics, 12,* 47–65.

*Harris, G. G. (1964). Considerations on the physics of sound production by fishes. In *Marine Bio-Acoustics,* W. N. Tavolga, ed., Pergamon Press: Oxford, pp. 233–247.

Hawkins, A. D. (1973). The sensitivity of fish to sounds. *Oceanogr. Mar. Biol. Ann. Rev., 11,* 291–340.

*Hawkins, J. E., and Stevens, S. S. (1950). The masking of pure tones and of speech by white noise. *J. Acoust. Soc. Amer.*, 22, 6–13.

Horch, K., and Salmon, M. (1973). Adaptations to the acoustic environment by the squirrelfishes *Myripristis violaceus* and *M. pralinus*. *Mar. Behav. Physiol.*, 2, 121–139.

*Jacobs, D. W., and Tavolga, W. N. (1967). Acoustic intensity limens in the goldfish. *Anim. Behavior*, 15, 324–335.

*Jacobs, D. W., and Tavolga, W. N. (1968). Acoustic frequency discrimination in the goldfish. *Anim. Behaviour*, 16, 67–71.

Köhler, D. (1973). A behavioural audiogram of juvenile carp. *Experientia*, 29, 125–127.

*Myrberg, A. A., Jr., Banner, A., and Richard, J. D. (1969). Shark attraction using a video-acoustic system. *Marine Biol.*, 2, 264–276.

Myrberg, A. A., Jr., Ha, S. J., Walewski, S., Banbury, J. C. (1972). Effectiveness of acoustic signals in attracting epipelagic sharks to an underwater sound source. *Bull. Mar. Sci.*, 22, 926–949.

*Nelson, D. R., and Gruber, S. H. (1963). Sharks: attraction by low-frequency sounds. *Science*, 142,, 975–977.

Nelson, D. R., and Johnson, R. H. (1972). Acoustic attraction of Pacific reef sharks: effect of pulse intermittency and variability. *Comp. Biochem. Physiol.*, 42A, 85–95.

Offutt, G. C. (1970). A proposed mechanism for the perception of acoustic stimuli near threshold. *J. Audit. Res.*, 10, 226–228.

Offutt, G. C. (1971). Response of the tautog (*Tautoga onitis*, teleost) to acoustic stimuli measured by classically conditioning the heart rate. *Conditional Reflex*, 6, 205–214.

Piddington, R. W. (1972). Auditory discrimination between compressions and rarefactions by goldfish. *J. Exp. Biol.*, 56, 403–419.

Popper, A. N. (1971). The effects of size on auditory capacities of the goldfish. *J. Audit. Res.*, 11, 239–247.

Popper, A. N. (1972a). Pure-tone auditory thresholds for the carp, *Cyprinus carpio*. *J. Acoust. Soc. Amer.*, 52, 1714–1717.

Popper, A. N. (1972b). Auditory threshold in the goldfish (*Carassius auratus*) as a function of signal duration. *J. Acoust. Soc. Amer.*, 52,, 596–602.

Popper, A. N. (1974). The response of the swim bladder of the goldfish (*Carassius auratus*) to acoustic stimuli. *J. Exp. Biol.*, 60, 295–304.

Popper, A. N., Chan, A. T. H., and Clarke, N. L. (1973). An evaluation of methods for behavioral investigations of teleost audition. *Behav. Res. Meth. Instru.*, 5, 470–472.

Popper, A. N., and Fay, R. R. (1973). Sound detection and processing by teleost fishes: A critical review. *J. Acoust. Soc. Amer.*, 53, 1515–1529.

Popper, A. N., Salmon, M., and Parvulescu, A. (1973). Sound localization by the Hawaiian squirrelfishes *Myripristis berndti* and *M. argyromus*. *Anim. Behaviour*, 21, 86–97.

Roberts, B. L., and Russell, I. J. (1972). The activity of lateral-line efferent neurones in stationary and swimming dogfish. *J. Exp. Biol.*, 57, 435–448.

Russell, I. J., and Roberts, B. L. (1972). Inhibition of spontaneous lateral-line activity be efferent nerve stimulation. *J. Exp. Biol.*, 57, 77–82.

Sand, O. (1974). Directional sensitivity of microphonic potentials from the perch ear. *J. Exp. Biol.*, 60, 881–899.

Sand, O., and Enger, P. S. (1973). Evidence for an auditory function of the swim bladder in the cod. *J. Exp. Biol.*, 59, 405–414.

Sand, O., and Enger, P. S. (1974). Possible mechanisms for directional hearing and pitch discrimination in fish. *Rheinisch-Wesfäl. Akad. Wiss.*, 53, 223–242.

Sand, O., and Hawkins, A. D. (1973). Acoustic properties of the cod swim bladder. *J. Exp. Biol.*, 58, 797–820.

Schade, R. (1971). Experimentelle Untersuchungen zum Hörvermögen an *Leucaspius delineatus*. *Biol. Zentralblatt*, 90, 337–356.

Scharf, B. (1970). Critical bands. In *Foundations of Modern Auditory Theory,* Vol. 1, J. B. Tobias, ed., Academic Press: New York.

Schuijf, A. (1975). Directional hearing of cod *(Gadus morhua)* under approximate free field conditions. *J. Comp. Physiol., 98,* 307–332.

Schuijf, A., Baretta, J. W., and Wildschut, J. T. (1972). A field investigation on the discrimination of sound direction in *Labrus berggylta* (Pisces: Perciformes). *Netherlands J. Zool., 22,* 81–104.

Schuijf, A., and Buwalda, R. J. A. (1975). On the mechanism of directional hearing in cod *(Gadus morhua* L.). *J. Comp. Physiol., 98,* 333–343.

Schuijf, A., and Siemelink, M. E. (1974). The ability of cod *(Gadus morhua)* to orient towards a sound source. *Experientia, 30,* 773–774.

*Tavolga, W. N. (1964). Sonic characteristics and mechanisms in marine fishes. In *Marine Bio-Acoustics,* W. N. Tavolga, ed., Pergamon Press: Oxford, pp. 195–211.

*Tavolga, W. N. (1967). Masked auditory thresholds in teleost fishes. In *Marine Bio-Acoustics,* Vol. 2, W. N. Tavolga, ed., Pergamon Press: Oxford, pp. 233–245.

Tavolga, W. N. (1971a). Sound production and detection. In *Fish Physiology,* Vol. 5, W. S. Hoar and D. J. Randall, eds., Academic Press: New York, pp. 135–205.

Tavolga, W. N. (1971b). Acoustic orientation in the sea catfish, *Galeichthys felis. Ann. N.Y. Acad. Sci., 188,* 80–97.

Tavolga, W. N. (1974a). Sensory parameters in communication among coral reef fishes. *Mt. Sinai J. Med., 41,* 324–340.

Tavolga, W. N. (1974b). Signal/noise ratio and the critical band in fishes. *J. Acoust. Soc. Amer., 55,* 1323–1333.

Tavolga, W. N.. (1976). Acoustic obstacle detection in the sea catfish *(Arius felis).* In *Sound Reception in Fish,* A. Schuijf, and A. D. Hawkins, eds., Elsevier: Amsterdam.

Tester, A. L., Kendall, J. I., and Milisen, W. B. (1972). Morphology of the ear of the shark genus *Carcharhinus,* with particular reference to the macula neglecta. *Pacific Sci., 26,* 264–274.

Vaitulevich, S. F., and Ushakov, M. N. (1974). Holographic study of swim bladder vibrations in *Cyprinus carpio.* [In Russian] *Biofizika, 19,* 528–533.

*van Bergeijk, W. A. (1964). Directional and nondirectional hearing in fish. In *Marine Bio-Acoustics,* W. N. Tavolga, ed., Pergamon Press: Oxford, pp. 281–299.

*van Bergeijk, W. A. (1967). Discussion of critical bands in hearing of fishes. In *Marine Bio-Acoustics,* Vol. 2, W. N. Tavolga, ed., Pergamon Press: Oxford, pp. 244–245.

*Weiss, B. A. (1967). Sonic sensitivity in the goldfish *(Carassius auratus).* In *Lateral Line Detectors,* P. Cahn, ed., Indiana University Press: Bloomington, pp. 249–264.

Wever, E. G. (1949). *Theory of Hearing.* Wiley: New York.

Wever, E. G. (1969). Cochlear stimulation and Lempert's mobilization theory. *Arch. Otolaryngol., 90,* 63.

SUMMARY OF QUANTITATIVE DATA

The following graphs, reprinted from Popper and Fay (1973), serve to summarize the quantitative data currently available on fish audition. References in the figure captions can be found in the bibliographies for Papers 1 and 2 in this volume.

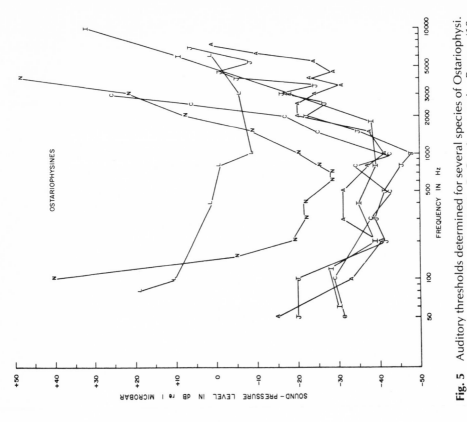

OSTARIOPHYSINES

Fig. 5 Auditory thresholds determined for several species of Ostariophysi. A, *Astyanax mexicanus*, Popper (1970); C, *Cyprinus carpio*, Popper (1972a); I, *Ictalurus nebulosus*, Poggendorf (1952); J, *Astyanax jordani*, Popper (1970); L, *Leucaspius delineatus*, Schade (1971); N, *Ictalurus nebulosus*, Weiss, Strother, and Hartig (1969). Reprinted from *J. Acoust. Soc. Amer.*, **53**(6), 1522 (1973); copyright © 1973 by the Acoustical Society of America

GOLDFISH

Fig. 4 Auditory thresholds for the goldfish (*Carassius auratus*) determined by several different workers. E, Enger (1966), speaker in air, classical conditioning; e, Enger (1966), speaker in water, classical conditioning; F, Fay (1969), speaker in air, classical conditioning; J, Jacobs and Tavolga (1967), speaker in air, avoidance conditioning; O, Offutt (1968), speaker in water, classical conditioning; P, Popper (1971), speaker in air, avoidance conditioning; W, Weiss (1966), speaker in water, avoidance conditioning. Reprinted from *J. Acoust. Soc. Amer.*, **53**(6), 1521 (1973); conditioning. Reprinted from *J. Acoust. Soc. Amer.*, **53**(6), 1521 (1973);

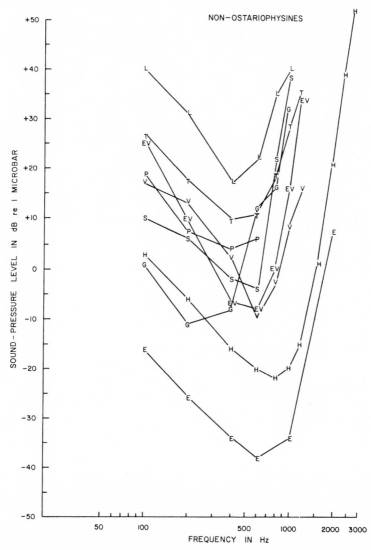

Fig. 6 Auditory thresholds determined for nine nonostariophysine species by Tavolga and Wodinsky (1963). E, *Equetus acuminatus;* EV, *Eupomacentrus leucostictus;* G, *Epinephelus guttatus;* H, *Holocentrus ascensionis;* L, *Lutjanus apodus;* P, *Prionotus scitulus;* S, *Haemulon sciurus;* T, *Thalassoma bifasciatum;* V, *Holocentrus vexillarius.* Reprinted from *J. Acoust. Soc. Amer.,* **53**(6), 1523 (1973); copyright © 1973 by the Acoustical Society of America

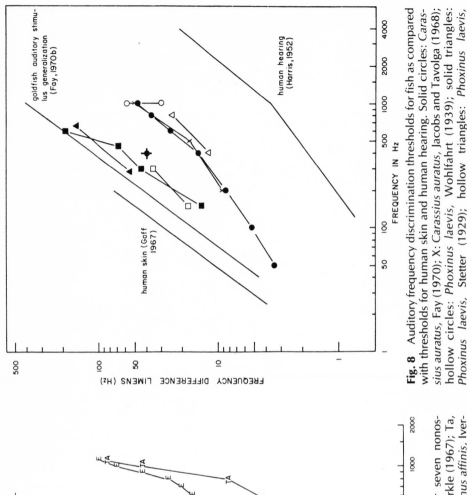

Fig. 8 Auditory frequency discrimination thresholds for fish as compared with thresholds for human skin and human hearing. Solid circles: *Carassius auratus*, Fay (1970); X: *Carassius auratus*, Jacobs and Tavolga (1968); hollow circles: *Phoxinus laevis*, Wohlfahrt (1939); solid triangles: *Phoxinus laevis*, Stetter (1929); hollow triangles: *Phoxinus laevis*, Dijkgraaf and Verheijen (1950); solid squares: *Sargus annularis*, Dijkgraaf (1952); hollow squares: *Gobius niger*, Dijkgraaf (1952); +: *Corvina nigra*, Dijkgraaf (1952). Human skin graph from Goff, G. (1967), Differential discrimination of frequency of cutaneous mechanical vibration, *J. Exp. Psychol.*, 74, 294. Human hearing graph from Harris, J. (1952), Pitch discrimination, *J. Acoust. Soc. Amer.*, 24, 750. Reprinted from *J. Acoust. Soc. Amer.*, **53**(6), 1525 (1973); copyright © 1973 by the Acoustical Society of America

Fig. 7 Auditory thresholds determined for seven nonostariophysine species. G, *Gadus morhua*, Buerkle (1967); Ta, *Thunnus albacares*, Iversen (1967); E, *Euthynnus affinis*, Iversen (1969); P, *Perca fluviatilis*, Wolff (1966); A, *Acerina cernua*, Wolff (1966); L, *Lucioperca sandra*, Wolff (1966); T, *Tautoga onitis*, Offutt (1971). Reprinted from *J. Acoust. Soc. Amer.*, **53**(6), 1524 (1973); copyright © 1973 by the Acoustical Society of America

Part II

DE AURE ANIMALIUM AQUATILIUM

Editor's Comments
on Paper 3

3   WEBER
On the Ears of Aquatic Animals

Ernst Heinrich Weber (1795–1878) was Professor of Anatomy at the University in Leipzig from 181, and Professor of Physiology from 1840. He is best known for his description of the chain of small bones that couple the swim bladder to the inner ear in ostariophysine fishes, and for his discovery of the nonlinear relationship between stimulus intensity and apparent sensation level. Both of these discoveries bear his name: the Weberian ossicles, and the Weber-Fechner Law.

In the first of his major works on the ears of aquatic animals, he not only provided precise descriptions of the inner-ear structures in a variety of forms, including crustaceans, octopus, ostariophysine and other fishes, and even some elasmobranchs (rays and sharks), but he theorized on the function of these structures. His was one of the early comparative studies in functional anatomy, and his conception of the swim bladder as a sound receiver was derived through brilliant intuition and remorseless logic. Knowing nothing of the evolutionary concepts of homology and common ancestry to burst on the scientific scene more than thirty years later, he reasonably compared the ostariophysine ossicles to the middle-ear bones in the human ear and named them accordingly: the *malleus* (the most distal one placed in contact with the swim bladder), the much smaller *incus,* and the blade-like *stapes*. He was faced with a fourth bone, closest to the inner ear and coupled directly to the endolymph. This one he called the *claustrum.* Following the nomenclature recommended by Bridge and Haddon more than sixty years later, these bones are now termed *tripus, intercalarium, scaphium,* and *claustrum.* Rather than being derived from jaw suspension elements as in the case of tetrapod middle-ear bones, the Weberian ossicles come from modified parts of

vertebral transverse processes. The functions of these bones were theorized by Weber, but it took more than 100 years for his theories to be
demonstrated experimentally and accepted.

In his later work, Weber described the fact that in human hearing
the just-noticeable-difference *(jnd)* in sound intensity is not the same at
all intensity levels. Indeed, he showed that the *jnd* is based on a proportion of the initial absolute sound level, and he was the first to document
this fact. Later, in 1860, Gustav Fechner, who established the science of
psychophysics, gave Weber's theory a mathematical formulation now
well-known as the Weber–Fechner Law.

With respect to the history of our knowledge of audition in fishes,
Weber's book on the ears of aquatic animals deserves to serve as the
starting point. In this book, the most trenchant observations are contained
in the figures drawn by J. F. Schroter, probably an assistant to the professor. With this in mind, we undertake to reproduce these illustrations
here.

There are few copies of Weber's 1820 book available, and one of the
few is in the library at the American Museum of Natural History. Unfortunately, there was some water damage to the book, but despite that,
G. Robert Adlington, of the Department of Invertebrates at the American
Museum, photographed the plates and retouched the negatives so as to
give the exquisite drawings a new life and precision.

The plate captions given here are not translations from the Latin but
are based on the current terminology in comparative anatomy wherever
possible. The author's original terms are given in a few cases, set off in
quotation marks.

Tab.I.

Fig.1.

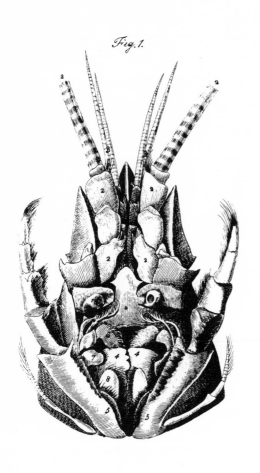

Fig. 3.

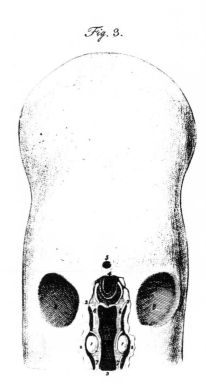

Fig. 2.

Fig.4.

Fig. 5

56

3

ON THE EARS OF AQUATIC ANIMALS

Ernst Heinrich Weber

*This translation was prepared expressly for this Benchmark
volume by William N. Tavolga from Ernest Heinrich Weber,
"De Aure Animalium Aquatilium," in* De Aure et Auditu
Hominis et Animalium, *Gerhard Fleischer, Leipzig, 1820*

PLATE I

Fig. 1 Ventral view of head and thorax of crayfish *(Astacus).*
1. Pore to statocyst
2. Major antenna
3. Minor antennae (antennule)
4. Mandible
5–8. Maxillipeds

Fig. 2 Brain and statocyst dissection, posterior view.
1. Right statocyst
2. Left statocyst, exposed
3. Optic lobes of "cerebrum"
4. Antenna levator muscle
5. Antennal nerve
6. Antennal depressor muscle
7. Statocyst nerve
8. Circumesophageal connective

Fig. 3 Dorsal view of head of lamprey *(Petromyzon).*
1. Labyrinth in cartilage
2. Cut skin
3. Opened cranium
4. Nasal cavity and membranes
5. External naris (unpaired)
6,7. Cranial cartilages
8. Orbit

Fig. 4 Lateral view of lamprey labyrinth.
1. Vestibular opening
2. Auditory nerve foramen
3. Minor vestibular opening
4. Cartilage

Fig. 5 Median view of lamprey labyrinth.
1. Cartilaginous labyrinth
2. Ampulla
3. Endolymphatic opening
4. Cartilage

Tab. II.

F. 6.

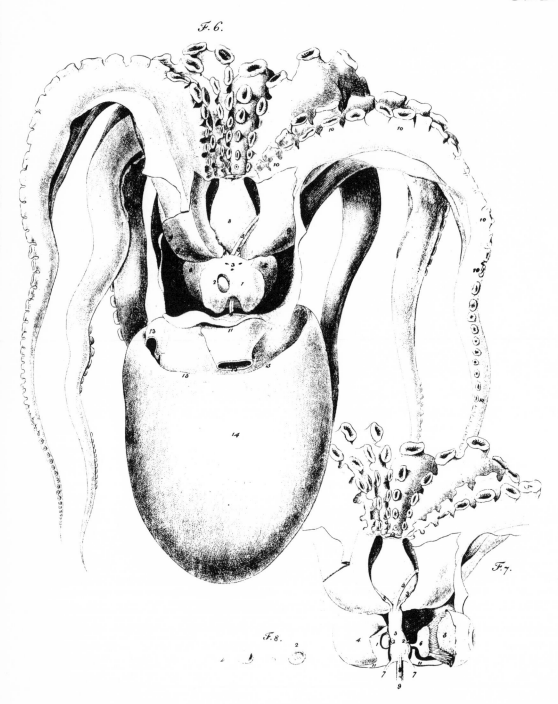

F. 7.

F. 8.

PLATE II

6   Dissection of octopus brain and auditory organ.

. Cartilaginous tuberosity
over the labyrinth
. Tuberosity exposed to show
labyrinth
. Blood vessel foramina
. Intestinal nerve

5. Pedal nerves
6. Orbit
7. Mouth opening
8. Buccal cavity
9. Arm bases
10. Suckers

11. Excurrent siphon
12. Siphon opening
13. Mantle margin
14. Mantle
15. Mantle lip

7   Dissection of head of octopus.

. Head cartilage enclosing
labyrinth
. Auditory nerves
. Pedal nerves

4,5. Eyes
6. Optic lobe
7. Mantle nerve
8. Intestinal nerve

9. Esophagus within brain
10. Mouth opening
11. Orbital cartilage
12. Cranial cavity

8   Otoliths of octopus.

. Otolith viewed from convex
surface

2. Medial, concave surface of otolith

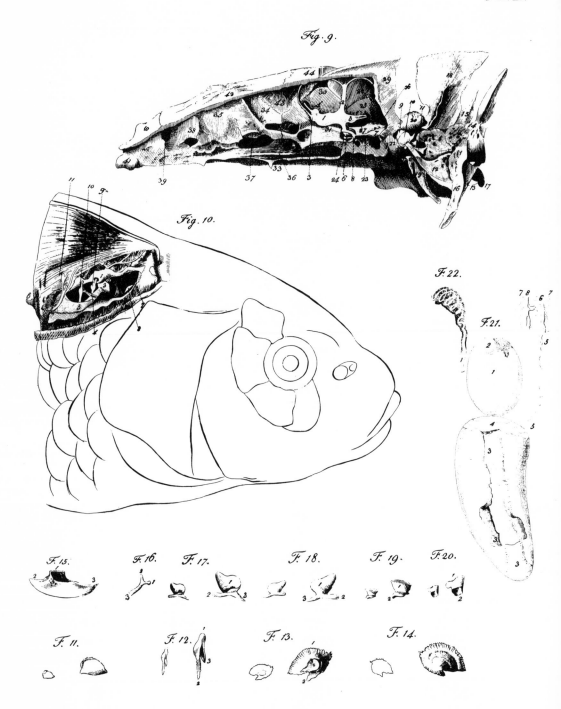

Tab. III.

Fig. 9.

Fig. 10.

F. 22.

F. 21.

F. 15. *F. 16.* *F. 17.* *F. 18.* *F. 19.* *F. 20.*

F. 11. *F. 12.* *F. 13.* *F. 14.*

PLATE III

Fig. 9   Median, sagittal view of skull and auditory apparatus of the carp *(Cyprinus carpio).*

1. Utriculus
2. Crus commune
3. Ampulla of anterior canal
4. Ampulla of horizontal canal
5. Ampulla of posterior canal
6. Sacculus
7. Sinus impar
8. Transverse canal
9. Claustrum
10. Scaphium ("stapes")
11. Intercalarium ("incus")
12. Tripus ("malleus")
13. Posterior apex of tripus
14. Fourth vertebra
15. Neural spine 3

16. Transverse process
17. Right transverse process
18. Neural spine 2
19. Transverse process 2
20. Neural spine 1
21 Transverse process 1
22. Basi-occipital
23. Perilymphic cavity
24. Otolith
25. Occipital
26. Trigeminal nerve foramen
27. Vagus nerve foramen
28. Supraoccipital
29. Occipital spine
30. Temporal

31. Temporal
32. Trigeminal foramen
33. Basi-sphenoid
34. Pterosphenoid
35. Orbitosphenoid
36. Parasphenoid
37. Optic nerve foramen
38. Ethmoid
39. Olfactory foramen
40. Nasal
41. Vomer
42. Frontal
43. Prefrontal
44. Parietal

Fig. 10   Head of carp *(Cyprinus carpio),* showing auditory apparatus.

1. Tissue membrane
2. Claustrum
3. Scaphium ("stapes")
4. Intercalarium ("incus")

5. Anterior arm of tripus
6. Posterior arm of tripus
7. Perilymphatic foramen
8. Trigeminal nerve branch

9. Spinal ganglion 1
10. Spinal ganglion 2
11. Spinal ganglion 3
12. Cut muscles

Fig. 11   Utricular otolith, natural size and enlarged.

Fig. 12   Saccular otolith, natural size and enlarged.

1. Anterior end

2. Posterior end

3. Lateral process

Fig. 13   Lagenar otolith, medial view, natural size and enlarged.

1. Serrated margin
2. Incision

3. Spine
4. Fossa

Fig. 14   Lagenar otolith, external surface, natural size and enlarged.

Fig. 15   Tripus ("malleus")

1. Articular process

2. Anterior end

3. Posterior end

Fig. 16   Intercalarium ("incus")

1. Vertebral process, set into foramen on second vertebra
2. Ligamental process, attached by ligament to second vertebra
3. Lateral extremity, in ligament between tripus and scaphium

Fig. 17   Scaphium ("stapes"), medial view, natural size and enlarged.

1. Shell

2. Inferior process

3. Superior process

Fig. 18   Scaphium ("stapes"), lateral view, natural size and enlarged.

1. Convex surface of shell

Fig. 19   Claustrum, lateral view, natural size and enlarged.

1. Ossicular surface
   (toward the scaphium)

2. Sinus impar surface

Fig. 20   Claustrum, medial-ventral view, natural size and enlarged.

Fig. 21   Swim bladder of the tench *(Tinca tinca),* with pneumatic duct opening into esophagus.

1. Tunica extern of anterior chamber
2. Tunica interna

3. Transverse muscle fibers
4. Circular muscle fibers
5. Pneumatic duct

6. Swelling at base of duct
7. Esophagus
8. Intestinalis branch of vagus

Fig. 22   Swelling in the pneumatic duct, magnified.

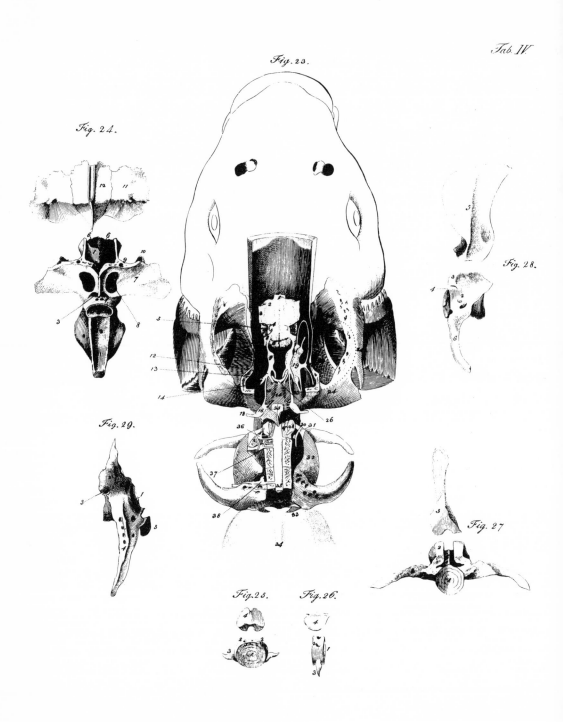

Fig. 23.

Tab. IV.

Fig. 24.

Fig. 28.

Fig. 29.

Fig. 27.

Fig. 25.

Fig. 26.

PLATE IV

Fig. 23 Head of carp *(Cyprinus carpio),* with cranium and auditory apparatus exposed. Parts of brain removed.

1. Cut surface of brain stem
2,3 Part of cerebellum
4. Auditory nerve
5. Part of cerebellum
6. Infundibulum
7. Optic lobe
8. Trigeminal nerve trunk
9. Auditory nerve ganglion
10,11. Saccular nerve
12–14. Auditory nerve branches
15. Ramus communicans

16–18. Spino-occipital nerve and branches
19. Membranous labyrinth
20. Anterior canal
21. Horizontal canal
22. Crus commune
23. Posterior canal
24. Dissected tissues
25. Sinus impar
26. Locus of fusion of transverse canals

27. Claustrum
28. Scaphium ("stapes")
29. Scaphium-intercalarium ligament
30. Intercalarium ("incus")
31. Intercalarium-tripus ligament
32. Tripus
33. Posterior process of tripus
34. Swim bladder
35. Spinal cord
36–38. Spinal ganglia

Fig. 24 Occipital portion of skull of carp *(Cyprinus carpio).*

1. Basi-occipital
2. Ventral process
3. Foramen magnum
4. Foramina leading to sinus impar

5. Articular surface
6. Cavities for sacculus
7. Lateral occipital
8. Cranial nerve foramina

9. Cavity of posterior canal
10. Cavity of horizontal canal
11. Part of occipital
12. Occipital spine

Fig 25 First vertebra, from posterior view.

1. Articular face
2. Foramen for attachment of scaphium

3. Transverse process
4. Neural arch and spine (detached)

Fig. 26 First vertebra, lateral view.

Fig. 27 Second vertebra, posterior view.

1. Articular face
2. Transverse process

3. Spinal canal
4. Neural spine

Fig. 28 Second vertebra, lateral view.

1. Articular face
2. Attachment point of intercalarium

3. Lateral body of vertebra
4. Spinal nerve incision

5. Neural spine
6. Transverse process

Fig. 29 Third vertebra, lateral view.

1. Articular face
2. Neural spine

3. Intervertebral incision
4. Transverse process

5. Part of transverse process penetrating swim bladder

63

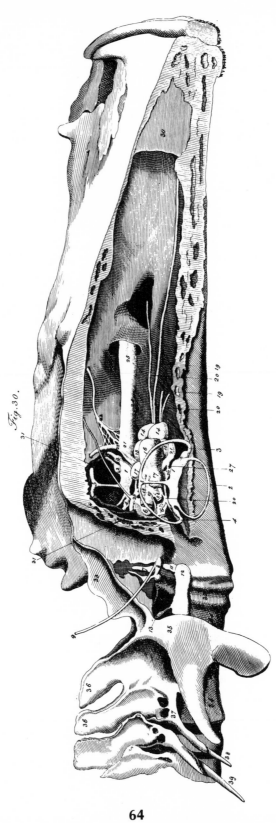

PLATE V

Fig. 30 Medial dissection of head of catfish (*Silurus glanis*), showing brain and auditory apparatus.

1. Utriculus
2. Horizontal canal
3. Anterior canal
4. Posterior canal
5. Crus commune
6. Sacculus
7. Locus of sinus impar
8. Scaphium ("stapes")
9. Probe entering sinus impar
10. Probe leaving sinus impar
11. Intercalarium ("incus")
12. End of tripus ("malleus")
13. Medial fulcrum of tripus
14. Olfactory lobe
15. Optic lobe
16. Anterior cerebellum
17. Lateral cerebellum
18. Medulla
19. Olfactory tract
20. Optic nerve (also vagus)
21. Trigeminal nerve
22. Trigeminal nerve branch
23. Trigeminal nerve branch
24. Locus of infraorbital trunk
25. Trigeminal ophthalmic trunk
26. Auditory nerve
27. Nerve ramus to trigeminal
28. Vagus nerve
29. Auditory nerve
30. Nasal septum
31. Bony labyrinth
32. Vertebra 1
33. Neural spine 1
34. Fused vertebrae 2 and 3
35. Transverse process 2
36. Neural spines fused
37. Transverse process 3
38, 39. Ribs

Tab. V.

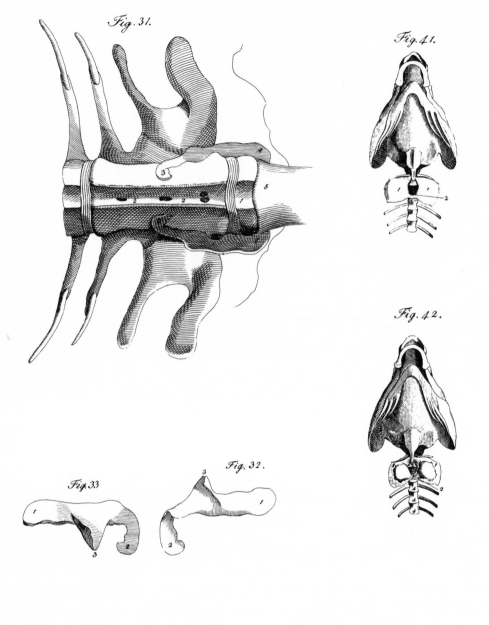

Fig. 31.

Fig. 41.

Fig. 42.

Fig. 33

Fig. 32.

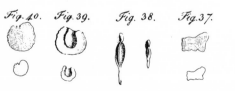

Fig. 40. Fig. 39. Fig. 38. Fig. 37.

Fig. 36. Fig. 35.

Fig. 34.

PLATE V, continued
Auditory Apparatus of the Catfish *(Silurus glanis)*

Fig. 31 First four vertebrae, ventral view, with tripus attached.
1. Vertebra 1
2. Fused vertebrae 2 and 3
3. Posterior end of tripus
4. Anterior end of tripus
5. Occipital

Fig. 32 Tripus ("malleus"), dorsal view.
1. Anterior end
2. Posterior end
3. Medial process

Fig. 33 Tripus ("malleus"), ventral view, labeled as above.

Fig. 34 Intercalarium ("incus").
1. End attached to scaphium
2. End attached to tripus

Fig. 35 Scaphium ("stapes"), lateral view.
1. Articular head, fitting into socket on first vertebra
2. Anterior surface, covering opening to sinus impar
3. Lateral tuberculum

Fig. 36 Ossicle from within the spherical sinus.

Fig. 37 Utricular otolith.

Fig. 38 Saccular otolith.

Fig. 39 Lagenar otolith.

Fig. 40 Lagenar otolith, convex surface.

Fig. 41 Cranium and vertebrae of the loach *(Cobitis barbaluta).*
1. Transverse processes 2 and 3 enclosing dual swim bladders
2. Locus of connection between swim-bladder chambers

Fig. 42 Cranium and vertebrae of the loach *(Cobitis barbatula),* as above but with swim-bladder chambers dissected.
1. Transverse processes
2. Swim-bladder transverse canal
3. Centra of vertebrae 2 and 3
4. Vertebrae 4, 5, and 6

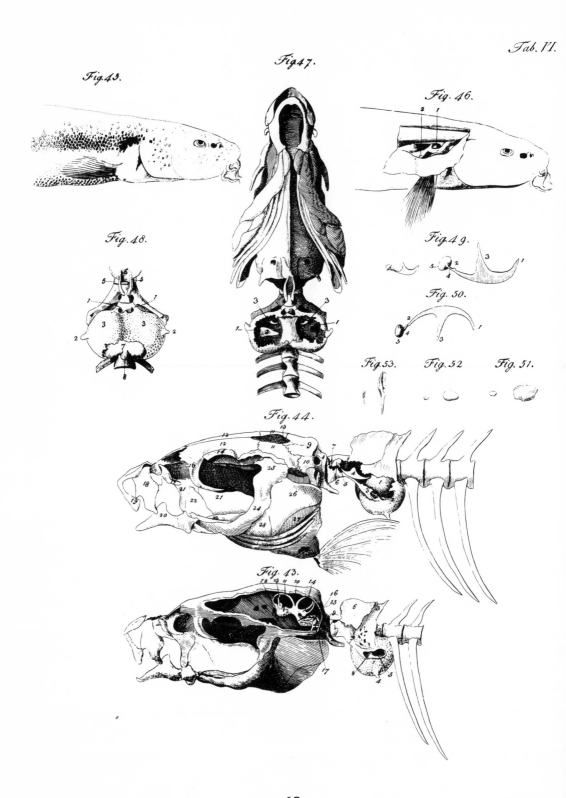

Tab. VI.

Fig. 45.

Fig. 47.

Fig. 46.

Fig. 48.

Fig. 49.

Fig. 50.

Fig. 53.   Fig. 52.   Fig. 51.

Fig. 44.

Fig. 43.

PLATE VI

Fig. 43   Head of a loach *(Cobitis fossilis)*, showing auditory apparatus.
1. Bony capsule of swim bladder
2. Centrum of third vertebra
3. Neural spine 3
4. Tip of transverse process 3
5. Opening of bony capsule
6. Neural spine 2
7. Transverse process 2
8. Process within bony capsule to which ossicles are attached
9. Neural spine 1
10. Crus commune
11. Anterior utriculus
12. Anterior canal ampulla
13. Horizontal canal
14. Posterior canal ampulla
15. Duct between utriculus and sacculus
16. Sacculus

Fig. 44   Head of loach, showing skeletal structure.
1. Swim-bladder capsule (opened)
2. Opening to swim-bladder capsule
3. Transverse process 2
4. Tripus ("malleus")
5. Intercalarium ("incus")
6. Scaphium ("stapes")
7. Claustrum
8. Basioccipital
9. Supraoccipital spine
10. Epiotic
11. Parietal
12. Frontal
13. Fontanelle
14. Supraorbital
15. Mesethmoid (dermethmoid?)
16. Prefrontal
17. Palatine
18. Maxillary
19. Premaxillary
20. Dentary
21. Ecto- and metapterygoid
22. Quadrate
23. Symplectic
24. Preopercular
25. Hyomandibular
26. Opercular
27. Subopercular
28. Interopercular

Fig. 45   Head and body of loach *(Cobitis fossilis)*.

Fig. 46   Dissection showing swim bladder.
1. Opening into swim-bladder capsule
2. Membranous connective tissues

Fig. 47   Ventral view of skull and vertebral column of loach *(Cobitis fossilis)*, swim-bladder capsules opened.
1. Swim-bladder capsule opening
2. Fibrous tissue covering opening
3. Inner opening of swim-bladder capsule showing end of tripus protruding

Fig. 48   Ventral view of swim-bladder capsules in the loach *(Cobitis fossilis)*.
1. Base of transverse process of capsule
2. Apex of transverse process of capsule
3. Bony capsule containing swim bladder
4. Transverse process 2
5. Centrum of vertebra 1
6. Basioccipital
7. Swim bladder exposed
8. Swim-bladder appendix

Fig. 49   Auditory ossicles of the loach *(Cobitis fossilis)*, natural size and enlarged
1. Posterior tip of tripus ("malleus")
2. Anterior tip of tripus
3. Articular process of tripus
4. Intercalarium ("incus")
5. Scaphium ("stapes")

Fig. 50   Medial view of auditory ossicles. Labels as above.

Fig. 51   Utricular otolith, natural size and enlarged.

Fig. 52   Lagenar otolith, natural size and enlarged.

Fig. 53   Saccular otolith, natural size and enlarged.

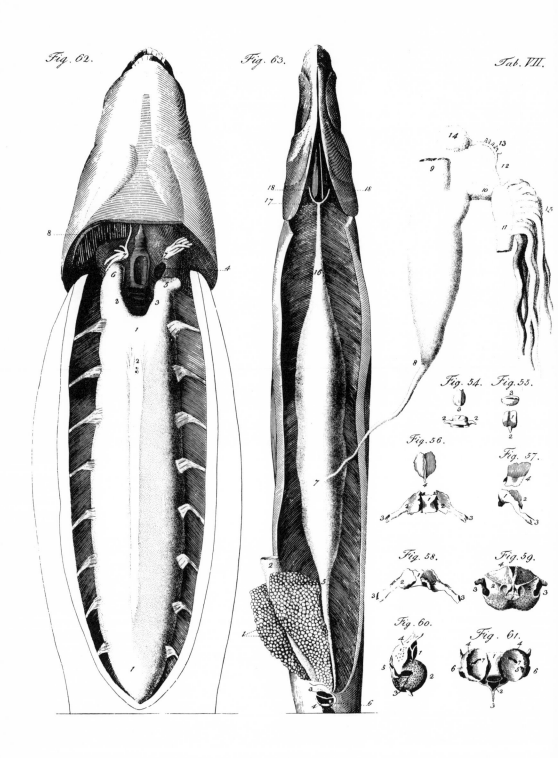

PLATE VII

Fig. 54   First vertebra of loach *(Cobitis fossilis).*
1. Centrum
2. Transverse process
3. Neural spine (top view)

Fig. 55   As above, side view.

Fig. 56   Second vertebra of loach *(Cobitis fossilis).*
1. Centrum
2. Transverse process
3. Opening of hollow bone
4. Neural spine

Fig. 57   As above, side view.

Fig. 58   As above, ventral view.

Fig. 59   Third vertebra of loach *(Cobitis fossilis).*
1. Centrum
2. Transverse process modified into vesicle for swim bladder
3. Opening into bony capsule
4. Neural spine

Fig. 60   As above, side view.

5. Anterior opening into swim-bladder capsule pierced by apex of tripus

Fig. 61   As above, ventral view with capsules opened.
1. Centrum
2. Spinal canal
3. Neural spine
4. Modified transverse process
5. External opening into capsule
6. Distal end of transverse process
7. Anterior opening pierced by apex of tripus

Fig. 62   Head and body of sea bream *(Sparus),* ventral dissection to show swim bladder and associated structures.
1. Swim bladder with rib attachments
2. Locus of entering and leaving blood vessels
3. Anterior caecum of swim bladder
4. Oval fenestrum in skull to which caecum is attached
5. Caecum shown pulled away from fenestrum
6. Caecum shown in normal position
7. Vagus nerve showing its many branches
8. Fifth gill

Fig. 63   Dissection of herring *(Clupea),* showing swim bladder and gut.
1. Ovary
2. Rectum
3. Anus
4. Genital pore
5. Posterior end of swim bladder
6. Small papilla end of bladder
7. Attachment of pneumatic duct
8. Base of pneumatic duct
9. Esophagus
10. Pylorus
11. Intestine
12. Ductus choledochus
13. Hepatic ducts
14. Gall bladder
15. Intestinal caecae
16. Anterior end of swim bladder
17. Anterior canal of swim bladder
18. Anterior canal extensions of swim bladder

71

Tab. VIII.

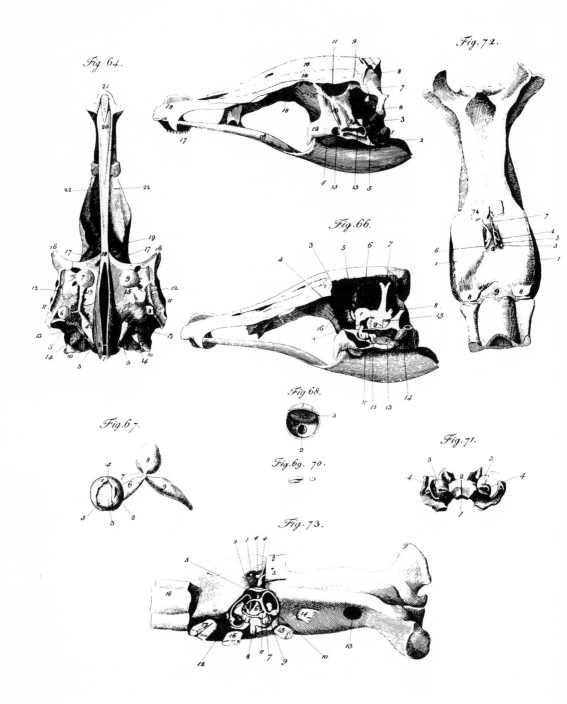

Fig. 64.

Fig. 72.

Fig. 66.

Fig. 68.

Fig. 67.

Fig. 69. 70.

Fig. 71.

Fig. 73.

PLATE VIII

Fig. 64   Ventral view of skull of herring *(Clupea).*
1. Occipital
2. Occipital processes
3. Locus of swim-bladder extensions
4. Enlargement above bony canal
6. Bony capsule terminus of posterior canal
7. Bony capsule terminus of anterior canal

8. Left posterior capsule
9. Left anterior capsule
10. Exoccipital
11. Pterotic
12. Fossa for hyomandibular
13. Locus of horizontal canal
14. Locus of posterior canal
15. Alisphenoid
16. Sphenotic

17. Orbitosphenoid
18. Parasphenoid, palatine fusion
19. Orbitosphenoid
20. Palatine
21. Premaxillary
22. Frontal

Fig. 65   Medial, sagittal view of skull of herring *(Clupea).*
1. Basioccipital
2. Opening for swim-bladder extension
3. Posterior capsule
4. Anterior capsule
5. Horizontal canal
6. Posterior canal

7. Exoccipital
8. Supraoccipital spine
9. Parietal
10. Frontal
11. Cranial cavity
12. Sphenotic
13. Pterotic

14. Alisphenoid
15. Pituitary foramina in skull
16. Parasphenoid
17. Palatine
18. Orbitosphenoid
19. Premaxillary

Fig. 66   Skull of herring *(Clupea)* showing brain and inner ear.
1. Anterior utriculus
2. Canal to sacculus
3. Appendix of anterior utriculus
4. Anterior capsule of swim bladder
5. Swim-bladder extension

6. Ampulla of horizontal canal
7. Crus commune
8. Base of posterior canal
9. Sacculus
10. Anterior swim-bladder capsule
11. Ampulla of anterior canal (left)

12. Ampulla of horizontal canal (left)
13. Horizontal canal (left)
14. Base of posterior canal (left)
15. Base of crus commune (left)
16. Trigeminal foramen

Fig. 67   Enlargement of bony capsule of swim bladder extension.
1. Anterior capsule, opened
2. Attachment point to utriculus
3. Membranous tissue within capsule

4. Annulus of utricular membrane attached to swim-bladder membrane
5. Margin of swim-bladder membrane

6. Bony anterior canal of swim bladder
7. External bony canal of swim bladder
8. Posterior capsule
9. Bony canal for swim-bladder

Fig. 68   Anterior swim-bladder capsule opened.
1. Surface bony capsule
2. Aperture entrance point of bony swim-bladder canal

3. Utricular membrane

Fig. 69   Saccular otolith.

Fig. 70   Lagenar otolith.

Fig. 71   Sphenoid and auditory region of skull, viewed from posterior.
1,2. Sphenoid-occipital complex
3. Anterior bony swim-bladder capsule

4. Opening into capsule normally penetrated by swim-bladder extension

Fig. 72   Skull of electric ray *(Torpedo),* dorsal view of chondrocranium.
1. Auditory bulla containing labyrinth
2. Endolymphatic fossa
3. Perilymphatic foramen

4. Endolymphatic foramen and duct
5. Cut muscle tissue
6. Muscle

7. Endolymphatic duct
8. Occipital condyle
9. Membrane over foramen magnum

Fig. 73   Lateral view of electric ray chondrocranium showing labyrinth.
1. Perilymphatic foramen (left)
2. Perilymphatic duct
3. Opening of endolymphatic duct
4. Endolymphatic duct
5. Endolymphatic duct within skull
6. Common vstibule (utriculus)
7. Anterior appendix of sacculus

8. Lagena
9. Crus commune
10. Ampulla of anterior canal
11. Ampulla of horizontal canal
12. Ampulla of posterior canal
13. Optic foramen
14. Oculomotor foramen

15. Abducens foramen (?)
16. Trigeminal foramen
17. Vagus foramen
18. Base of spinal column
19. Membrane between skull and spinal colum

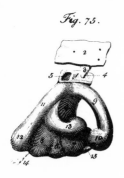

Fig. 75.

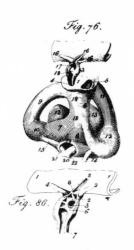

Fig. 76.

Tab. IX.

Fig. 77.

Fig. 86.

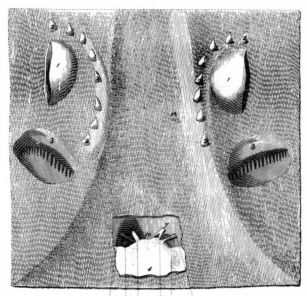

Fig. 74.

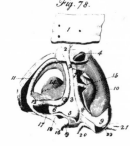

Fig. 78.

Fig. 80.

Fig. 81.

F. 82.   F. 83.   F. 84.   F. 85.

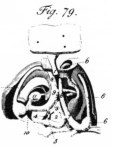

Fig. 79.

PLATE IX

g. 74 Top of head of ray *(Raja)*.
1. Eye
2. Denticle
3. Spiracle
4. Resected skin
5. Endolymphatic duct (left)
6. Endolymphatic duct (right— opened)
7. Endolymphatic duct penetrating chondrocranium
8. Perilymphatic foramen
9. Muscle
10. Perilymphatic fossa

g. 75 Cartilaginous labyrinth of ray *(Raja)*, lateral view.
1. Chondrocranium surface
2. Skin surface
3. Endolymphatic duct
4. Endyolymphatic duct penetrating skull
5. Perilymphatic foramen
6. Main vestibule (utriculus)
7. Anterior sacculus
8. Lagena
9. Anterior canal
10. Ampulla of anterior canal
11. Posterior canal
12. Ampulla of posterior canal
13. Horizontal canal and ampulla
14. Auditory nerve
15. Fine canal for nerves

g. 76 Cartilaginous labyrinth of ray *(Raja)*, medial view. Nos. 1–15 as above.
16. Endolymphatic ducts, opened
17. Endolymphatic duct, enlarged section
18. Crus commune
19. Internal meatus for nerve
20. Auditory nerve in meatus
21. Anterior ramus
22. Posterior ramus

g. 77 Cartilaginous labyrinth of ray *(Raja)*, anterior view. Labeled as above.

g. 78 Membranous labyrinth of ray *(Raja)*, medial view, dissected within cartilage. Labeled as above.
1. Skin surface
2. Swollen part of endolymphatic duct
3. Endolymphatic duct
4. Perilymphatic foramen
5. Sacculus
6. Anterior sacculus
7. Posterior canal
8. Utriculus of posterior canal
9. Ampulla of posterior canal
10. Cartilage over posterior canal
11. Anterior canal within cartilage
12. Ampulla of anterior canal
13. Utriculus of anterior canal
14. Ampulla of horizontal canal in cartilage
15. Part of horizontal canal
16. Auditory nerve
17. Anterior ramus
18. Anterior ramus
19. Posterior ramus
20. Accessory auditory nerve ramus
21. Auditory nerve ramus exiting
22. Foramen for exit of auditory nerve

g. 79 Membranous labyrinth of ray *(Raja)*, medial view dissected further than Fig. 78.
1. Endolymphatic duct
2. Sacculus
3. Base of endolymphatic duct (cut)
4. Anterior sacculus, opened
5. Septum of anterior sacculus
6. Posterior canal and ampulla
7. Posterior utriculus connection
8. Anterior canal
9. Anterior utriculus connection
10. Base of horizontal canal
11. Ampulla of horizontal canal
12. Common utriculus

g. 80 Membranous labyrinth, ventral view, dissected.
1. Anterior canal (cartilage)
2. Anterior ampulla (cartilage)
3. Anterior canal
4. Posterior canal (cartilage)
5. Anterior ampulla (cartilage)
6. Ampulla of anterior canal
7. Horizontal canal (cartilage)
8. Horizontal canal and ampulla
9. Anterior ramus, auditory nerve
10. Anterior nerve ramus
11. Branch of anterior nerve ramus
12. Branch of anterior nerve ramus
13. Posterior nerve ramus
14. Innervation of sacculus
15. Lagena and entering nerve
16. Accessory auditory nerve
17. Accessory nerve in foramen
18. Accessory nerve branch
19. Accessory nerve exiting cranium

g. 81 Ampulla of anterior semicircular canal and its innervation.
1. Part of anterior canal, opened
2. Ascending limb of anterior canal
3. Entering ampullar nerve
4. Septum within ampulla

g. 82 Otoconium from anterior sacculus.
1. Bony, upper portion
2. Gelatinous portion

g. 83 Otoconium from sacculus with lagenar extension.
1. Saccular portion
2. Lagenar portion

g. 84 Otoconium from sacculus with lagenar extension, ventral view.
1. Planar surface, with gelatinous portion attached
2. Lagenar extension

g. 85 Gelatinous (1) and bony (2) portions of otoconium.

g. 86 Endolymphatic duct detail.
1. Skin, reflected
2. Anterior canaliculi
3. Internal folds
4. Posterior canaliculus
5. Internal aperture of anterior canaliculus
6. Medial septum
7. Endolymphatic duct

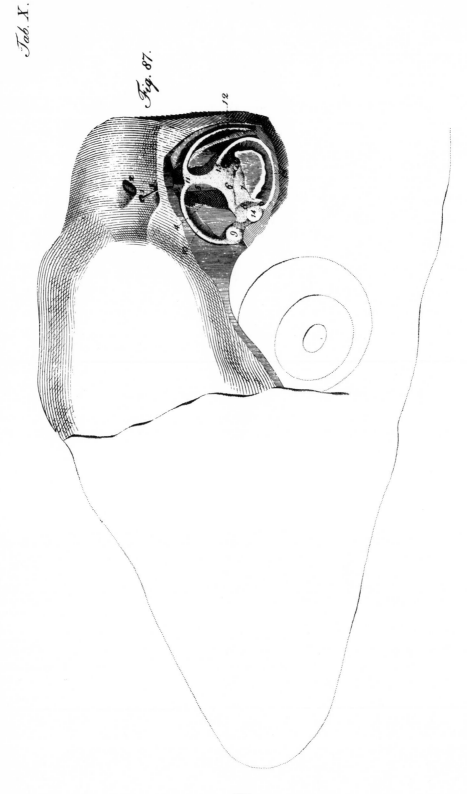

Tab. X.

Fig. 87.

PLATE X

Fig. 87 Head of shark (*Squalus*), dissected to show auditory apparatus.

1. Probe, showing perilymphatic foreamen
2. Endolymphatic foramen (right)
3. Endolymphatic foramen (left)
4. Perilymphatic space
5. Endolymphatic duct
6. Main vestibule (sacculus)
7. Sacculus
8. Anterior appendix of sacculus
9. Ampulla of anterior canal
10. Anterior canal
11. Crus commune
12. Posterior canal
13. Horizontal canal
14. Ampulla of horizontal canal
15. Base of horizontal canal

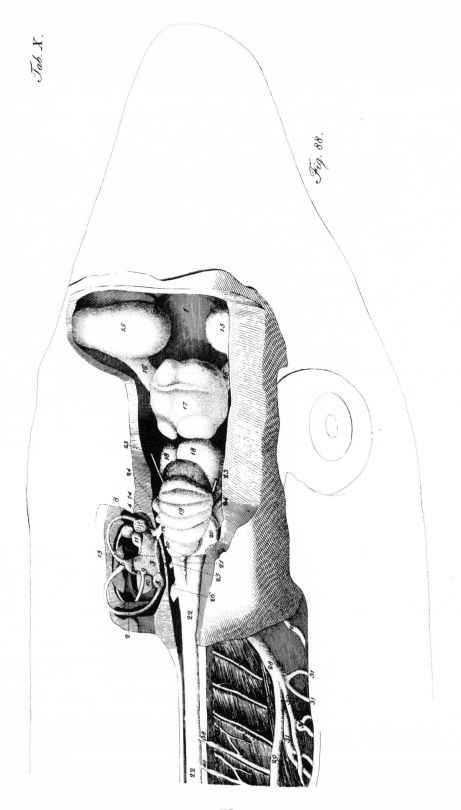

(PLATE X, continued)

Fig. 88 Brain and auditory apparatus of shark *(Squalus)*.

1. Cranial cavity
2. Vestibular cavity
3. Membranous labyrinth (sacculus)
4. Ampulla of anterior canal
5. Ampulla of posterior canal
6. Crus commune
7. Common utriculus
8. Ampulla of horizontal canal
9. Base of horizontal canal
10. Sacculus with otoconia
11. Anterior sacculus appendix
12. Auditory nerve
13. Posterior ramus
14. Anterior ramus
15. Olfactory bulb
16. Olfactory tract
17. Forebrain
18. Optic lobe
19. Cerebellum
20. Restiform body
21. Nuclei in medulla
22. Spinal cord
23. Trochlear nerve
24. Trigeminal nerve
25. Glossopharyngeal nerve
26. Vagus nerve
27. Hyomandibular branch of facial nerve
28. Vagus nerve
29. Lateralis branch of vagus
30. Visceral branch of vagus
31. Branchial branches of vagus
32. Spino-occipital nerve 1
33. Spino-occipital nerve 2
34. Spino-occipital nerve 3
35. Ventral root of spinal nerve 1
36. Spinal nerve 1
37. Ramus communicans of spinal nerve 1
38. Dorsal root of spinal nerve 1
39. Ventral root of spinal nerve 2
40. Dorsal root of spinal nerve 2

Part III
FISH *CAN* HEAR!

Editor's Comments
on Papers 4 Through 6

The controversy as to whether fish could or could not hear was in full swing at the turn of the century, and many well-known zoologists contributed both pro and con reports. One of the giants of American zoology made a significant mark in the field. George Howard Parker had a long and illustrious career, during which he generated major advances in the fields of comparative morphology and physiology of central nervous systems, of sense organs, physiology of color changes, and many aspects of behavioral and evolutionary biology. He also contributed to a classic textbook of general zoology which was used as a model for zoology teaching for two generations. Born in 1864, he became a member of the faculty at Harvard University in 1888. Even after his retirement in 1935, he continued active research and writing until his death in 1955. Among his most influential publications was his series of studies on the hearing in fishes. The 1903 lecture he gave on the subject (reprinted herein as Paper 3) represents not only a fine critical review of the current controversy, but a concise summary of his own very convincing experiments.

Surprisingly, there was still doubt as to the hearing ability in fishes, and in 1923 Karl von Frisch added his observations on catfish, and subsequently published some of the most stimulating reviews that have ever been written in the field. He was one of the first, for example, to recognize the difference between pressure and displacement energy as requiring significantly different receptor mechanisms. Born in 1886, Karl von Frisch is most famous, of course, for his work on the communicatory dances of bees, but during his long span as professor at the University of Munich, he has made major contributions in many aspects of zoology and behavior, and his studies on hearing in fishes certainly rank among the classics. He was awarded a Nobel prize in 1973, along with two equally renowned ethologists, Konrad Lorenz and Niko Tinbergen.

Papers 5 and 6 were chosen from among the several von Frisch had published on the subject of fish hearing. The first of these, published in 1923, was his initial effort in the field, and, in spite of its informal style, demonstrates von Frisch's incisive thinking and careful experimental design. The second paper (1938) is essentially an English version of his 1936 review, and also represents a milestone in the development of the study of fish audition.

4

Reprinted from *Amer. Naturalist,* **37**(435), 185–204 (1903)

THE SENSE OF HEARING IN FISHES.[1]

G. H. PARKER.

THE sense of hearing is unusual in several respects. Unlike the other senses, it is restricted to comparatively few groups of animals; for, though many experiments have been tried, there is no conclusive evidence, so far as I know, that a sense of hearing is possessed by coral animals, jellyfishes, worms, starfishes, crabs, oysters, snails, and their allies. It is true that the older naturalists described for many of these animals organs that they called ear-sacs and that were supposed to act as organs of hearing, but the experimental work of the last fifteen years has shown that these organs are without doubt means of controlling the equilibrium of the animals, and not organs of hearing. The only animals in which a sense of hearing may be said without reservation to be present are the higher arthropods, particularly the insects; and the four higher classes of vertebrates, the amphibians, reptiles, birds, and mammals. Excepting the arthropods and the vertebrates, it seems probable that the other animals cannot hear, that while they may be influenced by contact with the world about them, by its light, its odors, etc., they are uninfluenced by its sounds; in other words, they live as though surrounded by perpetual silence.

The sense of hearing is not only restricted to a very few groups of animals, but the animals possessing it are always the more highly organized members of their groups. Thus, among the arthropods, a group which includes the crabs, lobsters, myriapods, spiders, and insects, the sense of hearing, if not absolutely restricted to the most highly organized class, the insects, is at least best developed in them. So, too, in the vertebrates, though the frogs, toads, turtles and their like have a sense of hearing, the efficiency of this sense is low compared with that which it attains in the birds and particularly in the mammals, the highest

[1] A lecture delivered before the Department of Zoölogy of the Brooklyn Institute of Arts and Sciences, March 5, 1903.

vertebrates. It is thus evident that the sense of hearing is coupled with high organization.

When a survey of the whole animal kingdom is made, it is found that most sense organs are not restricted as the organs of hearing are ; for instance, eyes, often of a complicated structure, occur in such lowly organized animals as jellyfishes, starfishes, and worms, and these animals react with great precision to light. Not only do many of these lower animals possess eyes, but they also have organs of touch, taste, etc. ; in fact, the only important sense organ lacking in them is that of hearing. Since the sense of hearing is found only in the more highly organized animals and the other senses occur in the lower as well as in the higher animals, it follows that hearing is probably the most recently acquired of the senses.

If in accordance with these facts we endeavor to form some idea of the evolution of the sense organs in the animal series, we must picture to ourselves an early origin for all the important senses except hearing. This sense was undoubtedly the last important one to be differentiated and the reason for the lateness of its appearance I hope to make clear to you toward the close of this lecture.

It is a remarkable fact that the ear in the higher vertebrates, probably their latest important sensory acquisition, is an unusually perfect mechanism. Much has often been said about the perfection of the human eye and this organ undoubtedly displays a marvelously delicate construction, but in my opinion the efficiency of the ear as an organ of sense is as much beyond that of the eye as a modern chronometer is beyond an old-fashioned sundial. Evidence of the truth of this opinion can be seen in the many defects that are present in the eye as contrasted with the ear. For instance, what we call white light is well known to be any one of many possible mixtures of colored lights. Thus, when red light is combined with bluish green, the resultant is white ; orange and sky-blue likewise produce white, as do also yellow and violet, green and pink, etc. To all these combinations, which are totally distinct from a physical standpoint, the eye answers with but one sign, that for white light.

Color in light corresponds to pitch in sound, for both depend

85

upon wave lengths.   Thus, the keys of a piano when struck in sequence give rise to a series of tones that differ one from another much as the colors of the spectrum do, namely, in the lengths of their waves.   Although a trained eye cannot distinguish between white lights made by mixing different pairs of colored lights, even the unpracticed ear can distinguish between any pairs of tones when sounded on the keyboard, and, while the person may not be able to name the keys, the actual discrimination is easily accomplished.   Thus white light is a measure of the deception due to our eyes, a deception that the ear ordinarily never gives rise to.   Could we see the colors in ordinary light as we hear the tones in sound, the work of the most extreme French colorists would be dull in comparison with reality.   The eye, therefore, fails to give much information about light that is obtained from the ear about sound.

The occurrence of well-developed organs of hearing only among the insects and higher vertebrates suggests, since these animals are air-inhabiting forms, that possibly the sense of hearing is capable of development only in an organism surrounded by air. To test this supposition one naturally turns to the nearest aquatic relatives of the groups possessing this sense.   With the insects these relatives are probably the somewhat distantly related crustaceans, but with the vertebrates they are the fishes, a class closely allied to the other members of the vertebrate group.   If the sense of hearing can originate only in air-inhabiting animals, no traces of it should be found among fishes.   If it can arise in other situations, the fishes are probably the class in which its beginnings in the vertebrate series are to be sought for.   The problem of hearing in fishes, therefore, is a general one dealing with the possible origin of one of the most important senses of vertebrates, a sense probably the most recently developed of all and yet in many respects the most efficient.

Hearing in fishes can best be approached from the standpoint of the human ear.   The ear in man has long been known to be composed of three parts, the external, the middle, and the internal ear.   The external ear consists of a complicated fold of skin known as the concha and a somewhat twisted tube leading inward to the ear-drum.   The middle ear is a cavity in the head lying immediately internal to the ear-drum and connected with the mouth by the Eustachian tube. Through the cavity of the middle ear a bridge of small bones, the ear ossicles, passes from the ear-drum to the opposite wall of the middle ear where the innermost ossicle abuts against the cavity of the internal ear. The internal ear, which is situated somewhat deeper in the head than the middle ear, is a complicated fluid-filled sac with three semicircular canals and a spirally twisted portion, the cochlea. The nerve concerned with the sense of hearing ends in the walls of this sac. When the ear is normally stimulated, the sound-waves from the surrounding air beat against the ear-drum and set it in vibration. These vibrations cause the chain of ossicles to vibrate and thus the motion is handed on to the fluid of the internal ear. This fluid vibrates in turn and by some process not clearly ascertained stimulates the nerves on the walls of the ear-sac. As is well known the deafness caused by injuries to the external and the middle ear may often be relieved by various mechanical contrivances, but injuries to the internal ear are of an absolute kind and not open to amelioration, for the internal ear, as its nerve connections show, is the true organ of hearing, the middle and external ears being only means of conducting sound-waves to the true sense organ.

The form of ear just described is found only in the higher vertebrates ; in the lower ones this organ presents a somewhat simpler structure. Thus, in the frog, there is no external ear, but the ear-drum is exposed directly on the surface of the head and the whole auditory apparatus consists of only the middle and the internal ear. In fishes a still further reduction takes place in that the middle ear as such is not developed. Thus the fishes possess only the essential part of the organ of hearing, the internal ear, and even this is in an altered form, for their ear-sacs, though complicated in outline and usually provided with three semicircular canals, lack almost all traces of the spirally twisted part, the cochlea.

That fishes possess a sense of hearing seems to have been generally admitted by the older observers. Thus Isaac Walton, in his "Complete Angler" (1653), when asked if trout can see at night replies "Yes, and hear and smell too." He then describes some experiments made by Sir Francis Bacon to show that sound can pass through water, experiments that led Walton to crave the pardon of one whom he had laughed at for affirming that carp would come to a certain place in a pond to be fed, at the ringing of a bell or the beating of a drum. He thereupon declares that "it shall be a rule for me to make as little noise as I can when I am fishing, until Sir Francis Bacon be confuted, which I shall give any man leave to do," and he finally resolves "to advise anglers to be patient and forbear swearing, lest they be heard, and catch no fish."

The internal ears of the higher fishes were also known to the older observers. So far as I am aware they were first described by Casserius in 1610 and were studied in some detail in the following century by Geoffroy, Scarpa, Comparetti and the celebrated British physician, Hunter. The attitude taken by many of these early workers in the question of the ability of fishes to hear is well illustrated by a quotation from a paper on the organ of hearing in fishes published by Hunter (1782). This paper contains the following statement (1782, p. 383): "As it is evident that fish possess the organ of hearing, it becomes unnecessary to make or relate any experiment, made with live fish which only tends to prove this fact; but I will mention one experiment, to shew that sound affects them much, and is one of their guards, as it is in other animals. In the year 1762, when I was in Portugal, I observed in a nobleman's garden, near Lisbon, a small fish-pond, full of different kinds of fish. Its bottom was level with the ground, and was made by forming a bank all round. There was a shrubbery close to it. Whilst I was laying on the bank, observing the fish swim about, I desired a gentleman, who was with me, to take a loaded gun, and go behind the shrubs and fire it. The reason for going behind the shrubs was, that there might not be the least reflection of light. The instant the report was made, the fish appeared to be all of one mind, for they vanished instantaneously into the mud at the bottom, raising as it were a cloud of mud. In about five minutes after they began to appear, till the whole came forth again."

This passage shows very clearly that in the opinion of Hunter the internal ears of fishes, like those of the higher vertebrates, are organs of hearing. Without further experimental evidence, this view was accepted by the celebrated physiologist Müller (1848, p. 1238) in his well-known chapters on the physiology of the senses, and by many other eminent authorities such as Owen (1866, pp. 342 and 346), Günther (1880, p. 116), and Romanes (1892, p. 250). To these investigators the presence of the internal ear, seemed, as it did to Hunter, sufficient ground for assuming that fishes could hear.

Within recent years, however, this opinion has been called in question or even denied. Some of the grounds for this change of view may be stated as follows. The English zoölogist Bateson (1890, p. 251) in some investigations on the sense organs and perception of fishes, observed that the report from the blasting of rocks caused congers to draw back a few inches, flatfishes like the sole, plaice, and turbot to bury themselves, and pouting to scatter momentarily in all directions. Other fishes seemed to take no notice of the report. When the side of a tank containing pollack or soles was struck with a heavy stick, the fishes behaved as they did toward the report of the blasting. Pollack did not respond, however to the sound made by rubbing a wet finger on the glass window of an aquarium or to the noise made by striking a piece of glass under water with a stone, provided the means of producing the noise was not seen by the fishes. Bateson concluded that, while it may be regarded as clear that fishes perceive the sound of sudden shocks and concussions when these are severe, they do not seem to hear the sounds of bodies moving in the water but not seen by them.

Without knowledge of Bateson's observations, the Viennese physiologist Kreidl (1895) carried out a series of experiments with the view of testing the powers of hearing in the goldfish. This species was chosen because of the ease with which it could be kept in the laboratory and further because it is one of those fishes that have long been reputed to come at the sound of a bell. After an extended series of experiments Kreidl (1895, p. 458) concluded that normal goldfish never respond to sounds produced either in the air or in the water, though they do react to the shock of a sudden blow given to the cover of the aquarium.   To test whether such responses were dependent upon the auditory nerves, Kreidl removed these nerves and the attached ear-sacs from a number of goldfishes and subjected them to stimulation by sound.   In all cases they were found to respond precisely as the animals with ears did.   Kreidl, therefore, concluded that goldfishes do not hear by the so-called ear, but that they react to sound waves by means of an especially developed skin sense, or, to put the matter in other words, the goldfish *feels* sound but does not *hear* it (Kreidl, 1896, p. 581).   This condition is not so difficult to imagine as at first thought it seems, for we can not only hear sounds under water but we can also feel them, as anyone can prove by placing his hand under water near a loudly sounding body.

After Kreidl had reached his conclusion concerning goldfishes, he was led to take up a specific case of the response of fishes to the sound of a bell and an opportunity of doing this was found at the Benedictine monastery in Krems, Austria.   Here the trout of a particular basin were said to come for food at the ringing of a bell.   Kreidl (1896, p. 583), however, found that they would assemble at sight of a person and without the ringing of the bell.   If they were not then fed, they soon dispersed and no amount of bell-ringing would induce them to return.   If, however, a pebble or small piece of bread was thrown into the water, they immediately swam vigorously toward the spot where the disturbance had occurred.   Moreover, if a person approached the basin without being seen and rang the bell vigorously, the fishes did not assemble.   From these facts Kreidl (1896, p. 584) concluded that the assembling of the fishes was brought about through sight and the skin sense and not through hearing, and that the conclusion reached with the goldfish might be extended to other kinds of fishes.

While the problem of the auditory function of the ears of fishes was thus being investigated, a wholly different view as to the functions of these organs had been gradually opened up. Through the researches of Loeb (1888), Kreidl (1892), Bethe (1894), and Lee (1898) it became clear that whether the ears of fishes were auditory organs or not, they were, beyond doubt, organs for the control of the equilibrium of these animals, and in this respect they partook of the nature of the otocysts of the lower animals. My own few observations are fully in accord with this conclusion. When the nerves to the ears of the green killifish (Fundulus heteroclitus) are cut and the animal attempts rapid locomotion, it loses its bearings completely and swims in any position in spirals or even in circles. Thus the ear is in some way essential to the continued equilibrium of the fish. Although this conclusion has no direct bearing on the question of hearing in fishes, it makes it no longer necessary to assume that the presence of the internal ear in a given fish implies the ability of this fish to hear; hence the argument used by the older investigators is shown to be fallacious.

The conclusion arrived at by Kreidl that the ears of fishes like the goldfish, trout, etc. are not organs of hearing was supported and extended by the observations of one of our American physiologists, Dr. Lee of Columbia University, who studied the reactions of several species of fishes to such sounds as the human voice, the clapping of hands, and the striking of stones together in air and under water. In all his experiments Lee (1898, p. 137) obtained no evidence whatever of the existence of a sense of hearing as the term is usually employed; though he found that the fishes were exceedingly sensitive to gross shocks, such as the jarring of their tank or concussions upon its walls. From the observations and experiments of Bateson and of Kreidl and from his own work, Lee (1898, p. 138) believed that the conclusion is justified beyond doubt that fishes do not possess the power of hearing, in the sense in which the term is ordinarily used and that the sole function of the ear in fishes is equilibration. According to this view then, fishes resemble many of the lower aquatic animals, in that their so-called ears are not organs for hearing, but for controlling the equilibrium of their bodies; and, if they respond to sounds at all, they do so through the skin.

This general conclusion seemed to me not wholly in accord with certain well-known facts in the natural history of fishes. Most important of these is the undoubted ability on the part of some fishes to make sounds. Although it is conceivable that fishes, like some totally deaf persons, may produce vocal sounds that they themselves cannot hear, this conclusion is not probable and anyone that has ever heard a young swellfish (Chilomycterus schoepfi) make its characteristic sound when attacked by a hungry scup (Stenotomus chrysops) cannot but receive the impression that both fishes hear.   Moreover it is very difficult without assuming hearing to understand the economy of sound production where, as in the squeteague or weakfish (Cynoscion regalis), this function is limited to one sex, in this instance the males.   These habits raise the suspicion that notwithstanding the experimental evidence thus far brought forward, fishes may hear.   It was chiefly because of this suspicion that last summer at the invitation of the United States Fish Commission I undertook to investigate this question.

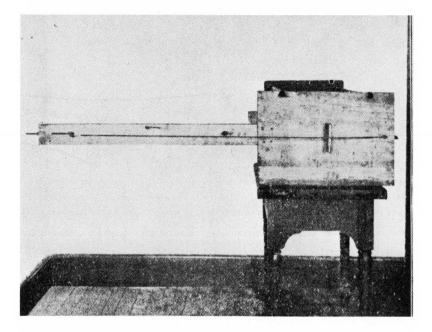

Fig. 1.

The apparatus used (Figs. 1 and 2) consisted of a large marine aquarium one end of which was replaced by a deal sounding board. On this board a bass viol string was stretched so that its vibrations could be transmitted through the board to the water in the aquarium. . By frequent adjustment the string was kept at forty vibrations per second, corresponding to a tone almost as low as any used in music. Within the aquarium was suspended from distant supports a small glass cage for the retention of the fishes to be experimented upon. The end of the cage toward the sounding-board was open except for a fine net, which, though it restrained the fishes from escaping from the cage, made no serious interference with the entrance of sound.

Fig. 2.

In testing fishes for the sense of hearing it must be evident from what has already been said that several precautions are necessary. First of all, the sounds used should be sustained and of relatively low intensity rather than of the kind that might produce a concussion or a shock. Next, care must be taken to determine whether these sounds influence the fish through its ears or through its skin; for if the ears are not stimulated, a sense of hearing cannot be said to be present. After some preliminary trials I finally resolved to use for my experiments the green killifish (Fundulus heteroclitus), a minnow common in the waters about the United States Fish ·Commission Station at Woods Hole, Massachusetts, where my work was done. This fish proved very hardy and in every way satisfactory for the work.

Three classes of killifishes were tested; first, those that were entirely normal; secondly, those in which the nerves to the ears had been cut; and, thirdly, those whose outer surfaces had been rendered insensitive by cutting the nerves to the skin. The fishes were easily etherized and cutting the nerves to the ears proved to be a simple though delicate operation. To render the skin insensitive, it was necessary to cut the fifth and seventh nerves, the lateral line nerves and the spinal cord, but from this apparently severe operation the fishes almost invariably recovered, fed well, and continued normally active for several weeks.

When a normal fish was placed in the cage and the bass viol string set in vibration, any one of four responses might be observed : first, the rate of the gill movements increased for a brief period; secondly, the pectoral fins, if quiet, were set in motion, or, if in motion, their rate was increased; thirdly, the tail fin often vibrated; and, finally, the whole fish might give a spring as if startled by the sound. Of these four reactions, the one most satisfactory for observation was the movement of the pectoral fins, and I subsequently used this almost exclusively in testing the fishes. Ten normal fishes when subjected each to ten tests with the sounding apparatus responded with the pectoral fins ninety-six times in the total hundred. This number may be taken as a basis of comparison for the fishes upon which operations had been performed.

To ascertain the importance of the ear in these responses, I next tested ten fishes in which the nerves to the ears had been cut and from ten observations on each fish I found that the number of responses to sound in a total of one hundred trials was only eighteen, and some of these eighteen were of doubtful character. It thus appears that cutting the nerves to the ears brings about a large reduction in the number of reactions and my results, therefore, are very different from those of Kreidl, who, it will be remembered, observed no difference in this respect between normal and earless goldfishes. Although at

first sight it might seem that these experiments proved conclusively that the ear of the killifish is, if not the only organ of
hearing, at least the chief organ for that sense, it is nevertheless
conceivable that the reduction in the number of reactions shown
by the earless fishes may be due not to the loss of the ear as a
sense organ but to the severity of the operation that the fishes
have undergone.

To determine how much weight should be given to this objection and at the same time to ascertain the part played by the
skin in these reactions, I tested ten fishes in which the skin had
been made insensitive but in which the ears were intact.   In a
total of one hundred trials, ten on each fish, there were ninety-
four responses to sound and six failures; in other words, these
fishes, though they had undergone more severe operations than
the earless ones, reacted almost exactly as normal fishes did.
These observations placed beyond a doubt the conclusion that
the ears of the killifish are stimulated by the disturbances set up
by the vibrating bass viol string, and the only question we have
to answer before a final conclusion can be safely drawn is,
whether these disturbances are really sound vibrations.

If the aquarium is observed closely when the bass viol string
is made to vibrate, not only will a sound be heard but the whole
aquarium will be seen to vibrate and ripples will be noticed passing over the surface of the water.   Is it not possible that the
fishes respond to the motion of the aquarium as a whole or to
the disturbance indicated by the ripples rather than to the true
sound-waves?   To determine this point, I substituted for the
bass viol string an electric tuning fork that gave a tone of 128
vibrations per second.   The fork was so placed that its base
could by a slight movement be brought into contract with the
sounding-board and thus, without jar or disturbance to the aquarium, the sound could be delivered to the contained water.

On testing fishes under these conditions, it was found that the
earless ones never responded to the tones from the tuning fork,
while those with ears very usually did respond.   I, therefore,
believe that I am entirely justified in drawing the final conclusion that the ears of the killifish are stimulated by sound-waves,
that is, that this fish hears.   It will be recalled that in the

experiments with the bass viol string the earless fishes responded eighteen times in the hundred trials. I believe that the tuning fork experiments, in which no earless fishes responded, make it probable that these eighteen responses were due not to the stimulating effect of sound on the skin of the fishes, as might be inferred, but to some other cause such as the trembling of the whole aquarium. I do not wish to imply, however, that the skin of a fish may not be stimulated by sound.

Although the conclusion that a fish hears is directly contrary to that arrived at by Lee, it is not at all necessary to suppose that the observations of this investigator and those of Kreidl should be regarded as incorrect. Neither Kreidl nor Lee worked on the killifish and the ears in this species may be different from those in the fishes studied by these two investigators. In fact, in my own work I tried on the smooth dogfish (Mustelus canis) the same experiments as those that I have just described for the killifish, but without obtaining the least evidence of hearing in this species. I am, therefore, quite prepared to believe that there are fishes in which the sense of hearing is undeveloped, and these may have been the very forms with which Kreidl and Lee worked; but that there are fishes that do hear I feel perfectly certain.

The ear is related to other sense organs in a way unusually well seen in fishes, and before closing I wish to call attention briefly to this aspect of the subject. The sense organs concerned are the skin and the lateral-line organs. Everyone is familiar with the skin as an organ of touch, but the lateral-line organs are less generally known for at least one obvious reason, namely, that man possesses none. Lateral-line organs occur only in the true aquatic vertebrates, the fishes and the amphibians, and in the latter only in those stages in which the animals inhabit the water. Thus in the frog, lateral-line organs are present while this amphibian is a tadpole, but, as soon as it takes on the adult form and emerges from the water, these organs disappear. Lateral-line organs, then, are in some way intimately associated with the water habit.

These organs form regular lines on the skin of an amphibian or a fish, though in the latter they are more frequently in grooves in the skin or in tubes that lie immediately under the skin and whose courses are indicated by numerous openings, the lateral-line pores.   In many fishes three such lines of pores can be recognized on the side of the head, one above the eye, a second immediately below the eye, and a third on the lower jaw.   From the union of these three near the back of the head, a fourth line passes posteriorly along the side of the fish, the lateral line, from which the whole system takes its name.

Modern embryology has shown that the ear is closely related to the lateral-line system.   The deep situation of the ear-sac at first sight seems to preclude this, but the ear-sac does not form in this situation.   In fishes, as in higher vertebrates, this sac forms as a pocket of skin pushed into the head as it were from the outer surface and in fishes it can be shown that the skin which is thus infolded is a portion of the lateral-line system. After the sac has been formed, it sinks into the deeper part of the head, generally loses its connection with the outer skin, and gradually takes on its final complicated shape by producing semi-circular canals, etc.   Thus the internal ear may be regarded as a modified part of the lateral-line system.   This system in turn develops from the skin, and when its organs lie in tubes, as they do in most fishes, the tubes are formed from groove-like depressions of the skin.   Thus the lateral-line organs are specialized sense organs from the skin.

These facts suggest at once interesting relations between the three sets of organs mentioned ; for, as the lateral-line organs may be regarded as derived from the undifferentiated sense organs of the skin, so the ear may be conceived to have been derived from the lateral-line organs.   Thus, we are dealing with what may be called three generations of sense organs : the skin representing the first generation, and giving rise to the lateral-line organs, the second, which in turn produce the third, the ears.

This view of the relations of these three sets of organs accords well with what I have been able to make out about their functions in the killifish.   It has already been shown that only such fishes as have their ears intact respond to the sound of a tuning fork.   Consequently we may conclude that such sounds do not stimulate either the lateral-line organs or the skin, but that they are a stimulus appropriate to the ear.

97

The lateral-line organs can also be shown to possess a stimulus peculiar to themselves.   These organs were originally supposed to be merely slime glands for the production of the slimy covering so characteristic of the skins of fishes.   In 1850 Leydig demonstrated their sensory character, and since then they have given rise to much speculation among naturalists.   Since they occur in fishes that have the usual five senses, Leydig (1868) regarded them as organs of a sixth sense quite distinct from any that we possess.   Schulze (1870) thought they served to detect mass movements of the water as when a current passes over the surface of a fish or the fish swims through the water.   Merkel (1880) believed that they were simply organs of touch, and Emery (1880) and P. and F. Sarasin (1887–1890) regarded them as accessory ears.   Fuchs (1895) brought forward evidence to show that they were pressure organs, and Richard (1896) believed they were in some manner connected with the production of gas in the swim-bladders of fishes.   Bonnier (1896) was of opinion that among other things they oriented the fish in reference to centres of disturbance in the water, and Lee (1898) thought them organs of equilibration.   Thus, much difference of opinion prevails as to the supposed function of these organs.

In the killifish the stimulus for the lateral-line organs is easily found.   If an aquarium in which a normal fish is sporting is made to undergo a slight inaudible oscillation by some means not visible to the fish, the latter will dart at once to the bottom.   This happens even when the oscillation is scarcely perceptible to the observer.   After the nerves to the lateral-line organs have been cut, the fish will no longer respond to these slight movements, but will continue sporting about even when the aquarium is made to tremble considerably.   The responses obtained from killifishes under these conditions are so invariable that I conclude that their lateral-line organs are stimulated, much as Schulze suspected, by a slight but inaudible movement of the whole mass of water, a movement that is too delicate to stimulate their skins.

The skin I found to be stimulated by the movements of the water in surface waves and in currents.   If a fish in which the lateral-line organs have been rendered inoperative swims into a region where surface waves affect it, it will swim downward out of the reach of these, though it does not go to the bottom of the aquarium as a fish with lateral-line organs does. If it is placed in a current of water, it will swim as vigorously against the current as a normal fish will. Thus the skin, though not stimulated by sound from a tuning fork or the slight inaudible trembling of the whole mass of water, is stimulated by currents and by surface waves.

Hence the three sets of sense organs under consideration may be regarded as having slightly different kinds of stimuli: the skin being affected by surface waves and by currents; the lateral-line organs by slight inaudible movements of the whole mass of water; and the ears by the still more delicate vibrations of water particles, sound. These three sets of sense organs, therefore, are not only genetically connected in that they represent so to speak three generations of organs, but their evolution has been toward more and more delicate means of stimulation. From this standpoint the lateral-line organs of the fishes and the amphibians may be said to be delicate organs of touch and even the ear as an organ of hearing may be looked upon as an exquisitely refined apparatus of much this same kind.[1] Hearing, then, is a most delicate form of touching, and the organ of hearing has developed late in the animal series because its processes are not original but are derived from those of the more primitive sense, touch. Many fishes possess at once the complete series of sense organs leading from touch to hearing, and in these animals the activities dependent upon such organs form doubtless a more or less homogeneous whole; but with us touching and hearing are very distinct things, a condition, however, that we can easily understand, for we have lost the intermediate sense, that of the

[1] At first sight it might seem that this view ignored completely the equilibration function of the ear, a function which may be the only one possessed by this organ in some of the lower fishes, but there are no facts so far as I know that prevent one from assuming that the stimulus for the lateral line organs may not be much the same as that for the ear as an equilibration organ and thus this function might indicate a sensory activity somewhat intermediate between that of the lateral line organs and of hearing. At least unless this is shown not to be the case, the equilibration function of the ear offers no real obstacle to the acceptance of the opinion expressed above as to the physiological relations of the skin, lateral line organs, and ear.

lateral-line organs.   Thus the consideration of the sense of hearing in fishes leads us to an understanding of a natural group of
sense organs whose genetic connections would never have been
suspected had we not been able to investigate them in these primitive aquatic vertebrates, the fishes.

Postscript.   Since this lecture was prepared Professor Tullberg's interesting paper (1903) on the functions of the ears of
fishes has reached me.   In this paper it is concluded (p. 20)
that the ears of fishes are not organs of equilibration and though
they may perhaps be to a certain extent organs of hearing, their
original and principal function is to receive stimuli from the
movements of the surrounding water, especially from currents.
Vibrations probably stimulate particularly the maculæ acusticæ
of the utriculus, the sacculus, and the lagena; currents affect
especially the cristæ acusticæ of the ampullæ.   Thus the ear is
held to be an organ directly concerned with the reactions of a
fish to a current of water (rheotaxis).

My own experiments have been directed to test the sense of
hearing in fishes rather than to ascertain what other functions
the ears in these animals may have, but some of my observations
bear on the questions raised by Professor Tullberg and I, therefore, call attention to them here.   Professor Tullberg believes
that the ears of fishes are not concerned with equilibration
because the disturbances in the equilibrium of fishes that follow
many operations on the ears and that have been taken to indicate this function, sooner or later disappear, and must, therefore,
be regarded as shock effects and not due to the loss of a special
sense organ.   I have observed much the same condition in *Fundulus heteroclitus* as that described by Professor Tullberg in
that two or three days after the eighth nerve has been cut
the fishes often swim quite normally.   If, however, they are
made to swim very rapidly, they invariably lose all orientation
and move in irregular circles and spirals.   I, therefore, believe
that the loss of the ear may have a *lasting* effect on the orientation of fishes in certain forms of locomotion, for these irregular movements were always observable in earless Fundulus
even up to the time of death, in some instances six weeks after
the cutting of the eighth nerve.   The apparent recovery after

the operation I attribute to the increased use of the eye as an organ for orientation and though this is an assumption on my part, it is one well supported by evidence from the invertebrates, and, until it is shown to be false for fishes, it seems to me to make Professor Tullberg's conclusion that the fish ear has nothing to do with equilibration at least premature.

My observations on the lateral line organs of Fundulus (Parker, 1903, pp. 59–62) are in entire agreement with those of Professor Tullberg (1903, pp. 8, 15) on these organs in other fishes in that I have found no evidence that these organs are essential to the normal swimming of a fish against a current. But since in Fundulus I could not persuade myself that the ear was not in some degree connected with equilibration, I was unable to devise a satisfactory experiment that would test in the absence of the ear, other organs of sense, such as the skin, that might be stimulated by water-currents. The only evidence I was able to obtain was that when fishes whose spinal cords and lateral-line nerves had been cut several days before, were held by the head near a gentle current of water the tails bent toward the current even though the action of the current on a cordless fish similarly held was to force the tail in the opposite direction. I am, therefore, entirely certain that the skin of the trunk of *Fundulus heteroclitus* is stimulated by water-currents, though I cannot say that these may not also stimulate the ears. I must confess, however, that Professor Tullberg's evidence (1903, pp. 11, 14,) on this point, namely, that after cutting both horizontal semicircular canals the fish no longer orients to a current, does not seem to me wholly conclusive, for this operation may bring about the observed condition by a slight interference with the equilibration function of the ear. In Fundulus swimming against a current of water is dependent in my opinion upon at least two factors: first, the retention of the normal position of the fish which is chiefly accomplished, I believe, by means of the ears as equilibration organs ,and, secondly, directive locomotion which is dependent upon the stimulating effect of the current on the skin of the fish. Under these conditions an interference with the ear might well give rise to a loss of rheotaxis though the primary stimulus for this form of response might be received by the skin.   Since the evidence that I have gathered from Fundulus seems to me to show conclusively that this fish uses the ears as organs of equilibration and since the skin in this species is stimulated by water-currents, I believe that the rheotaxis of this species probably is primarily dependent upon the skin, though it may be profoundly influenced by impulses originating in the ear either through a disturbance of equilibrium, as I have already suggested, or possibly directly, as Professor Tullberg believes.

BIBLIOGRAPHY.

1890 BATESON, W.   The Sense-organs and Perceptions of Fishes; with Remarks on the Supply of Bait.   Jour. Mar. Biol. Assoc. United Kingdom, new ser., vol. i, pp. 225–256, pl. 20.

1894 BETHE, A.   Ueber die Erhaltung des Gleichgewichts.   Biol. Centralbl., Bd. 14, pp. 95–114, 563–582.

1896 BONNIER P.   Sur le sens latéral.   C. R. Soc. Biol., ser. 10, tom. 3, pp. 917–919.

1880 EMERY, C.   Le Specie del Genere Fierasfer nel Golfo di Napoli e Regiori limitrofe.   Fauna u. Flora Neapel.   Monographie 2.   Leipzig, 76 pp., 9 Taf.

1895 FUCHS, S.   Ueber die Function der unter der Haut liegenden Canalsysteme bei den Selachiern.   Arch. ges. Physiol., Bd. 59, pp. 454–478, Taf. 6.

1880 GÜNTHER, A. C. L. G.   An Introduction to the Study of Fishes.   Edinburgh.   8°, xvi + 720 pp.

1782 HUNTER, J.   Account of the Organs of Hearing in Fish.   Phil. Trans. Roy. Soc. London, vol. 72, pp. 379–383.

1892 KREIDL, A.   Zur physiologischen Bedeutung des Ohrlabyrinthes.   Neurol.   Centralbl., Bd. 11, pp. 222–223.

1895 —— Ueber die Perception der Schallwellen bei den Fischen. Arch. ges. Physiol., Bd. 61, pp. 450–464.

1896 —— Ein weiterer Versuch über das angebliche Hören eines Glockenzeichens durch die Fische.   Arch. ges. Physiol. Bd. 63, pp. 581–586.

1898 LEE, F. S.   The Function of the Ear and the Lateral Line in Fishes.   Amer. Jour. Physiol., vol. i, pp. 128–144.

1850 LEYDIG, F.   Ueber die Schleimkanäle der Knochenfische.   Arch. Anat. Physiol., wiss. Med., Jahrg. 1850, pp. 170–181, Taf. 4, Fig. 1–3.

1868 —— Ueber Organe eines sechsten Sinnes.   Dresden, 4°, 108 pp., 5 Taf.

1888 LOEB, J. Die Orientirung der Thiere gegen die Schwerkraft der Erde. Sitzb. phys.-med. Gesell. Würzburg, Jahrg. 1888, pp. 5–10.

1880 MERKEL, F. Ueber die Endigungen der sensiblen Nerven in der Haut der Wirbelthiere. Rostock, 8°, 214 pp., 15 Taf.

1848 MÜLLER, J. The Physiology of the Senses, Voice, and Muscular Motions, with the Mental Faculties. Translated by W. Baly. London, 8°, xvii + pp. 849–1419 + 32 + 22 pp.

1866 OWEN, R. On the Anatomy of Vertebrates. Vol. I. London, 8°, xlii + 650 pp.

1903 PARKER, G. H. Hearing and Allied Senses in Fishes. Bull. U. S. Fish Comm., 1902, pp. 45–64, pl. 9.

1903[a] —— Sense of Hearing in Fishes. Science, new ser., vol. 17, p. 243.

1896 RICHARD, J. Sur les functions de la ligue latérale du Cyprin doré. C. R. Soc. Biol., ser. 10, tom. 3, pp. 131–133.

1892 ROMANES, G. J. Animal Intelligence. Internat. Sci. Ser., No. 44. New York, 8°, xiv + 520 pp.

1887–1890 SARASIN, P., und SARASIN, F. Zur Entwicklungsgeschichte und Anatomie der ceylonesischen Blindwühle Ichthyophis glutinosus, L. Ergeb. naturwiss. Forschung Ceylon. Bd. 2, 263 pp., 24 Taf.

1870 SCHULZE, F. E. Ueber die Sinnesorgane der Seitenlinie bei Fischen und Amphibien. Arch. mikr. Anat., Bd. 6, pp. 62–88, Taf. 4–6.

1903 TULLBERG, T. Das Labyrinth der Fische, ein Organ zur Empfindung der Wasserbewegung. Bihang till K. Svenska Vet.-Akad. Handlingar, Stockholm, Bd. 28, No. 15, 25 pp.

1653 WALTON, I. The Compleat Angler or the Contemplative Man's Recreation. London.

103

5

A CATFISH WHO COMES WHEN ONE WHISTLES TO IT

Karl von Frisch

*This article was translated expressly for this Benchmark
volume by the Department of Animal Behavior, American
Museum of Natural History, from "Ein Zwergwels, der kommt,
wenn man ihm pfeift," in* Biol. Zentralbl., **43,** *439–446 (1923),
with the permission of Veb Georg Thieme*

Very few questions of comparative physiology have given rise to such differences of opinion as that concerning whether fish can hear.

We know of no structural formation in the inner ear of fishes that corresponds to the basilar membrane of higher classes of vertebrates. One could conclude therefore that fish are deaf. This theory is supported by the fact that fish, as a rule, do not react to tones and noises. It is true that some observers admit they have some reactions to sounds, ranging from faint movements of the finds up to a hasty flight.[1]

Their data and opinions have been vigorously denied by the opposition.[2]

Investigations had negative results, and even a positive reaction to sounds could not be considered a proof of the capacity to hear as it could be produced through "feeling", via cutaneous tactile cells.

There is a serious problem here. Often stated is the fact that it is difficult to produce sound waves without displacements or mechanical waves. The fact is that generated sound is naturally linked with mechanical disturbances. It must be so, since all sound waves are nothing but a rhythmical disturbance of the medium. That is the reason that even human beings not only hear many sounds, but can also feel them at the same time. Among deaf people the capacity to feel sounds can be extraordinarily increased. Whether and to what degree it is developed among fishes we do not know. Whether, therefore, a fish, when it reacts to a sound, hears or feels it in the same way cannot be ascertained from theoretical assumptions but only by experiment. The possibility of a clear division between hearing and feeling can be deduced from comparative anatomy. Only if a reaction to tones or sounds is registered by the inner ear can we speak of a sense of hearing. Among invertebrates we lack this standard. For this reason the decision among them as to whether a reaction to sound is to be designated as hearing or feeling must be left more or less to other physiological measures.

We see that to prove a sense of hearing among fishes two things are necessary: First: To prove that fishes react to the generation of sound. Secondly: To prove that the reaction is caused by the internal ear.

Parker, Bigelow and Haempel have found among various species of fish (Fundulus heteroclitus, Mustelus canis, Carassius auratus, Amiurus nebulosus), not only reactions to sounds, but have stated that these reactions are only lessened, or are not to be seen at all, if the acoustic nerves are cut, or if the inner ear, especially the sacculus, are removed. Their statements were doubted and many objections were voiced against their experimental designs. To this date the conclusions of these three investigators have not yet been proven, and, indeed, every reaction of fish to sound waves is still doubted today.

In this conflict of opinions, the catfish (Amiurus nebulosus Raf.) plays an outstanding part.

Among 23 different fresh water and salt water species, H. N. Maier[3] could detect no reaction to the loud ringing of a bell which was rung in the water in the immediate neighborhood of the fish. He therefore became convinced that fish have no sense of hearing. He then observed as follows: In a large aquarium there was among other fish a catfish which was quite shy, and which, if anyone approached, hid itself among the stones. If one remained quietly standing before the aquarium the fish came out of its hole a few minutes later and swam about in the aquarium. On one such occasion Maier accidently whistled once. At the same moment the catfish turned around and hurried back to its hiding place as though frightened. Inside of two hours Maier repeated the experiment about fifteen times, and each time his whistling caused the fish flee at once. If he held his hand before his mouth so that the fish could not see the movement of his mouth the result was the same. Still skeptical, Maier in further experiments placed himself about five meters away from the aquarium so that he could not be seen by the fish and could not see it himself, but only the open and inverted hands of an observer placed before the aquarium. This observer gave the signal to whistle by closing his hands as soon as the catfish had left his hiding place. "Even in this experiment which excluded any perception of a movement of the observers or by me the catfish always reacted by immediate flight". All notes of any range which Maier could produce with his mouth, if they were not too faint, were effective, as was also loud calling. Among some hundreds of experiments not one failed if the sound made was loud enough. Maier, therefore, concluded that among all the fish investigated by him only the catfish was capable of hearing sounds, and this in a very pronounced degree.

Haempel[4] also found in catfish distinct reactions to whistles and the ringing of a bell, while four other species of fish did not react in any way to these sounds.

But the doubters were still on hand. Körner[5] also obtained catfish and whistled to them in many ways, but with very little result. "Whistling with the mouth and with a shrill bicycle whistle was in many experiments as ineffective as shrill whistling through the fingers and whistling with the Edelmann organ whistle from the Bezold "continuous scale", which produces very loud notes from c^2 to a^4 capable of penetrating the walls of a room. All these 18 notes were tried in rising and falling cadences with the necessary pauses, also in irregular sequence. The song scales and trills of a well known singer had no effect on the fish which lay quietly on the ground or swam between the plants seeking food, making no reflex dashes or without attempting to hide themselves." Notes and sounds produced in the water itself through membrane whistles, which were combined with another apparatus, remained entirely without effect. The successful experiments of Maier and Haempel are attributed by Korner to mistakes in experimentation "which confuse acoustical reflexes through the bringing about of optical or tactile stimuli", and he concludes that the catfish reacts just as little to sound stimuli as all the other fish species which have been investigated up to date.

Benjamin[6] also could not support the assumptions of Maier and Haempel. His catfish were entirely unresponsive to whistling and screaming, to singing and clapping and to the noise of a powerful electric bell which, enclosed in a lead container, was sunk in the aquarium.

It appears to me that the doubts expressed, especially by Körner, regarding the positive results obtained by Maier and Haempel, are just as applicable to the negative results obtained by Körner and Benjamin. Does every catfish have to react to whistling and ringing, or to the notes of a celebrated singer? Do these notes mean enough to the fish so that we can expect a reliable reaction? I do not think so. These are not biologically relevant stimuli, i.e., not stimuli that play a part in the life of the fish. If Maier's catfish responded to his whistling he had obtained by a lucky chance a particularly sensitive fish.

One could only count on reliable reactions by using biologically relevant sounds, but we do not know any such in the life of the catfish. Perhaps, however, we can make them. Perhaps we can make the fish perceive that a sound, which at first means nothing to it, can afterwards become important. This thought caused me to investigate the debated question again by training by sounds. I will now report briefly on the first experiments.[7]

105

On March 10th, a healthy catfish, 7 cm in length, was placed in a glass aquarium the floor of which was covered with 2 cm of sand and planted with Elodea.[8] In order to answer immediately any objection that optical stimuli were involved, I had blinded the fish in both eyes several days before. The blind fish learned very rapidly - principally assisted by his outstretched and touching barbels - to find his way about the aquarium. It preferred staying in a hollow pipe which had been put in the aquarium as a hiding place. It always swam into the pipe at the end marked "a" (see Plate 1), which was turned towards the room and remained with its head at the opening marked "b" (on the side of the window). All that could be seen of it was the end of its tail (at the "a" opening) or the point of its snout (at the "b" end - Plate 1).

From March 18-22 I fed the fish daily with raw sliced meat which I held in a glass tube in front of its nose. At the same time I whistled at a medium pitch with my mouth several times. The whistling at first had no visible effect on the fish. This changed on the sixth day, March 23rd. The catfish lay motionless as usual, in its pipe. When I now whistled, still holding the food rod in the air, the fish immediately jerked forward so that its head appeared at the opening of the pipe at "b", and inside of five seconds it was completely out of the pipe (Plate 2, p. 443), and swam freely around the aquarium seeking its food which was then given.

In the following weeks I repeated this simple experiment thirty times with the same animal.[9]

In view of the distrust with which all positive data regarding sound reactions among fishes is viewed, I was anxious to obtain witnesses. I wanted to try that experiment before various professors (names mentioned). Encouraged by the fact during six days of testing, the fish did not fail once in 30 consecutive experiments, I wished to venture showing it to a large group of spectators. Although I carried the aquarium as carefully as possible into the auditorium the blind fish became extremely excited. This excitement lasted for hours and was manifested by restless swimming here and there and by butting against a corner of the aquarium. Five hours later it again lay in its pipe. I whistled - no reaction! After repeated whistling he finally emerged after 30 seconds. Was it accidentally? I wanted to quiet the fish until the demonstration and left it alone for 2 days. On the morning of May 13 it lay in its dwelling pipe. I whistled to it for half a minute - the fish did not stir. Two repetitions were equally unsuccessful. It now occurred to me that a different position of the aquarium, perhaps on another table or other floor, might be significant. Who knows whether wave sounds are not transmitted through the floor. I therefore took him back to his old position. But he did not respond on that or on the next day. It appeared as though the excitement had made him forget what he had learned. The reaction remained uncertain for several days. After that, having again been trained he responded to the whistling as constantly as before.

On December 23rd, I began the same training with a second, smaller (4.5 cm long) catfish which had also been blinded. Here again I had positive results. My success, however, was not so impressive because the fish seldom retreated into the pipe, which was available but swam about almost constantly. As with the other catfish, I whistled before and after I fed it. In the first 24 feedings no distinct reaction to the whistling was to be seen. Only twice, when the catfish lay quietly, contrary to custom, did it respond to the whistling with a slight spreading of the pectoral fins. On the 25th feeding, the fish jumped when I whistled, then turned about and searched, although the feeding rod with the meat was still out of the water.

After the 55th observation, I set the aquarium on a 2/2 cm thick padding of white felt. The reactions of the fish were not lessened in the slightest. Accordingly, it is improbable that the stimulus is transmitted by way of the floor or support - a possibility which Korner questions in his sharp criticism of the Maier discoveries.

As a training sound I chose simple whistling with the mouth because, according to the data given in various works, it promised an earlier success. Experiments with physically better defined tone sounds have been begun - and have already succeeded. I intend to speak of this later, and then the question will have to be discussed as to whether the catfish can hear. As it now stands it is undecided. The behavior of my fish can be explained just as well by a highly developed sense of taste as by true hearing. In training using sounds, we have found a method which, I hope, in conjunction with better technique of surgery, will make possible the solution of the hotly contested subject of the hearing of fishes. For now, however, the question of whether the catfish responds to sounds can be said to be concluded.

[1] Zenneck, Parker, Bigelow, Maier, Haempel, Krausse have made statements to this effect.

[2] In addition to Kreidl and many other authors, Bernoulli and Körner could be mentioned as among the latest to state their opinions. I will not discuss this data here and will only refer to the statements of Mangold in Winterstein's Handbuch d. verl. Physiol.,vol. 4, Jena 1913, pp. 909-916 and to Körner: "Können die Fische hören?" Beiträge zur Ohrenheilkunde, Festschrift für A. Lucae, Berlin 1905, pp. 93-127, and to: "Über das angeblich Hörvermögen der Fische, insbesondere des Zwergwelses (Amiurus nebulosus)", Zeitschr. f. Ohrenheilkunde, vol. 73, 1916, pp. 257-272 -- cf. Krausse: "Kritische Bemerkungen und neue Versuche ueber das Hörvermögen der Fische", Zeitschr. für allgem. Physiol., vol. 17, 1918, pp. 253-286.

[3] H. N. Maier: "Neue Beobachtungen ueber das Hörvermögen der Fische", Archiv. f. Hydrobiologie und Planktonkunde", vol. 4, 1909, pp. 393-397.

[4] O. Haempel, "Zur Frage des Hörvermögens der Fische". Intern. Revue d. ges Hydrobiologie und Hydrographie, vol. 4, 1911, pp. 315-326.

[5] O. Körner. "Ueber das angebliche Hörvermögen der Fische, insbesonders des "Zwergwelses (Amiurus nebulosus)", Zeitschr. f. Ohrenheilkunde, vol. 73, 1916, pp. 257-272.

[6] Information from O. Körner: Investigations of Dr. C. E. Benjamins in Utrecht regarding the alleged capability to hear of the "Zwergwels" (Amiurus nebulosus), Zeitschrift. f. Ohrenheilkunde, vol. 74, 1916, pp. 109-110.

[7] As these experiments were already underway the works of McDonald - which had just been published - became known to me: (Ability of Pimephales notatus to form associations with sound vibrations", Journ. of Comp. Phychol., vol. 2, no. 3, p. 191, 1922. Also Westerfield's ("The ability of mudminnows to form associations with sounds", Journ. of Comp. Phychol., vol. 2, no. 3, pp. 187-190, 1922). Both investigators succeeded in training Pimephales

107

(a cyprinoid) and <u>Umbra limi</u> to respond to vibrating strings. This is only a brief allusion. I will refer again later to these authors and to other works on the subject.

[8] The aquarium stood on a wooden table, etc.

[9] At times the fish was only fed every second day.

6

Reprinted from *Nature*, **141**(3557), 8–11 (1938)

The Sense of Hearing in Fish*
By Prof. K. von Frisch, University of Munich

THERE is an old dispute as to whether fish are able to hear or not. It has seemed improbable that they can. Three main reasons have been brought forward against it.

(1) A biological reason : most fish seem to be dumb ; a sense of hearing would therefore not be of biological significance for them.

(2) An anatomical reason : the inner ear of mammals has two main functions. It is the organ of equilibrium and the organ of hearing. Perception of equilibrium is the function of the utriculus and the semicircular canals. It is not yet clear if the sacculus of mammals has to do with equilibrium or with hearing. At the sacculus we find the cochlea ; it is generally supposed that the cochlea alone is the organ of hearing. Comparative anatomy shows that there is no cochlea in the inner ear of fish. We find only a cavity of the sacculus, the lagena (Fig. 1, *L*), which is supplied with a stone and macula just like the sacculus (*S*) and utriculus (*U*). It has been suggested that fish cannot hear because the organ of hearing is not yet developed.

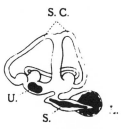

Fig. 1.

THE LABYRINTH OF A MINNOW. *U* = UTRICULUS ; *S.C.* = SEMICIRCULAR CANALS ; *S* = SACCULUS ; *L* = LAGENA.

(3) The third reason against the acceptance of a sense of hearing in fish was a physiological one. Many investigators tried to clear up the matter by making experiments, but they could not observe any reaction of fish to sound. But on this point there is no agreement. For example, American investigators, especially Prof. Parker and his collaborators, made experiments with various fish with positive results. Opponents, especially in Germany, could not confirm it. It was argued that if there is a reaction to sound it would be a reaction to the movement of water and not to sound vibration—it would not be true hearing.

So the question arises : What is hearing ? I think that, in vertebrates, it is not difficult to define it. Human beings can perceive very loud sounds by means of the skin and by means of the inner ear. Perception through the skin we call

feeling ; perception through the inner ear we call hearing. In all vertebrates the inner ear is a homologous organ. We should only speak about hearing' in the case of the perception of sound vibrations by means of the inner ear in vertebrates.

But the first question must be : Is there a reaction to sounds in fish ? There was no agreement on this point. Many observers could not see any reactions to whistling, or to notes from a violin, or to the voice of a singer, and so on. But that is not astonishing. The voice of a singer or the sound of a violin or whistle is not of the slightest biological significance for fish. We should not wonder, therefore, if they do not react to it.

I thought, however, it might be possible to give a biological significance to sounds. If we whistle every time when we give food to the fish, then whistling acquires a biological significance, because the food is announced by it. First I performed the experiment in the following manner. I had a little catfish, *Amiurus nebulosus*, in an aquarium. It lay mostly in an earthenware pipe put on the bottom of the aquarium. The fish was blind, both eyes having been removed, and so it could not see what happened. It got the food from a glass feeding-rod. When the food was brought near the opening of the pipe the fish perceived the meat by means of its chemical sense, came out and swallowed the food. Then, every time I gave it food, I whistled with my lips. Thus I tried to train the fish to the whistling. After some days the fish came out when I whistled before I put the feeding-rod into the water, swam upwards and sought for the food ; and always after that it could be called out by soft whistling not only from nearby but also from a considerable distance, for example, from the other side of a large room.

Later these experiments were continued by my collaborator, Dr. Stetter. He used various kinds of fish. The best results were given by our little minnows (*Phoxinus lævis*), and therefore they have been studied very thoroughly. To produce sounds tuning forks were generally used for low sounds and whistles for the higher ones. The sense of sight was eliminated by removal of the eyes. Then the fish was trained to a certain sound by four to five training feedings daily. After a few days the fish gives a very typical reaction to sound. The kind of reaction varies from individual to individual. When the sound is given, some fish dive down and snap for food on the bottom, others go up and snap on the surface, others stop and

---

** Substance of a lecture delivered at University College, London, on March 4, 1937.

snap vigorously on whatever spot they may be, but all snap and seek for food because they are accustomed to get the food when the sound is given. After a few seconds we put the feeding-rod into the water ; the fish gets the food, and so the training is continued.

There is not the slightest doubt that there are clear reactions to sound. Further experiments by Dr. Stetter gave a great many results. It seems to me that three of them are of special interest.

Dr. Stetter tried to train fish to very low and to very high sounds, and so to find out the limits of the sense of hearing. The upper limit in minnows is between D^5 and A^5 (about 5,000–7,000 vibrations a second). Training to higher sounds is without results. There are slight individual differences ; but there is a far greater difference between various species of fishes. Thus *Amiurus* gave positive results up to 13,000 vibrations a second. This is about the same upper limit as in human beings. Dr. Stetter was unable to find a lower limit. The lowest tuning fork, C_2 (frequency 16), gave good results.

A second result concerns the acuteness of the sense of hearing. A minnow was trained to E^3 (frequency 660). Then the sound of the whistle was diminished gradually to a very low intensity. The aquarium was put on a table in a long corridor and the soft whistle was given from farther and farther away in a series of experiments until reactions could no longer be obtained. Reactions could be obtained from a distance of about 200 feet. We ourselves could hear the whistle from that distance only as a very weak sound. But it is difficult to understand what this means, because we do not know to what extent the sound is weakened on entering the water. We therefore brought a large aquarium to the same spot and one of our students dived down and was tested in just the same manner as the fish. The experiment showed that our best fishes could hear as well as men in the aquarium, or even a little better than men. It was very surprising to us.

The third result concerns the discrimination of sounds. It is possible to prove that minnows can distinguish between different sounds. The following method was employed. A fish is trained to a certain sound, that is, the feeding sound. When there is a good feeding reaction, we introduce another sound one or two octaves higher or lower than the feeding sound. But at this sound no food is given, and if the fish begins to snap and seek for food, it is punished by a light blow with a glass rod. This other sound we call the warning sound, because it means a punishment. After some time of training, the fish gives the feeding reaction only to the feeding sound ; to the warning sound it gives no reaction, or even a very distinct flight reaction

to avoid the punishing blow. Now the interval between the two sounds can be gradually decreased, and thus we can find out what interval can be distinguished. Most fishes can easily be trained to distinguish between two sounds at an interval of one octave. The best fish could distinguish perfectly between the two sounds of a minor third, D^1/F^1 (frequencies 290 and 345).

During 1936, Dr. Wohlfahrt in our laboratory was able to improve these results by employing a new method. In the experiments of Dr. Stetter there was always a period of at least a quarter of an hour between the feeding sound and the warning sound. The fish, therefore, had to keep the sound in mind and decide by memory. It was clear from these experiments that the fish has some sense of absolute hearing—but not a very good one. Wohlfahrt gave short sounds so that they immediately followed one another, just like a trill. In this way he was able to show that minnows are able to distinguish even a half-tone interval.

Judging from all these results, it is very probable that there is a true sense of hearing in fishes. To be certain we must seek for the organ of perception.

Experiments have been published by Prof. Parker and his collaborators indicating that the inner ear especially has to do with hearing in fishes. Some observations seemed to show that the sacculus especially, or the lagena, would be the seat of the sense of hearing. But the results were not very convincing, because the methods employed to eliminate the sacculus and the lagena were not satisfactory. The method of training the fishes to sound, combined with careful operations, promised a clear result.

I removed various parts of the labyrinth in minnows. I tried first to remove the utriculus and the ampullæ and to leave the sacculus and the lagena intact. There is no difficulty in doing this. To perform the operation the fish is narcotized by means of a 0·5 per cent solution of urethane. As soon as the fish recovers from the narcotic we find that it has completely lost its sense of equilibrium. It lies on one side on the bottom of the aquarium, and when it swims it turns over and curves the body in a peculiar manner. Nevertheless, it is possible to train such fish to sounds as easily as normal ones. Training can be carried out in the same manner, in the same time, and within the same limits as in the case of normal fishes. There is not the slightest sign that the utriculus and the ampullæ have anything to do with the sense of hearing. They are only organs of equilibrium. It is more difficult to remove the sacculus and the lagena ; but I have succeeded in doing this. It was very surprising to see that such fish, with both sacculi and lagenæ and their large otoliths removed, swim in perfect equilibrium. But it is impossible to train them to sounds. Generally I did with each of them more than a hundred training feedings, but the fish gave no reactions to the sounds. Normal fish or fish only operated upon on one side gave reactions after five to fifteen training feedings. I carried out the experiment also in the following manner. I trained a normal fish to a sound. Then it was operated on on one side. The reaction was as clear as before. The fish was operated on on the other side, and then it was never possible to get any reactions.

All this applies only to sounds higher than C (frequency 130). The fish without sacculus and lagena can be trained to low sounds, if they are loud enough. It can even distinguish between different sounds in the low region as well as normal

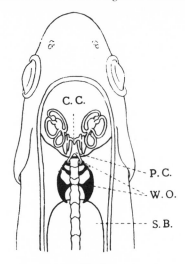

Fig. 2.

C.C. = CROSS CANAL, CONNECTING THE SACCULI WITH ONE ANOTHER ; *P.C.* = POSTERIOR CAVITY ; *W.O.* = WEBERIAN OSSICLES ; *S.B.* = SWIM BLADDER.

fish. The low sounds are perceived as well as before, even if the whole labyrinth is taken away or if the sense organs of the lateral line, too, are fully destroyed. We can therefore assume that the low sounds are perceived through the skin.

From special experiments it can be concluded that the lowest sounds are perceived only with the skin, low sounds from frequency 25 up to about 130 with the skin *and* with the inner ear, and all the middle high and very high sounds from about frequency 130 up to the upper limit only with the labyrinth. That is more or less the same as in human beings.

It is stated above that minnows, in the region of middle high sounds, can distinguish between different sounds even when there is an interval of

only half a tone. Now we know that these sounds are perceived by the sacculus and lagena. Thus we find that there is a remarkable ability to distinguish between different sounds in the fish labyrinth, in spite of the lack of a cochlea and therefore in the absence of a membrana basilaris. The function of the cochlea and of the membrana basilaris in higher vertebrates may be to improve the discrimination of sounds to the high degree known in man.

Certain anatomical facts are very important for understanding the acuteness of the sense of hearing in minnows. In minnows, as in all Cyprinids, there is a connexion between the labyrinth and the swim bladder by means of the Weberian ossicles. The sacculus of the right and left labyrinths are connected with one another by a cross canal (Fig. 2, *C.C.*) with a posterior cavity behind the labyrinth (*P.C.*) with one opening on each side. The opening is closed by a little bone connected with other bones by articulation (*W.O.*), the last of which is fixed to the anterior end of the swim bladder (*S.B.*). Sound vibrations in water must be transmitted to the swim bladder, from the swim bladder by means of the little bones to the cavity, from there to the cross canal and thence to the sacculus. Now it is very interesting that the shape of the otolith of the sacculus seems to make it suitable to take up the vibrations coming from the cross canal—a fact first recognized by the Dutch worker, Prof. de Burlet, in *Amiurus*.

We want to know, however, whether this connexion is necessary for sound perception. Consequently I took away the swim bladder through an incision in the ventral body wall of the minnow. I closed the wound by a suture and after recovering the minnows could be trained to sounds as before. But the acuteness of the sense of hearing was very much reduced. It seemed from these experiments that this connexion between the swim bladder and the sacculus might increase the acuteness of hearing.

If that were true, we should find a sense of hearing very well developed in all fishes possessing Weberian ossicles. All five species of Cyprinids which have been trained for sounds in our laboratory up to now have a very well-developed sense of hearing. The same is true for *Amiurus*, which belongs to the Silurids. They have Weberian ossicles too. On the other hand, in families having no connexion between the swim bladder and the inner ear, the sense of hearing is very poorly developed. We tried to train for sounds pike, perch, trout, eels and others. Some of them gave no results at all, others could be trained, but the sounds had to be made much louder than for *Amiurus* or for minnows, and the high sounds were never perceived.

Besides Cyprinids and Silurids there are two other families possessing Weberian ossicles : Characinidæ and Gymnotidæ. We trained a *Gymnotus* and some Characinidæ and found a well-developed sense of hearing in all these fish.

Now I wish to direct attention to a peculiar anatomical fact often mentioned in books of comparative anatomy, but never understood. In the Mormyrids, a family of African fish, there is a gas bladder on each side of the skull connected directly with the sacculus. In early embryological stages it is developed as a double cavity of the swim bladder, growing into the head. Later the connexion with the swim bladder is lost by degeneration and the two small air bladders lie completely separated in the skull. I thought that the function of these little air bladders might be the same as that of the big air bladder in minnows and other fishes possessing Weberian ossicles. Sound vibrations reaching the air bladders should cause vibration of them. In this case the stimulus can be transmitted directly to the sacculus, and therefore Weberian ossicles are not necessary. If that is true, we should expect a very well-developed sense of hearing in Mormyrids, although they do not have Weberian ossicles. It was rather difficult to get living Mormyridæ, and we looked for them for several years without success. But finally we got them. We began to train them for sounds with much interest, and we found with satisfaction that they could hear just as well as our best minnows. The anatomical peculiarities of these interesting labyrinths are now being studied in our laboratory.

It may well be asked for what purpose fishes are able to hear so well in silent water. It is not true that all fish are dumb. We know many species of sound-producing fish. There may be many more species of sound-producing fishes not yet known. Some years ago, Dr. Dykgraaf in our laboratory found out that minnows, too, are sound-producing fishes. If they are excited, a soft piping comes from the aquarium. The noise is very soft, but knowing the acuteness of the sense of hearing, we may be sure that it can be heard by the minnows. It is interesting that the production of sound by so well known a fish should have been overlooked for so long. There may be much to discover in the future about the language of fishes.

Part IV
HEARING MECHANISMS AND PSYCHOPHYSICS

Editor's Comments
on Papers 7 Through 10

The contributions of Sven Dijkgraaf to comparative physiology are certainly on a par with those of Parker and von Frisch. He was born in 1908, and educated at the University of Gröningen in The Netherlands, and, for a time, worked with von Frisch at Munich. Subsequently, he established the Laboratory of Comparative Physiology at the University of Utrecht, from which he retired recently (1975) as director. Like his illustrious colleagues, he will undoubtedly continue active research for a long time to come.

Paper 7, reprinted here in translation, is not his first report in the field by any means, but it was chosen for this compilation because it represents a culmination and peak of comparative studies on auditory mechanisms in fishes both with and without auditory specializations such as the Weberian apparatus.

In 1950, in collaboration with his student Frans Verheijen, Dijkgraaf provided the first quantitative study on the ability of fish to discriminate frequencies (Paper 8). In spite of what would now be considered coarse and unsophisticated equipment, the figures reported were remarkably accurate. Subsequent experiments by Jacobs and Tavolga (1968) and Fay (1970b) only refined the techniques and confirmed the earlier results (see Paper 2).

The first truly psychophysical approach to fish audition was that of Dietrich Poggendorf when he was at the University of Göttingen with the eminent H. Autrum. Poggendorf's work (Paper 9) was a major contribution in several ways. He certainly made it clear that the acoustical problems of working within a confined volume of water, such as an aquarium, were immensely complex. Unfortunately, many subsequent workers did not realize this problem, as well as the problem of confounding acoustic pressure energy (far-field) with displacement energy (near-field). Until Poggendorf's publication, the data available on hearing thresholds in fishes were primarily relative, or, at best, very crude approximations. Although his hearing threshold data are most often quoted, he also did some experiments on the mechanisms of sound reception, including extirpations of the Weberian ossicles, and elegant observations on the vibration patterns of the swim bladder.

Following the trend toward the use of psychophysical techniques and conditioned responses for the study of hearing in fishes, Paper 10, by Tavolga and Wodinsky, represents an important divergence from using goldfish, catfish, and other ostariophysines as experimental animals. This order contains only a small minority of teleost species, and the vast majority of marine forms do not have Weberian ossicles. In addition, this paper presented a technique, using avoidance conditioning, that has since become a widely used method in animal psychophysics. One other contribution, besides the actual threshold figures and audiograms, was the observation of apparently dual thresholds at low frequencies. The hypothesis was advanced that the animals were switching from one modality (inner ear) to another (lateral line), and this hypothesis has been supported by data reported by Cahn, Siler, and Wodinsky (1969) (see Paper 1).

115

7

INVESTIGATIONS INTO THE FUNCTIONS OF THE LABYRINTH IN MARINE FISHES

Sven Dijkgraaf

Zoological Station, Naples, and Institute for Comparative Physiology, Utrecht

This article was translated expressly for this Benchmark volume by Brigitte Cappelli, from "Untersuchungen über die Funktionen des Ohrlabyrinths bei Meersfischen," in Physiologia Compar. Oecologia, **2**, 81–106 (1949), *with the permission of W. Junk, Publisher*

INTRODUCTION

The question concerning the function of the various divisions of the labyrinth in fishes seems to have been solved by von Frisch and his collaborators, to the extent that it is known that the pars superior (utriculus and semicircular canals) exclusively serves a static-dynamic function, while the pars inferior (sacculus and lagena) receives sound (von Frisch, 1936). This result was obtained through experiments on ostariophysines, which have, in addition to the Weberian apparatus, a highly specialized pars inferior. That the pars inferior, and particularly the enormous sacculus, play the role of auditory organ in other fishes, seems to be supported by the fact that elimination of the sacculus does not generally entail (so far as has been noticed) disturbances of the equilibrium in vertebrates. However, this is a negative argument; the positive demonstration of sound reception is still to be made. This is true also for non-ostariophysines. Diesselhorst found some loss of hearing in the eel (Anguilla vulgaris) after elimination of the pars inferior; he found, however, the same thing after elimination of the pars superior, or even of the entire labyrinth, and concluded that "the role played by the various parts of the labyrinth in sound reception in the eel is so far totally unclear" (1938; p. 782).

That the above mentioned conclusions of von Frisch, in the form given, do not necessarily apply to all fishes, can be surmised simply by a consideration of the anatomic relationships of Clupeids. In these fish, (herrings, sardines) there are gas-filled chambers, which most probably serve to intensify sound stimuli, located close to the utriculus, a sensory receptor of the pars superior (Wohlfahrt, 1936). A direct proof of the vibratory function of the utriculus has been provided recently by electrophysiological experiments of Lowenstein and Roberts (1948), using the nervus acousticus of Raja clavata. Briefly summarized, these are the facts discovered in the labyrinth of the ray.

1. Both utriculus and sacculus transmit gravitational and sound stimuli, but reception is relegated to different portions of the maculae. For instance, sound stimuli are received by the utriculus only at the lacinia (a projection of the macula that is not covered by the otolith membrane), which, in turn, serves only that purpose; in the sacculus, a lateral part of the macula serves the same purpose.

2. The lagena transmits exclusively gravitational stimuli, in direct opposition to what von Frisch found in ostariophysines.

3. The macula neglecta, so far greatly disregarded in physiological work, is a particularly sensitive sound receptor.

These results demonstrate that, in the primitive chondrichthyes at least, there is as yet no functional separation between the pars superior and the pars inferior. Now the question is how the situation is in the non-ostariophysines.

In the present work, a contribution to the solution of this problem was intended.
    That the labyrinth, and especially the pars inferior, may be concerned with
audition is suggested partly by older experiments of Parker (1904, 1910), mostly
by the fact that damage to this section of the labyrinth does not always lead to
observable disturbances of equilibrium (Werner, 1929). DeBurlet (1929) argued
against an auditory function of the pars inferior in non-ostariophysines on
anatomical grounds.
    Though the majority of well-hearing ostariophysines are freshwater fishes,
the best known sound-producing fishes are marine. In some cases, as in the
Sciaenidae, sound production has without doubt biological meaning (Smith, 1905;
Dijkgraaf, 1948). For this reason it seemed logical to select a member of this
family in an investigation of the sense of hearing in non-ostariophysines. Such
a fish is Corvina nigra. Unfortunately, during my stay at the Naples Institute
(end of May - beginning of July, 1947), the late arrival of Corvina in the Bay
of Naples made it unavailable, and another species had to be used. (Resumption
and continuation of experiments with Corvina is planned). I selected the easily
obtainable Gobius paganellus. As all Gobiids, this species has a remarkably
large sacculus with a correspondingly large otolith (Fig. 1), which extends to
the vault of the cranium, and makes possible elimination of the pars inferior
alone, from above.
    Two sets of experiments were done. One to study equilibrium, the other,
sound reception. In both sets of experiments, the pars inferior was eventually
eliminated uni- or bilaterally, preserving the pars superior, and the effects
noted. Secondarily, observations were made of other senses, and of the hearing
of various other fishes.

METHODS

Testing of the equilibrium

    Imprisonment in a fish-holder was unsuited and unnecessary with this smooth,
thin-skinned bottom dweller, which will not keep still when it is not in contact
with the bottom. Instead, the fish were placed in a glass tube of suitable width,
in which they could neither turn, nor swim backward or forward. There was enough
room for bending along the body axis, and for fin- and eye-turning reflexes, which
were easily observed (Fig. 2). The glass tube was held submerged in one of the
large sea-water aquaria, and turned successively about its long, transverse, and
vertical axes. To observe eye-turning reflexes special lighting and a magnifier
were required. A gentle stream of water from front to back through the tube prevented asphyxia.
    All fish were further tested in this way. I allowed the fish (on the bottom)
to swim into an open glass tube slightly longer than body length, then raised it
gently horizontally to the surface where a sudden, horizontal backward pull freed
the fish, which was then suspended suddenly in the upper water layers (Fig. 3).
As a typical bottom dweller, every goby immediately and energetically attempts to
gain contact with the substrate. The animals which had been previously blinded
could be guided on their way down only by their sense of equilibrium, and any disturbance of that sense should have been noticeable. This method was often superi-
or for study than examination of the reflexes. Some animals were released in unnatural vertical or inclined positions, which makes increasing demands on their
sense of equilibrium.

Examination of sound perception

    To study sound perception, the animals were blinded by enucleation (urethane
anesthesia). They stood the operation well and often started feeding immediately
afterward. First we observed the spontaneous reflexes to sound and vibration,
but then we used more intense sound-training methods. Small pieces of sardine

117

were used as food, presented at the end of a thin glass rod. Some experience was necessary to recognize the gobies' food-reaction. Slight alarm is indicated by an unusual fanning of the fins, during which the animal remains immobile.

The sound sources were principally tuning forks (with thanks to the Inst. Phys. U. Naples). Wooden tension blocks were used to actuate them with constant, and controllable intensity; the vibrating fork was placed on the upper edge of the aquarium as quietly and smoothly as possible. For this each tuning fork was provided with a heavy brass handle, the end of which was machined to a slightly convex shape. This rounded end was covered by a double layer of (bicycle) inner tube, firmly held in place by a cuff of soft rubber (thick-walled rubber tubing). The vibrating fork was placed at such an angle on the aquarium wall that the cuff made contact first; then the fork was gently and steadily righted (Fig. 4). It was not until the end covered only by the inner tube came into contact with the glass, that the sound was noticeably transmitted to the aquarium. This was ascertained by direct auscultation with the naked ear, and by a hydrophone (see Dijkgraaf, 1947; p. 493). All experimental aquaria were carefully placed on solid supports. In spite of these precautions great care was necessary to prevent shaking of the tank during application of the tuning fork to the aquarium wall. For safety's sake, before starting each experiment, a silent fork was applied to the aquarium, at which time there was not supposed to be any reaction. Several fish were trained to noises produced in a variety of ways.

It was disturbing that occasionally blind fish became excited when I merely approached the aquarium. Considering their sensitivity, I tried to minimize light stimuli by avoiding both shadows, or increased illumination, on the aquarium (dark, rather than white laboratory coat). As the fish were very sensitive to vibrations transmitted through the ground, I always wore soft rubber soles during the experiments. Even then, careful approach was necessary, especially in fish kept in out of the way rooms.

Surgical technique

The operation to eliminate the pars inferior was done as follows. Under urethane anesthesia, the fish lay on the operating table under the binocular microscope; artificial respiration was provided. The dorsal skin was incised, approximately over the region of the sacculus, and the underlying muscles spread apart with watchmaker's forceps, down to the vault of the skull. The wound was kept open by two hooks, attached to small lead weights by a thin thread; the weights hung free over the edges of the operating table. After the skull above the sacculus had been exposed, it was opened by removing small pieces of bone with forceps (Fig. 5). Then the sacculus was opened, and the otolith lifted out. After that the small lagena, lying deeply caudally, was carefully brought up, loosened from the nerve, and removed together with its tiny otolith. Pulling on the posterior ampulla and its nerve had to be avoided. Now, starting from the dorsal aspect, the otolith wall of the sacculus was loosened from the other parts of the labyrinth (first from the anterior semicircular canal) until the sacculus nerve was clearly visible below. The nerve was then completely severed from the macula by means of a fine-tipped, curved watchmaker's forceps. In this operation as well, pulling or compression of adjacent parts of the labyrinth and their nerves had to be avoided. Removal of the macula without pulling on other organs was extremely difficult (even though in Gobius there is no direct connection between the pars superior and inferior; Retzius, 1881; Wohlfahrt, 1933) and was attempted only exceptionally. In view of the rapid regeneration (as will be shown later) this operation would have been most advantageous.

In some operations only the sacculus otolith was removed. Within three days, otolith regeneration was apparent on the macula, some stones having already attained the size of the lagena-otolith. After 14 days, the entire otolith wall of the sacculus was covered with a large number of small otolith regenerates, which generally looked like small, clear glass pearls, and stuck fairly evenly distributed to the wall. The macula region of and the margin were covered with pearls earlier than the rest of the otolith wall. In one instance all the regenerated otoliths had a small green spot at the center. Oddly, the lagena otolith, not touched during the operation, had a stripe of the same green substance along its convex border whereas the utriculus otolith had no such marks. Otoliths also regenerate after separation of the macula from the nerve.

Troublesome were the frequent wound infections. The operation per se was well supported. In general the animals were quite normal shortly after the operation, and often started feeding at once. One fish displayed (sexually) to his aquarium mates within 1.5 hours after the operation. But after 15-20 hours, the animals began to refuse food, while the wound appeared inflamed (swelling, turbidity), later infected (pus). Usually these symptoms were soon followed by secondary disturbances of the equilibrium; in these cases examination always revealed extension of the infection to segments of the pars superior. The initially high incidence of wound infections increased further as the temperature increased (up to 35° during June). The effect of temperature was also evident in enucleation. Toward the end of May, during cool weather, not one of 30 Gobius paganellus was lost after enucleation; toward the end of June about one-third of the operated animals developed orbital wound infections, and had to be discarded. Unfortunately, time was too short to allow a search for corrective measures. The conditions explain why some of the data are considered preliminary, especially those pertaining to hearing. Exactly to determine the effects of the functional elimination of various organs would have required longer post-operative training than was usually possible.

RESULTS

A. Observations on G. paganellus

I. Equilibrium before and after blinding

G. paganellus, as other Gobiids, usually lives on the bottom. Resting attitude and swimming behavior agree with those of G. jozo, described by Werner (1929), with this difference that G. paganellus occasionally swims to the surface. Especially single individuals, kept isolated in large aquaria often swam about freely. In this connection it may be pointed out that G. paganellus, in opposition to G. jozo, has a swim-bladder (length: 2 cm with 12.5 cm body length). Usually, however, in spite of their swim bladder, the fish were disequilibrated, and clearly too heavy.

In turning the previously mentioned glass tube (Fig. 2), several equilibration reflexes were clearly recognizable, though some fish reacted more vigorously than others. Involved were eye- and fin-movements, and bending of the body axis. The eyes always turned away from the direction of turning, and the fin movements always opposing the induced movement. In addition, "fixation" of the fish in unusual positions elicited corresponding positional reflexes. The following fin-reflexes and body bendings were noted during rotation about long-, transverse-, and vertical axes:

119

Long axis: The upper edge of the pectoral swings toward the direction of turning. If the movement continues, the leading pectoral fin works against the movement; the dorsal fins, and especially the posterior margin of the second dorsal also bend in the direction of motion.

Transverse axis: Upper edge of the pectorals as above. Tilting forward causes the dorsals to be maximally fanned out, and the head to rise; tilting toward the tail causes the dorsals to be collapsed, and the head to bend forward.

Vertical axis: Pectorals, as above; the caudal peduncle and the caudal fin are bent in the direction of turning.

Concerning the eye-reflexes, it must be added that rotation about the transverse axis cause them to follow the turn in small jumps (nystagmus). Lifting the tail caused several small jumps, raising the tail produced fewer, larger ones. Positioned reflexes of the eyes occurred only in unnatural positions, i.e., by turns about the long or transverse axis; no positional reflexes followed turns about the vertical axis.

These equilibrium reflexes were elicited just as well in blind fish. To test this, animals were blinded by transsection of the optic nerve, without touching the oculomotor muscles, and leaving the eyeball in situ. The operation was easy under the binocular, using a fine scissors bent into a hook. Especially the jerking motions (nystagmus) of the eyes during turns about the transverse axis were sometimes more pronounced after nerve section than before.

Sighted gobies, lifted in a glass tube from the bottom, seeing the ground disappear, became greatly excited, and tried to dive through the glass tube. Blind individuals remained quiet. But both sighted and blind individuals immediately dove after swimming out of the tube, or after the tube was pulled away from them. Even blind fish were always in good equilibrium.

II. Equilibration after elimination of the pars inferior of the labyrinth.

In 31 specimens (12 sighted, 25 blind, of which 6 had been tested while still with sight) the pars inferior was partially or wholly eliminated functionally on one or both sides, and equilibration was observed before and after each operation. In partial elimination either the sacculus otolith alone was removed, or the sacculus nerve was also cut close to the macula, leaving the lagena intact. Occasional further observations could be made on fish used for sound-training in which the entire pars inferior had been removed uni- or bilaterally.

In most cases the fish displayed no marked disturbances of equilibrium, such as always develops after injury to the utriculus or the ampullae of the semicircular canals. Unfortunately, as already mentioned, wound infections prevented prolonged observations. Disturbances that did develop subsequently were obviously caused by secondary injury (infection with pus) of the pars superior, always clearly recognizable under the binocular microscope.

The more or less frequent deviations from normal behavior in the operated fish can be summarized in their characteristic forms as follows:

1. The operated fish usually does not swim down immediately after liberation from the tube; instead it lets itself sink, i.e., it floats down gradually with alternate fanning of the two pectorals, horizontally and forward, while swaying slightly about its long axis in rhythm with the movements of the pectorals. In some cases, both fins rowed simultaneously. Most remarkable was a strange paralysis (relaxation) of the posterior end of the body. The caudal peduncle and the tail usually sank a little or trailed passively during swim-

ming. The rowing motions of the pectorals seemed to be caused by the lack of propulsion from the caudal fin.

2. The operated fish remains horizontally suspended for about 1/2 - 1 sec. after withdrawal of the tube, then dives steeply. But the fish does not swim straight down, the way an ordinary blinded goby does; instead it describes a short arc, ending backside down, below its point of departure. Only at that moment, or shortly before, does it perform a half-turn about the long axis - to right or left - so that it lands in a normal position (Fig. 3). The entire movement is usually rapid, and continuous. The somewhat variable radius of the arc was at least 10 cm. In many cases an intermediate behavior was observed: the fish did not go head-over-heels, but dove straight down until its nose hit the bottom.

3. After surgery, there is a disturbance in the filling of the swim bladder; the fish becomes buoyant, its anterior end particularly tending to float up.

4. Rotation about the transverse axis causes the eyes to make circular rolling turns, but nystagmus was missing.

A control animal, merely anesthetized, on awakening developed none of the abnormalities described above, though nystagmus was lacking for some hours.

In the following we shall discuss to what extent the observed anomalies of behavior are to be attributed to the elimination of the pars inferior. Unless otherwise stated, all disturbances appeared immediately after surgery.

Relaxation of the caudal portion of the body occurred in all 5 animals with complete, bilateral elimination of the pars inferior. Unilaterally operated fish (13, including one of the above 5) did not develop it. A bilaterally operated, sighted fish swam normally; only after exhaustion (because of attempted immobilization) did it develop a transitory wobble about the long axis. It may be that the disturbances of motion were optically corrected in this specimen, because another sighted fish, who had only suffered bilateral elimination of the sacculus (otolith removed, nerve sectioned, lagena intact) swan normally before blinding; after blinding, swimming was disturbed. The behavioral abnormalities were typically evident in some of the animals which had lost only the sacculus otolith, i.e., in 3 of 7 seeing, in 6 of 8 blinded fish. Three of the 8 blinded animals had been tested before blinding; 1 specimen was not disturbed either before or after enucleation, 1 both before and after, 1 not before, but after, which again points to a compensating action of the eyes.

After what has been said one has the impression that the behavioral abnormalities discussed here are actually caused somehow by elimination of the pars inferior, or by removal of the saccular otolith. That they are not caused by shock following surgery is suggested by the fact that unilaterally operated animals never demonstrate the behavioral abnormalities, whereas after operation of the second side they not only developed promptly but continued, in one case, for several days. In addition, the abnormalities sometimes developed only after blinding, an operation that, by itself, never caused such changes of behavior. Still unexplained is the fact that after bilateral otolith removal part of the animals developed abnormalities, while others did not. There is, finally, the possibility of an effect on the pars superior, by the surgery, even if it were only due to the opening of the cranium and the removal of the pars inferior.

The second type of abnormality (head-over-heels swimming), on the other hand, developed in some of the animals after either uni- or bilateral elimination of the entire pars inferior, as well as after removal of the sacculus otolith, and in seeing as well as blind animals. The number of animals that showed head-over-heels swimming in the different categories was:

OPERATION	SEEING ANIMALS	BLIND ANIMALS
Bilateral elimination of the entire p. inferior	0 of 1	3 of 4
Unilateral elimination of the entire p. inferior	0 of 3	6 of 11
Bilateral removal of sacculus otolith	4 of 7	2 of 7
Unilateral removal of sacculus otolith	-	0 of 2

One blind fish, in which the sacculus only was eliminated unilaterally swam down vertically. In 2 cases, sighted animals after labyrinth operation (unilateral elimination of the entire pars inferior, or removal of both sacculus otoliths) swam down without disturbances of equilibrium; but after blinding they developed typical head-over-heels swimming. There seems little doubt that in both these cases, disturbances were compensated optically. Sometimes operated fish, especially seeing ones, displayed no abnormalities when they were allowed to swim quietly in their normal position from the tube, but did show them when they were excited, or when they had to leave the tube in an unusual, e.g., head up, position.

Most normal reflexes (rotational and positional reflexes of the body, fins and eye-movements) could usually be elicited after operations on the pars inferior, even in fish in which the organ was completely eliminated bilaterally. Only after rotation about the transverse axis did some fish display minor symptoms of the operation. Of 4 gobies with bilateral removal of the sacculus otolith, only one (blind) reacted with normal body and fin reflexes; one animal (sighted) showed no reflexes at all; a second (sighted) one, only weak bends of the body during lowering of the tail; a third (sighted) one, clear reflexes when the tail was lowered, none when it was raised; this animal could be tilted forward until it was lying on its back; then it corrected its position by a twist of 180° about its long axis. This behavior was absolutely atypical. It corresponds to the disturbance that is manifest during head-over-heels swimming. All fish had normal reflexes when rotated about their long and their transverse axes.

It made me suspicious that some of the fish - even some bilaterally operated, blind ones - would absolutely not display head-over-heels swimming, or other abnormalities. A clear relation between surgical intervention and disturbances of movement could not be demonstrated (see previous Table). It seemed reasonable to think of an associated, involuntary trauma of other parts of the labyrinth, and especially of the semicircular canals. I would like to recall that the animals, after withdrawal of the tube, first retained their position; the disturbance did not appear until the animal was turned. Of course, I first paid attention to the vertical semicircular canals. Seen from above, the posterior canal - shortly before reaching the anterior one - crosses the posterior portion of the sacculus otolith; from their junction, both canals extend down, closely applied to the sacculus (see Fig. 5). It does not seem impossible that, during the removal of the otolith, this canal was sometimes squashed. A goby in which only the two posterior semicircular canals were squashed at the indicated region with a forceps displayed the head-over-heels swimming of Fig. 3. As in this case the sacculus was in no way damaged, it appears certain that the behavioral anomaly cannot have been caused primarily by elimination of the sacculus or of the pars inferior. As a matter of fact, in another fish, section of the posterior canals dorsal to the sacculus otolith did not elicit head-over-heels swimming; the animal wobbled about its long axis and only occasionally swam straight down. Maybe the disturbance, in those fish in which the entire pars inferior was eliminated, was brought on by some tension on the nerve-branches to the ampullae. The nerve for the horizontal ampulla courses together with the sacculus nerve; the nerve to the posterior ampulla, together with the lagenal branch. A third possibility: junctional elimination of the ampullae by infection; this could have developed only after some time, whereas the disturbance was noted immediately after surgery. Further, it should be mentioned that Werner (1929) observed still more pronounced head-over-heels swimming in G. jozo ("partly in large, partly in short arcs, and up to 12 times in succession") after centrifuging the animals. Here, too, exact correspondence between anatomical conditions and physiological reactions could not be established (exactly what happened in the labyrinth during centrifugation is, as a matter of fact, not clear).

To summarize: head-over-heels swimming most probably is not caused directly by damage to, or elimination of, the pars inferior, but by involuntary damage to other parts of the labyrinth, e.g., the vertical semicircular canals. A remarkable, and not entirely understandable fact is the appearance of swimming anomalies after unilateral operation (see above). Disturbances of the swim bladder (buoyancy) were observed in 9 of 46 blind, operated fish. In 4 cases these were animals with unilateral removal of the pars inferior first, followed two days later by total elimination of the contralateral pars inferior. The effect developed, weak at first, two days after the second operation. Finally, all 4 fish hung with more or less buoyancy at the surface. A fifth fish, in which the time interval between the two perations was 12 days, developed a transitory buoyancy of 1 - 2 days duration two days after the operation. One animal, operated bilaterally at one session, also developed some buoyancy three days later. These animals moved over the vertical glass walls with the same ease as previously over the bottom. The ninth animal displayed minor buoyancy one day after the removal of both sacculus otoliths.

As far as the cause of this phenomenon is concerned, it should be mentioned that disturbances of the swim bladder quite generally develop in blinded animals which are prevented by any means from swimming about normally, i.e., to control their equilibrium constantly by contact with the bottom (von Frisch, 1934; Dijkgraaf, 1942). And as, among our fish, 7 of 9 displayed disturbances or equilibrium and (on autopsy) purulent infection of the pars superior, the same interpretation may apply to them. Why the other two animals developed buoyancy remains unclear. It should be added, however, that in a non-operated, but blind fish, strong buoyancy developed; the animal hung for days with a distended swim bladder at the surface. Whether the opposite disturbance, underfilling of the swim bladder also occurred, was not determined. It should be remembered that our gobies are normally not in static equilibrium, but clearly too dense. We come now to the compensatory rolling of the eyes. This reflex was studied in 7 bilaterally operated gobies. In 2 (blind) the pars inferior was eliminated; in the other 5 (sighted; 2 subsequently blinded) only the sacculus otolith was removed. Postoperatively, all animals displayed compensatory eye rolling movements during turns about the transverse axis, in either direction, but the nystagmus corrections were missing at first. In the 5 fish which had their otoliths removed, nystagmus had returned after 20 (in one case after 6) hours. The two subsequently blinded fish developed only very sporadic eye jerks and in the two fully operated fish they did not return at all (observed for 39 hours, when wound infection made continuation of observation useless). In a control animal (sighted) in which only the cranium was exposed, nystagmus returned after 4.5 hours quite normally. The total lack of nystagmus in the two fish mentioned may have been due to section of the optic nerves, which also resulted in wound infections. That elimination of the pars inferior is not responsible for the lack of nystagmus is proven by the fact that in two (sighted) fish with bilateral removal of the entire labyrinth (excepting the ampulla of the posterior semicircular canal) nystagmus and eye rolling during turns about the transverse axis were present also after about 20 hours.

In summary, we find that of all the observed disturbances of behavior following elimination of the pars inferior (relaxation of the caudal appendage, head-over-heels swimming, buoyancy, disappearance of nystagmus) only the first can be attributed to elimination of the pars inferior, or of the sacculus otoliths.

III. Equilibration after interventions in the pars superior of the labyrinth.

The primary object of the current investigations was elucidation of the role of the pars inferior. No systematic investigations were done on the pars superior. The observations presented here are the result of occasional elimination experiments in 7 animals, and are reported for comparative purposes.

In one sighted goby, both pars superiors were eliminated in a single operation. For this, the anterior semicircular canal was exposed (without damaging the sacculus) and used to pull up the utriculus. After section of the utricular nerve, the utriculus was removed and the ampullae of the anterior and external semicircular canals were destroyed. The posterior ampulla was left intact as it is difficult to remove without damage to the pars inferior. In open water, the fish swam with wildly spiralling and weaving motions. On the bottom it righted itself.

Turns about its long and vertical axes showed a complete loss of righting and positional reflexes. Though the animal noticed that it was being moved, its reflexes were quite unspecific, i.e., undirected, and merely an expression of anxiety. In a wide tube the fish could be turned carefully by as much as 30° to the left or right about its long axis before it even moved (anxiety caused by tactile stimuli from the floor: the fish were always too dense). In a narrow tube it remained quietly in any position, even on its back. Normal gobies react specifically to the slightest displacement about the long axis and correct their position correspondingly.

During turns in either direction about the transverse axis, only compensatory eye movements (rolling, nystagmus) remained, which continued, though weaker, even after additional elimination of the pars inferior.

The entire right labyrinth (with exception of the posterior ampulla) was removed from one specimen. In open water the animal spiralled to the right. In the reflex-tube, it showed compensatory eye movements during left or right rotations about the long axis, but fin reflexes and positional correction only after rotation to the left. Toward the right, in a narrow tube, it could be rolled about at will without showing any reaction. During rotation about the vertical axis the tail bent feebly in the direction of the turn, in either direction. Turns about the transverse axis elicited (in both directions) eye rolling and nystagmus. After removal of the second labyrinth (without posterior ampulla) this animal behaved exactly as the previous one: during transverse rotation all reflexes except feeble ones of the eyes had disappeared. Once eye movements were also seen during rotation about the long axis. At all other times the fish allowed itself to be turned into any position in a narrow tube; in a wide one, it showed signs of disquiet at deviations of 30° from the vertical.

On the 5 other blind gobies observations were made after section of specific semicircular canals, or of the nerves leading to them. Section of the two posterior canals resulted, once, in head-over-heels swimming, and once in weaving

about the long axis. After section of the two anterior canals, one fish, when
chased, rolled several times halfway or completely about its long axis, a typical disturbance of equilibrium. A second fish swam normally, but in the tube
displayed only positional reflexes during rotation about the body axis, i.e.,
the extremely sensitive fin reflexes at the start of the rotation were missing.
In the fifth fish, both pars inferiors were lacking, and nerves to the external
and posterior ampullae were cut. The animal weaved about both long and vertical
axes while swimming.

In summary: all manipulations of the pars superior caused disturbances of
equilibrium. Complete elimination destroys nearly all positional and rotational
reflexes, and the fish weave in the water. Contrast with the minimal, oft hardly
noticeable, effects of elimination of the pars inferior is striking.

IV. Ability to receive sound

Tuning fork sounds

Twenty-one gobies were trained to the sounds of tuning forks. During training to 100 Hz, the 5 fish responded positively after 3 - 4 feedings, i.e., they
showed signs of excitation and made searching motions. During training to 340
Hz, 16 fish responded positively after 4 - 5 feedings. Training gave rapid results. One fish even became excited spontaneously the first time he was exposed
to a sound (340 Hz) (tuning fork sounds of 50 Hz somewhat excited most gobies
spontaneously, i.e., without any training). After training some fish did, and
some did not, respond to an intercalated sound of 200 Hz; after training to 340
Hz all fish equally well responded to 480 and, in so far as they responded at
all, to 640 Hz. At that level the approximate upper limit of hearing was reached.
Only 2 fish responded (one poorly, and clearly) to 770 Hz; none to 1024 Hz.

Trained fish reacted equally well whether in contact with the bottom or swimming in open water, without any contact with solid objects. One goby, kept in a
large tank (40 X 80 cm; water depth 30 cm), behaved as follows. It reacted to
strong tones of 340 and 480 Hz at all distances from the point of application of
the tuning fork (aquarium wall, below the water surface); to weaker sounds, however, and to those of 640 Hz, it reacted (when it was swimming in open water) only at close proximity to the point of application, which it seemed to localize.
Frequently, for instance, it swam past the right point, hesitated, turned, and
snapped in the direction of the sound. This observation was repeated many times.
At greater distances, the fish reacted only, but then immediately, when it had
made contact with the wall or the bottom of the aquarium. At the wall, the reactions may have occurred just before actual contact. It was our impression
that perception of the sound under these circumstances was primarily tactile.
Occasionally, the free-swimming fish did seem somewhat excited, and appeared to
be deliberately making contact with the wall, as if to ascertain that there
really was a sound. Once, and only once, did it snap toward the bottom while
lying on it (340 Hz). A second fish in a large tank behaved similarly; in smaller
aquaria the behavior was less evident, most probably because of the lesser dimensions (21 X 29 cm; water depth 16 cm).

Noises

Before the tuning forks became available, 9 fish were trained to a variety
of noises, 3 of them very loud hums from an electric buzzer with a sound cone.
The fish reacted after 6 - 9 feedings to this sound, directed toward the wall
of the aquarium, when the source was held no further than 30 - 35 cm from the

wall. Only one fish, on a good day, responded when the distance was 150 cm. The continuous Neapolitan street noises, and noises in the building, may have vitiated the results. Whistling (with the mouth) had no effect in one goby after 13 feedings. Air sounds are thus more poorly received than the naturally more intense tuning fork sounds. This indicates a relatively low auditory acuity, as might be expected from the non-ostariophysine fish (see von Frisch, 1936).

Four gobies were trained to the sound made by a damp finger sliding along the aquarium wall under slight pressure. Frequency varies greatly, depending on the speed of motion, but was below about 400 Hz. The animals reacted spontaneously to this sound by signs of excitation (e.g., erection of the fins), and learned to search for food after 3 - 4 feedings.

Two animals, finally, were trained to a soft, but somewhat adjustable (in intensity) sound, made by stroking the roughened edge of the all glass aquarium (21 X 29 X 24 cm; water depth 16 cm; wall thickness 3 - 5 mm) with a water color brush or a piece of filter paper. The brush was laid across the edge, and then moved. One fish responded positively regularly after the third feeding, though only when the sound was relatively intense (brush hairs placed on the aquarium wall's edge close to their origin). Slighter brushing sounds (middle of hairs) produced only occasional responses (fin-fanning, see "noticing", p. 84), and soft brushes with the tip of the hairs, none at all. When, after 11 training sessions, the fish had shown no reaction, the brushing was once intensified, whereupon the animal responded with a clear feeding response. The second animal was first trained to the noise made by a piece of filter paper, but then also reacted to stimulation from the paint brush, as described above.

V. Sound reception after functional elimination of the pars inferior

As already mentioned, these experiments have been greatly vitiated by the high incidence of wound infections. As the operation per se is well supported, several animals could be tested shortly after surgery, i.e., before onset of the infection, leading to valuable information concerning the ability to receive sounds. For the rest, I had to rely on fish which did not become infected, or which had recovered. An additional complication was the exceedingly rapid regeneration of otoliths and nerves. The latter effects became manifest only during autopsy, performed on all fish still living shortly before the end of the Neapolitan stay. For these reasons, the following results are not as definitive as one might wish; but they do seem to point out certain things.

Reception of tuning fork sounds

Of the 21 fish trained to sound, from tuning forks, the pars inferior was unilaterally removed in 6, bilaterally (in 2 stages) in 7, and bilaterally (in one stage) in 4.

Of 6 animals in the first group, only 3 could be used, but these, and the other seven after the first (i.e., unilateral) stage of the operation, reacted without exception, and apparently just as well, to the learned sounds (from 100 to 770 Hz).

All told, ten animals were available for testing after bilateral removal of the pars inferior: 3 did not react at all, 4 only weakly (i.e., with reduced expression), 3 quite well. The animals that did not respond, and the 3 that responded well, all came from the second group (2 stage bilateral labyrinthectomy); that this is not accidental will be seen from the following.

First the three negative cases. Tests were at 340 Hz (also a lower tone in one fish), to which unilaterally or non-operated animals always react excellently.

One case should really be excluded, as the animal not only did not react after the operation, but also did not feed well. It died after 4 days; the other 2 animals fed well.

During 27 feedings, (340 Hz, and lower), one animal reacted twenty times completely negatively, five times doubtfully, and twice positively (200 Hz, presented for the first time at the twentieth feeding, i.e., on the sixth day after the second operation). The reaction consisted merely in a cessation of breathing movements while the fish was lying on the bottom. Autopsy (21 days after the first, 9 days after the second operation) revealed that the sacculus on the side that was operated first was not infected, but glassy clear and healed. Some 20 otolith regenerates had formed on the inner wall, like glass beads, and about the size of the lagena otolith (Fig. 1); the sacculus nerve had partly reestablished connection with the macula in the form of 6 or 7 fine strands. On the side that was operated later, the entire region of the sacculus was filled with a turbid pus; regeneration was out of the question there. Infection had spread to the ampulla of the anterior semicircular canal; the animal showed, from the second postoperative day equilibrium disturbances on the corresponding side, i.e., occasional rolling to that side, transitory buoyancy. In this animal, the few positive sound responses may have been mediated via the organs of the side that had healed.

In the second fish, the interval between operations was only 1.5 days. After elimination of function on the one side, the animal immediately responded well to sound. About 1 day after the second operation, a disturbance of equilibrium developed (buoyant spiralling toward the side that was operated first). Most of the time the fish hung quietly from the surface; but it ate well. During 18 feedings it did not once react to the tone (340 Hz), though the latter was presented with as much intensity as possible, not even after surgical emptying the swim bladder allowed the fish to lie in contact with the ground. Yet the fish ate well when food was presented. At autopsy (8 days after the last operation), the following was noted. On the side that was first operated, the sacculus was inflamed, and neither nerve nor otoliths had regenerated. Part of the pars superior was also infected and full of pus, including the utriculus and the ampulla of the anterior semicircular canal (note equilibrium disturbances!). On the controlateral side, the sacculus was also filled with pus, but the focus lay further back and infection had spread to the ampulla of the posterior semicircular canal. The other parts of the pars superior were, however, unaffected. It is to be noted that in this animal, in which both pars inferiors were anatomically non-functional, there was never any reaction to sound, contrary to what happened in the fish previously described.

Now we come to the three positive cases.

The first fish was trained to a tone of 100 Hz, and reacted to it as well after the first as after the second operation, carried out 2 days later. For this tone, not even auditory acuity seemed greatly diminished. This was determined by allowing the tuning fork to "run down" (after setting it going at a constant intensity) until the fish just barely gave a clear reaction. It was interesting that the fish continued to react sensitively to the training tones, though it refused to eat after the second operation, and developed some buoyancy; its actual reaction was to make spitting movements, during presentation of the tone, as well as during presentation of food. As bilateral removal of the pars inferior had not affected hearing, I also removed the two pars superiors on the third day. Before this, the freely swimming fish had had good equilibration, indicating that the pars superiors were largely undamaged. After the operation, the animal reacted just as well to a tone of 100 Hz (spitting motions) while hanging freely at the surface because of buoyancy; even after elimination of

127

the entire lateral line system (by cutting of the facial and vagus nerves, easily accessible after removal of the labyrinth) (see Dijkgraaf, 1934), the animal still clearly reacted to the tone. Perception at this frequency therefore seems to be largely a function of the integumental sense organs (see von Frisch, 1936). The wall of the swim bladder must also be considered as a possibility.

In the second fish, a few days after the first operation, some disturbances of equilibrium (rolling to operated side) developed, but they cleared later, even when specifically tested. The fish was trained to 340 Hz; 22 days postoperatively, the pars inferior of the second side was eliminated. The fish swam well and reacted to the tone as before. Autopsy on the following day revealed that the operation had completely eliminated the pars inferior on that side, but that on the other side, (the one previously operated) the sacculus had partly regenerated. Though there was a pus pocket in the musculature of the old wound, the sacculus had healed completely and was clear as glass. On its inner aspect small otolith regenerates had developed in 8 - 10 spots. The largest of these had the approximate diameter of the utriculus otolith. In addition, a small bundle of regenerated sacculus nerves was clearly visible at the approaches to the macula. In this case the reaction to sound may have been mediated by the regenerated organ.

Still more revealing in this respect was the third fish. Before the first operation, it reacted well to tones of 340 and 480 Hz, and, at great intensities, of 640 Hz. After the operation it responded equally well to all frequencies, even 640 Hz; even a tone of 770 Hz was occasionally answered. Because of a strong hemorrhage during the operation, it was not certain whether the sacculus nerve had been completely severed. Six days later, after the second operation (fully successful) the animal reacted to all frequencies (340, 480, 640, once even 770 Hz). At autopsy 4 days later, the suspicion that the sacculus nerve had not been entirely severed and had remained in contact with the macula, was confirmed. The unsevered part was the outermost portion of the nerve, which contains the longest fibers. During surgery I had spared that bundle, as I was afraid that it was the nerve leading to the ampulla of the horizontal semicircular canal. But the latter had merely been obscured by the operation. At several places on the macula, including the part that had remained innervated, otolith regenerates had formed. The wall of the sacculus had closed, about this otolith (much smaller than the utriculus otolith), forming a glass clear bubble, a sort of miniature sacculus. Sound perception in this fish may also have been due to the remaining sacculus. But it would be remarkable if such a small remnant (both lagenae and the second sacculus had been eliminated) could mediate such extensive hearing to the upper limits of frequency reception.

Now we must still discuss the 4 gobies in which the bilateral operation was carried out in a single session, and all of which still responded in a limited way to the tones.

The first specimen had reacted, preoperatively, to all tones (340, 480, 640, and once at 770 Hz). It was operated on during the evening, and the very next morning signs of infection were apparent. Nevertheless, at noon the fish still responded to a very intense sound at 340 Hz. It was lying on the bottom of the aquarium, though it could also swim freely with good equilibrium (with paralyzed caudal). During the evening the animal refused food and was killed because of its worsening condition. Autopsy revealed complete purulent involvement of both pars inferiors. The perception of an intense tone at 340 Hz is thus possible without this part of the labyrinth. In connection with the previously obtained results, the skin sense is probably to be suspected.

The second fish showed this even more clearly. This fish was kept in a large aquarium, and, before the operation, responded to 340, 480, and 640 Hz. It spent most of its time lying on the bottom. The tuning fork was applied to the front wall of the aquarium about 15 - 20 cm above the bottom. While the fish responded to 480 Hz at any distance from the point of application, it responded to 640 only when very close by, and when the tones had high intensity. Once we observed that the animal, that was sinking down gradually, did not notice a 640 Hz sound until it touched the bottom (snapping reaction). Two days after the operation the animal responded to a strong tone of 340 Hz at the first trial, but not in the usual manner. It was lying at the bottom, close to the front wall. A tuning fork was first applied, 15 cm above and to the right of the fish, which reacted slightly to this tone by twitching one of its pectorals (lifting the tip of the fin slightly from the ground). Immediately after this, the tuning fork was again applied to the wall, this time directly above the fish still about 15 cm away. To this it reacted similarly but more strongly by twitching and lifting both pectorals from the ground. Eleven more tests during the next 4 days were completely negative 9 times (7 times to 340, twice to 480 Hz, intense tones), and only twice dubiously (340 and 200 Hz). Yet he was eating well. After the third day postoperatively, slight disturbances of the equilibrium became manifest. Before killing (sixth day) equilibrium was specifically tested with the tube. The fish swam in left handed spirals and fell over forwards. Autopsy revealed complete elimination without regeneration of both pars inferiors. Of the pars superior, on the right side, only the ampulla of the posterior semicircular canal was slightly inflamed; on the left side, however, most of the pars superior, including the utriculus and the ampullae of the two vertical semicircular canals were completely purulent. In this case too, complete bilateral elimination of the pars inferior went hand-in-hand with loss of sound perception. The only positive reactions were clearly mediated by the tactile sense (bottom vibrations).

The third goby had reacted, preoperatively, regularly to 340 and 480 Hz while lying on the bottom, but never to 640 Hz. For 6 days after the operation, the animal failed to respond (20 feedings, at which the accepted food was sometimes spit out again); 17 times to 340, 3 times to 100 Hz (intercalated toward the end). On the seventh day the fish reacted for the first time positively to 100 Hz, but not to 340; the next day it answered 200, and the following day 340 (intense); on the eleventh day it responded well to 480 Hz, and auditory acuity at 340 Hz had improved; on the thirteenth day, acuity to 480 had also improved; the animal never reacted to 640 Hz. The long latent period of 3 - 4 sec. between the start of the sound and the response was remarkable. Before killing, equilibrium was tested; the fish had a tendency to veer to the right, to roll, and to turn head-over-heels occasionally. At autopsy, on the left side the sacculus was pus-filled towards the back, as was the ampulla of the posterior semicircular canal. There was hardly any regeneration; only one tiny otolith-regenerate was found on the sacculus wall, and there was no visible regeneration of the nerve. On the right side, however, the sacculus had completely healed and was glass-clear. On the medial surface were a large number of regenerating otoliths, which formed a circular line corresponding approximately to the circumference of the original otolith; others formed a strip along the macula; a few fibers of the sacculus nerve had clearly regenerated, and were in contact with the macula. The gradual return of hearing power in this animal may have been caused by the regeneration of the one sacculus. The lagena was removed totally at every operation, and nothing was suggested of regeneration.

We now come to the fourth and last, fish of this group. This animal was not trained to sound (100 Hz) until 2 days postoperatively. It reacted positively after the fourth trial with spitting movements; there was loss of appetite during the first three days. It always lay at the bottom. In spite of the highest intensity, it did not, at first, react to 340 Hz. On the fifth day it reacted to 200, on the sixth to 340 Hz, but in a strange manner: in addition to the spitting motion (it continued to refuse food), it twitched the abdominal fin (ground sensation). The sound had to be intense. On the seventh day it also reacted weakly for the first time to a tone of 480 Hz, with a similar display. In this fish too, the reaction time (3 - 4 sec.) was extremely long. At autopsy (ninth day) both sacculi were entirely purulent. The swollen stumps of the sacculus nerves were "glued to" the maculae, but there was no indication of regeneration of the nervous connection. Except for a few tiny kernels lying in the pus of one sacculus, no otolith regeneration was apparent. On one side the pars superior was untouched, on the other filled with a purulent fluid (ante mortem, there had been equilibrium disturbances). If, as we suspect, both pars inferiors were completely eliminated functionally, even sounds of 480 Hz can be perceived through some other organ during contact with the ground, possibly through the skin. The type of reaction supports this assumption. Compared with the previous fish, it was noted that the sounds had to be much stronger, and that the reactions were weaker, and of a different type.

In summary we find that the ability to hear a tone of 100 Hz is not greatly affected by the bilateral elimination of the pars inferior; the fish react even without contact with the ground. Higher tones (340, 480 Hz) are received only when very intense, and if the fish is in contact with the ground. It is assumed that reception occurs through an integumental sense, or possibly the wall of the swim bladder. Maintenance of even a small fraction of the sacculus nerve on one side is sufficient to allow perception of tones up to the upper auditory threshold (770 Hz).

Perception of noise

Two specimens were trained to respond to humming sounds from an electric buzzer. Both reacted positively after the sixth feeding when the buzzer-to-aquarium distance was about 35 cm. After unilateral elimination of the pars inferior one animal did not respond three times in three feeding sessions, though it ate well; then it died. The second animal responded after the first operation as well as before. After the second operation (3 days later) it developed buoyancy for which a puncture of the swim bladder was necessary. In 12 trials over 4 days the fish responded negatively 8 times, dubiously 4 times, but it did not eat well, and both labyrinths were badly infected.

Three fish were trained to the sound of a finger sliding along the aquarium wall. As one animal did not want to eat, it was trained by punishment: each time the signal was given, it received a mild shock. It reacted both before and after elimination of the pars inferiors to the noise, but after the operation, the noise had to be louder. The two other fish were trained to food. Both responded well after the first operation, but after the second one, rarely and weakly.

In one goby, trained to react to the sound of the paint brush, both saccular otoliths were removed simultaneously; thereafter the animal reacted only to very intense stroking noises. At autopsy, one sacculus was completely filled with pus, the other one, normal, and already containing many small otolith-regenerates, some (after only 69 hours) of the size of the lagena otolith.

In general, we found that removal of the pars inferior decreased auditory acuity.

IV. Other observations of sense organ physiology

During the experiments on labyrinthine function, incidental observations
were made of the structure, function, and significance of other senses in Gobius
paganellus. Their chemical sense was very keen; they rapidly found the sardine
meat presented at the feedings. On the head, and, in part, on the body there
are many taste buds. The animals were also extremely sensitive to stimulation
of the lateral line organs, i.e., to the approach of foreign objects. During
tests with a small glass disk attached to a rod (see Dijkgraaf, 1934) many fish
reacted to stimulation of the side of the body by bending tail and dorsal fin
toward the stimulus. When the disk was brought into the vicinity of the head,
the fish snapped at it. The trembling end of a 1 mm thick glass needle, held
as quietly as possible, elicited - when stimulating the left side of the caudal
peduncle - a rapid turn to the right, and vice versa. The mouth always came to
the exact place of stimulation. How sensitive the fish were to these stimuli,
is evident from the following figures. The involuntarily trembling glass needle
was noticed, in the vicinity of the tail fin at a distance of 2 - 3 cm, near the
head at a still greater distance; a 5 mm thick glass rod at a distance of 4 - 5
cm (the reaction was always a turn toward the rod). A wooden slat 2.5 cm wide,
however, brought about flight at a distance of 10 - 20 cm, so that it is clear
that the size itself was perceived.

The lateral line system of Gobius paganellus is built in a characteristic
way. The many sensory buds, which lie free in the skin are arranged on small,
wart-like integumental protuberances, which are particularly noticeable on the
head (see Fig. 5). With the correct light, one can see that each sensory bud
has a movable columnar cupula, just as in the minnow (Phoxinus laevis, Dijkgraaf,
1934; Schulze, 1861, 1870). The lateral line canal system is greatly reduced;
it occurs only in certain places on the head (dorsal side; see the openings,
Fig. 5). Most interesting are conditions about the lower jaw. The canal has
here degenerated into an open trench, at the bottom of which, tightly packed,
is a long row of sensory buds (with cupulae). Oddly, there is nevertheless an
accompanying row of free sensory buds (also with cupulae) packed even more closely on the margin of the trench.

In addition to the perception of food and enemies, another biologic function of the lateral line organs became evident during mating displays, which nearly all gobies displayed in the aquarium, immediately after being set in the tank,
from the end of May on. (A blind Gobius surprised me by dropping numerous eggs
in her small, bare experimental tank; she ate the eggs on the following day).
Both sighted and blind animals displayed to one another, in all possible combinations, and all in the same manner. It was quite remarkable with what sureness
the blind gobies, moving jerkily over the bottom, could recognize and locate one
another (stimulation of the lateral line organs by displacement phenomena, see
Dijkgraaf, 1934, 1947). When a sexually active fish approached another goby, it
performed an unusually slow undulation of the body, to which the partner then
responded with a similar movement. They faced one another head-on, their heads
next to one another, (about 1 - 3 cm) or at the level of the partner's side.
Their behavior was reminiscent of that of Macropodus (Dijkgraaf, 1934) under similar conditions. The undulations were frequently alternating, one animal undulat-
ing while the other remained quiet, after which the roles were reversed. It looked
as if the fish were asking and answering questions. The episode usually ended when
the fish interlocked their mouths.

The mating display motions were usually accompanied by a great deal of excitement; the animals went into a very dark phase, and every unpaired fin was
erected to the fullest - the dorsal retaining a green cast, an imposing picture,

131

though the blind fish could hardly see it. The erection of the fins, however, is not only an optical but a mechanical device (stimulation of the lateral organs, especially by movements of the caudal fin). The display undulations were easy to elicit artificially, for example with a glass disk, brought near to the fish; under such circumstances, however, the fish soon noticed that something was wrong, and withdrew. During June not all the animals were eager to display, and simply swam away. In one such case I observed an animal that remained quietly lying down, but reacted by making the posterior end of the dorsal flutter as if it were a little flag, while fanning with the pectorals. During this negative display, the fish remained in the light phase. The importunating partner several times jostled the fish near the gill slit, but then stopped, and chased another fish.

Very remarkable, too, was the light sensitivity of blinded gobies. They react to both shade and light, and are extraordinarily sensitive to every change in illumination. That this had to be taken into account during the training experiments has been previously mentioned. Most probably the reception of light differences occurs, as in the minnow, in the mesencephalon (mid brain) (Scharrer, 1928). At least, there is a window in the meninges at that point, where the iridiocytes and melanophores, elsewhere closely crowded, are lacking. It was also noticed that the blind gobies were not darker than the seeing fish, contrary to conditions in the minnow.

In addition, one must still mention a reaction to mechanical stimulation, such as the start given by most fish, including gobies, when the wall of the aquarium is jabbed with the tip of an outstretched finger. In the minnow, the reaction was prevented by removal of the Weberian ossicles, (Dijkgraaf, 1942), indicating that the stimulus in those fish is perceived principally via the labyrinth. But a Gobius, during its recovery from urethane anesthesia, during which both his labyrinths had been removed, responded to each knock at the aquarium wall, and to each knock at the table upon which the aquarium stood, by a twitch of the body, the jaws and opercula, from which one can conclude that the stimulus is also perceived by organs outside the labyrinth. Incidentally, the fish did not respond to a tuning fork tone of 50 Hz, though a normal Gobius, at least when lying on the bottom, does (by swimming upward).

B. Observations of the Sound Sensitivity of Other Fishes

Other species were also observed. A 50 Hz tone was responded to by blinded specimens of Scyllium canicula, Serranus cabrilla, and Trigla corax, without any training, i.e., spontaneously. In each instance, the fish was lying on the bottom. The reactions consisted of spreading and fanning of the fins and (in Scyllium) by keeping open the eye lids (nictitating membranes?). Other kinds of grossly mechanical stimuli (pressure-pulse, sound of the finger being rubbed over the aquarium wall) were also sometimes answered spontaneously, e.g., in Scyllium (by arrest of respiratory movements) and in Trigla (spreading of the beautifully colored pectoral fins).

Training experiments to tuning forks were also carried on with one blinded specimen each of Trigla corax and Corvina nigra. Trigla reacted to 340 Hz positively after the ninth feeding. The fish always lay on the bottom (it has no swim bladder). A few seconds after the start of the sound, the fish began to crawl with the unwebbed rays of its pectorals (these rays transmit taste receptions (Scharrer, 1935) and are important in the search for food). Unfortunately, the fish was lost from the tank before it could be tested for higher tones.

The Corvina (about 30 cm long) always swam about quietly and freely. After the sixth feeding it responded without exception to 340 Hz, and after that also to

480, 640, 770, and even 1024 Hz. The reactions were imposing and well-defined: stopping, snapping, tilting, fin-spreading, etc. Most impressive however, was the localization of the sound source at the wall of the aquarium. Again and again, I made sure that the fish answered to the tone, and not to the contact between the tuning fork and the aquarium wall. The fish responded in a lively way to every frequency (higher ones were not available), coming from any point of the aquarium (40 x 160 cm; water depth 40 cm). Localization of the sound (i.e., turning toward the source and snapping) however, took place only when the fish was in immediate vicinity of the source-point on the aquarium wall. Once the fish also responded to a silent tuning fork, when it was set accidentally onto the glass with a jar, in immediate vicinity of Corvina. In this connection one must mention the greatly developed lateral line canal system in the head, where the sense for touch-at-a-distance (Ferntastsinn) is located (Dijkgraaf, 1934). The fact that Corvina responds to tones up to, and probably beyond, 1024 Hz, while swimming freely in the water, indicates that it probably detects them through the labyrinth. Experience with other fish suggests that such high frequencies are not received via the sense of touch in the skin, and that the lateral line system is specialized for the reception of quite a different type of water movement than occurs in sound waves (von Frisch and Stetter, 1932; Dijkgraaf, 1934, 1947).

DISCUSSION

Our attempts at functional elimination in G. paganellus have led to the following results:
1. Though there may be minor disturbances of equilibrium, these are so slight that they do not suggest that static control is a major function of the pars inferior; in fact, such disturbances may have been due to accidental involvement of the pars superior. Only the queer "paralysis" of the caudal peduncle we consider a direct physiologic effect of sacculus-elimination. (It was also observed by Werner (1929)). The value of his other experiments is reduced by the fact that he did not blind his fish (Gobius jozo). It is clear, and the present work has confirmed, that some disturbances of equilibrium, caused by the functional elimination in the labyrinth, may be compensated optically. Further, Werner only removed the sacculus otolith, which operation does not completely eliminate the pars inferior functionally. Of course, electrophysiological tests would be welcome. Rigorously, it is possible that an equilibrational disturbance is immediately compensated by transference of the function to other parts (especially utriculus) of the labyrinth. This is not likely. Destruction of the pars superior, saving the pars inferior, promptly abolished all equilibrium reflexes.
2. Reception of sound was unaffected by unilateral elimination of the pars inferior, much reduced after bilateral elimination. Sounds and tones had to be much more intense, if they were to be heard at all. Reactions were different, in part tactile (twitches of body parts touching the vibrating bottom). The upper auditory threshold was normally between 640 and 770 Hz. The highest frequency to which a bilaterally operated fish responded was 480 Hz. Auditory acuity for this and lower (340 Hz) tones was clearly reduced. But a tone of 100 Hz was clearly detected, not only after elimination of both labyrinths entirely, but after the additional elimination of the lateral line system. It is thus to be assumed that the skin contributes to the perception of sounds at low frequencies (as in the minnow). The results agree remarkably well with those of Diesselhorst (1938) on the eel, in which elimination of the labyrinth also reduced the upper threshold from 600 to 400 Hz, and reduced acuity.
Concerning the general auditory performance, our experiments with G. paganellus have confirmed the contrast between ostariophysines and non-ostariophysines, or,

more particularly, of fish with and without a sound intensifying apparatus. A comparison illustrated this.

In ostariophysines, the upper auditory threshold lies between 1000 Hz (Gymnotus electricus) and 13,000 Hz (Amiurus nebulosus). Auditory acuity is about comparable to that of man. The limit of relative discrimination of frequencies is one-third of a tone in the minnow (Phoxinus laevis; Wohlfahrt, 1939). (Above 1000-1260 Hz, to the upper auditory threshold of 5000-6000 Hz, tones are not distinguished by their frequency but by their intensity (Dijkgraaf and Verheijen, 1950). Perception of the tones comes through the pars inferior, and both the sacculus and the lagena are involved over the entire range of frequencies (von Frisch, 1938) (with the possible exception of sounds above 3000-6000 Hz, which may be received through the sacculus alone). The sharpness of hearing of the ostariophysines depends upon the presence of the Weberian ossicles, which transmit the vibrations detected by the wall of the swim bladder to the sacculus, which is stimulated nearly exclusively via this pathway. The lagena, on the other hand, seems to respond directly to the water-borne vibrations; possibly the lagena-window at the side of the skull may be important for this role. However, even the very slow vibrations of hydrostatic pressure are perceived in the pars inferior after transmission via the Weberian ossicles (Mohres, 1940; Dijkgraaf, 1941).

Among non-ostariophysines, similar hearing is known only for Mormyrids and labyrinth fishes (upper threshold about 3000 Hz; acuity as in ostariophysines). In these fishes the labyrinth lies close up against gas filled spaces that intensify the sound (Diesselhorst, 1938; Stipetic, 1939; Schneider, 1941). A fairly high upper threshold was also found in young Lebistes reticulatus (1000-1200 Hz) (Farkas, 1936) and, here, in the sciaenid Corvina nigra (above 1024 Hz). Otherwise, one has found in non-ostariophysines significantly lower auditory acuity, and a much lower upper threshold (if sound reactions could be obtained at all). The upper thresholds of Anguilla vulgaris and adult Lebistes reticulatus were about 500-600 Hz (Diesselhorst, 1938; Farkas, 1936); in G. paganellus I found it to lie between 600 and 800 Hz. It is clear that all sound detection values are only valid for normal intensities. At abnormally high intensities, higher tones may be effective in all fish; under such conditions (bone conduction) even man's upper threshold extends far into the ultrasonic (up to 175 kHz, Kunze, 1949).

There are no indications as yet of the limits of relative tone discrimination in non-ostariophysines. Training in labyrinth fishes was possible to an absolute discrimination down to a sixth (Schneider, 1941), in mormyrid fishes to a minor third (Stipetic, 1939); in the eel only an octave was reached (Diesselhorst, 1938). In none of these experiments, by the way, was any account taken of intensity differences, which thus reduces the validity of the determinations (Dijkgraaf and Verjeijen, 1950).

It is important that after elimination of the resonator in labyrinth fishes (the air-filled respiratory cavity) by filling with water, the upper threshold is reduced from 3000-4500 Hz to 500-650 Hz (i.e., 2-3 octaves) and that auditory acuity is greatly diminished (Schneider, 1941). This value is about that of the non-ostariophysines, which do not have a natural sound-intensifying apparatus (except in young Lebistes and Corvina). Unexplained still remains the unusually high threshold of the minnow after removal of the swim bladder (about 3000 Hz, possibly higher; von Frisch and Stetter, 1932; von Frisch, 1938).

After elimination of the pars inferior, ostariophysines still respond to strong low tones (about 100-150 Hz in the minnow; von Frisch and Stetter, 1932), in Ides melanotus and Carassius auratus maybe even to 500 Hz (von Frisch, 1938; Boie, 1943). As additional elimination of the pars superior and of the lateral line organs did not alter this in the minnow, it was assumed that reception was through the touch sense of the skin. But it should be noted that in these experiments the elimination of the labyrinth was never complete, so that reception may have been via the remaining ampulla of the posterior semicircular canal or the papilla neglecta.

How to picture the stimulation of the otolith organs is still not entirely clear. It can be imagined that, at the relatively long wavelengths (at 500 Hz = 3 m) and with the relatively small density difference between fish and water, the entire fish vibrates back and forth, while the otoliths are held back by inertia and exert tension on the sensory epithelium of the macula. Yet the otoliths are apparently not essential for the perception of sound (von Frisch, 1938; also here). Farkas's attempts to deny (1942) any action of the otolith on the maculae on histologic grounds (no matter how beautiful the preparations) are probably to be dismissed out of hand. As a matter of fact one can easily ascertain how loosely the otolith lies on the sensory epithelium of the sacculus, and how mobile it is by examining living or just dead fish (e.g., Gobius). One need not even open the skull; just changing the position of the fish's head is enough to show the displacement of the heavy otolith (X-rays made by Dr. M. De Vries (Physical Laboratory, Groningen) show that in Acerina cernua the otolith shifts about 0.2 mm in the direction of its greatest dimension (measured against the bony wall of the sacculus) when the fish is tilted from head-down to head-up position).

Still not solved is the functional effectiveness of the various "windows" in the skull. According to Schneider (1941), macropodids with a well-developed window at the sacculus (elastic membrane) displayed better hearing, at least in the higher registers, than fish with a smaller window. The effect is easily understood here, because the membrane is in direct contact with the air-filled respiratory cavity. But in many other cases there are merely remarkably thinned out regions in the skull bones next to the sacculus and the lagena (for instance, von Frisch, 1938). Such a window in the bone is also present in Gobius, at the ventral aspect of the sacculus. Systematic investigation of these structures in the different fishes would no doubt reveal many new things of interest, and is most desirable.

Electrophysiological investigations in ostariophysines and non-ostariophysines have revealed that in the sacculus, the lagena, and the utriculus, sounds cause potential changes that have the same frequency as the tone (Adrian, Craik, and Sturdy, 1938; Pumphrey, 1939; Zotterman, 1943; Dijkgraaf, 1948). They correspond the "microphonic effect" first described by Wever and Bray in the cochlea of the mammal. Similar potential changes during the presentation of a sound were also recorded from the ampullae of the semicircular canals, and from the organs of the lateral line (De Vries, 1948; De Vries and Bleeker, 1949), though none of these organs, any more than the utriculus of the ostariophysines, are used in sound perception. The origin and physiologic significance of these potential changes, which are purely local is still in controversy. It would be more important to know what happens in the acoustic nerve during sound stimulation. So far there is little information about this (Zotterman, 1943; Lowenstein and Roberts, 1948), and the essentials have already been mentioned in the introduction.

In our experiments both Gobius and Corvina could, to some extent, localize the source (point of application of the tuning fork) of a sound. But they could only do this when they were close to the source; at greater distances, their responses were unoriented. Such localization as was observed may therefore have had its origin in the simultaneous stimulation of other sense organs (skin touch receptors, lateral line organs). Similar results were obtained previously in feral tests on the minnow (von Frisch and Dijkgraaf, 1935), in which case, however, the experimental situation was better suited to determine any recognition of the direction of a sound from a distance. Whether the non-ostariophysines have this ability is therefore still an open question. (The Viennese diver-zoologist Hans Hass has noticed that sharks are attracted by the movements of harpooned breams; other fish were frightened by a rapid movement of the arm or leg, though direct sight had been in some cases impossible (oral communication). These suddenly appearing reactions can therefore have been elicited only mechanically, and the distance suggests that displacement phenomena (lateral line organs) are not, or at least only little, involved, so that sound waves may have been the cause.

SUMMARY

In a first series of experiments, the effect of uni- and bilateral elimination of the pars inferior of the labyrinth on the equilibrium of Gobius paganellus was studied. The animals were also blinded to prevent optic orientation, and they were made to swim in open water so that they would not be able to orient themselves by tactile sensations. Movement and position reflexes (fins, eyes, body) were tested. Strong disturbances of equilibrium did not develop. A few abnormal effects (head-over-heels swimming) were described; they are to be attributed probably to secondary effects on other parts of the labyrinth. Only a certain paralysis of the caudal peduncle seems to be caused directly by the bilateral elimination of the pars inferior (or the sacculus otoliths). Elimination of the pars superior always gave rise to characteristic disturbances of equilibrium.

In a second series of experiments, the effect on hearing of eliminating the pars inferior was examined. Gobius was easy to train to tuning fork tones and other sounds that were transmitted directly to the aquarium or to the table on which it stood. Training to air-borne sound gave poor results; auditory acuity was relatively slight. The upper auditory threshold was around 600-800 Hz. Unilateral elimination of the pars inferior did not disturb auditory perception. After operation on the controlateral side, noticeable worsening occurred, decreasing the upper threshold to about 500 Hz, and causing irregular responses only to the most intense sounds, or after contact with the bottom. Low tones (e.g., 100 Hz) were still heard just as well (even after additional elimination of the pars superior and of the lateral line organs). In this case apparently the skin sense organs, or the wall of the swim bladder are involved.

In connection with these matters, a few other senses of G. paganellus are discussed, among them the structure and function of the lateral line organs, the significance of touch-at-a-distance in mating behavior, the light sensitivity of blind animals, and the reaction to a pressure shock. Also described were the reactions to sound of Scyllium canicula, Serranus cabrilla, Trigla corax, and Corvina nigra. This last fish reacted, after training, to a tone of 1024 Hz (higher tones were not tested). We see in this some evidence that in this fish, too, the labyrinth is concerned with the reception of sounds.

The hearing performance of G. paganellus a non-ostariophysine is discussed in comparison to the hearing of other fish.

[*Editor's Note:* In the original, an English summary follows the German article.]

LITERATUR.

ADRIAN, E. D., K. J. W. CRAIK and R. S. STURDY, 1938. *The electrical response of the auditory mechanism in cold-blooded vertebrates.* Proc. R. Soc. Ser. B. **125**, 435—455.

BOIE, H. J.,˙ 1943. *Untersuchungen über den Gehörsinn von Carassius auratus L. (Goldfisch).* Z. vergl. Physiol. **30**, 181—193.

BURLET, H. M. DE, 1934. *Vergleichende Anatomie des stato-akustischen Organs. Die innere Ohrsphäre.* Handb. vergl. Anat. **2** 2, 1293—1380. Berlin und Wien.

DIESSELHORST, G., 1938. *Hörversuche an Fischen ohne Weberschen Apparat.* Z. vergl. Physiol. **25**, 748—783.

DIJKGRAAF, S., 1934. *Untersuchungen über die Funktion der Seitenorgane an Fischen.* Z. vergl. Physiol. **20**, 162—214.

DIJKGRAAF, S., 1941. *Über die Bedeutung der Weberschen Knöchel für die Wahrnehmung von Schwankungen des hydrostatischen Druckes.* Z. vergl. Physiol. **28**, 389—401.

DIJKGRAAF, S., 1942. *Über Druckwahrnehmung bei Fischen.* Z. vergl. Physiol. **30**, 39—66.

DIJKGRAAF, S., 1947. *Über die Reizung des Ferntastsinnes bei Fischen und Amphibien.* Experientia **3**, 206—208.

DIJKGRAAF, S., 1947. *Ein Töne erzeugender Fisch im Neapler Aquarium.* Experientia **3**, 493—494.

DIJKGRAAF, S., 1948. *Über den Gehörsinn mariner Fische.* Rev. Suisse de Zool. **55**, 260—264.

DIJKGRAAF, S. und F. J. VERHEIJEN. 1950. *Neue Versuche über das Tonunterscheidungsvermögen der Elritze.* Z. vergl. Physiol. **32**, 248—256.

FARKAS, B., 1936. *Zur Kenntnis des Hörvermögens und des Gehörorgans der Fische.* Acta Oto-Laryngol. **23**, 499—532.

FARKAS, B., 1942. *Untersuchungen über das Ohrlabyrinth der ostariophysen Fische.* Acta Zool. Univ. Szeged. **1**, 102—122.

FRISCH, K. v. und H. STETTER, 1932. *Untersuchungen über den Sitz des Gehörsinnes bei der Elritze.* Z. vergl. Physiol. **17**, 686—801.

FRISCH, K. v., 1934. *Über eine Scheinfunktion des Fischlabyrinthes.* Naturwiss. **22**, 332—334.

FRISCH, K. v. und S. DIJKGRAAF, 1935. *Können Fische die Schallrichtung wahrnehmen?* Z. vergl. Physiol. **22**, 641—655.

FRISCH, K. v. 1936. *Über den Gehörsinn der Fische.* Biol. Rev. **11**, 210—246.

FRISCH, K. v., 1938. *Über die Bedeutung des Sacculus und der Lagena für den Gehörsinn der Fische.* Z. vergl. Physiol. **25**, 703—747.

KUNZE, 1949. *Der Ultraschall in der Medizin.* 18. Zürich.

LOWENSTEIN, O. and T. D. M. ROBERTS, 1948. *Oscillographic analysis of the gravity and vibration responses from the labyrinth of the Thornback Ray (Raja clavata).* Nature (London) **162**, 852—853.

MOEHRES, F. P., 1940. *Untersuchungen über die Frage der Wahrnehmung von Druckunterschieden des Mediums.* Z. vergl. Physiol. **28**, 1—42.

PARKER, G. H., 1904. *Hearing and allied senses in fishes.* Bull. U.S. Fish. Comm. **22/1902**, 45—64.

PARKER, G. H., 1910. *Structure and function of the ear of the Squeteague.* Bull. U.S. Bur. Fish. **28**, 1213—1224.

PARKER, G. H., 1910. *Influence of the eyes, ears and other allied sense organs on the movements of the dogfish, Mustelus canis.* Bull. U.S. Bur. Fish. **29**, 43—57.

PUMPHREY, R. J., 1939. *Microphonic potentials from the utricle.* Nature (London) **143**, 898.

RETZIUS, G., 1881. *Das Gehörorgan der Wirbeltiere.* 1. Stockholm.

SCHARRER, E., 1928. *Die Lichtempfindlichkeit blinder Elritzen.* Z. vergl. Physiol. **7**, 1—38.

SCHARRER, E., 1935. *Die Empfindlichkeit der freien Flossenstrahlen des Knurrhahns (Trigla) für chemische Reize.* Z. vergl. Physiol. **22**, 145—191.

SCHNEIDER, H., 1941. *Die Bedeutung der Atemhöhle der Labyrinthfische für ihr Hörvermögen.* Z. vergl. Physiol. **29**, 172—194.

SCHULZE, F. E., 1861. *Über die Nervenendigung in den sogenannten Schleimkanälen der Fische usw.* Arch. Anat. Physiol. wiss. Med.

SCHULZE, F. E., 1870. *Über die Sinnesorgane der Seitenlinie bei Fischen und Amphibien.* Arch. mikrosk. Anat. **6**.

SMITH, H. M., 1905. *The drumming of the „drumfishes" (Sciaenidae).* Science N.S. **22**, 376—378.

STIPETIC, E., 1939. *Über das Gehörorgan der Mormyriden.* Z. vergl. Physiol. **26**, 740—752.

VRIES, H. DE, 1948. *Die Reizschwelle der Sinnesorgane als physikalisches Problem.* Experientia **4**, 205—213.

VRIES, H. DE and J. D. J. W. BLEEKER, 1949. *The microphonic activity of the labyrinth of the pigeon.* Acta Oto-Laryngol. **37**,˙ 298—306.

WERNER, C. F., 1929. *Experimente über die Funktion der Otolithen bei Knochenfischen.* Z. vergl. Physiol. **10**, 26—35.

WOHLFAHRT, T. A., 1933. *Das Ohrlabyrinth des Schlammspringers (Periophthalmus schlosseri Pall.)* Z. Anat. Entw. gesch. **102**, 298—306.

WOHLFAHRT, T. A., 1936. *Das Ohrlabyrinth der Sardine (Clupea pilchardus Walb.) und seine Beziehungen zur Schwimmblase und Seitenlinie.* Z. Morph. Ökol. d. Tiere **31**, 371—410.

WOHLFAHRT, T. A., 1939. *Untersuchungen über das Tonunterscheidungsvermögen der Elritze (Phoxinus laevis Agass.).* Z. vergl. Physiol. **26**, 570—604.

ZOTTERMAN, Y., 1943. *The microphonic effect of teleost labyrinths and its biological significance.* J. Physiol. **102**, 313—318.

137

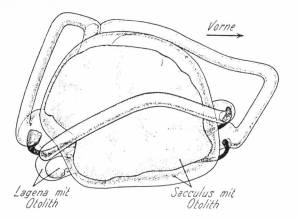

Vorne

Lagena mit Otolith

Sacculus mit Otolith

Fig. 1 Right labyrinth of a gobii (*Gobius niger*), seen from the oute aspect (the sacculus otolith of G paganellus extends still farther up ward). After Retzius. *Lower left* lagena with otloith; *lower right,* sac culus with otolith; *upper right* cephalad. Reprinted from *Physiologi. Compar. Oecologia,* **2,** 81–106 (1949) copyright © 1949 by W. Junk, Pub lisher

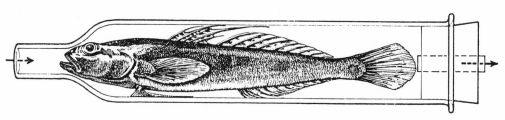

Fig.2 Glass tube for testing the equilibrium of *G. paganellus* by turning about the longitudinal, transverse, and vertical axes. Reprinted from *Physiologia Compar. Oecologia,* **2,** 81–106 (1949); copyright © 1949 by W. Junk, Publisher

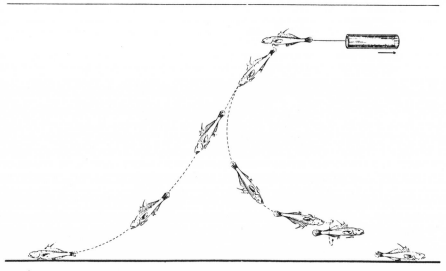

Fig. 3 Behavior of a blind *G. paganellus* after withdrawal of the glass tube. *Left,* normal; *right,* head-over-heels swimming after labyrinthectomy. Reprinted from *Physiologia Compar. Oecologia,,* 81–106 (1949); copyright © 1949 by W. Junk, Publisher

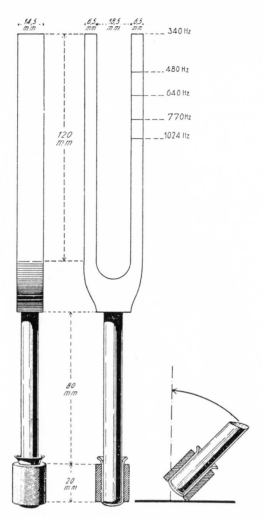

Fig. 4 Tuning fork for the training of *G. paganellus, Trigla corax,* and *Corvina nigra. Lower right,* position of the handle at the moment of application to the aquarium wall (cross-hatching: rubber cuff). Reprinted from *Physiologia Compar. Oecologia,* **2,** 81–106 (1949); copyright © 1949 by W. Junk, Publisher

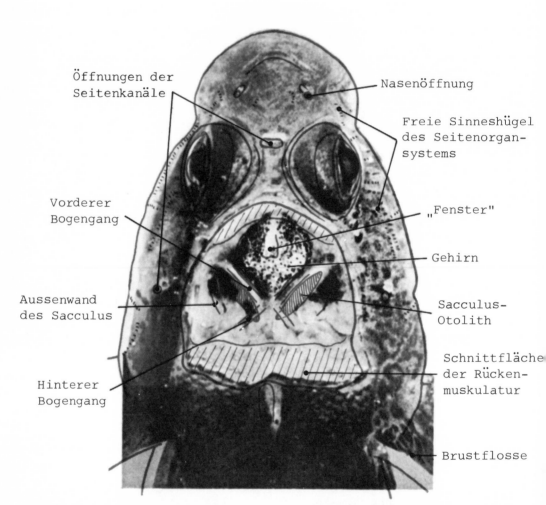

Öffnungen der
Seitenkanäle

Nasenöffnung

Freie Sinneshügel
des Seitenorgan-
systems

Vorderer
Bogengang

„Fenster"

Gehirn

Aussenwand
des Sacculus

Sacculus-
Otolith

Schnittfläche
der Rücken-
muskulatur

Hinterer
Bogengang

Brustflosse

Fig. 5 Head of *G. paganellus*, dorsal view. The roof of the skull is partially exposed by removal of skin and muscles; brain and labyrinth are dimly seen (the pearl-like structures on the skin and muscle surfaces are air bubbles). Observe the "window" in the light-absorbing meninx above the mid-brain. *Left, top to bottom,* opening of the lateral line canals; anterior semicircular canal; outer wall of the sacculus; posterior semicircular canal. *Right, top to bottom,* naris; free sensory hillocks of the lateral line system; "window"; brain; sacculus otolith; cut surface of dorsal musculature; pectoral fin. Reprinted from *Physiologia Compar. Oecologia*, **2**, 81–106 (1949); copyright © 1949 by W. Junk, Publisher

8

NEW EXPERIMENTS WITH THE SOUND DISCRIMINATING ABILITY OF THE MINNOW

Sven Dijkgraaf and Frans J. Verheijen

This article was translated expressly for this Benchmark volume by Brigitte Cappelli, from "Neue Versuche über das Tonunterscheidungsvermögen der Elritze," in Zeitschr. Vergleich. Physiol., **32,** *248–256 (1950), with the permission of Springer-Verlag, Berlin, Heidelberg, New York*

INTRODUCTION

It is known that in humans the ability to discriminate various pitches of sound is well developed. The threshold of frequency discrimination is less than 1%, a fraction of a whole tone (=12% frequency difference). Even the dog can discriminate at least one-quarter tone. It is generally assumed that the cochlea has an important part in the discrimination of sound. Even though the old Helmholtz resonance hypothesis has to make way for new ideas, it is still valid that the basilar membrane, which increases in width from one end to the other, must be considered as the peripheral analyzer of sound frequencies.

The fish labyrinth has no basilar membrane. It was therefore not surprising when Stetter, while attempting to train the minnow (Phoxinus laevis), found the threshold of pitch discrimination to be on an average of one octave (=100% frequency difference). He mentioned that the performance of a particularly gifted minnow was the discrimination of a minor third (=19% frequency difference; Stetter, 1929; von Frisch, 1936). These values are apparently located far above the human threshold; though in reality they are not comparable. What Stetter determined, was not the "relative" but the "absolute" threshold of sound discrimination. The sounds to be discriminated (food signal vs. warning signal) were not presented immediately following each other but with ever increasing time intervals. The fishes had to discriminate the sounds from memory (by "absolute pitch"). Under these circumstances even the performance of a human would hardly be better.

It therefore represented substantial progress when Wohlfahrt (1939) determined the threshold of the relative sound discrimination of the minnow. For this purpose, the fish was presented with a feeding signal at a specified sound frequency, in the form of rhythmically repeated sound pulses. Sound pulses in the same rhythm represented the warning signal, with the difference that two sounds of different frequencies alternated, of which the lower one (lower) is at the frequency of the feeding signal (Fig. 1). The frequency difference between the two, that combined to form the warning signal, was now slowly decreased, until the fish ultimately began to confuse the feeding and the warning signal. In this manner Wohlfahrt found the relative threshold of the sound discriminating ability of the Elritze to be about one-third of a tone (=4% frequency difference) in the tested sound range of around 977 Hz.

Although the frequency discrimination of the ear of the minnow was about 10 times poorer than in humans, this performance, considering the absence of a basilar membrane (or a similar structure, that would qualify as a peripheral sound frequency analyzer) appeared to us to be very remarkable. In view of the still outstanding physiological interpretation we found a clarification of the state of affairs to be in order.

In conjunction with the investigations by Wohlfahrt it should next be systematically examined in this work, how the frequency discrimination varied at higher frequencies. Concerning this, Wohlfahrt made only the following statement: One minnow, that was trained for a whole tone interval of 775-870 Hz, reacted positively and without additional training to interspersed tests of

141

lower or higher whole tone intervals throughout the entire range of 581 to 1550 Hz.

Wohlfahrt brought out that it is not necessarily certain that the sounds were discriminated according to the frequency. "It is also possible, that the test animals responded to the sound pressure difference, which at a medium sound intensity in the frequency range tested (d^2 to g^3; 581-1550 Hz) a whole tone step (=12% frequency difference) is nevertheless great enough that a sensitive organ could conceivably detect it". To prove the possibility, Wohlfahrt attempted to conduct a discrimination training, whereby the warning signal was at the same frequency as the feeding signal (775 Hz), except that the sound pulses were alternately loud and soft. This intensity training however had negative results, from which Wohlfahrt concluded, that the discriminations could only have been made by the frequency difference.

In the following we also investigated this question, but using an improved training method, which led to positive results.

First we took a number of blinded minnows and trained them according to the above mentioned method (Wohlfahrt, 1939) to react to a whole tone interval, at 400, 800, 1600 and 3200 Hz. The drawback of this method showed itself to be the poor tolerance the minnows had for the punishment stimulus. The fishes became especially confused at the higher sound levels and made false responses, often searching for food at the sound of the warning signal.

In a second test series we proceeded differently and eliminated the punishment stimulus. The rhythmically interrupted sound (=feeding signal in Wohlfahrt's method) was now offered frequently and in long duration, without feeding the fish. The fish was not permitted to react to this neutral signal in any way. For a feeding trial, the neutral signal was first switched on, then, after 10 minutes, it was suddenly switched to the alternating signal (=warning signal in Wohlfahrt's method) without any break in the rhythm. Whereupon the minnow was fed (Fig. 2). Thus, Wohlfahrt's feeding signal in our method was the "neutral signal", and Wohlfahrt's warning signal was our "food signal".

For the production of the sounds we had one loudspeaker and 2 Philips sound generators (type GM 2307) at our disposal. The GM 2307 permitted a continuous regulation of the intensity and of the frequency in the range of 30-16,000 Hz. The sound impulses in the first series of experiments (Wohlfahrt's method) were produced by manual switching in the rate of 2 pulses a second (each having a duration of approximately 1 second). The production in the second series (our method) was maintained mechanically. An oscillating lever, driven by an electric motor, alternately closed 2 of 4 contacts producing 100 sound pulses per minute. During the "neutral" signal all 4 contacts were connected with the same sound generator. To switch on the "feeding" signals 2 of the 4 contacts were connected with the sound generator by a manually operated double switch (between 2 sound pulses), so that the sound pulses were now alternately supplied by the two generators.

The minnows were kept separately in unplanted metal-framed aquaria (20 x 30 cm, 18 cm deep).

RESULTS

A. Experiments according to Wohlfahrt's method

Discrimination training for whole tone discrimination succeeded readily with this method at 400 and 800 Hz. While Wohlfahrt could train minnows successfully to one-half tone discrimination at 977 Hz, but not to one-quarter tone, he assumed the discrimination threshold to be one-third of a tone. In our experiments we

142

successfully trained two investigated minnows to around one-quarter of a tone
(=3% frequency difference) at 400 and 800 Hz (smaller intervals were not examined) so that the threshold is even lower than Wohlfahrt assumed.

At 1600 and 3200 Hz however neither the training to a whole tone nor to a
smaller or greater interval was successful. The experiment was made with 13
minnows; each animal received in excess of 100 learning trials. In 2 of these
cases, the animal showed good frequency discrimination at lower frequencies
(400 and 800 Hz). It was obvious that the high sounds were detected; we found
the upper limit to be about 5000 Hz. Frequency discrimination in this sound
range (1600 Hz and higher) was obviously not possible. Even training to intervals up to 7 whole tones (=octave + whole tone) was unsuccessful.

B. Experiments according to our method

Starting with fish trained to a whole tone discrimination, we could demonstrate discrimination of one-quarter of a tone at 400 and 800 Hz. In contrast
to the above described results, minnows reacted to the whole tone step not only
at 400 and 800 Hz, but at 1600 Hz. However it turned out that the discrimination in this case depended upon intensity differences. If instead of using the
two-tone feeding signal, alternate sound pulses of the neutral signal were soft-
er or louder, the animal also reacted by searching for food. The ability to
discriminate sound intensities could be established in the entire frequency
range tested (400-3200 Hz). Wohlfahrt's negative results concerning intensity
discrimination and his conclusions appear to be wrong (see Introduction).

After these preliminary experiments, which seemed to indicate that the upper limit of the ability to discriminate frequencies was between 800 and 1600
Hz, 5 minnows were trained systematically in the 615-1600 Hz range. This sound
range contained 8 whole tones. The training interval always amounted to one major third (=2 whole tones). Furthermore the reaction to intensity discrimination was avoided or extinguished in all test sequences by repeated offering of
the signal without the feeding. As a control, we presented trials with intensity differences interspersed with the frequency discrimination tests. The results of these controls together with the frequency training results are found
in Table 1.

After a number of training trials the Weberian apparatus of minnow No. 4
was removed (bilateral removal of incus + malleus under urethane anesthesia;
see Dijkgraaf, 1942) and with it, in effect, the sound receiving function of
the sacculus (von Frisch, 1938). Renewed tests showed no changes in the sound
frequency discrimination. Apart from discriminations of a major third, the lagena alone was as effective in this connection as the whole pars inferior.

The Table shows that the 615-800 Hz interval was discriminated almost without error; the discrimination of 800-1000 Hz interval was still good (an average
of more than 75% clearly positive reactions); the 1000-1260 Hz interval, by comparison, was only imperfectly discriminated (less than 25% positive reactions);
and the 1260-1600 Hz interval was not at all detected. Fig. 3 shows the data
graphically.

Finally frequency discrimination tests were attempted as follows. In this
case the feeding signal was derived from the neutral signal by generating,
simultaneously with every alternate sound pulse, a higher frequency tone from
a second loudspeaker. Here the intensity difference was also controlled by
trials in which the second tone was made equal in frequency to that of the neutral signal, and withholding the feeding reward. In these experiments, the
range around 1260 Hz was found to be the limit, above which no frequency discrimination occurred. The highest interval discriminated was 1120-1420 Hz.

DISCUSSION

Because of our new discrimination training method, in which we used only reward (the effect of the second stimulus is extinguished not by punishment but by training), it was possible for the first time to establish discrimination of sound intensity in the minnow by contrast to the negative results of previous authors (Stetter, 1929; Wohlfahrt, 1939). Strictly speaking, Wohlfahrt's demonstration of frequency discrimination also becomes invalidated, because his fishes could have responded to intensity differences. In the range above 1260 Hz, this seems quite likely to us, because of the fact that Wohlfahrt found discrimination of a whole tone interval, while according to our results frequency discrimination no longer occurs in that range (however, there is intensity discrimination). In other cases too, Wohlfahrt might have been deceived in part, especially because in his experiments he used flutes and other instruments similarly difficult to regulate. Furthermore we also found the ear of the minnow to be amazingly sensitive for frequency discrimination, with a threshold exceeding one-quarter of a tone (=3% frequency difference). This value is located somewhere in the middle between the threshold of the human ear (0.1 - 0.3% in the middle sound region) and the sense of vibration of the human skin (10 - 35% frequency difference). We are currently investigating, with our methods, the sense of vibration sensitivity of the skin of the minnow (von Frisch and Stetter, 1932).

The physiological interpretation of the frequency discrimination in the minnow is difficult. Perhaps it is important that the discrimination limitation is at 1260 Hz, discovered by us, as well as the establishment that the lagena seems as capable of sound discrimination as the intact pars inferior. The first fact brings to mind an analogy with hearing in man, whose ear, when properly stimulated, responds far into the ultrasonic range. So stimulated, the ear "hears" the highest of its normal hearing range. The latter was predicted on the strength of new discoveries (Galambos and Davis, 1943). However, it would be too early to draw further conclusions as to the hearing of the minnow from these facts. Discrimination experiments with other species of fish, and electrophysiological experiments with the minnow's acoustic nerve are in progress, and we await results.

SUMMARY

1. With discrimination training tests in minnows, according to the method by Wohlfahrt, it was easy to demonstrate frequency discriminating at 400 and 800 Hz. The discrimination threshold was not yet reached at around one-quarter of a tone (=3% frequency difference).
2. With the same method and some of the same animals, the frequency discrimination training at 1600 and 3200 Hz failed completely, even at intervals up to and above one octave (7 whole tones). The sounds were doubtlessly perceived, for the upper threshold was found to be at around 5000 Hz.
3. A new discrimination training method was instituted, which only used reward; the effect of the counter-stimulus is not extinguished with punishment, but with habituation.
4. It was established with this method, that minnows can be trained to intensity differences in the entire tested sound range (400-3200 Hz). This finding stands in contrast with the negative results of Stetter and Wohlfahrt.
5. In regard to the frequency discrimination, the above mentioned findings were confirmed and the limits above which sound frequency discriminations were no longer possible, was determined to be at around 1260 Hz, by systematic experiments with five minnows.

6. Removal of the Weberian apparatus (according to von Frisch this is identical with elimination of the sacculus as a sound receiving organ) had no noticeable influence on the ability to discriminate frequencies (major third). The lagena alone is apparently as effective as the entire pars inferior.

Table 1. Training attempts with minnows for the discrimination of a major third. Results by variation of the sound intensity from 615-1600 Hz.

+ clearly positive feeding reaction; ? weak positive or doubtful reaction; - no reaction.

Fish No.	No. of reactions to intensity discriminations			Neutral Tone (Hz)	Feeding signal (Hz) frequency interval-always major third	No. of reactions to frequency discriminations		
	+	?	-			+	?	-
4	2	12	41	800	800-1000	50	8	1
	16	15	13	1000	1000-1260	16	22	22
4 (after re-moval of Weberian apparatus)	1	6	28	615	615- 800	37	3	0
	5	9	32	800	800-1000	58	7	1
	8	7	19	1000	1000-1260	25	14	12
				1260	1260-1600	No reaction, even at greater inter-vals.		
8	1	5	8	615	615- 800	14	6	0
	2	11	14	800	800-1000	32	11	1
	3	4	1	1000	1000-1260	1	4	11
				1260	1260-1600	No reaction.		
15	0	1	14	615	615- 800	17	0	0
	0	12	43	800	800-1000	57	13	6
	6	6	9	1000	1000-1260	0	9	22
				1260	1260-1600	No reaction.		
17	2	6	27	615	615- 800	32	7	1
	1	13	22	800	800-1000	42	6	0
	5	6	4	1000	1000-1260	8	6	4
				1260	1260-1600	No reaction.		
18	2	8	22	615	615- 800	29	7	0
	13	12	25	800	800-1000	35	27	10
	10	6	18	1000	1000-1260	7	13	30
				1260	1260-1600	No reaction.		

Literatur.

DIJKGRAAF, S.: Über Druckwahrnehmung bei Fischen. Z. vergl. Physiol. 30, 39 (1942). — FRISCH, K. v.: Über den Gehörsinn der Fische. Biol. Rev. 11, 210 (1936). — Über die Bedeutung des Sacculus und der Lagena für den Gehörsinn der Fische. Z. vergl. Physiol. 25, 703 (1938). — FRISCH, K. v., u. H. STETTER: Untersuchungen über den Sitz des Gehörsinnes bei der Elritze. Z. vergl. Physiol. 17, 686 (1932). — GALAMBOS, R., u. H. DAVIS: The response of single auditory-nerve fibers to acoustic stimulation. J. Neurophysiol. 6, 39 (1943). — STETTER, H.: Untersuchungen über den Gehörsinn der Fische. Z. vergl. Physiol. 9, 339 (1929). — WOHLFAHRT, TH. A.: Untersuchungen über das Tonunterscheidungs-vermögen der Elritze (Phoxinus laevis Agass.). Z. vergl. Physiol. 26, 570 (1939).

— — — — — — — — —

Futtersignal   Warnsignal

Fig. 1 Threshold determination of frequency discrimination according to Wohlfahrt's method. *Left,* feeding signal; *right,* warning signal. Reprinted from *Zeitschr. Vergleich. Physiol.,* **32,** 249 (1950); copyright © 1950 by Springer-Verlag, Berlin, Heidelberg, New York

Neutraltonsignal   Futtertonsignal

Fig. 2 Threshold determination of the frequency discrimination with the new method. *Left,* neutral signal; *right,* feeding signal. Reprinted from *Zeitschr. Vergleich. Physiol.,* **32,** 250 (1950); copyright © 1950 by Springer-Verlag, Berlin, Heidelberg, New York

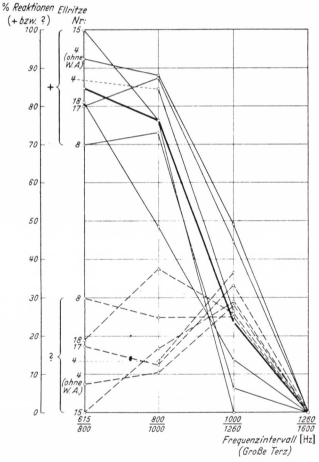

Fig. 3 Discrimination of a major third in the sound range 615–1600 Hz (see Table 1). *Light solid line,* percentage of positive reactions to the presentation of an interval of a third; *dashed lines,* percentage of doubtful reactions; *ohne W.A.,* after removal of the Weberian apparatus; *heavy solid line,* average percentage of positive reactions. Reprinted from *Zeitschr. Vergleich. Physiol.,* **32,** 253 (1950); copyright © 1950 by Springer-Verlag, Berlin, Heidleberg, New York

9

THE ABSOLUTE THRESHOLD OF HEARING OF THE BULLHEAD (*AMIURUS NEBULOSUS**) AND CONTRIBUTIONS TO THE PHYSICS OF THE WEBERIAN APPARATUS OF THE OSTARIOPHYSI

Dietrich Poggendorf

This article was translated expressly for this Benchmark volume by Helmut E. Adler and Brigitte Cappelli, from "Die absoluten Hörschwellen des Zwergwelses (Amiurus nebulosus*) und Bieträge zur Physik des Weberschen Apparates der Ostariophysen," *in* Zeitschr. Vergleich. Physiol., **34,** *222–257 (1952), with the permission of Springer-Verlag, Berlin, Heidelberg, New York*

I.   Introduction

The sense of hearing in fish has been thoroughly investigated from the comparative-physiological point of view (Diesselhorst, 1938; Dijkgraaf, 1949; von Frisch, 1936 and 1938; von Frisch and Stetter, 1932; Schneider, 1942; Stipetić, 1939; Wohlfahrt, 1950). Hearing ability is most highly developed in the ostariophysines in which the anterior part of the swim bladder, the Camera aerea Weberiana, is connected with the labyrinth by means of the Weberian ossicles. The Camera aerea Weberiana, the Weberian ossicles and the perilymphatic and endolymphatic spaces of the labyrinth (apparently concerned with sound conduction), are designated as the Weberian apparatus (Chranilov, 1927). If the Weberian apparatus is eliminated, the hearing ability of ostariophysines is weakened, their upper thresholds lowered (von Frisch, 1938; von Frisch and Stetter, 1932).

The physical events taking place in the organ of hearing in fishes have not as yet been analyzed. Also lacking are measurements of the absolute threshold of hearing, as they have been obtained in man (Sivian and White, 1933), the bullfinch (Schwartzkopff, 1949) and the grasshopper (Autrum, 1941). The reasons for this lack are primarily methodological: it is difficult to set up suitable experimental conditions for acoustical investigations on biological subjects under water.

The present work is designed as a contribution to the solution of the following questions:
1. The generation of an experimental sound field suitable for investigating aquatic animals.
2. Determination of the effective sound field for the organ of hearing when normal and with the Weberian apparatus eliminated.
3. Determination of the absolute threshold of hearing in an ostariophysine with and without its Weberian apparatus.
4. Analysis of physical processes in the Weberian apparatus.

II.   Apparatus

A.   The sound tank

It is difficult to produce a quantitatively determined field of sound on a tank of water bounded on all sides. The local distribution of sound is dependent in a complicated manner on the acoustical properties of the surrounding media (walls of the tank, surface of the water) and the shape and size of the tank; and cannot be determined in advance. In addition, sound waves corresponding to the tank dimensions will produce standing waves between the limiting surfaces, which complicate conditions still further.

* = *Ictalurus nebulosus* (Ed. note).

The experimental conditions utilized the sound cage pictured in Figure 1, whose dimensions were chosen as small as possible in order to avoid standing waves over as great a range of frequencies as possible. The sound source was incorporated rigidly into the bottom of the tank in order to obtain a good sound distribution. An electrodynamic speaker was chosen, because its amplitude of oscillation at constant frequencies is proportional to a great extent to the A. C. current flowing through its solenoid and can be extrapolated at low sound intensities from the voltage across the coil.

The bottom and two opposite walls of the sound tank consisted of brass 8 mm thick, the other two walls were glass 7 mm thick. The inside dimensions of the vessel were 148 x 152 x 116 mm; it was filled to within a few millimeters from the top. The oscillating piston (St) (43 mm dia.) was set into the bottom. It was made watertight yet moveable by the rubber washer (D) held in place by the lockring (Kr). The immersible coil (T), connected to the oscillating piston, was inserted into the strong permanent magnet (M).

B. Measuring sound pressure under water

The only parameter of a sound field that can be measured satisfactorily under water is the sound pressure, since amplitude and velocity of the water particles are much smaller under water, at the same sound intensity, than of the particles of a sound field in air.

Sound pressure was measured by means of a piezoelectric microphone (pictured in Tamm, 1941). Two 3 x 3 x 6 mm crystals of Rochelle salt lie opposite one another in the cylindrical head of the microphone (dia. 12 mm, height 8 mm). Their outside covering is directly connected to the brass housing of the head, their inner covering (a thin silver plate) is interconnected by means of a fine copper wire. The crystals are therefore electrically coupled with one another. The (microphone) head was carried on a brass tube, approximately 3 mm thick and 50 cm long, containing the insulated copper wire.

In the interest of the best possible resistance and capacitance characteristics, the terminals of the microphone were directly connected to the grid and cathode of the adjacent A. C. amplifier. Microphone voltages were amplified by the A. C. amplifier, whose frequency dependent amplification was determined for each measurement, and measured by a VTVM at its terminal. A pair of earphones could be substituted for the VTVM for direct acoustical control.

The voltage yield of a piezoelectric crystal is proportional to its mechanical deformation and therefore to the sound pressure it receives, as long as the frequencies used lie below the natural frequency of the crystal, as was the case in all experiments. The charge (Q) generated at a given sound pressure flows across the circuit loaded by resistance R and capacitance C, so that voltage V occurs at the grid of the tube (Schafer, 1941). A constant sound pressure, V increases the smaller the value of C and the greater the value of R. On the other hand, the lower limit to which the frequency characteristics of the microphone are approximately linear, is given by $\omega = 1/RC$. C, therefore, must not be too small in order to keep the limit low. Increasing the sensitivity of the microphone is therefore connected with deviations from the linearity of transmittance at the lower frequencies.

In measuring sound pressure the resistance R was $10^8 \Omega$ in round numbers, the capacitance C (essentially line capacitance) 1.2×10^{-10} F. The lower limit is 10-20 Hz in this case, sufficiently much below the lowest frequency (60 Hz) at which measurements were still made.

The sensitivity of the Rochelle salt is constant in the region -18 to 24°C; this was checked for temperatures from 0 to +20°C. All sound pressures were measured at +15 to 20°C. The microphone was calibrated at +16.7°C[1]. The

---

[1] I thank Dr. K. Tamm (III. Physikalisches Institut, Gottingen) for the calibration of the microphone.

wavelength of the sounds was large at all frequencies measured, compared to the dimensions of the microphone head, so that the sound field was not disturbed by the microphone.

C. Behavior of the sound field parameters in the sound tank

The A. C. voltage at the immersible coil, which was easily measurable, served as measurement of the sound intensity inside the tank. Sound pressure in water is, however, a function of frequency and location as well as of immersed coil voltage. Separate calibration had therefore to be carried out for these two variables.

The effect of frequency on sound pressure. Sound pressure in the middle of the tank increases to about 600 Hz with frequency at constant coil voltage. It is high between 600 and 1700 Hz but is difficult to measure due to its strong dependency on frequency changes. Between 1700 and 5000 Hz it is relatively constant, forming a maximum at 6750 Hz. It was not measured above 10,000 Hz. Frequencies of 60, 120, 200, 400, 800, 1600, 3000, 5000, 6000, and 10,000 were selected for the training experiments. They were chosen before the acoustical properties of the tank were known sufficiently. It turned out later on that at some of them, for example at 800 Hz, sound pressure was difficult to measure, because of its strong dependence on small changes of frequency. However in order to allow comparison of results of the training experiments among each other, frequencies once chosen were retained in the further course of experimentation.

Sound pressure in the middle of the tank at the training frequencies is shown in Fig. 2, at the same time demonstrating the wide dispersion of measurements. This variability becomes understandable if the dependence of sound pressure on small changes of frequency, the fact that at low frequencies the sound pressure differed only slightly from the noise level of the amplifier, and the large extent of decay of the sound pressure over distance are taken into account. The final calculation of the absolute sound pressure was made from the geometric mean (logarithmic representation) of each of the measurements.

The decay of sound pressure over distance is considerable, especially in the vertical direction. The course of distribution of sound pressures in the vertical in the center of the tank at different frequencies is shown in Fig. 3. The abscissa is the distance of the head of the microphone from the bottom of the tank, the ordinate is the relative sound pressure in decibels (dB), where the highest value measured right above the bottom was chosen as the 0 decibel. Sound pressure always shows a minimum at the water surface; its gradient is strongest near the surface. [At 10,000 Hz there is a further minimum at a deeper water level (Fig. 3c)]. The horizontal lines represent dimension and position of the training cages in the water.

Sound pressure in the training cages is therefore not constant; the difference in sound pressure within a cage is especially large when the cage is close to the water surface and is then about 10 dB, at greater depth it is about 5 dB.

After the absolute sound pressure in the middle of the sound tank at various frequencies had been measured (Fig. 2), it became possible to calculate the sound pressure from its known decay at these frequencies for each point of the vertical in the middle of the tank (Fig. 3).

Decay in the horizontal is much less at constant voltage and frequency. In general it decreases from the middle to the edge, although the reverse happens occasionally. With increasing frequency and water depths horizontal decay becomes steeper. This decay is however not equal in directions, its distribution is often unsymmetrical. The measurements are hard to replicate. An example of the measurements is given in Table 1. Sound pressure was measured for a series

of frequencies at two depths in the middle of the tank. In addition the microphone was moved horizontally by 4 cm in different directions. (A distance of
4 cm just corresponds to half the length of the training cage). The difference
in dB between the final lateral results and the vertical at tank center is recorded.

<u>Behavior of sound velocity</u>. Apart from the spatial distribution of sound
pressure, we are also interested in sound velocity - which could not be measured.
Since sound velocity is proportional to the gradient of sound pressure one can
estimate its behavior from the sound pressure measurements. It is highest at
the water surface and decreases with increasing depth underwater. Near the surface vertical components predominate, while the horizontal components increase
with increasing depth. In the immediate vicinity of the sound source the situation is unclear.

Sound pressure underwater at a given point with frequency held constant, is
proportional to the voltage across the immersible coil, as checking measurements
confirmed. It is therefore permissible to extrapolate to sound pressures that
could no longer be measured from the voltage across the immersible coil.

When an experimental animal was placed into the water and moved back and
forth, the sound pressure changed little, if at all. The sound field, then,
was not disturbed by the presence of the experimental animal.

D. Production of training signal

The variable A. C. needed for the electro-dynamic speaker was provided by
an oscillator in connection with an amplifier. Its voltage at the immersible
coil could be measured by a VTVM. It could be set quickly to any desired value
by a system of adjustable resistances R, calibrated in dB's. A total range of
voltages of about 100 dB was available. A logarithmic potentiometer served to
turn on the training signal gradually. In training to low frequencies a capaci-
tor was switched into the system in order to suppress high frequency noise.

III. The auditory threshold of the bullhead

A. Threshold determination by a training method

1. The course of training experiments

During training, experimental animals should be confined to a small portion
of the experimental tank in which the values of the sound field were known with
sufficient accuracy. The animals were therefore confined to a small cage which
served as their abode at all times for the duration of the experiment - in extreme cases almost for a whole year. These cages had to be large enough to allow the animals sufficient room to move about, but, on the other hand, they had
to be of a small enough size so that the falling off of the sound field values
within them remained within limits. In addition, they were not supposed to influence the acoustical data of the sound field to any marked degree.

Plastic cages measuring 8 x 2.5 x 2.5 cm were therefore employed. Their
walls were pierced by numerous holes. Celluloid had proved itself in preliminary experiments as a material which did not influence the acoustical data of the
sound field in any measurable way. These cages were hung at the desired height
in the sound tank during the training periods, and in the same manner in the
resting tank during rest periods.

Minnows (<u>Phoxinus laevis</u>) could not get used to the narrow training cages.
Bullheads (<u>Amiurus nebulosus</u>) were therefore used for the experiments. Body

length of A_1 - A_4 and A_{10} - A_{12} amounted to about 5 - 6 cm, that of A_5 - A_9, A_{13} and A_{14} was about 6 - 7 cm.

All experiments were carried out on animals which had not been blinded. A bullhead enucleated provisionally (A_3) swam about in its cage so agitatedly that it was not possible to coordinate feeding with the training signal. Animals with intact vision learned very much better.

Visual capacities nevertheless seemed of only minor importance. Reaction to optical stimuli was never observed. During training, animals snapped at the food most of the time only when it was held immediately next to a barbel or was moved close to the animal or if the training cage was shaken lightly. At the beginning of the experiments it appeared as if the approach of the experiments before the start of a training session was noticed. A fish lying quietly at the bottom of the cage would then start to swim about its cage agitatedly.

A cardboard screen, containing a peephole through which the whole cage could just be surveyed, was placed between the sound tank and the location of the experiments, in order to avoid errors caused by inadvertent cues. All manipulations, such as switching the potentiometer, the baiting of the feeder pin, etc. were invisible to the animal. Food was presented across the top of the screen only when the animal had definitely reacted to the training tone. The fact that optical sources of error were eliminated is shown by the check series described.

Training of each animal took the following course: After a fish had become habituated to the training cage and after he had learned to take the proffered food from the feeding pin he was brought into the sound tank for the first time and fed only there from then on. He was then trained to follow the food held in front of him into one of the corners of his cage and would get his food only there. This food training was the most difficult part of the preliminary training procedure. Since the feeding pin had to be inserted through one of the holes in the top of the cage it was difficult to move it in a horizontal direction. The fish noticed the food only when it was held immediately in front of his barbels. If one tried, now, to draw the food away just before the fish snapped it up, in order to tease it into a typical indicator response, the cage tended to be shaken slightly. This shaking frightened the fish so that he would swim wildly into the walls of his cage, after which he would often fall into a typical cataleptic state that would make him temporarily useless for any further experiments. Slowly the fish would get used to feed from one of the four <u>upper</u> corners of his cage. From then on the training tone was turned on simultaneously with the offering of the food. After a few feedings the training tone was turned on a few seconds before the food so that the success of the training procedure could be observed.

On each day experiments were conducted, several animals in succession were trained in the same sound tank. For each experimental run the animal with its cage was lifted from its tank, in which it had remained during rest pauses, and carried in a small container, filled with water, to the sound tank, filled with water at the same temperature. During the change the fish was kept below the water surface so that it was disturbed as little as possible. After a lapse of time two hours at the start, later just as successfully after a few minutes, the trials commenced. Each day on which experiments were conducted was followed by a day of rest so as to make sure that the animals were sufficiently hungry for the next day's trials.

Training started at a tone of 800 Hz (except for one animal each at 400 Hz and 1600 Hz) because this tone possessed the greatest intensity under water at the given voltage of the submersible coil. The number of trials to the first successful response, to the criterion of learning and to the first threshold determination, as well as the total number of trials are shown in Table 2.

The first successful response generally consisted of the animal giving a short start at the sound of the tone. The typical response pattern developed only later. It consisted of a sustained searching and "burrowing" of the animal into one of the four upper corners of the cage, mostly those closest to the animal at the moment.

In the early stages of training the animals would often try to find a way out of the cage and "burrowed" with similar movements but into the bottom corners of their cage, so that these efforts could be distinguished from the trained response pattern. They gave up these escape attempts later but got into the habit of searching in one of the upper corners of the cage even without the training tone. These spontaneous search movements were undistinguishable from the trained responses and had to be taken into account during the evaluation of the results.

Interspersed during the training trials there were blank runs during which all movements, including the turning on of the potentiometer, were carried out. However, only the noise (AC hum etc.) of the audiogenerator and the power amplifier were turned on instead of the training tone. The blank trials allowed an estimate of the frequency of spontaneous search behavior. At the same time they prevented conditioning to acoustical stimuli stemming from the AC source (electrical noise) or from the environment of the tank. These noises were many dB's lower than the training tone, but could have become a source of error in case the fish were more sensitive to their freqencies than to those of the training tone. Indeed in one instance a bullhead being trained to 10,000 Hz reacted to almost every blank trial. Apparently there occurred in this case conditioning to the noise instead of the training tone. This error could be eliminated by conditioning against this response and the threshold for 10,000 Hz could be determined.

The trials were evaluated on the following scale:

(a) Training trials

1. + + + = very good response
2.   + + = good response
3.   + = weak response, but still clearly distinctive
4.   ? = questionable response

(b) Blank trials

6.   + = no searching
7   ? = questionable result
8.   - = accidental search

Responses of the first three types were added together in later analysis.

With training successful to a given tone, its intensity was decreased in steps of 5 or 10 dB's. Each new intensity step had to be responded to without error, before proceeding to the next step. Eventually intensities were reached at which the response pattern always remained unsteady. Once this level was reached the trial series to determine the threshold were carried out.

At a very low sound intensity the animals generally reacted only after a long latency (up to 10 sec.). Each training tone therefore remained on for 10 seconds. If the response took place during this period was used in the blank trials and all spontaneous search responses falling into this period were also counted.

When the threshold had been successfully determined for any frequency, a new frequency was tested. The change of conditioning to the new tone, as well as the descending series to the threshold level progressed exactly like it had in the case of the first frequency - only faster.

2. Evaluation of training experiments

The experimental series were evaluated by taking the percentage of searching responses in the sum of positive and negative trials (Example in Table 3a). In training trials this was the percentage of positive responses, in the blank trials the percentage of negative responses. The latter generally amounted to 0-30%, rarely more. In case it went beyond 50%, an error in carrying out the experiment had to be assumed (for example in case of the training to 10,000 Hz).

In general it was sufficient to run 3 series for determining the threshold at a given frequency. Occasionally, however, the level at which the responses became unsure decreased gradually in the course of several series of trials, so that the experiments had to be continued to the point where reproducible results could be obtained. The results were evaluated as shown in the example in Table 3b. At each intensity level and for the blanks, average percentages for each series were calculated. The average of the training trials decreases with decreasing intensity and approaches that of the blanks. At a sufficiently low intensity (for example at -35 dB) the average and each of the separate values of the training trials cannot be distinguished from those of the blank trials. They both appear to be samples of the same population (of responses).

If one assumes (null hypothesis) that the positive responses found at a given intensity belong to the same population as those counted in the blank trials, i.e., that one is dealing merely with spontaneous search responses, one can give the probability p that such a difference would occur between these two types of results according to a method given by Patan (1939), that was developed for a small number of cases. Should the intensity be sufficiently high then p becomes so small (for example at -20 and -25 dB) that both series may be considered as being different. As intensity decreases, p increases rapidly (Table 3b). It is a matter of convention at what probability level the difference between the two series can be considered statistically just significant.

The sample record in Table 3b is displayed graphically in Fig. 4. The abscissa shows the relative voltage of the coil, the ordinate the percentage of search behavior per trial. The unbroken line connects the average percentage of positive training trials, the dash and dock line, parallel to the abscissa, marks the percentage of searching responses during the blank trials. At high and low intensities the percentage of positive searching responses is independent of intensity: At high intensities the animal reacts almost all the time; at low intensities only spontaneous search movements are found. At this point the solid and the dot and dashed lines coincide. Between these levels there is an intensity interval in which the curve changes from the one to the other, where, in other words, there is a slope change. The increase of the percentage of positive responses as a function of intensity extends over a range of intensities of about 15-20 dB in all animals and at all frequencies.

The threshold of hearing must lie within this range.

The gradual change points to two factors. 1. Interval factors: A threshold stimulus will just lead to a response in one case and not in another. 2. External factors: During an experiment the fish crosses his cage in which the sound field intensity will not have the same value every where; the stimulus will be above threshold at one point, and not at another, and will be responded to accordingly.

One has a certain amount of choice what point within this range one wishes

153

to consider the threshold. Two possibilities appear most useful:

    1. One defines the threshold as that intensity at which, on the average, 50% of all responses are positive.

    2. One defines it as the intensity at which a preselected value of the above mentioned probability p occurs.

In the present work threshold definition 1. has been chosen. The probability p usually has a value of about 0.05 at that intensity, a value that can be considered as just sufficient for statistical significance of a difference between both series of measurements. Thus both definitions happen to coincide in this case.

In a preliminary publication of these results (Autrum and Poggendorf, 1951, Poggendorf, 1951) that intensity had been chosen as threshold where the percentage of positive responses to the training tone equaled the spontaneous searching responses (in the example in Fig. 4 at about -35 dB). In addition a correction, due to the difference of capacitance during calibration and measurement with the Rochelle salt microphone, had not been considered. In what follows, the threshold sound pressures are therefore given as larger by about 15 dB (a linear factor of about 5-6) than in the preliminary report. The shape of the auditory threshold curve is not changed thereby.

B. Operations on the Weberian apparatus

1. Extirpation of the malleus [= tripus, ed. note]

The largest ossicle of the Weberian apparatus, the malleus, which is connected to the Tunica externa of the swim bladder, can easily be removed in bullheads by means of an operation.

For purposes of the operation the fish was anesthetized by means of a 0.5% Urethane solution to a point where it would no longer react to mechanical stimuli, but where breathing movements remained visible. It was then fastened to a wax basin, lying on its side. The body bulges clearly caudally and dorsally at the origin of the pectoral fins. That is the spot where the fully filled swim bladder reaches to just below the skin. A 3 mm incision was made 1-2 mm ventrally of the lateral line and parallel to it. The incision reached forward to the pectoral girdle. Cautiously the skin was pulled apart with retractors, revealing the frontal part of the side of the swim bladder. The dorsal edge of the swim bladder was pushed somewhat ventrally and caudally with the probe. Now one inserted fine tweezers into the opening between swim bladder and spine and, with some practice, it was easy to grasp the malleus blindly, by sliding along the spinal column. The malleus could then be pulled out. Its connection to the incus [= claustrum, ed. note] broke by itself, its attachment to the swim bladder was cut with fine scissors. During the operation the swim bladder was pulled slightly out of place, but it could be replaced easily. It was not damaged in the operation, only the Tunica externa showed a slight rip. The filling of the swim bladder was not disturbed by this fact however. The skin wound was closed after the operation by means of several sutures of fine nylon thread. In closing up care was taken not to damage the lateral line. For the same reason the skin incision had been made sufficiently far away from it, although a somewhat more dorsal course would have been more convenient. The malleus on the other side was extirpated the next day in the same manner.

Animals A_{14}, A_{11} and A_{10} were operated; in A_{10} and A_{11} the threshold of hearing had previously been taken, A_{14} was only trained after the operation. All three animals remained alive until the end of experimentation. There was no abnormal finding on autopsy. The swim bladder was fully inflated and undamaged except for a small wound in the Tunica externa at the attachment of the mallei.

2. Elimination of the swim bladder

Elimination of the swim bladder by extirpation is not possible in the bullhead as the swim bladder on its dorsal side is attached to the spine and cannot be taken out without damage to the experimental animal. Thus the only possibility that remained was to destroy the acoustical properties of the swim bladder. Since it was impossible to collapse the bladder or to fill it with Ringer's solution, as it would soon be filled again with air by secretion or via the Ductus pneumaticus from the intestines, it was attempted to fill it with as neutral as possible a material, that would not be reabsorbed easily, and thus could replace a certain volume of air. For this purpose the swim bladders of A_1, A_4, A_7 and A_{12} were filled with paraffin oil. The operation, the details of which will be omitted here, apparently damaged the animals badly. They could be trained further, but the results were uncertain. The animals died at the latest two months after the operation. Various results showed on post mortem examination. There were always small remainders of air in the swim bladder, the paraffin oil had mostly disappeared. It remained uncertain, whether the swim bladder had not occasionally been fully filled with air during the course of the experiments.

C. Results of the training experiments

1. Normal animals

Mode of sound reception. A sound receiver may be actuated either through changing sound pressure or by displacement of the particles of the medium. The question, which parameter of the sound field effects the fish organ of hearing can be solved by determination of the auditory threshold at various water depths. With respect to the effective magnitude of the sound field, the auditory threshold would remain the same at different locations within the sound tank, with respect to the submerged coil, however, it would have to change with the depth at which the fish is swimming, as sound pressure and speed depend on water depth at constant voltage of the submerged coil.

Fig. 5 demonstrates two examples at two frequencies, one series taken in deep water and one just under the water surface. A in Fig. 4, the percentage of positive responses is shown as a function of coil voltage. The region of thresholds taken below the water surface is clearly displaced in the direction of higher voltages compared to the other series. The apparent rise in the threshold corresponds - within the range of error ($\pm$ 10 dB) - to the falling off of sound pressure with distance from the bottom surface (Fig. 3). At 800 Hz this correspondance is not quite as good. This is understandable: At 800 Hz the horizontal decrease of sound pressure with water depth is particularly strong (Table 1). Since the calculation of the difference of sound pressure between bottom and surface is based on the sound pressure on the middle vertical line and horizontal decay had been ignored, but since, on the other hand it is just the average sound pressure in the cage, which is hard to calculate, that determines the threshold, it seems clear that the drop of sound pressure in the vertical direction had been estimated somewhat too large.

The auditory threshold of the bullhead is therefore constant at each frequency, with respect to the sound pressure under water. We conclude then that the organ of hearing is a receiver for sound pressure. This fact is understandable considering the role of the swim bladder in reception and conduction of sound.

The auditory thresholds. On the basis of the results showing that the organ of hearing of the normal bullhead is a pressure receiver it makes sense to
calculate the absolute sound pressure from the relative sound thresholds obtained. Table 4 lists all measured results, Fig. 6 the achievement of the best
experimental animal (A4). Each point represents the threshold sound pressure
in the center of the training cage.

Measurements on a given fish for a particular frequency at different water
depths deviate widely, but these deviations lie within the wide range of error
that results from the unavoidable drop of sound pressure within the cage and
from errors in measuring absolute sound pressure as well as from the threshold
determination by means of the training method. This range of error is estimated
to be $\pm$ 10 dB. (The variance dispersion is greatest at 800 Hz. The reasons for
this fact are the same as those mentioned before).

Comparing thresholds on different animals, one is struck by the large differences in the absolute values, which may, in extreme instances, amount to two
orders of magnitude. (40 dB; at 800 Hz the lowest value for A4 was found to be
0.005 μ bar, the highest threshold value for A2 was 0.48 μ bar). Large individual differences in hearing capacities of fishes have also been observed by previous authors (see, for example, Stetter, 1929 and Hafen, 1935).

If one chooses the threshold sound pressure at 800 Hz (all fish were tested
at this frequency) as the basis of comparison, one can calculate the curve of
relative hearing thresholds (Fig. 7) from the averages of all animals. It has
the same form as the threshold curve of the best experimental animal (A4).

The sound pressure threshold of the bullhead is, according to this curve,
particularly constant at the lower frequencies; it only rises noticeably at values above 1600 Hz. As shown by the deviations of the extreme values from the
average, variance is also quite large in this case.

2. Operated animals

Auditory thresholds after extirpation of the malleus. Table 5 lists the
auditory thresholds of three animals after bilateral extirpation of the malleus.
In Fig. 8 the auditory threshold curve (calculated from the average of the obtained values) is compared with that of two animals before their operation. The
threshold sound pressure is increased by 30 to 100 times (30-40 dB) throughout
the frequency range. The shape of the auditory threshold curve remains the same
as before; At low frequencies of 60-800 Hz the threshold remains almost constant,
the first increase lies between 800 and 3000 Hz.

The operation sharply reduces the hearing range of the animal (in agreement
with investigations of von Frisch, 1938 and von Frisch and Stetter, 1932). The
organ of hearing remains now as then a pressure receiver, since the threshold remains constant with respect to sound pressure at varying water depths.

The two values at 120 Hz for animal A10 (see Table 5) were not included in
the graphic display (Fig. 8) since they were considered to be in error. The
threshold of the two other animals were not taken at this frequency.

Measurements after filling of swim bladder. The thresholds after filling
of the swim bladder with paraffin oil are shown in Table 6. At some frequencies
hearing of the animals was almost normal, at other frequencies it was elevated,
without any connection being apparent. The experimental conditions (success of
operation) were so unclear that an evaluation of the results is impossible.

IV. Acoustical properties of the swim bladder

A. General part

The swim bladder of fish as a first approximation can be considered from a physical point of view to be a gas bubble in water. The acoustical properties of small spherical gas bubbles in liquid are knonw (Meyer and Tamm, 1939): The volume of an enclosed quantity of gas is inversely proportional to pressure at constant temperature. An air bubble in water must therefore change its volume periodically under the influence of sound pressure, it is forced to pulse at the sound frequency. Like all bodies capable of vibration, it has its natural frequency and a certain damping factor that determine the way in which their frequencies depend on the frequency of the source. The natural frequency of such a bubble may be calculated from the elasticity of the gas volume and the mass of the vibrating medium. It is, unless one can neglect surface tension between gas and liquid at very low frequencies, inversely proportional to the diameter of the bubble. For air bubbles in water at normal air pressure the following relation holds:

$$f_0 \cdot d = 6.57 \text{ kHz} \cdot \text{mm}$$

where f_0 is the natural frequency of the bubble in kHz and d its diameter in mm.

The swim bladder also must follow the vibrations of a sound field in water. One cannot tell a priori to what extent the laws of vibration valid for free spherical air bubbles also hold for the swim bladder of complex shape. Since the swim bladder of Ostariophysi certainly plays an important role in their auditory capacities, the physical properties of their swim bladders were investigated.

Compared to air bubbles in water, the swim bladder shows the following characteristics, which may influence its mode of vibration:

1. It is not spherical, but of a complicated shape. In many Ostariophysi it consists in fact of two parts, separated by a deep constriction, of which only the frontal part, the Camera aerea Weberiana is connected to the chain of the Weberian ossicles.

2. The volume of air within the bladder is separated from the outside by several layers of different material and diverse structure (Tunica interna and externa; in some fishes, e.g., Cobitis and Nemachilus in addition by a bony capsule with few openings. (Chranilov, 1927)).

3. The membranes are themselves not uniform (fibrous structure, insertion of Weberian ossicles and various ligaments, attachment to spine and other bones).

4. Outside its specific membranes the swim bladder is not surrounded by water but by the soft and bony parts of the body.

5. The interval pressure of the swim bladder does not equal the external pressure, but may be higher (tension of swim bladder membrane; Evans and Damant, 1928).

Experimental investigation of the swim bladder inside the body of the fish was not feasible. The swim bladder had to be dissected out. A part of the conditions existing within the body of the fish could therefore not be considered in these investigations. In any case some important conclusions could be based on the acoustical behavior of the isolated swim bladder.

Measurements were made on the swim bladder of the minnow (Phoxinus laevis), which can be dissected easily from the body. In the minnow the swim bladder is divided into two almost completely separate parts. Only the auterior part, the Camera aerea Weberiana is connected to the last and largest of the Weberian

157

ossicles, the malleus, and therefore of importance for hearing. Morphologically (Chranilov, 1929) and physiologically the whole of the swim bladder of the bullhead corresponds to this part. Since it was impossible to dissect out both parts of the swim bladder of the minnow without injury and to hold them in their natural relation to one another without disturbing supports in the water, the influence of vibrations of the second part of the swim bladder on the Camera aerea could not be investigated. The uniform swim bladder of the bullhead should generally behave like the Camera aerea of the minnow.

B. Preparation of the Camera aerea of the minnow

The minnow was decapitated and its ventral side cut open to the vent. The intestines on the ventral side of the swim bladder were pushed aside, the Ductus pneumaticus ligated and cut between the ligature and intestines. After removal of the intestines the Tunica externa of the Camera aerea was torn open and the fully inflated Tunica interna carefully removed with a blunt probe. It was now held only by the narrow connecting canal between both parts of the bladder. This canal was also ligated and the posterior chamber severed just behind the ligature. The Camera aerea was now removed from the body, carefully cleaned again of still attached bits of tissue, and then was ready for the experiment in its natural filled state.

The thick, fibrous and easily torn Tunica externa, which encloses the Tunica interna loosely and which can be moved in all directions with respect to it, unfortunately, could not be removed intact from the body, as it is grown on to ligaments and the mallei. When, in the following account, the swim bladder is mentioned, it refers only to the Camera aerea surrounded by its Tunica interna.

The swim bladder was fastened by means of a thread, that also served to ligate the other part of the bladder, to a fine wire hook, held by a glass rod, at a distance of about one cm.

C. Method of measurement

The method of Meyer and Tamm (1939) was used to measure the vibrations of the swim bladder. In this method the shadow of the freely suspended bladder is allowed to image underwater on a photocell. The size of the shadow on the photocell changes with the volume of the bladder and therefore varies the electric current generated by it. This method is rather sensitive.

Method. A point source of light delivered a practically parallel beam of light of even density via a condenser. The swim bladder was illuminated, as it was floating in the water, through the glass panes of the sound tank and imaged on the photocell after magnification by a second lens. The swim bladder appeared on the photocell as a sharply bounded shadow, since at the water and air boundary within the bladder the light rays were for the most part totally reflected. Only those rays which fell perpendicularly on the wall of the swim bladder passed through it to fall on the photocell and permitted the interior of the shadow to appear brighter than the outside. This bright center in the shadow could be darkened by means of a central stop introduced into the light path at a suitable place, so that the whole shadow surface could be darkened evenly. A second stop, close in front of the photocell, could eliminate as big a portion of the shadow of the swim bladder as one might want, so that portions of the edge of the swim bladder could be investigated separately. For measuring the vibrations of the whole swim bladder, the major part of the illuminated surface of the photocell was covered, in order to increase sensitivity, and only a strip about one mm wide around the edge of the shadow was left free. The photocell was a selenium element with a flat response curve; its current output was proportional to the illuminated surface. When the shadow of the swim bladder changed its surface in the rhythm of the sound waves, an A.C. output with a frequency equal to vibrations of the swim bladder became impressed on the always present D.C. output of the photocell. This A.C. output was passed to the first grid of an A.C. amplifier via an R.C. coupling and then measured by a VTVM (vacuum tube voltmeter). The excursion of the VTVM was proportional to the amplitude of the swim bladder vibrations. Ear phones could be substituted for the VTVM for direct acoustical checking.

At the time the swim bladder vibrations were being investigated, measurement of absolute values of the sound pressure underwater had not yet been made possible, and it was sufficient to measure the amplitude of the displacement of the swim bladder wall in relative terms. In addition, the sound tank was filled to different depths during the various tests. The acoustical data of the swim bladder investigation therefore do not correspond to all those described on page 224.

The apparatus was most sensitive to extraneous vibrations. This fact was most noticeable when small portions of the edge of the swim bladder were being investigated separately. In this case the least shaking of the suspended swim bladder affected the illuminated surface of the photocell relatively strongly. These, mainly low frequency, vibrations could not be eliminated mechanically. They were therefore cut off electrically in the amplifier.

D. Results

Oscillations of the swim bladder could be observed in the frequency range of 200 to almost 3000 Hz. There was no measurement at lower frequencies, at higher frequencies the excursions of the VTVM could no longer be distinguished from the amplifier noise.

All swim bladders showed particularly large oscillations in the frequency range between 400 and 1100 Hz. At these frequencies, however, sound pressure also was high and hard to measure, so that the observed amplitudes appeared to be less determined by the mechanical properties of the swim bladder than by apparatus conditions. All later measurements were therefore carried out only at frequencies above 1100 Hz at which sound pressure was more or less constant.

The resonant frequencies of swim bladders on the basis of their volume would be expected at frequencies above 1100 Hz according to conditions holding for free air bubbles.

Each frequency curve indeed shows a maximum above 1100 Hz depending on swim bladder size. The resonant frequencies of some swim bladders are entered in Table 7. If one calculates the volume of a sphere equivalent to the volume of the swim bladder and multiplies its diameter by the appropriate resonant frequencies, one obtains values which average to 7.2 kHz. (The bladder volume was not measured directly but calculated, the bladder being taken as cylindrical in shape as a first approximation). The product 7.2 Hz mm deviates only slightly from the value for air bubbles (6.57 kHz mm).

The isolated swim bladder underwater therefore shows a clearly defined resonant frequency in spite of its deviation from spherical shape. This frequency is inversely proportional to the diameter of a sphere of equal volume.

As an apparatus check resonant frequencies of air bubbles in water were determined in the same way. Table 7 illustrates some numerical examples. The product of bubble diameter and resonant frequency amounts to 6.0 kHz mm on the average. It shows therefore also only a slight deviation from the expected value.

It could naturally be expected that the swim bladder vibrations would be damped more strongly compared to those of free air bubbles. The wall of the swim bladder offers resistance to the vibrations that would increase the damping. Since the resonance curve of the swim bladder, i.e., its amplitude as a function of frequency (at constant sound pressure), could be recorded easily, one can calculate the damping from the half-widths Δf. Some resonance curves of air bubbles and swim bladders are shown in Fig. 9. The half-widths determined graphically from these curves and the damping calculated from them are also entered in Table 7. The logarithmic decrement δ of swim bladder vibrations is about twice that of air bubbles.

The difference between the two means is statistically significant, as the probability of accepting the null hypothesis of equality of the two series is less than 0.0002. The dependency of damping on sound frequency described by Meyer and Tamm (1939) lies below the limits of accuracy of my apparatus at the frequency range used.

At the levels used, resonant frequency and natural frequency of the swim bladders and air bubbles practically coincide.

The question of how great a damping of the swim bladder might occur in its natural surrounding cannot be answered by direct measurement. It was attempted, therefore, to embed the swim bladder in a watery medium of a consistency closer to that of living tissue than that of pure water: A swim bladder was embedded carefully in a stiff gelatine solution and a small rectangular block, containing the swim bladder, cut out of the gelatinous mass. The resonance curve of a swim bladder before and after embedding is shown in Fig. 10. The decrement of the bladder in water before and after embedding in gelatine amounted to 0.22 and 0.27 respectively, whereas in the gelatine it was 0.42. In addition, the resonant frequencies of the swim bladder were shifted to lower frequencies in the gelatine. This shift in resonance cannot be explained as merely due to the higher degree of damping.

The maximum amplitude of a system under forced vibrations coincides with its natural frequency only when the damping $\delta=0$. At $\delta>0$ it is shifted to lower frequencies. The following relation holds:

$$f_m = f_0 \sqrt{1 - \frac{\delta^2}{2\pi^2}}$$

where f_m designates the frequency of the amplitude maximum (see, for example, Trendelenburg, 1950).

The observed shift in resonance would call for a damping effect $\delta=1.25$. The shift in resonance must therefore have another reason (for example, expansion of the swim bladder during embedding in the slightly warmed gelatine and persistence of this expansion after cooling due to tension in the gelatinous mass). After freeing the swim bladder from the gelatine the old resonant frequency was again measured (Table 7). The slight increase in damping from 0.22 to 0.27 lies within the uncertainty of measurement.

Qualitatively, the measurements point to the fact that the tissues surrounding the swim bladder in the living animal must sharply damp the vibrations of the swim bladder wall. The damping is therefore surely much stronger than the decrement of the isolated <u>Camera</u> <u>aerea</u> would indicate.

During the measurement it was noted that the amplitude of vibrations was not the same at all locations on the wall of the swim bladder. Their amplitudes were therefore further measured separately in the following way: The shadow imaged on the photocell was closed off by the diaphragm except for a small round hole. A portion of the shadow equal to the length of the hole's diameter was then projected through the hole. Photocell and diaphragm were rigidly connected and could be moved simultaneously in the image plane. Thus the whole edge of the shadow of the swim bladder could be scanned. The swim bladder was excited in its resonant frequency and the edge of its shadow traced several times in succession in some 30 sections. Eventually means were taken of five measurements of each section. Fig. 11 shows the typical vibratory mode of a swim bladder. The inner line represents the outline of the shadow of the swim bladder, illuminated from the dorsal side. It is divided into the sections used in measurement. The average relative amplitude of vibration is entered in the center of each section perpendicular to the edge and the points connected by the outside line. The stationary representation of the swim bladder vibrations clearly shows that some parts are subject to greater displacement than others. Specially affected appears to be the cranial side of the swim bladder (and particularly the lateral corners) and certain parts of the lateral edge. The attachment of the mallei occurs on the cranial side of the swim bladder, somewhat on the dorsal side, however, and could not be included precisely in this experiment. But at least in their vicinity the swim bladder carries out particularly large excursions.

The differences in the magnitude of the amplitudes can be explained by locally different properties of the Tunica interna. One might expect that the tissues surrounding the swim bladder in the body of the fish also influence the amplitudes. How large this influence is and whether the places of attachment of the Weberian ossicles possess preferred amplitudes cannot be stated. One might assume that differences in amplitude, as large as those observed in the experiment, may be traced to the high sound pressure used and to the isolation of the swim bladder.

In this connection it must be mentioned that embedding the swim bladder in gelatine eliminates completely the differences in amplitudes.

V. Discussion of results

A. Importance of the swim bladder in hearing

The physical processes in the organ of hearing of Ostariophysi can be described as follows: The swim bladder is excited by the changing sound pressure to pulsating vibrations. This process transforms the changes in pressure into movement of the swim bladder wall (physical transformation of stimulus, according to Autrum, 1942). The movement of the swim bladder wall is transmitted to the endolymph of both labyrinths by means of the sound conducting apparatus (Weberian ossicles, Sinus impar Canalis communicans transversus) and there stimulates the specific sensory cells in Sacculus and Lagena in which the physical stimulus is transformed into excitation (physiological transformation of stimulus).

The stimulus acting on the sensory cells is therefore determined primarily by the movement of the swim bladder wall. The function derived from the general equation for forced vibrations that holds for the amplitudes of vibration of the swim bladder wall is given by $A = A_s \cdot R$ (see, for example, Trendelenburg, 1950). Where R is a resonant function of the form

$$R = \frac{1}{\sqrt{(1 - \nu^2) + \frac{\delta^2}{\pi^2} \nu^2}}$$

($\nu = f/f_0$, f = sound frequency, f_0 = natural frequency of swim bladder, δ =

logarithmic decrement of swim bladder vibrations) and A_S is a function of sound pressure, therefore constant at constant sound pressure. The amplitudes of vibrations of the swim bladder wall therefore depend only on one variable, the sound frequency f.

The average natural frequency f_0 of the swim bladder, in case of the bullheads examined, can be estimated from the size of the swim bladder at about 1200 Hz. Damping is certainly as great as in the Camera aerea of the minnow. However, it influences the dependency of amplitudes on frequency only in the vicinity of the locations where resonance occurs, so that in the following calculations the rounded value of $\delta = 1$ can be assumed without doing violence to the data.

The amplitude of the vibrations of the swim bladder wall as a function of frequency at constant sound pressure is plotted in curve A of Fig. 12. Amplitudes in dB are given on the left ordinate. They are constant below the natural frequency f_0 of the swim bladder and decrease with increasing frequency above f_0 (sign of ordinate!). The peaking at $\nu = 1$ is quite small. The sensitivity of the organ of hearing is inversely proportional to the threshold sound pressure.

Sensitivity is constant at low frequencies and decreases above a specific frequency (the swim bladder's natural frequency) with increasing frequency, since the threshold sound pressure increases above this point (cf. Fig. 7). The relative sensitivity of the auditory organ is also entered on Fig. 12. The values were taken from Fig. 7. The appropriate relative threshold sound pressure is entered on the right ordinate. As both ordinates are given in logarithmic scale, the dB values for threshold sound pressure on the right ordinate must have the reverse of the sign of the sensitivity (left ordinate) to which they are inversely proportional.

The sensitivity curve (only obtained values are plotted) follows the amplitude curve pretty well over a wide range of frequencies. They diverge only at very high frequencies (above 3000 Hz). Up to 3000 Hz, then, sensitivity of the organ of hearing and amplitude of vibration of the swim bladder wall are proportional. Or in other words: The threshold sound pressure is just large enough to cause a constant threshold amplitude of vibrations of the swim bladder wall. Above 3000 Hz the sensitivity of the organ of hearing is less, threshold sound pressure is higher and in this connection a greater threshold amplitude of the swim bladder wall vibrations is necessary to just elicit a threshold excitation.

In addition to the frequency characteristics, Fig. 12 also has entered on it velocity $S(= A \cdot \omega)$ and acceleration $B(= A \cdot \omega^2)$ of the swim bladder wall. The left ordinate is valid for them also. These curves can be displaced up or down at will, since the ordinate only refers to their relative values, and their crossing at 800 cps is arbitrary. The sensitivity curve does not agree with these two curves, the amplitudes of vibration of the labyrinthine endolymph possess the same frequency characteristics as the amplitudes of the swim bladder vibrations. One can make the following statement regarding changes in frequency characteristics of the sound conducting apparatus: It is a system of coupled oscillators. Each section is excited by the vibrations of the one before it and transmits its vibrations to the next one. This transmission occurs at all frequencies in equal amounts only when the frequency of the previous vibrations lie below the natural frequency of the following section. Frequencies above the respective natural frequencies are transmitted the worst, the higher their frequency. In addition, as in man's ossicles (Dahlmann, 1929, 1930), the coupling of the Weberian ossicles may be less also, at higher frequencies. This fact must also lead to a poorer transmission of higher frequencies. If the frequency characteristics of the swim bladder vibrations are changed at all during their transmission to the labyrinth, this change would have to be noted primarily by a poorer transmission at higher frequencies.

We can understand, therefore, why the threshold sound pressure has to be higher at the upper frequencies, than would be necessary to achieve a constant amplitude of swim bladder vibration. Apparently, it is important that the effective amplitude at the labyrinth remain constant at all frequencies. In order to achieve this constancy, the threshold sound pressure (and with it naturally the amplitude of swim bladder wall vibrations) has to be higher, the poorer the transmission of the sound conducting apparatus.

Since a definite minimum amplitude, that is independent of frequency, appears to be necessary, one can conclude that the amplitude of vibrations in the labyrinth constitutes the adequate stimulus for the sensory cells of the sacculus and in the lagena.

This assumption is supported by the investigations of Steinhausen (1933) and Lowenstein and Sand (1940) on the function of the semicircular canals of the labyrinth and the work of von Holst (1950) on the function of the utriculus in fish. They reveal that the adequate stimulus for the sensory cells of cristae of the semicircular canals and the macula utriculi consists of the lateral displacement (shearing) of the haircells. They respond then to the same physical stimulus as the sensory cells of sacculus and lagena. Since all sensory epithelium of the labyrinth originates from a common source, this response to the same form of stimulation is understandable.

The manner of stimulation of the sensory cells in detail is unclear. Presumably the otoliths lying on top of the sensory epithelium play a role. DeVries (1950) determined the natural frequency of the dilation vibrations of the sacculus otoliths in the perch (Perca) at approximately 40 Hz. These otoliths must therefore behave as rigid bodies with respect to frequencies which lie considerably higher. Whether findings valid for the perch otoliths (perch is not an ostariophysine) apply to the otoliths of the much smaller bullhead appears questionable.

The labyrinthine sensory cells of the ostariophysi are stimulated not only by vibrations originating in the swim bladder and transmitted to the sound conducting apparatus of the labyrinth, but also by direct stimulation by water particles vibrating due the sound field in the water. These vibrations must also be transmitted to the labyrinth in some way. After elimination of the Weberian apparatus (including the swim bladder) these vibrations alone will act on the labyrinth: A comparison suggests itself between the amplitudes of vibration of an underwater air bubble that are caused by the same sound pressure.

The particle amplitudes in such a sound field may be calculated from the relationship:

$$\frac{p}{A_T \, 2\pi \, f} = \rho \cdot c$$

Those of the air bubble by the relationship:

$$A = A_s \cdot R$$

In the latter case one has to determine the constant A_s, which can be calculated for a spherical air bubble from the formula:

$$A_s = \frac{r_0 \, \rho}{3\chi \, P_0}$$

Derivation of the equation for A_c: If a sound pressure p, in addition to the hydrostatic pressure P_0, is exerted on an air bubble of volume V_0 then the following law holds:

$$(P_0 + p) \, v^\chi = P_0 \, V_0^{\chi}.$$

163

From this we get:

$$V = V_0 \cdot \left(1 + \frac{p}{P_0}\right)^{-\frac{1}{\chi}}$$

and for a spherical volume:

$$r = r_0 \cdot \left(1 + \frac{p}{P_0}\right)^{-\frac{1}{3\chi}} .$$

As sound pressure p is always small compared to the hydrostatic pressure P_0 we have approximately:

$$r = r_0 \cdot \left(1 - \frac{p}{3\chi P_0}\right).$$

The displacement of the bubble surface is then:

$$A_s = r_0 - r = r_0 - r_0 + \frac{r_0\, p}{3\chi P_0} = \frac{r_0\, p}{3\chi P_0} .$$

The following terms are used in these equations:

A = Amplitude of vibrations of air bubble surface
A_s= Static displacement of air bubble surface
A_T= Amplitude of vibrations of water particles
c = Sound velocity in water (= $1.4\ 10^5$ cm/sec)
f = Sound frequency
p = Sound pressure
P_0= Hydrostatic pressure on air bubble (assumed to be 10^6 μbar in this case)
r_0= Radius of air bubble
R = A resonance function (see p. 247)
χ = Adiabatic coefficient (1.4 for atmospheric air)
ρ = Density of water (= 1 gm/cm^3)

The relationship:

$$\frac{A}{A_T} = \frac{r_0\, 2\pi\, \rho L}{3\chi\, P_0} \cdot fR$$

tells us how much greater will be the amplitude of vibrations of the air bubble surface than the amplitude of vibrations of the water particles in an undisturbed sound field. Under the assumption of an air bubble radius of 0.28 cm, a corresponding natural frequency f_0 of 1200 Hz and a damping factor $\delta = 1$ (valued approximately true for the swim bladders of the bullheads examined), one obtains the following values at the frequencies indicated.

Frequency (Hz)	50	100	200	400	800	1600	2400	6000	10000
A/A_T		3	6	12	24	79	110	48	11	7

From these calculations the advantage is clearly apparent that the transformation of sound pressure into movement of the swim bladder wall gives to the hearing ability of Ostariophysi, since the amplitude of vibrations of air bubble surfaces (and therefore also the amplitude of vibrations of the swim bladder wall) is larger over the whole range of frequencies examined than that of the particles of water. Of course the numerical values given here apply only under the stated conditions (to a sound field with progressing sound waves and a spherical air bubble of stated size).

The true relationship of the swim bladder amplitude versus that of the undisturbed sound field and the value that this proportion may reach in the labyrinth remain unknown. An ideal progressive sound field as that on which we have based these considerations, is of course never to be found under natural conditions in the animal's environment and nor is it found in laboratory experimentation.

The fact that the organ of hearing of the normal bullhead is a receiver for sound pressure appears to be understandable, since the oscillations of the swim bladder wall which are transmitted to the labyrinth, are caused by the changing sound pressure. After interruption of the sound conducting apparatus by extirpation of the mallei [= tripus (ed.)] we would then expect that there would be no more sound pressure reception. This requirement appears to be contradicted by the experimental findings in which the threshold of hearing, after extirpation of the mallei, depended on water depth of the fish in the same way as before. According to these findings, then, there still appeared to be pressure reception. These results, however, are open to various interpretations:

1. The decision on whether sound pressure or particle movement reception occurred was based on the fact that sound pressure decreased with distance from the bottom surface of the sound tank, whereas sound velocity (and the amplitude of oscillations of water particles proportional to it) increased. This increase of amplitude in the oscillation of water particles with increasing distance from the bottom surface concerns, however, only the vertical component of amplitude, the horizontal component may behave similar to sound pressure, i.e., decrease also with increasing distance from the bottom surface. If the sensory cells of the labyrinth respond preferentially to the direction of oscillation in the frontal plane of the animal and the horizontal component shows about the same drop as the sound pressure, then pressure reception may only be simulated.

It appears not unlikely that sensory cells are able to respond preferentially to a certain direction of oscillation, if one considers that the Weberian ossicles which normally conduct the stimulus to the sensory cells, also oscillate preferentially in the frontal plane of the animal.

2. The oscillations of the swim bladder wall are not limited to this wall alone, but disperse in the adjoining medium. The amplitude of the particles becomes less as distance from swim bladder increases. In this manner the vibrations reach the labyrinth also in a direct manner, i.e., without the mediation of the sound conducting apparatus, only these vibrations are smaller, when they arrive there, than if they had been transmitted via the ossicles. The swim bladder will then have to vibrate at a greater amplitude so that the vibrations may end up with the same amplitude in the labyrinth. The threshold sound pressure would therefore have to be higher, since the vibration transmitted via the swim bladder apparently is the decisive factor. The shape of the threshold curve depends then, as before the operation, on the resonance characteristics of the swim bladder (cf. Fig. 8).

Accordingly, the swim bladder may also be important for the hearing capacity of nonostariophysi, which lack a sound conducting apparatus.

A clarification of this question might have been made possible by filling or extirpating the swim bladder. Experiments aimed in this direction did not yield useable results, however, since, among other things, it was not possible to judge clearly whether the swim bladder (or even the intestines) were possible filled partially or completely by air. von Frisch and Stetter (1932) were successful in extirpating the swim bladder of the minnow. The operated animal still possessed a clearly apparent, but weakened, hearing ability. The auterior part of the intestines was always filled with air. Air bubbles in the intestines may also possibly of course be of importance for the hearing ability of fishes.

B. Comparison of the auditory threshold of
the bullhead with that of other animals

A clear picture of the performance of the sense of hearing in bullheads can
be gained from a comparison with other animals and with man. The following physical magnitudes are available for this purpose:
1. Threshold sound pressures;
2. The sound energy impinging on the organ of hearing at threshold; best
rendered by the energy density (Watt sec/cm^3) of the undisturbed sound field;
3. The threshold amplitude at the organ of hearing.
The threshold sound pressure for man (see Sivian and White, 1933) and bird
(bullfinch, Schwartzkopff, 1949) are practically equal (7 x 10^{-5} and 1 x 10^{-4}
μbar respectively) in the optimum hearing range (about 3200 Hz for both). The
threshold sound pressure for the bullhead amounts to 5 x 10^{-3} to 2 x 10^{-2} μbar in
the optimal hearing range of about 800 Hz, on the average to 1 x 10^{-2} μbar (see
Table 4). It is then considerably higher.
The energy density E_R in a sound field with progressive waves can be calculated from the sound pressure p according to the relationship

$$E_R = \frac{p^2}{\rho c^2}$$

(see, for example, Trendelenburg, 1950) in which ρ is the density of the medium
and c the velocity of sound. For the human ear the least still perceptible energy
density of the undisturbed soundfield then amounts to 3 x 10^{-22} Wsec/cm^3. In their
optimal hearing range, animals living in an atmospheric and an aquatic medium are
consequently of equal sensitivity, if one compares the energy required to reach
threshold in the optimal range. At low frequencies the bullhead has much better
hearing than man (at 60 cps, for example, the proportion of energy densities at
the threshold is 1:10^4 [5 x 10^{-21} to 6 x 10^{-17} Wsec/cm^3]), at high frequencies,
however, his hearing is much worse (at 10,000 Hz, for example, the energy densities are 10^6:1). The threshold curves for man, bullfinch and bullhead are presented in Fig. 13.
The amplitude of the vibrations of the swim bladder wall can be calculated
if one assumes that the swim is spherical as a first approximation. The following relationship then applies:

$$A = \frac{r_0 \ p}{3_X \ P_0} \quad x \ R.$$

Utilizing the values for the swim bladder mentioned, one finds a minimum amplitude of vibrations at 1600 Hz. At a threshold sound pressure of 1 x 10^{-2} μbar,
the amplitude of vibration would be 7 x 10^{-10} cm in this scale. Wilska (1935)
found a value of 6 x 10^{-10} cm for the threshold amplitudes of the human eardrum
in the optimal frequency range (2000 - 3000 Hz). Schwartzkopff (1950) found a
threshold value of 10^{-10} cm for the amplitude of vibrations at the ear drum of
the bullfinch. The vibration sensitive organ of the cockroach *Periplaneta* still
responds to an amplitude of the substrate of 2 x 10^{-10} cm (Autrum, 1943). The
threshold vibration amplitudes of the bullhead swim bladder are consequently
only slightly larger than the threshold amplitudes cited for the ear drum of the
other animals.
Of the cited values, threshold energy density and displacement amplitude
agree for animals in an atmospheric and aquatic environment, sound pressures differ by two orders of magnitude. The energy density (= intensity) at the sense

organ allows an immediate comparison, because its definition is independent of the medium and almost independent of the specific physical characteristics of the sound receptor. It tells us how much energy has to be present to make the sense organ respond. The displacement amplitudes are comparable because the sound can get to the sensory endings only via the movement of the sound receptor membranes. The fact that among the displacement values, the amplitude in the fish ear should be accorded a special position, has been discussed. Of course the agreement between threshold amplitudes of swim bladder wall and ear drum may be only due to chance, in that it is not known at all, what amplitudes reach the sensory cells themselves. The agreement in the order of magnitude of displacement threshold amplitude in animals living in an atmospheric environment, air chamber walls in fish and extremities of insects are indeed remarkable.

Threshold sound pressures are unsuitable for comparison, as: 1. these organs do not respond to pressure itself, but to the movement caused by this pressure (sound pressure is not an adequate stimulus for organs) and 2. the same pressure magnitude in air at the ear drum, on the one hand, and in water at the air chamber, on the other hand, produce very different amplitudes.

Summary

The absolute thresholds of hearing in the frequency range 60 - 10,000 Hz are determined for the bullhead (<u>Amiurus nebulosus</u>). The method described, only permits measurements whose error must be estimated at about ± 10 dB.

The organ of hearing of the bullhead is a sound pressure receptor, so that the hearing thresholds may be given in units of sound pressure (μbar = dyn /cm^2).

In the range from 60 - 1600 Hz the threshold sound pressure is approximately constant; above 1600 Hz it rises sharply with frequency (see Fig. 7).

After bilateral extirpation of the <u>malleus</u> [= <u>tripus</u> (ed.)] sensitivity fell 1/30 - 1/100 (about 30 - 40 dB), however the shape of the auditory threshold curve remained the same (see Fig. 8).

Attempts to eliminate the swim bladder remained unsuccessful.

The natural frequency and damping of pulsations were measured for the isolated <u>Camera</u> <u>aerea</u> (auterior chamber of swim bladder) of the minnow. The natural frequency of the swim bladder is, inversely proportional to its mean diameter. The logarithmic decrement of its vibrations averages 0.25. One may assume that damping is greater inside the fish body.

The shape of the threshold sound pressure curve can be understood on basis of the acoustical properties of the Weberian apparatus, if one assumes that a minimum amplitude of endolymph vibration in the labyrinth, independent of frequency, is necessary for threshold stimulation of the sensory cells.

A comparison between displacement amplitudes of a spherical air bubble in water and the particles of an underwater soundfield with progressive waves, at the same sound pressure, shows the advantage conferred by the transformation of sound pressure to displacement of the swim bladder wall on the hearing ability of ostariophysi.

The sensitivity to sound of bullheads (demonstrated by threshold energy density in an undisturbed sound field), in its optimal frequency range (about 800 Hz), is equal to that of man and bird (bullfinch) in their optimal sound range (about 3200 Hz); on the other hand, the sensitivity of the bullhead to sound at low frequencies (for example 60 Hz) is considerably higher, at high frequencies (for example 10,000 Hz), however, it is considerably lower than that of man or bird (see Fig. 13). The calculated threshold displacement amplitudes of the swim bladder wall are only slightly larger than those of the human or avian tympanic membrane.

Table 1. Decay of sound pressure along the horizontal in the sound tank.

Frequency Hz	Difference in sound pressure between a point 4 cm from the center to the value in the center. (dB)								
	Direction of microphone in degrees								
	0	45	90	135	180	225	270	315	360=0
	(a) At a plane 6 cm above bottom								
60	No measureable difference								
120	No measureable difference								
200	Difference < 1 dB								
400	-2,5	-2,5	-2,5	-2	-1	-2	-2	-2,5	-2
800	-6	-6	-2,5	-1	-0,5	-2	-2,5	-8,5	-6
1600	0	0	-1,5	-4,5	-4,5	-4	-2,5	-1	0
3000	-5,5	-5,5	-4	-4	-3	-5	-3	-5	-4
6000	-3	-3	-3	-2,5	-2,5	-3,5	-2,5	-3	-2
10000	Violent uncontrollable variations at the least movement of the microphone. Largest difference about - 8 dB.								
	(b) At a plane 3.5 cm above bottom								
60	No measureable difference								
120	No measureable difference								
200	No measureable difference								
400	-1,5	-1,5	-0,5	-0,5	-0,5	-1,5	-1,5	-1,5	-1,5
800	-6	-11	-2,5	0	+2,5	0	-2,5	-8,5	-8,5
1600	0	0	0	-2	-4	-3,5	-1	-0,5	0
3000	-6	-5	-3	-4	-5	-6	-6	-6	-6
6000	-3,5	-3,5	-2	-2	-2	-2	-2	-2	-2
10000	-2	-1,5	+3,5	+5,5	+5,5	+6,5	+5,5	-0,5	-1,5

Table 2

Training Behavior of Normal Bullheads

Animal No.	Frequency (Hz)	1st resp.	Criterion	Threshold	End
			at trial no.		
A_1	800	47	66	560	3303
A_2	1600	39	69	385	2204
A_4	400	41	53	540	3083
A_5	800	18	112	472	1395
A_6	800	13	198	-	620
A_7	800	8	145	491	1416
A_8	800	19	173	491	842
A_9	800	62	93	-	326
A_{10}	800	11	21	336	931
A_{11}	800	13	31	371	1025
A_{12}	800	18	52	389	389
A_{13}	800	12	52	421	421

Table 3a

Example of Evaluation of Trial Series

	Training trials at intensity in dB				Blank Trials	
	-20	-25	-30	-35		
+	8	5	2	2	+	8
-	1	4	6	6	-	2
%+	89	56	25	25	%-	20

Table 3b

Determination of Threshold for A_{11} at 200 Hz

	Training trials - %+							
Trial Day	Intensity in dB						Blank Trials %-
	-10	-15	-20	-25	-30	-35	
26.6.51	100	100	90	80	57		11
28.6.51			89	56	25	25	20
30.6.51			78	67	50	14	10
Average	(100)	(100)	86	68	44	20	14
p.100	-	-	0.02	0.2	4.5	29	-

Table 4

Absolute Threshold of the Normal
Bullhead in μ bar = dynes/cm^2.

(h = high, m = middle, t = low; cf. Fig. 3a-c.)

Animal	Height in Tank	Frequency in Hz									
		60	120	200	400	800	1600	3000	5000	6000	10,000
A$_1$	h	-	0.03	-	-	0.0062	-	-	-	-	-
	m	0.041	0.025	0.13	0.063	0.031	0.012	0.27	1.9	-	41
	t	-	0.027	-	-	0.030	-	-	-	-	-
	Average	0.04	0.03	0.1	0.06	0.02	-	-	-	-	-
A$_2$	m	-	0.5	0.27	-	0.55	0.48	0.68	-	-	-
	t	-	-	-	-	0.48	-	-	-	-	-
	Average	-	0.5	-	-	0.5	-	-	-	-	-
A$_4$	h	0.038	-	0.011	-	0.005	-	-	-	-	-
	m	0.015	0.038	0.043	0.020	0.022	0.015	0.14	-	4.6	41
	t	0.027	-	0.0068	-	0.012	-	-	-	-	-
	Average	0.03	0.04	0.01	0.02	0.01	-	-	-	-	-
A$_5$	h	-	-	-	-	0.04	-	-	-	-	-
	m	-	-	-	-	0.14	-	-	-	-	-
	t	-	-	0.86	-	0.21	-	-	-	-	-
	Average	-	-	0.9	-	0.1	-	-	-	-	-
A$_7$	h	-	0.019	-	-	0.012	-	-	-	-	-
	m	-	-	-	-	0.08	-	-	-	-	-
	t	-	0.051	-	-	0.076	-	-	-	-	-
	Average	-	0.03	-	-	0.04	-	-	-	-	-
A$_{10}$	t	-	-	0.03	-	0.06	0.074	0.34	-	-	-
A$_{11}$	t	-	-	0.03	-	0.07	0.12	0.34	-	-	-
A$_{12}$	t	-	-	-	-	0.5	-	-	-	-	-

170

Table 5

Absolute Threshold of Bullhead in μ bar (= dynes/cm^2)
After Bilateral <u>Malleus</u> Extirpation.

Animal	Height in Tank	Frequency in Hz						
		60	120	200	400	800	3000	6000
A_{10}	h	-	(0.028)	0.89	1.2	-	-	-
	mt	2.7	(0.071)	2.7	3.2	-	30	-
	Average	3	-	2	2	-	30	-
A_{11}	h	1.3	-	2.2	-	0.85	2.1	-
	mt	-	-	1.1	-	2.9	7.6	550
	Average	1	-	2	-	2	4	550
A_{14}	h	-	-	2.0	-	0.54	-	-
	mt	-	-	6.7	-	2.6	54	-
	Average	-	-	3	-	1	54	-

Table 6

Absolute Threshold of Bullhead in μ bar (= dynes/cm^2)
After Filling of Swim Bladder with Paraffin Oil.

Animal	Height in Tank	Frequency in cps			
		120	200	400	1600
A_1	h	-	-	0.38	0.8
	t	-	-	1.5	5.0
A_4	h	0.28	-	0.021	0.45
	t	2.0	-	0.027	3.2
A_{12}	h	-	0.63	0.0096	18
	t	-	1.1	-	-

Table 7

Resonant Frequencies and Damping of Air
and Swim Bladders in Water.

	Dia. d of the bubble mm	Resonant Frequency f_0 kHz	$f_0 \cdot d$ kHz·mm	Half Value Δt kHz	Log. decrement δ
a) Air bubbles	4.67/5.78	1.03	4.8/6.0	-	-
	3.78	1.50	5.7	0.05	0.10
	3.12	1.96	6.1	0.10	0.16
	2.67	2.33	6.2	0.07	0.09
	2.34	2.60	6.1	0.09	0.11
	1.78	3.35	6.0	0.11	0.10
	1.45	3.68	5.3	0.13	0.11
					0.11
b) Swim bladders (Camera aerea of minnow)	5.24	1.40	7.3	0.10	0.22
	4.58	1.54	7.1	0.16	0.33
	4.69	1.55-1.60	7.4	0.15	0.30
	4.15	1.68	7.0	0.12	0.22
	4.41	1.68	7.4	0.15	0.28
	4.14	1.70	7.0	0.10	0.19
	4.36	1.72	7.5	-	-
	4.44	1.72	7.6	0.12	0.22
	4.44	1.72	7.6	0.15	0.27
	4.1	1.74	7.1	0.13	0.23
	3.8	1.78	6.8	-	-
					0.25
c) Swim bladders in gelatine: Before embedding	4.44	1.72	7.6	0.12	0.22
In gelatine	-	1.65	-	0.22	0.42
Returned to water	4.44	1.72	7.6	0.15	0.27

Literatur.

AUTRUM, H.: Über Gehör und Erschütterungssinn bei Locustiden. Z. vergl. Physiol. **28**, 580 (1941). — Schallempfang bei Tier und Mensch. Naturwiss. **30**. 69 (1942). — Über kleinste Reize bei Sinnesorganen. Biol. Zbl. **63**. 209 (1943). — AUTRUM, H.. u. D. POGGENDORF: Messung der absoluten Hörschwelle bei Fischen *(Amiurus nebulosus)*. Naturwiss. **38**. 434 (1951). — CHRANILOV, N. S.: Beiträge zur Kenntnis des WEBERschen Apparates der Ostariophysi. I. Vergleichend-anatomische Übersicht über die Knochenelemente des WEBERschen Apparates bei *Cypriniformes*. Zool. Jb., Anat. u. Ontog. **49**, 501 (1927). II. Der WEBERsche Apparat bei *Siluroidea*. Zool. Jb., Anat. u. Ontog. **51**, 323 (1929). DAHLMANN, H.: Zur Physiologie des Hörens; experimentelle Untersuchungen über die Mechanik der Gehörknöchelchenkette, sowie über deren Verhalten auf Ton und Luftdruck. Z. Hals- usw. Heilk. **24**, 462 (1929); **27**, 329 (1930). — DIESSELHORST, G.: Hörversuche an Fischen ohne WEBERschen Apparat. Z. vergl. Physiol. **25**, 748 (1938). — DIJKGRAAF, S.: Untersuchungen über die Funktionen des Ohrlabyrinthes bei Meeresfischen. Physiol. comp. et oecol. (Den Haag) **2**, 81 (1949). — EVANS, H. M., and G. C. C. DAMANT: Observations on the physiology of the swimbladder in cyprinoid fishes. Brit. J. of Exper. Biol. **6**, 42 (1928). — FRISCH, K. v.: Über den Gehörsinn der Fische. Biol. Rev. Cambridge Philos. Soc. **11**, 210 (1936). — Die Bedeutung des *Sacculus* und der *Lagena* für den Gehörsinn der Fische. Z. vergl. Physiol. **25**, 703 (1938). — FRISCH, K. v., u. H. STETTER: Über den Sitz des Gehörsinnes bei der Elritze. Z. vergl. Physiol. **17**, 686 (1932). — HAFEN, G.: Zur Psychologie der Dressurversuche. Z. vergl. Physiol. **22**, 192 (1935). — HOLST, E. v.: Die Arbeitsweise des Statolithenapparates bei Fischen. Z. vergl. Physiol. **32**, 60 (1950). — LÖWENSTEIN, O., and A. SAND: The mechanism of the semicircular canal. A study of the responses of singlefibre preparations to angular accelerations and to rotation at constant speed. Proc. Roy. Soc. Lond., Ser. B **129**, 256 (1940). — MEYER, E., u. K. TAMM: Eigenschwingung und Dämpfung von Gasblasen in Flüssigkeiten. Akust. Z. **4**, 145 (1939). — PÄTAU, K.: Zur statistischen Beurteilung von Messungsreihen. (Eine neue t-Tafel.) Biol. Zbl. **63**, 152 (1943). — POGGENDORF, D.: Über Hörschwellenmessungen an Fischen. Verh. Dtsch. Zool. Ges. Wilhelmshaven. 1951. — SCHÄFER, O.: Das elektrische Ersatzschema piezoelektrischer Schallempfänger. Akust. Z. **6**, 326 (1941). — SCHNEIDER, H.: Bedeutung der Atemhöhle der Labyrinthfische für ihr Hörvermögen. Z. vergl. Physiol. **29**, 172 (1942). — SCHWARTZKOPFF, J.: Über Sitz und Leistung von Gehör und Vibrationssinn bei Vögeln. Z. vergl. Physiol. **31**, 527 (1949). — SIVIAN, L. J., and S. D. WHITE: On minimum audible sound fields. J. Acoust. Soc. **4**, 288 (1935). — STEINHAUSEN, W.: Über die Funktion der *Cupula* in den Bogengangsampullen des Labyrinthes. Z. Hals- usw. Heilk. **34**, 201 (1933). — STETTER, H.: Untersuchungen über den Gehörsinn der Fische, besonders von *Phoxinus laevis* L. und *Amiurus nebulosus* Raf. Z. vergl. Physiol. **9**, 339 (1929). — STIPETIC, E.: Das Gehörorgan der Mormyriden. Z. vergl. Physiol. **26**, 740 (1939). — TAMM, K.: Ein- und zweidimensionale Ausbreitung von Wasserschall im Rohr bzw. Flachbecken. Akust. Z. **6**, 16 (1941). — TRENDELENBURG, F.: Einführung in die Akustik, 2. Aufl. Berlin: Springer 1950. — VRIES, HL. DE: The mechanics of the labyrinth otoliths. Acta otolaryng. (Stockh.) **38**, 262 (1950). — WILSKA, A.: Eine Methode zur Bestimmung der Hörschwellenamplituden des Trommelfelles bei verschiedenen Frequenzen. Skand. Arch. Physiol. (Berl. u. Lpz.) **72**, 161 (1935). — WOHLFAHRT, TH. A.: Über die Beziehungen zwischen absolutem und relativem Tonunterscheidungsvermögen sowie über Intervallverschmelzung bei der Elritze. Z. vergl. Physiol. **32**, 151 (1950).

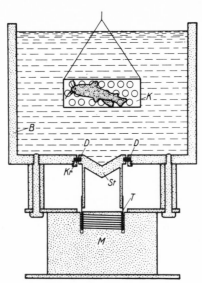

Fig. 1 Experimental conditions for determination of the hearing threshold of the bullhead, 1:3. B, brass walls of the sound tank (front and rear walls are glass); D, rubber washer; K, plastic training cage with experimental animal; Kr, lock-ring; M, magnet; St, oscillating piston; T, submerged coil. Reprinted from *Zeitschr. Vergleich. Physiol.,* **34,** 222–257 (1952); copyright © 1952 by Springer-Verlag, Berlin, Heidelberg, New York

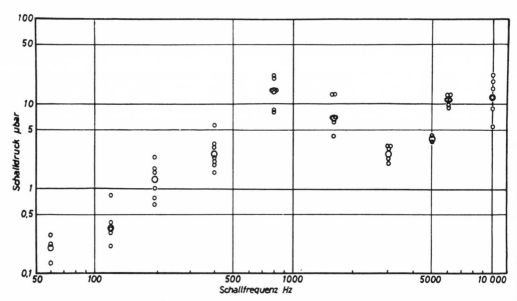

Fig. 2 Sound pressure (in μbars on the ordinate) in the center of the experimental tank, as shown in Fig. 1, at the frequencies (in Hz on the abscissa) used in training at constant voltage (100 mV). *Small circles,* values obtained on different days in the course of 1 year; *large circles,* geometric mean of measurements. Reprinted from *Zeitschr. Vergleich. Physiol.,* **34,** 222–257 (1952); copyright © 1952 by Springer-Verlag, Berlin, Heidelberg, New York

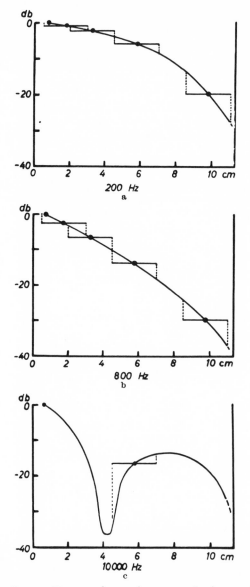

Fig. 3 a–c   Decay of sound pressure in the vertical in the center of the tank at different frequencies. Abscissa: height of the microphone above the bottom of the experimental tank, cm; ordinate: relative sound pressure (relative to the highest measurement just above the tank bottom), dB. *Curved lines,* extent of training cage at different water depths. Reprinted from *Zeitschr. Vergleich. Physiol.,* **34,** 222–257 (1952); copyright © 1952 by Springer-Verlag, Berlin, Heidelberg, New York

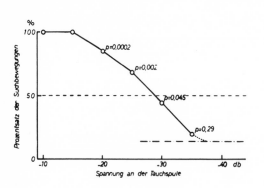

Fig. 4 Percentage of positive responses (on the ordinate) as a function of voltage of submerged coil (in dB on the abscissa) at a tone of 200 Hz. Animal A_{11}: Cage in middle of sound tank (Table 3b). *Dashed line,* threshold of hearing; *dashed-and-dotted line,* average percentage of spontaneous search movements. At each observed value the probability p of a chance positive result is given. Reprinted from *Zeitschr. Vergleich. Physiol.,* **34,** 222–257 (1952); copyright © 1952 by Springer-Verlag, Berlin, Heidelberg, New York

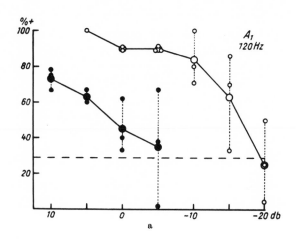

Fig. 5a and b Relative auditory threshold as a function of water depth. Abscissa: voltage of submerged coil, dB; ordinate: percentage of positive responses to the conditioned tone. *Small filled circles,* measured values and their average *(large filled circles)* closely below water surface (cage position *h;* see Fig. 3). *Small open circles,* measured values and their average *(large open circles)* close to the bottom of the tank (cage position *t;* see Fig. 3). *Dashed line,* average percentage of spontaneous searching responses. Reprinted from *Zeitschr. Vergleich. Physiol.,* **34,** 222–257 (1952); copyright © 1952 by Springer-Verlag, Berlin, Heidelberg, New York

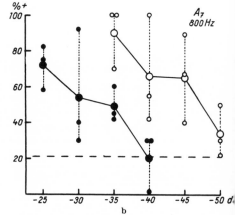

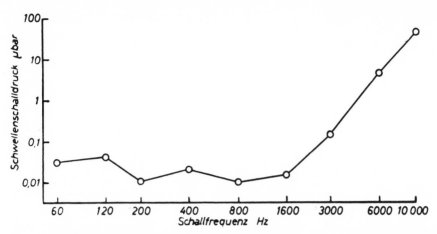

Fig. 6 Bullhead: absolute threshold curve with reference to sound pressure. Abscissa: frequency, Hz; ordinate: sound pressure, μbars (dynes/cm²). Averages of best animal (A_4). Reprinted from *Zeitschr. Vergleich. Physiol.*, **34,** 222–257 (1952); copyright © 1952 by Springer-Verlag, Berlin, Heidelberg, New York

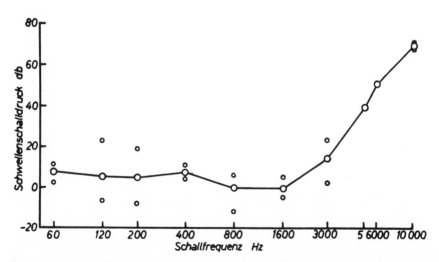

Fig. 7 Relative threshold of hearing in the bullhead. Abscissa: frequency, cps; ordinate: relative sound pressure, dB. *Large open circles,* average threshold sound pressure of all animals with reference to the value at 800 Hz (=0 dB); *small open circles,* extreme values found in single animals. Reprinted from *Zeitschr. Vergleich. Physiol.*, **34,** 222–257 (1952); copyright © 1952 by Springer-Verlag, Berlin, Heidelberg, New York

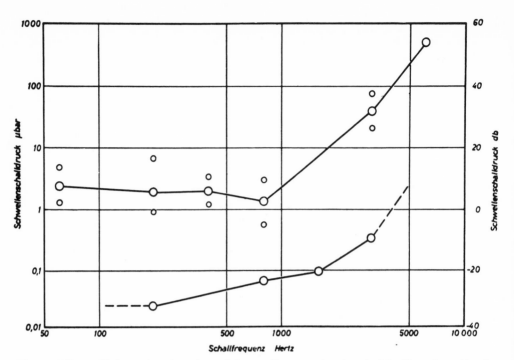

Fig. 8 Effect of bilateral extirpation of the *malleus* on the threshold of hearing. Abscissa: frequency, Hz; ordinate: threshold sound pressure μbar and dB, respectively. Lower curve: threshold, of A_{10} and A_{11} prior to operation (values of both animals agreed almost completely). *Small open circles,* measurements; *dashed line,* presumed further course of threshold curve (see Fig. 6). Upper curve: thresholds of A_{10}, and A_{14} postoperatively. *Large open circles,* averages; *small open circles,* extreme values found in single animals. Reprinted from *Zeitschr. Vergleich. Physiol.,* **34,** 222–257 (1952); copyright © 1952 by Springer-Verlag, Berlin, Heidelberg, New York

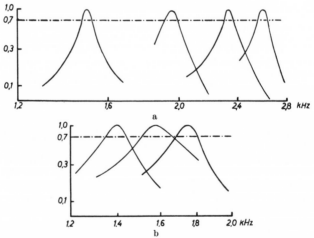

Fig. 9a and b Resonance curves of air bubbles (a) and swim bladders (b) in water. Abscissa: frequency, kHz; ordinate: relative amplitudes (effective values). The dashed-and-dotted line marks the half-width of the resonance curves. Reprinted from *Zeitschr. Vergleich. Physiol.,* **34,** 222–257 (1952); copyright © 1952 by Springer-Verlag, Berlin, Heidelberg, New York

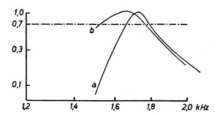

Fig. 10 Resonance curve of a swim bladder in water (a) and in gelatine (b). Coordinates as in Fig. 9. Reprinted from *Zeitschr. Vergleich. Physiol.*, **34,** 222–257 (1952); copyright © 1952 by Springer-Verlag, Berlin, Heidelberg, New York

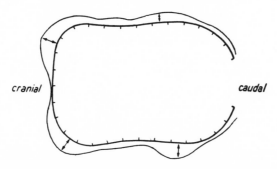

Fig. 11 Stationary representation of the vibrations of an isolated *Camera aerea* of the minnow. Inside line: outline of swim bladder (dorsal aspect); outside line: connecting line of relative amplitudes of vibration (plotted perpendicularly to the center of each measured section). Arrows show main vibration directions. Amplitudes are greatly exaggerated. Reprinted from *Zeitschr. Vergleich. Physiol.*, **34,** 222–257 (1952); copyright © 1952 by Springer-Verlag, Berlin, Heidelberg, New York

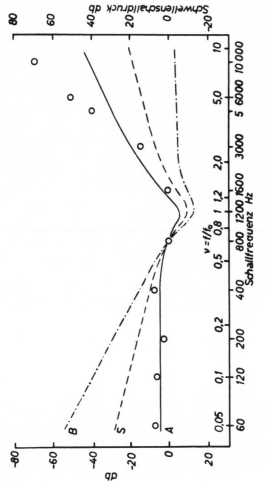

Fig. 12 Relationship between amplitude of vibration of swim bladder wall and sensitivity to sound of bullhead. Abscissa: sound frequency, cps, and proportion sound frequency f to natural frequency f_o of the swim bladder, respectively. Left ordinate: relative amplitude A, relative velocity S, and relative acceleration B of the swim bladder wall (in dB), calculated for a spherical bubble, and the relative sensitivity for sound of the bullhead (= reciprocal of the threshold sound pressure). Right ordinate: relative threshold sound pressure as in Fig. 6. Further explanation in text. Reprinted from *Zeitschr. Vergleich. Physiol.*, **34**, 222–257 (1952); copyright © 1952 by Springer-Verlag, Berlin, Heidelberg, New York

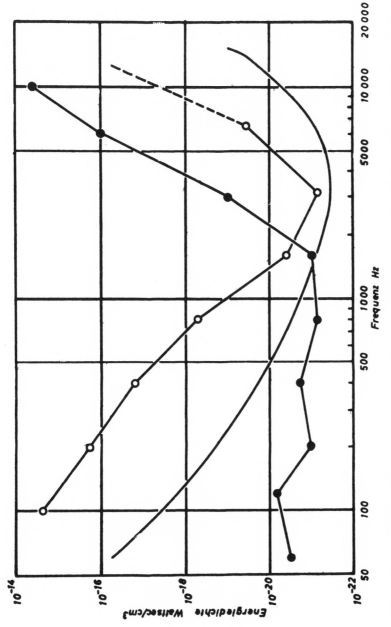

Fig. 13 Comparison of auditory thresholds of man: *solid curve*, after Sivian and White 1933; *curve with open circles*, after Schwartzkopff (1939); and *curve with closed circles*, bullhead (A₄). Abscissa: sound frequency, Hz; ordinate: energy density of the undisturbed sound field, Wsec/cm³. Reprinted from Zeitschr. Vergleich. Physiol., **34**, 222–257 (1952); copyright © 1952 by Springer-Verlag, Berlin, Heidelberg, New York

10

Reprinted from *Bull. Amer. Mus. Nat. Hist.,* **126,** 177, 179–239 (1963)

AUDITORY CAPACITIES IN FISHES

•

PURE TONE THRESHOLDS IN NINE SPECIES OF MARINE TELEOSTS

WILLIAM N. TAVOLGA

Research Associate, Department of Animal Behavior
The American Museum of Natural History

JEROME WODINSKY

Department of Psychology
New School for Social Research
New York, New York
Presently in the Department of Psychology
Brandeis University
Waltham, Massachusetts

INTRODUCTION

NOT UNTIL THE EARLY DECADES of the present century was it actually established that fishes could hear and respond to sound vibrations in the water. Parker's (1918) investigations conclusively proved that such capacity existed in a number of teleosts. Quantitative work on the frequency range of teleost hearing was undertaken mainly in Germany by von Frisch (1936) and his coworkers. The site of auditory reception in the labyrinth was located at the sacculus and lagena by Dijkgraaf (1949) and his colleagues in The Netherlands. Over the past 30 years, there have been numerous studies on the frequency range, auditory sensitivity, and discrimination in fishes. The literature has been thoroughly reviewed by Kleerekoper and Chagnon (1954).

The methods of most of the investigators consisted of conditioning the animals to a "feeding sound," and the positive response was the approach of the subject to the feeding area. Many workers also used an unconditioned reaction to sound as a sign of a positive response. In terms of the Pavlovian school of animal psychology, this would be called an "orientational reflex." Responses conditioned by a negative stimulus, such as an electric shock, have been used by relatively few investigators. Prominent among these have been Bull (1928), Froloff (1925), Maliukina (1960), Rough (1954) and, recently, Dijkgraaf (1963). In no case was instrumental conditioning (e.g., bar pressing) utilized.

The main problem with the feeding, orientational, and conditioned responses as reported heretofore has been that no clear-cut positive response was used as a criterion. Rather, the responses have been variously described as an approach, "fright reaction," increase in movement, or in similar nonspecific terms. Attempts to obtain a measurable activity change were made by Bull (1928), but in many reports the exact criteria for a positive response were not even described.

The use of such generalized responses, although adequate for qualitative work, is not sufficient for threshold determinations. It is well known, from the study of sensory thresholds, that the response of the subject becomes variable and erratic as the threshold is approached (Ash, 1951), which is to be expected, since a threshold is actually a statistically determined point and there is some probability of positive responses both above and below the calculated threshold point. What is needed, therefore, is a positive response on the part of the subject that is clear and unambiguous to the observer. The search for such responses led to the development of instrumental and avoidance conditioning techniques. On this basis we decided to use the avoidance response in a modified shuttle box as described by Horner, Longo, and Bitterman (1961), as a means of determining sound intensity and frequency thresholds in marine teleosts. Prior work by Behrend and Bitterman (1962) and Wodinsky, Behrend, and Bitterman (1962) demonstrated the feasibility of using this technique for a number of species.

In the majority of previous studies on teleostean auditory capacities, the objective was to determine the upper frequency limits to which the animals could respond. Only in a relatively few studies were absolute intensity thresholds attempted (Autrum and Poggendorf, 1951; Diesselhorst, 1938; Kritzler and Wood, 1961; Maliukina, 1960; Poggendorf, 1952; Stetter, 1929; von Boutteville, 1935), and, in these reports, only one or a few selected frequencies were actually tested. With the exception of the work of Griffin (1950), the intensity measurements were only approximations. Griffin's determinations were based on measurements taken with calibrated hydrophones, amplifiers, and decibel meters. For the present report, equipment was assembled that would give sound pressure measurements with considerable accuracy, i.e., within 1 decibel, an accuracy probably beyond that of the auditory apparatus of the fish.

Interest has always centered on those fishes that possess a Weberian apparatus, the Cypriniformes (Ostariophysi). Species such as the minnow (*Phoxinus*) and the catfish (*Ameiurus*)[1] have been studied most, since it was evident that the Weberian ossicles could act

---

[1] The well-known generic name *Ameiurus* has been synonymized with *Ictalurus*, but many recent references still use the older name.

183

in a manner analogous to the mammalian middle ear bones and transmit sounds received by the swim bladder to the inner ear. It has been clearly shown by many workers that the Cypriniformes possess a higher frequency response and lower auditory threshold than most other forms. This group includes mostly fresh-water forms and some estuarine species. Truly marine forms and those that lack a Weberian apparatus have been investigated only sporadically as to hearing capacity. Most prominent of such studies is that of Maliukina (1960).

The nine species chosen for this report included some of the most common ones in the vicinity of Bimini Island, Bahamas. They can be considered as being representative of a large percentage of the shallow-water fauna of the Caribbean.

With the recent rise in interest in sound production among marine fishes (Fish, 1954; Tavolga, 1960; Schneider, 1961) it becomes of importance to determine what are the hearing capacities of the sound producers, and to what extent these sounds can be detected by other fishes. Also it would be desirable to know how much of the normal ambient water noise can be heard by fishes.

The purpose of this investigation, then, was to determine sound pressure thresholds at various frequencies and thereby enable the construction of an audiogram for several representative species of marine teleosts.

The technique and the apparatus used in the present study are described in detail in later sections of this report. The animals were trained and tested in an avoidance conditioning apparatus. This consisted of an aquarium tank, with two compartments separated by a barrier. The water level was adjusted so that the fish could swim across the barrier but would not remain there. The animal was exposed to a selected tone, produced by an under-water speaker concealed under the barrier, and this was followed in a short time (usually 10 seconds) by a series of intermittent electric shocks. During initial training, the fish learned to escape the shock by crossing the barrier, thus breaking a light beam to a photoelectric cell which terminated the trial. After a period of escape training, the animal began to cross the barrier after the onset of the sound (the conditioned stimulus) and before the onset of the shock (the uncon-

ditioned stimulus). This behavior, therefore, was an objective index of the fact that the fish responded to the sound. The sound was virtually a pure tone of a single frequency, and its intensity was measured, in terms of acoustic pressure, by a calibrated monitoring system. After the avoidance response was judged sufficiently reliable, the level of the sound was reduced in graded steps with each successive trial, until the subject failed to avoid, i.e., it crossed the barrier only after being shocked. The threshold for each given frequency was determined by the staircase or "up-and-down" method commonly used in psychophysical studies, and from a series of such determinations at various frequencies audiogram curves were constructed for each of the species tested.

ACKNOWLEDGMENTS

Financial support for this project was obtained through Contracts Nonr 552 (06) NR 301-322 and 522 (07) NR 104-511 between the Office of Naval Research and the American Museum of Natural History.

The facilities of the Lerner Marine Laboratory, Bimini, Bahamas, were made available through the courtesy of Mr. Robert F. Mathewson, Resident Director.

We are greatly indebted to Dr. John Steinberg, of the Institute of Marine Science, University of Miami, Mr. Robert Laupheimer, of the Courant Institute of Mathematical Sciences, New York University, Dr. E. E. Suckling, of the New York State Downstate Medical Center, and Dr. M. E. Bitterman, of the Department of Psychology, Bryn Mawr College, for their advice on many technical problems.

We are also grateful to Dr. Lester R. Aronson and Dr. T. C. Schneirla, of the Department of Animal Behavior, the American Museum of Natural History, for their helpful comments on the manuscript of this report.

Dr. G. G. Harris and Dr. Willem A. van Bergeijk, of the Bell Telephone Laboratories at Murray Hill, New Jersey, were kind enough to advise the authors on many problems of under-water acoustics and calibration of the equipment, and to comment on the manuscript.

The illustrations were prepared by Mrs. Frances W. Zweifel.

THE FOLLOWING NINE species of marine fishes were tested for this report:

Squirrelfish, *Holocentrus ascensionis* (Osbeck), Holocentridae

Dusky squirrelfish, *Holocentrus vexillarius* (Poey), Holocentridae

Cubbyu, *Equetus acuminatus* (Bloch and Schneider), Sciaenidae

Blue-striped grunt, *Haemulon sciurus* (Shaw), Pomadasyidae

Schoolmaster, *Lutjanus apodus* (Walbaum), Lutjanidae

Blue-head wrasse, *Thalassoma bifasciatum* (Bloch), Labridae

Beau-gregory, *Eupomacentrus leucostictus* (Müller and Troschel), Pomacentridae

Red hind, *Epinephelus guttatus* (Linnaeus), Serranidae

Slender sea robin, *Prionotus scitulus* (Jordan and Gilbert), Triglidae

These forms were chosen on the basis of several criteria. The species are representatives of different teleost families which are some of the major groups of shallow-water forms in the Bimini area. They are also representative of a number of very different configurations of swim-bladder structure. Included are species that are well known to be sound producers. All are quite common in the region.

The choice was restricted by the time available to train and test the animals, and in addition it was found that some species were not testable by the methods described here. Some preliminary attempts at avoidance conditioning were made with the goby, *Bathygobius soporator*, the toadfish, *Opsanus* sp., and numerous plectognaths such as puffers, triggerfish, and cowfish. The main reason for failure with these species appeared to be that their response to the electric shock was usually a freezing reaction, and a reliable escape response could not be elicited under the conditions used. Modifications of the apparatus or, possibly, the use of positive or reward conditioning will be required for adequate threshold determinations in such forms.

With the possible exception of the squirrelfish, all the species tested were strictly diurnal in habit. They were collected locally in traps or by hook and line. The squirrelfish and red hind were captured in the neighborhood of Turtle Rock, a rocky outcropping a few miles south of Bimini. The others were collected near the laboratory dock.

SQUIRRELFISH (*Holocentrus ascensionis*)

The family Holocentridae is represented by only a few species in this area. The systematics of the western Atlantic forms was reviewed by Woods (1955), and the identification of this species, which is by far the most common in Bimini, was based on the descriptions given in that paper.

In captivity, squirrelfish are hardy but quite timid and usually seek out dark corners or shelters. As daylight wanes, they become more active and feed more readily. Their activity rhythm is distinctly crepuscular and possibly nocturnal (Moulton, 1958). The distinctive large eyes are obviously excellent light-gathering devices. In the field, they are usually to be found among rocks and corals. Territorial behavior has been reported by personal communications from many skin divers but has not yet been confirmed. Sex differences in behavior or external structure are not known, nor is there any information on reproductive behavior.

This species is of particular interest in auditory studies since it is well known to be a sound producer. In the Bimini area, *H. ascensionis* is probably one of the most regularly vociferous fishes. Moulton (1958) and Winn and Marshall (1960) have described the sound bursts that are emitted when the animals are threatened or sometimes merely approached by other squirrelfish or other species. The sonic mechanism has been described as consisting of a pair of muscles stretched across the dorsal surface of the swim bladder and attached to the anteriormost ribs (Winn and Marshall, 1963).

The probability that the squirrelfish has a good hearing apparatus is enhanced by the fact that the anterior end of the swim bladder in *H. ascensionis* is almost in contact with the otic region of the skull (Nelson, 1955), separated only by a tough band of connective tissue. If we assume that the swim bladder acts as a receiving transducer, then the direct or indirect physical contact with the skull should increase the efficiency of sound transfer to the inner ear in a manner analogous to that of the Weberian apparatus in the Cypriniformes.

A total of five *H. ascensionis* were used in threshold determinations, and several additional animals were used in preliminary tests. All specimens were mature and ranged in size from 17 to 20 cm. in standard length. This is a hardy species, and it submitted to handling without any damage. All the animals were kept in a large, concrete, holding tank (about 100 gallons) on the laboratory grounds. Running sea water was supplied, and the specimens were fed about every two days on pieces of conch (*Strombus*). The training and testing took place daily. Since the animals were kept in a single holding tank, each specimen was identified by fin clipping.

DUSKY SQUIRRELFISH
(*Holocentrus vexillarius*)

This is a smaller species, 5 to 8 cm. in standard length, usually found in rocky tide pools. Little is known about the behavior or ecology of *H. vexillarius*, and it is not known to be a sound producer. Dissections revealed that this species has the same type of swimbladder structure as does *H. ascensionis*.

Three specimens of *H. vexillarius* were conditioned and tested. They were kept together in a 10-gallon aquarium and marked by fin clipping.

CUBBYU (*Equetus acuminatus*)

This is probably the only representative of the family Sciaenidae that is found in the Bimini area. The species is not common but can be collected sporadically in the bay.

The swim-bladder structure in this species is very similar to that of the grunts and snappers. Schneider and Hasler (1960) reported the existence of "drumming" muscles in the lateral body wall of *E. lanceolatus*, but no sound-producing mechanism could be located in the specimens used here. *Equetus* has not been specifically reported as a sound producer.

There is no information on the auditory capacities of this species. Indeed, there has been no published study of hearing of any sciaenids, with one exception. The European genus *Corvina* was shown to have a high sensitivity to sound. Maliukina (1960), by the use of classical conditioning, demonstrated thresholds of −45 decibels (re 1 microbar) at 320 cps. and −50 decibels at 500–600 cps.

The data in the present report are based on determinations made on three specimens, 8 to 12 cm. in standard length.

BLUE-STRIPED GRUNT (*Haemulon sciurus*)

This is certainly the most common member of the Pomadasyidae in the Bimini area. Small individuals are always present in the vicinity of the laboratory dock, and specimens can be collected in traps or by hook and line almost anywhere along the shore.

The species is not territorial in habit and is entirely diurnal. All the grunts are well known as sound producers. Burkenroad (1930) described the mechanism as being the pharyngeal teeth. The scraping of these patchs of rasp-like denticles is presumably amplified by the swim bladder into the grunt-like sound heard when the fish is handled (Moulton, 1958). It is not known if these animals produce a sound under water during the course of their normal behavioral repertoire. Thus far the evidence appears to be negative.

There is no information on sound reception in any of the Pomadasyidae.

The swim bladder in *Haemulon* can be considered as typical in general form. It extends for almost the full length of the abdominal cavity. It protrudes into the perivisceral cavity and can be separated from the body wall easily, except just along the middorsal line. It is composed of tough, inelastic connective tissue and is rounded cephalad where it ends short of the occipital region of the skull.

Threshold determinations were based on four specimens. All were young, immature individuals of about 8 cm. in standard length. They were kept in individual 2-gallon aquaria and were trained and tested daily.

SCHOOLMASTER (*Lutjanus apodus*)

This species was chosen as an easily available representative of the large snapper family (Lutjanidae). Young specimens of *L. apodus* were readily collected in traps around the laboratory dock.

The schoolmaster sometimes occurs in groups of up to a dozen individuals that remain in one general area for long periods of time. However, this species is not territorial, and the loose aggregations cannot be considered schools. None of the members of the Lutjanidae is known to be a sound producer, and there is no information on sound reception in this group.

The swim bladder in *Lutjanus* is essentially the same in general structure as that of *Haemulon*.

Threshold determinations were based on three specimens. All were young, immature individuals of about 10 cm. in standard length. They were kept in individual 2-gallon aquaria.

BLUE-HEAD (*Thalassoma bifasciatum*)

The blue-head (*Thalassoma bifasciatum*) and the slippery dick (*Halochoeres bivittatus*) are the most abundant wrasses (family Labridae) in the shallow waters around Bimini. Curiously, *Halochoeres* turned out to be completely unsuitable for this type of conditioning in that individuals would not learn to escape the shock but remained in a corner of the tank and simply endured the shock until it almost killed them. *Thalassoma*, however, learned the escape and the avoidance problems readily. Specimens were captured in traps within 100 yards or so of the laboratory dock.

These wrasses are generally found in or around hiding places such as rock crevices, corals, and shells, but they are not territorial in habit. None of the labrids is known to be a sound producer. The only information on hearing in this group is the report of Bull (1928) who demonstrated the ability of *Crenilabrus melops* to respond to a sound of 128 cps. in frequency. However, the same species was not able to discriminate between the sound of a tuning fork and that of an electric buzzer (Bull, 1929).

The swim bladder in *Thalassoma* is small, ovoid, and in the posterior third of the abdominal cavity. It is less than one-fifth of the length of the cavity and is loosely attached to the dorsal body wall.

Threshold determinations were based on four specimens. These were all mature males, as judged by the predominant blue and black coloration of the head and body (Stoll, 1955), and they were about 5 to 7 cm. in standard length. The animals were kept in individual 2-gallon aquaria.

BEAU-GREGORY (*Eupomacentrus leucostictus*)

This species is probably one of the most strongly territorial among the many reef-dwelling members of the Pomacentridae. It is quite common in the vicinity of the laboratory dock at Bimini, living in and around conch shells and pilings. Breder (1950, 1954) described some factors in their territorial behavior. Both males and females defend their selected shelters and areas vigorously. In captivity, it is usually necessary to keep the animals in separate aquaria, since they fight one another or other fishes until severe damage is inflicted.

Knudsen, Alford, and Emling (1948) reported the "damozel" as producing a "drumming, tapping" sound, presumably with its pharyngeal teeth. The specific identification is doubtful, but the animals were very likely to have been pomacentrids. *Eupomacentrus leucostictus* was definitely identified as a sound maker by Moulton (1958). Faint snapping sounds were produced by individuals in aquaria when one attacked another or when darting for cover (confirmed by observation, Tavolga, unpublished).

There is no information on the sound reception in this species or any other member of the Pomacentridae.

The swim bladder in *Eupomacentrus* is unlike that of any of the other species studied here. The bladder is essentially triangular in cross section, with the apex pointed dorsally. It is tightly wedged between the dorsolateral body walls, and on dissection of the perivisceral cavity, only the thin, flat ventral wall of the bladder is visible. The anterior end of the bladder does not abut the otic region as in *Holocentrus*. If the bladder acted as a transducer in sound reception, its coupling to the inner ear would be indirect, e.g., lateral musculature and ribs to vertebral column to skull.

Threshold determinations were based on four specimens. All were presumably mature individuals of about 7 to 8 cm. in standard length. They were kept in individual 2-gallon aquaria supplied with running sea water and fed about every two days on conch.

RED-HIND (*Epinephelus guttatus*)

This species is considered representative of the family Serranidae, which includes the many species of sea basses and groupers. Specimens of *E. guttatus* were commonly captured on hook and line in the vicinity of Turtle Rock, south of Bimini. Nothing specific is known of the territorial habits of this form, but it is usually found in or around rock crevices, as are its close relatives, the rock hind (*Epinephelus adscensionis*) and Nassau grouper (*E. striatus*).

Sound production has been described for the latter species by Moulton (1958) as consisting of "vibrant grunts" when the animals were disturbed or approached by a foreign object. Tavolga (1960) obtained series of sound beats from the black grouper (*Mycteroperca bonaci*). These sounds were also elicited when the animal was disturbed or, in some cases, were produced when another fish swam close by. Electrical stimulation of the common sea bass (*Centropristis striatus*) resulted in drum-like thumps (Fish, 1954). Moulton (1958) believed that the sounds were produced by vibrations of the lateral body musculature, while Fish (1954) and Tavolga (1960) thought that the pounding of the operculum against the pectoral girdle was the mechanism involved. The swim bladder itself lacks drumming muscles. The quality of the sounds of these serranids is that of a low-pitched grunt or thump, with a fundamental frequency of 100 to 200 cps. Hazlett and Winn (1962) described the lateral body musculature involved in sound production in the Nassau grouper (*Epinephelus striatus*).

The swim bladder of the red hind, like that of all the serranids, is large and thin-walled and extends the full length of the abdominal cavity. It is composed of tough, inelastic, connective tissue and, anteriorly, there is no direct connection with the occipital region of the skull. Essentially, it is similar to that of *Haemulon* and *Lutjanus*.

Although a number of specimens were used, the threshold determinations given here are based on the responses of a single animal. This one was immature, about 27 cm. in standard length.

SLENDER SEA ROBIN (*Prionotus scitulus*)

The sea robins, as are most of the Triglidae, are well known as sound producers, and references to this ability go back hundreds of years. The sonic mechanism was described by Tower (1908) as consisting of a pair of muscles attached to the lateral walls of the swim bladder. The muscles are intrinsic, i.e., completely detached from the lateral body wall. The studies of Moulton (1956) showed that sound production in *Prionotus* may be involved in some form of communication.

The auditory capacity of a sea robin (*Prionotus evolans*) was investigated by Griffin (1950). In a preliminary study, he showed that this species can respond to a sound of 100 cps. at a pressure level of about 17 decibels re 1 microbar, but such response was not construed to be a threshold value.

Although this species is normally not common in the Bimini area, three specimens of 15 to 20 cm. in standard length were collected, and threshold determinations were made.

BRIEFLY STATED, THE EQUIPMENT used consited of five systems: (1) the experimental aquarium tank in which the animals were trained and tested, (2) the test sound-producing system, (3) the sound monitoring and measuring apparatus, (4) the electric shock system for the unconditioned stimulus, and (5) the control apparatus interconnecting all of the above.

THE EXPERIMENTAL AQUARIUM

A standard glass aquarium tank was lined on the inside with a 2-inch layer of rubberized hair on the sides and floor. The rubberized hair was the type commonly used as padding within packages containing fragile items. The insulating material was found, after prolonged tests, to be inert as far as any deleterious effects on fish were concerned. It consists of a mixture of curled horse and hog hair impregnated with latex. As an under-water sound insulator, it decreased the background noise level in the tank by about 20 decibels, and, as a sound baffle, it virtually eliminated sound reflections and standing waves. One important property of this material was that, when water was introduced into the tank, it penetrated through the insulation without significant trapping of air bubbles. Air bubbles are known to be excellent sound reflectors, and these could be eliminated by slowly filling the tank with its interior insulation. This material possesses some of the sound-absorbing properties of various materials of fiber type (Tamm, 1957) and has been widely used as an acoustical curtain in under-water sonic studies. To eliminate further the effects of background noise, the tanks were set on 2-inch cushions of foam rubber at the corners. Most low-frequency noise was eliminated in this way.

Two experimental tanks were constructed. One was a 20-gallon aquarium, and the other a 5-gallon size. The larger one was used for testing squirrelfish (*Holocentrus ascensionis*) and red hind (*Epinephelus*), while the smaller one was used for the other, smaller species.

Transversely, across the center of each experimental tank, a partial barrier was constructed of rubberized hair (solid, flat surfaces were avoided to prevent sound reflections and possible standing waves). The tank, therefore, was divided into two equal compartments, with the floor slanted up toward the center divider. The water level was adjusted so that the center barrier was covered by an inch or so. The fish was able to swim from one compartment into the other, but in doing so was forced to cross the barrier on its side or with a large part of its dorsal surface protruding out of water.

The water level over the center barrier was found to be a critical dimension. It had to be high enough to permit the fish to swim over, although with some difficulty, yet low enough to inhibit the animal from remaining in this center area. In training, the water level was generally higher, but, as intertrial crossings of the barrier increased, it was gradually dropped to a level optimal for each species. A light beam to a photoelectric cell was placed so that the crossing of the barrier could be detected.

The under-water speaker was concealed under the center barrier. The shocking electrodes were inserted into the inner insulator walls on the sides of each compartment. The hydrophone was placed in the tank usually at one of the ends farthest from the sound source, but it was normally not left in the tank during the course of a training or testing run. A mirror was clamped in a position above the tank, so the center barrier could be observed.

Figure 1 is a diagrammatic section of the small experimental tank. The large tank and its dimensions are shown in figure 2.

The water in the small tank was changed completely after each series of trials, and the large tank was supplied with running sea water which was turned off temporarily during threshold determinations to lower the level of ambient noise.

SOUND-PRODUCING SYSTEM (THE CONDITIONED STIMULUS)

In all this work, single frequency sine waves were used as the conditioned stimulus. The system was arranged so that the conditioned stimulus was virtually a pure tone (as determined from the sound monitoring system). The sine wave was generated by an

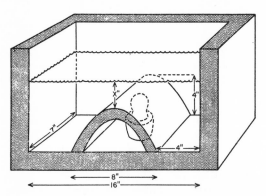

FIG. 1. Diagrammatic longitudinal section of the small experimental aquarium used in the testing of auditory capacities in seven species of marine fishes. The dimensions are in inches. The insulating material was 2 inches thick, and the entire structure was set inside a glass aquarium. The height of the water above the central barrier (X) was varied with the species used. The underwater speaker was within the central barrier, as shown.

audiogenerator (Heath Model AG-1A) that possessed an output meter, which permitted constant control of the output level. After appropriate calibration by means of the sound-monitoring system, the intensity of the output from the speaker could be controlled with this meter alone.

The power amplifier was a 14-watt unit (Heath Model EA-3), the gain and tone controls of which were set to produce the output of least distortion consonant with the generator output and the frequency and intensity required for the conditioned stimu-

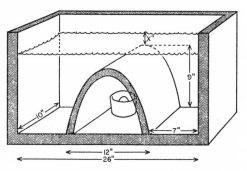

FIG. 2. Diagrammatic longitudinal section of the large experimental aquarium used in the testing of two of the species (*Holocentrus ascensionis* and *Epinephelus guttatus*). Except in size, this tank was essentially like that shown in figure 1.

lus. The switching of the signal took place, by means of the control system, between the generator and the amplifier. The snapping noise or transient click of the switch was not detectable by the monitoring system and was probably far below background noise level in intensity. Some blank trials were included in random fashion in the testing and training series in which the gain control of the generator was turned down to the minimum level and the shock system was disconnected. The possible conditioning of the animals to the transients of switching noise was largely eliminated.

The under-water loud-speaker in the small tank was constructed of a public address driver unit (University Model SA-HF) with a stiff rubber bulb attached over the horn end. The entire unit was waterproofed with tar, tape, and rubber. The rubber bulb served as a good coupling device for transmitting the sound into the water, and there was enough air inside so that the excursions of the voice coil were not inhibited. Distortion-free sine waves were obtainable from this unit in the 200– to 5000–cps. range at pressure levels of up to 50 decibels above 1 microbar. At lower frequencies, however, harmonic distortion and clipping took place at levels above 30 to 35 decibels. The acoustic pressure was measured with the monitoring system at distances of 6 to 8 inches from the sound source, and distortions were observed through the monitoring system on an oscilloscope screen.

The large tank was equipped with an under-water speaker designed by University (Model MM-2), with a plastic expansion bulb as the driving surface. Under the conditions of the present investigation, the frequency response and distortion level of this unit were slightly superior to those of the one described above.

In the process of testing the frequency response of the speakers, it was found that the rubberized hair insulation eliminated standing waves in the tanks, at least at the frequencies and acoustic pressures that were used.

SOUND-MONITORING SYSTEM

The hydrophone used as the pick-up unit was a disc-shaped barium titanate unit (Model SB-154C, Chesapeake Instrument Co.)

approximately 5 cm. in diameter and 1.5 cm. in thickness. The output was given by the manufacturer as −89 decibels (re 1 volt per microbar of sound pressure) and a frequency response essentially flat from 50 cps. When the output was monitored from the speaker, the hydrophone was always placed in the same position in the tank, i.e., suspended at the wall farthest from the sound source.

The pre-amplifier was a transistor unit designed by Robert Laupheimer of the Courant Institute of Mathematical Sciences, New York. Its frequency response was flat from 50 cps., and it had a calibrated gain control with settings at 40, 60, and 80 decibels. Its internal noise level was below 1 microvolt at the output. It possessed a cut-off switch at 5, 10, and 20 kilocycles per second.

The sound levels were measured on an audio volt meter (Heath Model AV-3) the calibration of which was checked against a standard root-mean-square decibel meter. In all, the accuracy of the sound pressure determinations at the frequencies and intensities used was in the order of ±0.5 decibel.

All the decibel measurements given here refer to acoustic pressure levels rather than acoustic intensity *per se*. Albers (1960) makes the distinction between these two values clearly. "Acoustic intensity" is measured in ergs or watts per square centimeter and is proportional to the square of the pressure. "Acoustic pressure" is given in terms of dynes per square centimeter and, for arithmetic convenience, is usually expressed in decibels in reference to some standard value such as 1 microbar (=1 dyne per square centimeter). The following formulas for acoustic power, intensity, and pressure will facilitate the conversion of our data into other units.

Acoustic power: $P = p^2 A / \rho c$ (in ergs per second)

Acoustic intensity: $I = p^2 / \rho c$ (in ergs per square centimeter), or $I = (10^{-7} p^2)/\rho c$ (in watts per square centimeter)

Acoustic pressure:

$$p = \sqrt{\frac{10^7 P \rho c}{A}}$$

(in dynes per square centimeter), or $p = 20 \log_{10} (p/p_0)$ (in decibels)

In the above equations for plane waves, A is the area in square centimeters through which the acoustic energy must flow. The factor ρc is the acoustic resistance of the medium (the acoustic ohm) and is the density of the water times the velocity of sound in this medium. The value of this factor for water is usually taken as 150,000 grams per square centimeter per second, and for air it is 42 grams per square centimeter per second. Temperature and salinity, of course, affect both the density and velocity figures. In the last equation, p_0 is the reference value of acoustic pressure. All measurements given in this report are in reference to 1 microbar (which equals 1 dyne per square centimeter), rather than the idealized and commonly used 0.0002-microbar threshold of human hearing at 1000 cps. In under-water acoustics, the human threshold actually has little real meaning and the 1-microbar reference level is becoming more widely used (Horton, 1959). Most of the earlier reports use the 0.0002 level as 0 decibel, which is equivalent to −74 decibels re 1 microbar, so that conversion is a simple arithmetic matter.

Although the distance of the hydrophone from the sound source was constant in all determinations, the distance of the fish from the sound source varied. The transmission loss of sound energy over the length of the experimental tank had to be considered. Based on the data and equations given by Albers (1960) and Horton (1959), the attenuation of the sound pressure because of scattering, absorption, and air-bubble effects is negligible over the distances and frequencies involved in these experiments. The loss of energy from spreading or divergence, however, follows the inverse square law. Since intensity varies as the square of the pressure, the sound pressure should vary in inverse proportion to the distance from the sound source. Assuming a point source of sound in our experimental tanks and measuring the range of distances from the sound source where the experimental animal was most likely to position itself at the start of a trial, we calculated that the transmission loss was about 2 decibels in the small tank and 3 decibels in the large tank. By placing the hydrophone in different positions in the experimental tank, we found that the actual transmission loss was somewhat more than the theoretical value. In the large tank, there

TABLE 1

Ambient Noise Levels in Experimental Tanks

Band Width in Cycles per Second	Sound Pressures in Decibels (re 1 Microbar)	
	Large Tank	Small Tank
37.5– 75	< −50	−43
75– 150	< −50	< −50
150– 300	−50	< −50
300– 600	−46	−43
600–1200	−43	−39
1200–2400	−39	−34
2400–4800	−35	−29
4800–9600	−20	−20

was a 5-decibel decrease in sound pressure from the base of the central barrier to the wall farthest from the speaker, a distance of about 6 inches. The corresponding loss in the small tank was 3 decibels. Height above the bottom made no perceptible difference, but, if the hydrophone was in direct contact with the insulating material of the central barrier which covered the speaker, the increase in sound pressure was about 2 decibels. Thus, if the starting points for the fish were randomly distributed within its compartment, the accuracy of the sound determination with respect to the actual pressure received by the fish was ±3.5 decibels in the large tank and ±2.5 decibels in the small tank. Actually, the threshold determinations made were more accurate, since the fish generally made a habit of assuming the same position during the intertrial period. For most individuals, this starting position was close to the far wall of the compartment of each fish, although there were many exceptions. This question is discussed in greater detail in the section on Results, below.

The total ambient noise levels in the experimental tanks ranged from −10 to −15 decibels (re 1 microbar). The actual background sound was mostly a combination of high-frequency hissing produced by the running sea-water system in other aquaria in the laboratory and some low-frequency ground vibration. Both noises were considerably reduced by the rubberized hair insulation and the foam rubber padding beneath the tanks. The noise, as measured by the sound monitoring system, also included electrically in-

duced and intrinsic noise, i.e., 60-cps. hum and transistor and tube thermal noise. The noise spectrum was determined by the insertion of an Allison band filter into the system. Table 1 shows the band widths and background sound pressures (the system was not accurate below the −50-decibel level).

From table 1 it can be seen that in the range used in this work (50 to 3000 cps.), the noise level was quite low and at least 10 decibels below the lowest auditory threshold obtained for any of the species tested.

Electric Shock System (the Unconditioned Stimulus)

The source for the unconditioned stimulus was the output from a variable autotransformer (Fisher Powerstat). In some of the preliminary work, a direct-current source, i.e., battery, was used, but the autotransformer output was more easily variable and the electrodes were not polarized. The voltages, as measured at the output of the transformer, ranged from 5 to 30 volts. By trial and error, the optimal voltages for each species were determined, and it was found that some forms could not tolerate more than about 7 volts, while others showed no response until 25 or 30 volts. The optimal voltages are given in the Results section for each species tested.

The shocking electrodes had to be of some material that could withstand the corrosive effect of sea water and be highly conductive and yet yield no toxic by-products. Short pieces of silver solder (a type of brazing material) were found to be satisfactory. These were twisted into circles, a pair for each compartment of the experimental tank, and attached to the side walls by our inserting them into the stiff insulating hair. During a shock pulse, the electrical field was strong enough to affect the fish at any point in the experimental tank.

The shock was applied intermittently by the control system in pulses of about one-tenth of a second in duration and at a repetition rate of approximately 40 pulses per minute.

Because of the high conductivity of sea water, it is assumed that the amount of current passed between the electrodes was high, but no means were available for actual measurement of this factor. All that can be said is that the shock level was adjusted so that a clear response could be obtained from the fish without damaging it. The fact that some animals were tested daily for up to two months with no deleterious effects shows that such a level was empirically achieved.

The range of shock intensities was affected by several variables: species differences in tolerance; development of tolerance with training; changes in effective shock intensities as a result of corrosion of the electrodes; changes in the position of the fish; and line-voltage fluctuations. The shock intensities used for each species are given in the Results section.

In cases in which the shock level was too high but still not lethal, the effect on the behavior of the fish was immediately apparent. Both avoidance and escape responses ceased, even in fish that had been well trained previously. On the basis of a number of such observations, we concluded that, if the shock level were too high, both avoidance and escape behavior were disrupted, and that in the majority of our tests the shock was below the disruptive levels. Short of this extreme, we are not in a position to evaluate the effects of variations in shock intensities on the threshold determinations.

CONTROL SYSTEM

The apparatus was essentially the same as that used in shuttle-box avoidance conditioning by Horner, Longo, and Bitterman (1961), Behrend and Bitterman (1962), and Wodinsky, Behrend, and Bitterman (1962).

To begin a trial, the "start" button was pressed, which turned on the switch between the audiogenerator and the power amplifier, i.e., the conditioned stimulus was on. Simultaneously, an electric clock (graduated to one one-hundredth of a second) was started. A standard interval between the onset of the sound and the shock of 10 seconds was used.

If the animal crossed the barrier from one compartment into the other during this period, it broke a light beam to a photoelectric cell. This stopped the sound and the clock.

If the animal did not "avoid" during the 10-second period, the shock was applied with a pulse repetition rate of about 40 per second. The sound continued. When the animal escaped by crossing the barrier, the shock, sound, and clock were stopped. The time for an animal either to avoid or to escape was shown on the clock. After an appropriate intertrial interval, the trial was repeated, with the animal crossing the barrier in the opposite direction.

Wodinsky, Behrend, and Bitterman (1962), using some of the same species but with light as the conditioned stimulus, found that 10 seconds was an optimal interval between the conditioned and unconditioned stimuli for the response to take place. Generally, if the animal did not avoid within that time, it did not do so if given more time. In addition, a longer interval led to a confusion between an avoidance response and an intertrial response. If the time before onset of the shock were too long, the association (contiguity learning) between the two stimuli was not developed. If the interval between the stimuli were too short, the slow-reacting species or individuals lacked enough time to respond.

The intertrial interval had to be varied for the species used, i.e., ranging from one-half of a minute to five minutes. In addition, for each series of trials, the intertrial interval was varied in a random fashion to prevent the animal from anticipating the onset of a trial. For example, if an intertrial interval of two minutes were chosen for a particular series, the actual intervals were one minute, two minutes, and three minutes, varied at random, i.e., averaging two minutes. The specific intervals are given below in the sections under the various species.

METHODS

Training Techniques

INITIALLY, THE ACOUSTIC STIMULUS LEVEL was set at a point some 20 or 30 decibels above the estimated threshold level. In the early experiments, no estimates were available, and in some cases this initial training level turned out to be as much as 50 decibels above or 10 decibels below the actual threshold. The frequency of the training tone was varied with different animals, but often we began at 400 or 440 cps. Some fish were trained at other frequencies to check points on the audiograms.

The shock level was also estimated. After some trial and error, including the death of some specimens, the optimal shock levels were determined for each species.

The first series of trials can be termed "escape training." The test animal was placed in one of the compartments in the test tank, the start button on the control apparatus was pressed, and the trial was begun. The interval between the onset of the sound and the shock was uniformly 10 seconds (with one exception, i.e., *Prionotus*).

At the onset of the intermittent shocks the animal reacted with visible, violent twitches to each shock and an increase in general activity. The shock levels during these early trials were kept as low as possible, so as not to produce any damage to the fish. The water level over the barrier was usually at least twice the optimal value (see below under Results), so that the fish had no difficulty in crossing the barrier.

In the majority of cases, no crossing took place in the first few trials, and, in order to prevent the animals from receiving an excessive number of shocks, the fish was guided or pushed across the barrier, after the fish had received not more than 20 or 30 shocks.

The escape response consisted of the fish's swimming across the barrier after receiving one or more shocks. Once the animal escaped a number of times, the technique of guiding the fish was discontinued, unless there was no response for about 20 seconds in the duration of shocks. In the majority of cases, the escape training was achieved in the first day of trials. Twenty-five trials per day were used as a standard during the training period, but was varied from 10 to 50 on a few occasions. The latency of each response was measured on an electric clock which was part of the control apparatus.

The intertrial period was varied in random fashion so that the animal should not become conditioned to the time intervals and to control for the coincidence of intertrial crossings with the onset of the sound stimulus. The average intertrial periods for each species are reported in the Results section.

Once escape training was on its way, the water level across the barrier was lowered to such a point that the crossing of the fish was not prevented but intertrial crossings were inhibited. Often the lowering was not done until later testing trials, since intertrial crossings rarely took place during the training period.

The intensity of the shock usually had to be raised as escape training progressed. The animals seemed to develop a tolerance for the shock, and the level for each species, as given in the Results section, was that used during the test trials.

During training, the subject had to learn two things. First, it had to learn to cross the barrier in response to the shock, which we call "escape training." Second, it had to associate the sound with the shock and learn to cross over as soon as the sound came on, which we call "avoidance training."

With each day's trials, the number of avoidances increased. Often, in a series of avoidance responses, the response time gradually increased from one or two seconds to a maximum of 10 seconds. This was followed by one or more escape responses; then the animal began to avoid again. The number of training days for an adequate number of avoidances to be achieved varied, ranging from three days for *Equetus* up to 12 days for *Lutjanus*, at 25 trials per day.

Since the rate of learning to avoid was not the primary concern of this investigation, only rough indications of this rate can be given. In some cases, the intensity of the conditioned stimulus had to be raised during the course of initial training, because the starting levels were too close to threshold values, and avoidance learning was abnormally slow. The number of trials per day was not constant during the training period. Also, if an animal did not escape during the first day's trials, it was guided across the barrier with a plastic paddle, to reduce the total number of electric shocks received by the subject. For these reasons, then, the conditions during early training were not constant, and the records do not provide a reliable index of the rate of learning to avoid. With an average of 25 trials per day, most of the animals reached a criterion of 90 per cent avoidance within five or six days. This compares favorably with the results reported by Wodinsky, Behrend, and Bitterman (1962) who used light as the conditioned stimulus.

A behavioral feature common to most of the animals tested was their slow response at the beginning of any given day's series of trials. Even after the animals were well conditioned and had been tested a number of times, they rarely avoided on the first few trials, even though the sound level was initially 20 decibels above threshold. It was as though the animals required a short "refresher course." These "warm-up" trials at the beginning of each series were characteristic of nearly all the animals tested. The criterion,

therefore, for successful avoidance training was set at a minimum of 18 avoidances out of 20 trials, with the first five trials in a day's sequence discarded as "warm-up" trials.

Figure 3 presents the entire training sequence of one animal, a squirrelfish (*Holocentrus ascensionis*). The response times (in seconds) are plotted on the ordinate. P on the graph represents cases in which the animal was guided or prodded across the barrier in order to prevent its receiving too many shocks. Note that this had to be done in 20 out of 25 trials during the first day but only sporadically on other trial days. The second and third days of the trials showed good escape learning and a few avoidances. On the fourth day there were eight avoidances in 25 trials, and on the fifth day the criterion of avoidance learning was attained with 22 avoidances in 25 trials.

Figure 4 shows a threshold determination made for the same animal, the training protocol of which is illustrated in figure 3. This threshold was taken immediately following the twenty-fifth trial on the fifth training day. After each avoidance response, the conditioned stimulus level was reduced by 5 decibels at the subsequent trial. If there was no avoidance, the animal usually escaped promptly, and at the next trial the condi-

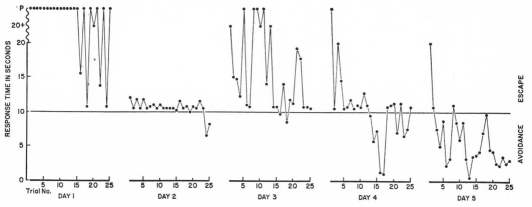

FIG. 3. Example of a five-day training sequence of a squirrelfish (*Holocentrus ascensionis*, no. DF-2), with the use of 25 trials per day and an interval of 10 seconds between the onset of the sound and the onset of the shock. The conditioned stimulus in this case was a tone of which the frequency was 1600 cps. at a pressure level of 30 decibels (re 1 microbar). In the first 15 trials, the responses were forced, i.e., after about 30 seconds from the start of the trial, the animal was pushed across the barrier with a plastic paddle. These forced responses are indicated by P on the ordinate. Response times of over 20 seconds are all grouped together, indicated by 20+ on the ordinate. All responses under 10 seconds were avoidances.

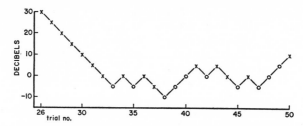

Fig. 4. An example of a threshold determination made for the same animal the training protocol of which is illustrated in figure 3. After each avoidance response (indicated by X), the sound pressure was reduced by 5 decibels. After each escape response (indicated by O), the sound pressure was increased by 5 decibels. The calculated threshold for this series of trials was -1.25 decibels re 1 microbar.

tioned stimulus level was raised by 5 decibels.

TESTING TECHNIQUES

Once the animal achieved a high enough score of avoidances, it was clear that the acoustic stimulus was perceived and that we could begin to test for the threshold level for that particular training tone.

The acoustic pressure of the test tone was generally 20 to 30 decibels above the estimated threshold, and, with each avoidance response, the stimulus level was lowered for the subsequent trial. For most of the species, the stimulus level was lowered in steps of 2 decibels. In two cases (*Holocentrus ascensionis* and *Epinephelus guttatus*), 5-decibel steps were used, because it was found that these animals stopped responding after more than 40 or 50 trials, and coarser steps had to be used.

When the stimulus level was dropped to a point near or below the range of the threshold, the animal did not avoid during the 10-second interval and received one or more shocks. In these cases, the escape was usually a prompt one, often occurring after a single shock. In the next trial, the stimulus level was raised the appropriate 2- or 5-decibel step. In short, each time the animal avoided, the stimulus was lowered, and each time there was no avoidance (i.e., the subject escaped after being shocked) the stimulus was raised in intensity.

In this manner, the threshold range could be bracketed. The technique is a modification of the method of minimal changes, often called the "staircase" or "up-and-down" method (Guilford, 1954).

With increased practice, the fish became more efficient in crossing the barrier, and the number of intertrial crossings increased to a point at which a test trial response could not be distinguished from an intertrial crossing. The animals also may have learned to respond on a time basis. In such situations, the water level was lowered to inhibit these intertrial responses, and the intertrial interval was increased (sometimes up to 15 minutes) to give the animal a chance to settle down. General activity was always higher immediately after a trial, and the subject often crossed the barrier back and forth a few times after which it became quiescent in its typical position in the compartment.

Since it was evident that intertrial crossings increased in frequency as the threshold range was approached, such responses are properly to be considered as false positives or "false alarms." In our study, we attempted not to count these responses but rather, by adjusting the water level at the barrier, to reduce their occurrence.

The fish learned rapidly that the place of the light beam and the top of the barrier were of critical importance. Some of the subjects learned to remain in the beam and partially across the barrier, which, of course, made a trial impossible, since the sound was turned off as soon as the trial was begun, and the fish did not make the required response. The solution, again, was to lower the water level to a point that would inhibit any attempt on the part of the subject to remain in the beam, but not low enough to prevent avoidance or escape responses.

A similar situation was one in which, at the onset of the sound, the fish swam up to the light beam and broke it, but did not cross over to the other compartment, by nosing the beam or breaking it with a fin movement. These partial or accidental responses were considered a true avoidance response for two reasons. If it be assumed that the fish had learned the relevance of breaking the beam or approaching the barrier to the occurrence of the sound, these partial responses are just as objective and meaningful as is the complete avoidance response, and they should be treated as such. If the breaking of the beam were a chance occurrence, it would fall in the same category as an apparent avoidance response that was due to a chance intertrial crossing by the fish. Selected sampling of intertrial crossings indicated that the obtained threshold data cannot be accounted for by the frequency of their occurrence. A chance response or "false alarm," therefore, was counted as a positive response.

An additional behavioral observation in a few cases was that, for reasons unknown to us, the fish developed an asymmetry in the avoidance response. That is, a given fish avoided from one compartment and ceased to avoid from the other compartment. This asymmetrical response occurred at intensities that were sufficiently high to eliminate all possibility that it was the result of an unequal sound level in the two compartments. There were also no differences in the two compartments as measured by our monitoring system. This one-sided avoidance took one of two forms. First was the simple form of one-sided avoidance. This problem was handled by our presenting each sound level twice, so that at least one stimulus was presented to the fish in the compartment from which he was avoiding. In the second form, not only was there one-sided avoidance, but the fish also showed a preference for remaining in a given compartment during the intertrial interval. That is, if the fish crossed from compartment 1 to compartment 2 as a result of a trial (escape or

avoidance), it then returned to compartment 1 shortly thereafter, during the intertrial interval. The result was that the fish was always presented with the conditioned stimulus in only one compartment. Such a one-sided avoidance presented no problem, providing that the preferred compartment was the one from which the fish avoided. The problem would become almost insoluble if the fish simultaneously developed one-sided avoidance and a preference for the compartment from which it did not avoid. Fortunately, this behavior pattern was manifested infrequently among the subjects, and, when it did appear in an individual fish, it lasted for only a few days. An attempt was made to break it by shocking the fish whenever it entered the non-avoiding compartment. At times this was successful, but the total amount of shock that the subject received on that day made the threshold determination somewhat questionable, and these data were excluded from the results presented here.

CRITERIA OF THRESHOLD

A graph of a threshold determination (fig. 4) appears as a series of vertical zigzags. The range between the peaks and valleys of this graph includes the threshold. This is essentially the "up-and-down" or "staircase" technique used by Dixon and Mood (1948), Dixon and Massey (1951), Blough (1958), and others in their method of minimal changes for determining visual thresholds in birds and other animals. The well-known audiometer paper of von Békésy (1947) described this technique for human auditory studies.

One problem in this method is to select the point in the graph at which to begin the calculation. In all of our studies, we started the test trials with a suprathreshold stimulus and gradually worked the animal down to the threshold range, but the slope of this initial part of the graph was often not smooth. The question, then, was: At what point in the graph can it be said that the asymptote was reached? No statistical manipulation is known to us that gives a satisfactory answer to this problem. As shown in several of the figures in this report, the point from which the calculation was made was chosen on the basis of its apparent relation to the beginning of an asymptote. All the points of inflection from there on were used for the calculation of the threshold. A recent description of this staircase technique was given by Cornsweet (1962).

Each segment of the broken zigzag line represents a range that includes the threshold value. We assume, therefore, that the threshold is on a midpoint between each peak and valley of the graph. The mean value of all these midpoints for the entire graph, then, becomes the calculated threshold value. This represents a theoretical point at which the signal is received and responded to 50 per cent of the time and is essentially the same as the calculations used for the method of limits (Guilford, 1954). The calculations were also checked by the frequency analysis method of Dixon and Massey (1951), and the results were virtually identical.

The curves for the several audiograms shown in the following figures were fitted to the data by the method of orthogonal polynomials (Pearson and Hartley, 1956) except in cases of large gaps, in which the lines were drawn in by visual inspection and approximation.

The total number of trials for a test series varied. In training, 25 trials per day were used as a standard, and the range in a threshold determination was from 25 to 150 trials per fish per day. Often a series of a given day was terminated by the animal. In such instances, it simply stopped all avoidances and sometimes even ceased escape behavior. In many cases, the trials for the day were stopped when it appeared that the threshold data obtained were sufficient for a reliable calculation. In general, the criterion was considered reached after at least 10 consecutive reversals of response from avoidance to escape to avoidance, and so on. In some cases, more than 40 such reversals were achieved in a single test series.

Once a threshold for a particular frequency in a given specimen was determined, on the following day the frequency of the test tone was changed and the animal was retested on the new frequency. Eventually some of the animals were retested at the same frequencies, and in most cases the thresholds for different frequencies were replicated at least once by other specimens of the same species.

The number of cases on which an individual threshold is determined is not necessarily the only or the best indication of the reliability of that determination. If an individual threshold falls in line with the slope of an audiogram curve and is consistent with the thresholds obtained with higher and lower frequencies around it, its validity is increased regardless of the number of cases on which it is based. Thus, there is a great deal of confidence in the current audiograms for the higher frequencies. On the other hand, among the low frequencies, where there seem to be at least two threshold functions, not only is a large sample size necessary, but great care must be invoked in fitting any obtained threshold into an appropriate function.

The previous amount of training and the previous number of testing sessions may influence the obtained threshold. A large body of data (Adams, 1957; Teichner, 1954) suggests that the thresholds change as a function of practice. An attempt has been made in the present research to control for this factor by testing some of the animals of a given species in ascending frequencies, and some in descending frequencies. After thresholds were determined for various fish at different frequencies, some new fish were then trained at selected frequencies for the purpose of adding additional subjects, and for checking the obtained values, as well as checking the effect or previous training on the threshold.

In addition to the appearance of the graph of avoidances and escapes, the adequate number of points of inflection as the asymptote is reached, and the consistency of the results with other threshold determinations, another criterion for a reliable threshold was the range of variability in the test series. A maximum acceptable variability was set at 10 decibels, but the range between the maximum and minimum inflection points was usually less. All results reported present the arithmetic means and standard deviations based on the points of change between avoidance and escape. Most of the standard deviations varied from ± 2 to ± 3.

RESULTS

PART 1

THE THRESHOLD DETERMINATIONS on the three species described in the present part (*Holocentrus ascensionis*, *H. vexillarius*, and *Equetus acuminatus*) were consistent at all the frequencies tested. Variation among different individuals within a species was small. The tabular data are arranged on the basis of the frequencies tested.

AUDITORY THRESHOLD DETERMINATIONS IN *Holocentrus ascensionis*

During the preliminary escape training, the optimum shock levels for this species were determined to be 15 to 20 volts. After the avoidance response became well established and the specimens received fewer actual shocks, the shock level was raised to 25 volts. The intertrial intervals were varied on a random basis, but it was found that the minimum was three minutes. Shorter intertrial intervals resulted in a general increase in activity and numerous intertrial crossings. The interval was varied randomly from three to five minutes, with an average of four minutes. Longer intervals were occasionally introduced if intertrial crossings took place at frequencies greater than one per minute. Intervals up to 10 or 15 minutes usually gave the animal a chance to settle down in a corner.

The water level over the barrier was a critical variable. The squirrelfish, unlike the other species tested, rarely turned on its side to cross over, even if the water level was very low. Levels of 5 cm. or more were readily traversed, even though the dorsal fin and a large part of the dorsum protruded from water during the crossing. At a water level of 2.5 cm., crossings were greatly inhibited, and the animal often went part way over and then dropped back. After initial training, a level of from 3.5 to 4.0 cm. was found to be optimal, i.e., spontaneous crossings were not very frequent and escape or avoidance crossings were not inhibited.

Once the training parameters were established, i.e., the intertrial interval, the shock level, water level, and so on, it took about four to six days for a squirrelfish to reach a

reliable criterion of avoidance. The animal was given 25 trials per day. On the first day, it had to be helped across the barrier by a plastic paddle in the first five to 10 trials. Help was given to speed up the escape learning, because, for purposes of this work, the learning time was not important. On the second and third days, escape from the shock was regular and rapid, usually after the first one or two stimuli, and there were sporadic avoidances. By the fifth day, the number of avoidances was usually over 50 per cent (it was 90 per cent in one instance). By the sixth or seventh day, the animal was avoiding in 80 to 90 per cent of the trials. Most avoidances took place within five seconds of the onset of the conditioned stimulus. In almost every day's series of trials, however, there was a "warm-up" period in which, for the first five or 10 trials, there were no avoidances, and thereafter the response was close to 100 per cent. This warm-up period persisted even

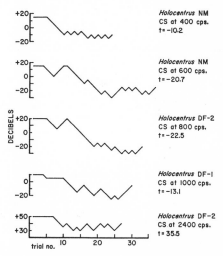

FIG. 5. Five examples of threshold determinations made on the squirrelfish (*Holocentrus ascensionis*). The initial horizontal line represents the "warm-up" trials; the downward slopes represent avoidance responses, and the upward slopes are escape responses. The sound frequencies (conditioned stimulus = CS) and the calculated threshold values (t), in decibels, are given for each protocol.

199

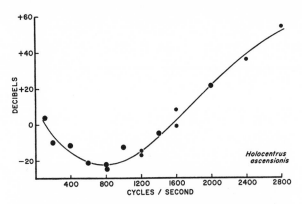

FIG. 6. Summary of threshold determinations made for five specimens of the squirrelfish (*Holocentrus ascensionis*). The data are given in table 2. The larger spots indicate two or more values at almost the same point.

after more than 30 days of testing in some individuals.

When an individual fish was tested, it was found that after 40 or 50 trials the avoidance responses became sporadic and often ceased entirely. In many instances even escape responses became slow and irregular. It was as if the animal tired or the response became extinguished. To keep the animals from getting shocked too frequently, the trials were terminated for the day when the avoidance responses became obviously slow and unreliable.

Once avoidance responses became stabilized and a threshold determination was in progress, the animals consistently took up the same position in the compartment during the intertrial interval. This position faced into a corner or against the far wall of the compartment, i.e., about where the hydrophone was placed for sound measurements. It is fair to say, therefore, that the accuracy of the threshold measurements for *Holocentrus* was probably in the order of ±2 decibels, if equipment variability and small changes in the initial position of the animal at the onset of the conditioned stimulus are allowed for.

Figure 5 shows five sample records obtained with *Holocentrus* auditory threshold determinations.

Figure 6 and table 2 summarize all the data on threshold determinations in this species. A total of five animals were used. The larger spots on the graph indicate two or more threshold values of almost the same value.

This species was one of the most sensitive tested. Its lowest threshold was at 800 cps. at an acoustic pressure level of below −20 decibels. The squirrelfish also possessed the broadest frequency-response spectrum, exhibiting reliable thresholds at 2400 and 2800 cps.

AUDITORY THRESHOLD DETERMINATIONS
IN *Holocentrus vexillarius*

The general behavior of this smaller species of squirrelfish was remarkably similar to that of *H. ascensionis*.

The optimum shock levels were 15 to 20 volts, and the level was maintained at 20 volts in most of the threshold determinations. The intertrial periods were varied from one to three minutes, with occasional periods of up to 10 minutes when intertrial crossings became too frequent. The water level at the barrier was extremely critical, with 2 cm. as the optimal value. Seven to eight days of training were usually required, with 25 trials per day, until the 90 per cent avoidance criterion was reached. The interval between the onset of the sound and the delivery of the shock was 10 seconds. This species was tested at sound-pressure changes of 2 decibels, i.e., after each avoidance the sound level was reduced 2 decibels or raised 2 decibels after an escape. Like *H. ascensionis*, these animals also regularly took up a position against the far wall of the compartment between trials.

Figure 7 and table 3 present the data on threshold determinations in *H. vexillarius*. Three animals were used. There were some clear differences between this species and *ascensionis*. The lowest threshold values were

at 600 cps. instead of 800 cps., and these were higher by more than 10 decibels over the lowest values in *ascensionis*. The audiogram of *H. vexillarius* showed a steeper rise both above and below the point of highest sensitivity. Although attempts were made to test these animals at frequencies above 1200 cps., no reliable threshold determinations could be

TABLE 2

Auditory Threshold Determinations in the Squirrelfish, *Holocentrus ascensionis*

Fish No.	Date	Frequency, in Cycles per Second	N^a	T^b	Mean, in Decibels	σ
NM	7/10	100	15	18	4.1	2.3
LP	7/16	100	10	21	3.8	2.1
LP	8/2	100	12	15	3.6	1.7
LP	7/15	200	11	23	−10.0	4.3
LP	8/3	200	17	21	−9.8	2.1
NM	7/9	200	10	12	−10.2	1.5
NM	7/11	400	14	16	−10.2	2.5
LP	8/5	400	15	22	−13.5	1.4
NM	7/14	400	10	12	−12.8	1.2
NM	7/12	600	11	16	−20.7	2.8
DF-1	7/9	600	13	14	−21.0	3.1
DF-1	7/11	800	13	17	−24.6	2.2
NM	7/13	800	9	11	−23.2	1.1
UC	7/11	800	12	18	−24.1	3.5
DF-2	8/5	800	11	15	−22.5	4.6
DF	7/12	1000	8	19	−13.1	6.5
UC	7/9	1000	12	22	−12.7	5.4
DF	7/13	1200	16	24	−17.0	3.1
UC	7/13	1200	15	20	−15.2	2.9
DF-1	7/15	1400	13	17	−5.2	2.8
UC	7/15	1400	9	12	−4.3	4.5
UC	7/21	1600	12	19	8.3	3.4
DF-2	7/31	1600	12	21	−1.3	2.5
UC	7/22	2000	7	9	20.7	2.4
DF-2	8/2	2000	5	9	21.5	1.3
DF-2	8/3	2400	11	17	35.5	1.9

[a] Number of points of inflection in the threshold determination curve.
[b] Number of trials on which the threshold determination was made.

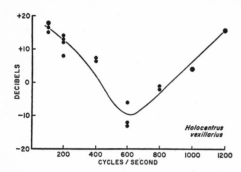

FIG. 7. Summary of threshold determinations made for three specimens of the dusky squirrelfish (*Holocentrus vexillarius*). The data are given in table 3. The larger spots indicate two or more values at almost the same point.

made because of extremely erratic avoidance behavior.

AUDITORY THRESHOLD DETERMINATIONS IN *Equetus acuminatus*

The optimum shock voltage was 12 to 15 volts. The intertrial intervals averaged two minutes. The water level above the barrier was varied from 2.5 to 3.0 cm. The interval between sound and shock was 10 seconds, and the sound level was varied in steps of 2 decibels during the threshold determinations. Three specimens were used.

This species learned the avoidance problem by far the most rapidly. For example, initial training of specimen A at 600 cps. was begun

TABLE 3

AUDITORY THRESHOLD DETERMINATIONS IN THE DUSKY SQUIRRELFISH, *Holocentrus vexillarius*

Fish No.	Date	Frequency, in Cycles per Second	N^a	T^b	Mean, in Decibels	σ
A	7/13	100	9	21	15.0	2.2
B	7/10	100	12	32	17.3	3.2
C	7/13	100	14	27	16.4	3.0
B	7/16	100	15	30	17.8	2.1
A	7/13	200	10	27	8.2	1.1
B	7/12	200	16	31	14.1	1.8
C	7/12	200	19	23	12.2	1.8
B	7/17	200	23	47	12.5	2.1
A	7/12	400	18	44	6.4	1.9
B	7/13	400	20	43	7.3	3.2
A	7/10	600	9	26	−6.0	2.7
B	7/11	600	13	28	−13.2	1.8
A	7/11	600	15	27	−12.4	1.2
A	7/14	800	18	40	−1.0	2.3
C	7/14	800	20	38	−2.2	2.5
A	7/14	1000	19	42	3.8	2.0
C	7/14	1000	12	26	4.2	2.1
A	7/15	1200	15	36	16.1	1.8
C	7/15	1200	21	39	15.5	2.4

[a] Number of points of inflection in the threshold determination curve.
[b] Number of trials on which the threshold determination was made.

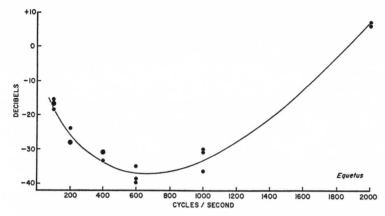

FIG. 8. Summary of threshold determinations for three specimens of the cubbyu (*Equetus acuminatus*). The data are given in table 4. The larger spots represent two or more congruent points.

TABLE 4

AUDITORY THRESHOLD DETERMINATIONS IN THE CUBBYU, *Equetus acuminatus*

Fish No.	Date	Frequency, in Cycles per Second	N[a]	T[b]	Mean, in Decibels	σ
A	6/27	100	14	34	−8.3	2.7
B	6/28	100	23	36	−5.4	1.2
C	6/29	100	20	34	−6.2	2.2
C	6/30	100	18	25	−7.1	1.8
C	7/1	100	16	24	−6.5	2.4
C	7/2	100	19	28	−6.8	1.0
B	6/27	200	8	16	−24.0	1.2
A	6/28	200	13	29	−28.1	2.4
C	6/27	200	17	30	−27.4	2.3
C	7/3	200	22	38	−27.7	3.1
A	6/26	400	11	25	−31.3	2.8
B	6/26	400	12	26	−33.3	1.0
C	6/26	400	15	34	−30.5	3.2
A	6/24	600	8	18	−35.0	1.2
B	6/25	600	9	22	−39.8	1.3
C	6/25	600	14	24	−38.8	1.9
A	6/29	1000	18	34	−36.3	1.7
B	6/30	1000	25	38	−30.1	2.2
B	7/1	1000	27	37	−30.7	1.9
A	6/30	2000	19	30	6.2	3.4
A	7/1	2000	10	22	7.3	2.9

[a] Number of points of inflection in the threshold determination curve.
[b] Number of trials on which the threshold determination was made.

on June 21. In 25 trials, the first two had to be forced escapes (i.e., the animal was prodded across the barrier), but in the remaining trials of this first day, the subject avoided on the tenth trial and escaped rapidly in all the others. On the second day, this animal avoided in 12 out of 25 trials. On the third day, it avoided in 48 out of 50 trials. On the fourth day, June 24, its threshold at 600 cps. was determined.

During preliminary trials, intertrial crossings were virtually absent, but, as in all other species tested, as the threshold was approached, the animals continued to cross the barrier every five to 10 seconds shortly after a

trial, but within one to two minutes they settled down to a stable position. This position was usually close to the center of the compartment, facing the barrier. Avoidances were usually rapid, usually about two seconds after the onset of the sound.

Coincident with the rapid learning of the avoidance problem, this species exhibited the lowest threshold values of any of the forms tested. Table 4 and figure 8 show the threshold determination results for *Equetus*. Thresholds as low as almost −40 decibels at 600 cps. were determined. There was little variability among the three animals tested.

PART 2

This group consists of four species: *Haemulon sciurus*, *Lutjanus apodus*, *Thalassoma bifasciatum*, and *Eupomacentrus leucostictus*.

At frequencies above 400 cps., all the members of these species gave threshold values that showed only small variations among different individuals of the same species, but at the low frequencies a high degree of variability began to appear as the animals were retested and the points on the audiograms were replicated. These variabilities took two forms. One was an abrupt change in the threshold determinations as compared to values obtained in early tests, and the other was the appearance of a temporary threshold during a given series of test trials.

SECONDARY LOW-FREQUENCY THRESHOLDS

A feature exhibited by several of the animals tested was the presence of what appeared to be two very different thresholds for the same frequency. This was evident only at frequencies below 500 cps. During the replicating of the low-frequency threshold determinations, it was found that some of the subjects showed a drop in threshold values of as much as 20 decibels below the previously determined levels. This occurred only after the animals had been tested over a period of several days or weeks. As an example, in grunt no. 3 (*Haemulon sciurus*) the threshold values for 100 cps. and 200 cps. were determined to be +11.3 and +12.1 decibels when the fish was tested on June 20 and June 21, respectively. After additional testing at these

and other, higher frequencies, the thresholds at 100 cps. and 200 cps. became −17.3 and −16.4 decibels on August 20 and August 15, respectively. The data on these low frequencies, therefore, had to be divided into two groups—early and late determinations. It

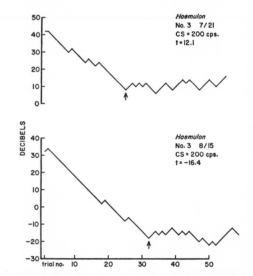

FIG. 9 Graph of two representative threshold determinations made on a specimen of grunt (*Haemulon sciurus*, no. 3). The arrow indicates the point at which the calculation of the threshold was begun. CS is the frequency of the conditioned stimulus. Note that the threshold values (t) of the two determinations are 28.5 decibels apart. The lower value was obtained after the animal had had considerable testing experience (see table 5).

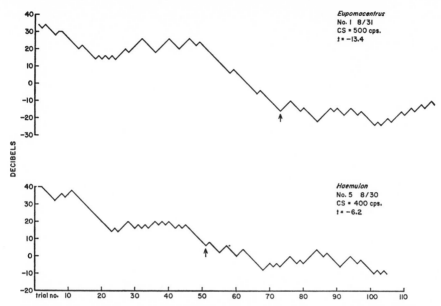

FIG. 10. Two graphs of threshold determinations that illustrate the plateau effect. The arrow indicates the point at which the calculation of the threshold was begun. The upper graph is for a beau-gregory (*Eupomacentrus*, no. 1), and the lower is for a grunt (*Haemulon*, no. 5).

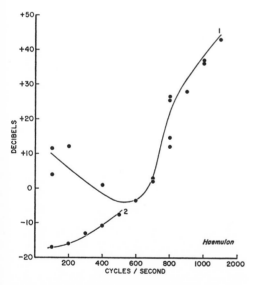

FIG. 11. Summary of threshold determinations for the grunt (*Haemulon sciurus*, no. 3). The values are listed in table 5. Curve 1 represents the primary threshold determinations made during the period July 13 to August 14. Curve 2 is the secondary low-frequency series of determinations made August 15 to 27.

was evident that the testing procedure itself constituted additional training and that an improvement in the performance would not be surprising. What was surprising, however, was the abrupt and major change in the threshold values. In species in which this change occurred, we grouped the threshold data into two separate curves. The first determinations (both low and high frequencies) we call the "primary threshold curve." The later low-frequency determinations comprise what we call the "secondary low-frequency threshold curve." These are described in detail in the sections under each species and are shown in the tables and graphs.

The data in the tables for these species are presented in chronological order for each individual subject, so that the threshold changes with time can be seen.

PLATEAU EFFECT

During the course of many of the threshold determinations at frequencies below 500 cps., a temporary threshold effect was obtained as the sound level was lowered or raised in the step method described above. As trials were

205

TABLE 5

AUDITORY THRESHOLD DETERMINATIONS IN A
SINGLE SPECIMEN (NO. 3) OF THE BLUE-STRIPED
GRUNT, *Haemulon sciurus*

Date	Frequency, in Cycles per Second	Threshold, in Decibels
7/10	700	1.3
7/13	400	0.5
7/20	100	11.3
7/21	200	12.1
7/23	100	3.7
7/24	600	−3.9
7/25	800	25.2
7/26	800	26.4
7/28	700	2.7
7/31	800	11.9
8/3	900	27.5
8/9	1000	35.8
8/11	1100	42.7
8/12	1000	36.7
8/14	800	14.4
8/15	200	−16.4[a]
8/20	100	−17.3[a]
8/22	300	−13.4[a]
8/25	400	−11.1[a]
8/27	500	−7.7[a]

[a] Secondary low-frequency thresholds.

continued, the record of avoidances showed a sharp drop and an eventual stabilization at a lower sound pressure. We call this temporary threshold the "plateau effect."

The plateau was usually of brief duration, usually involving fewer than 10 points of inflection in the test series, but on a few occasions as many as 20 such points were included in a plateau. After the appearance of a plateau, the threshold curve sometimes dropped as much as 20 or 30 decibels before becoming asymptotic (fig. 9).

We are not able to state with any certainty whether these plateaus are caused by high sound or shock intensity, stage of practice, or a shift in sensory modality. One difficulty that is introduced by the presence of these plateaus is the uncertainty as to whether or not the asymptote of any individual threshold has been reached. Most of the thresholds reported here are based on 10 to 20 points of inflection. The fact that plateaus of comparable duration can occur invites caution, to

assure that the reported values are true thresholds and not merely plateaus and thus preludes to lower thresholds.

The plateau effect and the secondary low-frequency thresholds seem to be related in that they occur only at frequencies below 500 cps. The repeated trials, either in a single day's series or over many days of testing, add to the experience of the subject and lead to the expression of either the plateau effect or the secondary threshold.

AUDITORY THRESHOLD DETERMINATIONS IN *Haemulon sciurus*

The optimum shock levels were 7 to 10 volts, and the intertrial intervals averaged two minutes. The water level at the barrier ranged from 0.4 to 1.2 cm. At 25 trials per day, the animals learned to avoid regularly in four or five days. The interval between the onset of the sound and the shock was 10 seconds, and the staircase method of testing used steps of 2 decibels. Intertrial crossings (i.e., "false alarms") were infrequent and occurred only occasionally when the sound

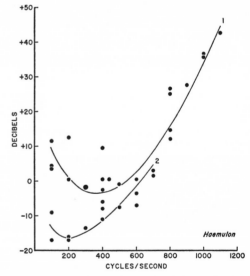

FIG. 12. Summary of threshold determinations made for four specimens of the blue-striped grunt (*Haemulon sciurus*). The data are given in table 6. Curve 1 represents the primary thresholds, and curve 2 is the secondary low-frequency series of determinations. The larger spots indicate two or more values at almost the same point.

TABLE 6

AUDITORY THRESHOLD DETERMINATIONS IN THE BLUE-STRIPED GRUNT, *Haemulon sciurus*

Fish No.	Date	Frequency, in Cycles per Second	N^a	T^b	Mean, in Decibels	σ
1	8/4	100	11	25	4.0	2.4
3	7/20	100	16	31	11.3	3.2
3	7/23	100	20	38	3.7	2.6
3	8/20	100	14	18	−17.3[c]	1.5
5	9/5	100	20	44	−9.1[c]	3.2
1	7/31	200	11	20	0.3	1.8
3	7/21	200	16	32	12.1	1.9
3	8/15	200	17	29	−16.4[c]	2.6
5	9/3	200	15	31	−16.6[c]	1.7
1	7/26	300	27	46	−2.2	3.9
3	8/22	300	15	22	−13.4[c]	1.5
5	9/1	300	21	48	−1.8	2.5
1	7/17	400	21	48	−2.9	4.0
1	7/25	400	20	30	9.2	2.1
3	7/13	400	15	28	0.5	2.9
3	8/25	400	20	36	−11.1[c]	2.2
4	7/18	400	14	29	−7.7[c]	2.7
5	8/30	400	21	39	−6.2[c]	3.5
4	7/11	440	9	18	0.4	2.1
4	7/14	440	19	35	−11.8[c]	2.0
3	8/27	500	25	44	−7.7[c]	2.4
5	8/29	500	11	19	−0.9	3.2
1	8/6	600	11	25	−7.3	1.5
3	7/24	600	34	57	−3.9	2.3
4	7/20	600	23	36	0.6	2.5
3	7/10	700	14	32	1.3	4.6
3	7/28	700	28	61	2.7	3.6
3	7/25	800	41	73	25.2	4.1
3	7/26	800	13	25	26.4	2.9
3	7/31	800	21	40	11.9	3.6
3	8/14	800	17	28	14.4	2.7
3	8/3	900	29	59	27.5	4.3
3	8/9	1000	39	93	35.8	5.8
3	8/12	1000	19	36	36.7	6.6
3	8/11	1100	29	61	42.7	3.6

[a] Number of points of inflection in the threshold determination curve.
[b] Number of trials on which the threshold determination was made.
[c] Secondary low-frequency thresholds.

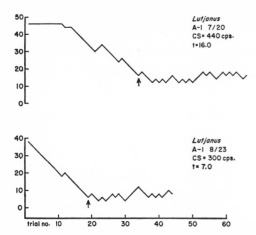

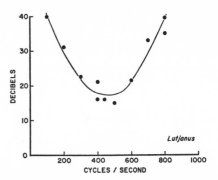

FIG. 14. Summary of the first 11 threshold determinations (see table 7) made for a single specimen of schoolmaster (*Lutjanus*, no. A-1) during the period July 16 to 30. This represents the primary threshold curve for the specimen.

FIG. 13. Two graphs of threshold determinations made on a specimen of schoolmaster (*Lutjanus*, No. A-1). The arrow indicates the point at which the calculation of the threshold was begun. The upper graph is an example of a long "warm-up" period, while the lower graph shows no "warm-up."

level was close to threshold. The usual position of the animal just prior to a test was against the far wall of the compartment, but sometimes it remained in the center of the compartment with its snout pointing toward the barrier. Four specimens were used in these determinations.

Figure 9 shows two representative threshold determinations of *Haemulon* no. 3 at 200 cps. The arrow in the graph indicates the point from which the threshold value was calculated. Note that the threshold values of these two determinations are 28.5 decibels apart. The upper graph was a determination made during the early stages of testing on July 21. Prior to this test, this animal had three previous threshold tests at 100, 400, and 700 cps. The lower graph was a threshold measurement taken on August 15 after this animal had had 15 threshold determinations at frequencies of from 100 to 1100 cps. This latter value is considered here as representing a secondary low-frequency threshold.

Figure 10, lower, is an exceptionally long record consisting of more than 100 trials. In contrast to records as exemplified in figure 9, this showed a plateau effect from the twentieth to the forty-fifth trial. Such plateaus were generally evident in tests of frequencies of 400

cps. or below and also, in most cases, occurred during the later periods of testing, i.e., when the secondary low-frequency thresholds began to appear.

Table 5 lists the threshold data in chronological order for a single animal (no. 3), and figure 11 shows these data in graph form. The curve labeled "1" represents the primary thresholds (as defined above), which were determined during the period July 13 to August 14. Replications of the low-frequency thresholds at later dates (August 15 to 27) showed an abrupt change in value. These determinations, labeled "2" on the graph,

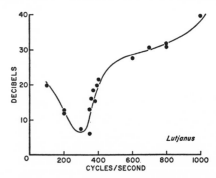

FIG. 15. Summary of 16 threshold determinations (see table 7) made for the same specimen as is represented in figure 14 (*Lutjanus*, no. A-1) during the period August 7 to September 4. The portion of the curve below 400 cps. represents the secondary low-frequency thresholds for this specimen. Comparison of this graph with that of figure 14 shows the effect of repeated threshold testing on the low-frequency sensitivity.

TABLE 7

AUDITORY THRESHOLD DETERMINATIONS FOR A
SINGLE SPECIMEN (NO. A-1) OF THE SCHOOL-
MASTER, *Lutjanus apodus*

Date	Frequency, in Cycles per Second	Threshold, in Decibels
7/16	400	15.9
7/20	440	16.0
7/22	400	21.2
7/23	600	21.2
7/24	800	35.1
7/25	800	39.1
7/26	700	32.8
7/27	300	22.6
7/28	200	30.9
7/29	100	39.7
7/30	500	14.7
8/7	600	27.4
8/9	700	30.4
8/11	800	31.5
8/13	800	30.4
8/14	1000	39.6[a]
8/16	200	12.3[a]
8/19	200	11.9[a]
8/21	100	19.3[a]
8/23	300	7.0[a]
8/24	400	21.3
8/26	350	5.5[a]
8/28	380	15.1
8/30	390	19.6
8/31	470	18.0
9/2	360	15.8
9/4	350	12.6

[a] Secondary low-frequency thresholds.

represent the secondary low-frequency thresholds by virtue of a drop of more than 10 decibels from the earlier determinations. The determination at 500 cps. is considered as part of the secondary curve only because it was obtained after the subject had considerable experience in the testing situation.

Figure 12 is a composite graph for all four subjects of all the determinations listed in table 6. From 700 cps., the audiogram curve resembles that of *Holocentrus* and that of *Equetus* in general shape and consistency. Below 400 cps., the data break into two distinct groups, with the lower values being the later determinations of subjects nos. 3 and 5. The 400- to 600-cps. region shows a high degree of variability. This is evidently where

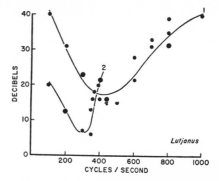

FIG. 16. Summary of threshold determinations for three specimens of the schoolmaster (*Lutjanus apodus*). The data are given in table 8. Curve 1 represents the primary thresholds, and curve 2 is the secondary low-frequency series. The larger spots indicate two or more congruent values.

the primary and secondary curves overlap. The curves as drawn in figure 12 are only approximations and interpretations.

AUDITORY THRESHOLD DETERMINATIONS IN *Lutjanus apodus*

The optimum shock level was 7 volts; this species was extremely sensitive to higher voltages. The intertrial intervals averaged two minutes. The water level at the barrier ranged from 0.6 to 1.3 cm. This species was one of the slowest to learn the avoidance problem. As many as 12 days were required before avoidances became regular enough for threshold determinations. The interval between sound and shock was 10 seconds, and the sound level was varied in steps of 2 decibels during testing. Intertrial crossings were very infrequent. There was some tendency to establish a "preferred" side, and, after an avoidance or escape, the animal immediately crossed the barrier to return to the original compartment. The positions of the animals prior to a test varied widely but usually showed some orientation with respect to the barrier which indicated a readiness to respond. One common position was with the snout leaning against the top of the barrier in such a way that a single flip of the tail sent the fish across the barrier. Three specimens were used.

Figure 13 shows two sample threshold determinations in *Lutjanus*. The upper graph

TABLE 8

Auditory Threshold Determinations in the Schoolmaster, *Lutjanus apodus*

Fish No.	Date	Frequency, in Cycles per Second	N^a	T^b	Mean, in Decibels	σ
A-1	7/29	100	33	47	39.7	4.7
A-1	8/21	100	31	42	19.3^c	4.3
A-1	7/28	200	31	42	30.9	2.2
A-1	8/16	200	23	34	12.3^c	3.2
A-1	8/19	200	19	28	11.9^c	2.2
A-1	7/27	300	21	30	22.6	3.7
A-1	8/23	300	17	27	7.0^c	1.5
N	9/9	300	24	41	23.3	2.3
A-1	8/26	350	22	47	5.5^c	5.1
A-1	9/4	350	21	46	12.6	2.9
A-1	9/2	360	13	48	15.8	4.4
A-1	8/31	370	11	38	18.0	2.7
A-1	8/28	380	24	40	15.1	2.5
A-1	8/30	390	18	30	19.6	1.6
A-1	7/16	400	7	18	15.9	2.3
A-1	7/22	400	25	46	21.2	2.0
A-1	8/24	400	23	33	21.3	2.1
P-4	7/11	440	17	29	15.5	2.6
P-4	7/13	440	20	42	14.6	3.1
A-1	7/20	440	24	34	16.0	1.8
A-1	7/30	500	11	51	14.7	3.3
A-1	7/23	600	33	44	21.2	2.3
A-1	8/7	600	21	81	27.4	3.1
A-1	7/26	700	29	39	32.8	1.9
A-1	8/9	700	10	35	30.4	2.2
A-1	7/24	800	19	35	35.1	5.2
A-1	7/25	800	33	42	39.1	2.2
A-1	8/11	800	17	26	31.5	1.3
A-1	8/13	800	11	17	30.4	1.2
A-1	8/14	1000	17	41	39.6	3.1

[a] Number of points of inflection in the threshold determination curve.
[b] Number of trials on which the threshold determination was made.
[c] Secondary low-frequency thresholds.

TABLE 9

AUDITORY THRESHOLD DETERMINATIONS IN THE BLUE-HEAD, *Thalassoma bifasciatum*

Fish No.	Date	Frequency, in Cycles per Second	N^a	T^b	Mean, in Decibels	σ
1	8/18	100	21	41	27.1	2.8
1	8/22	100	25	35	20.4	2.2
1	8/6	200	15	28	6.0	1.9
2	8/6	200	13	22	5.5	1.6
2	8/18	200	21	35	9.4	2.8
4	9/10	200	12	31	22.3	4.7
1	8/3	300	14	25	11.9	2.4
1	8/25	300	15	24	1.5	1.4
2	8/4	300	14	23	14.4	1.6
3	9/9	300	11	17	17.4	1.4
4	8/4	300	15	42	17.2	4.3
1	8/15	400	19	39	9.9	3.1
2	8/15	400	17	37	10.7	3.5
3	9/3	500	22	51	4.8	2.8
1	8/8	600	15	27	9.0	1.9
2	8/8	600	19	30	10.1	2.9
1	8/10	800	21	33	19.3	1.8
2	8/10	800	25	39	23.6	2.0
1	8/11	900	15	30	22.9	3.2
2	8/14	900	17	26	29.4	1.8
1	8/13	1000	11	16	26.1	1.0
2	8/12	1000	21	37	31.3	2.6
1	8/14	1200	13	25	34.8	2.2

[a] Number of points of inflection in the threshold determination curve.
[b] Number of trials on which the threshold determination was made.

is an example of a long "warm-up" period. Here the first 10 trials were not avoidances, and the sound level was not changed. After the eleventh trial, the sound pressure was reduced 2 decibels with each avoidance or increased 2 decibels after each escape. In contrast, the lower graph shows a case in which there were no "warm-up" trials, and the sound level was reduced regularly until the threshold range was reached.

As in *Haemulon*, a secondary low-frequency threshold curve was present in *Lutjanus*.

Figures 14 and 15 show this. Figure 14 is a graph of the first 11 threshold determinations made for specimen no. A-1, during the period July 16 to 30. This graph represents the primary threshold curve. Figure 15 is a graph of 16 threshold determinations made for the same specimen during the period August 7 to September 4. The upper portions of these curves, from 500 cps., are similar. At 100 and 200 cps., however, the later determinations (fig. 15) show as much as a 20-decibel drop in the thresholds, and a 15-decibel drop at 300

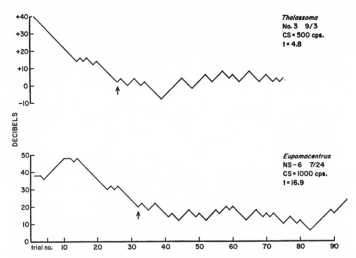

FIG. 17. Two graphs of threshold determinations. The arrow indicates the point at which the calculation of the threshold was begun. The upper graph, for a blue-head wrasse (*Thalassoma*, no. 3), illustrates the absence of a "warm-up" period and a trace of the plateau effect. The lower graph, for a beau-gregory (*Eupomacentrus*, no. NS-6), illustrates a prolonged "warm-up" period.

cps. The region of overlap at 400 to 500 cps. shows a high variability but no clear threshold drop.

Table 7 lists, in chronological order, all the determinations made on the above specimen, A-1. The results at 800 and 600 cps. show a high degree of consistency between tests made in July and those made more than a week later in August, whereas, when the animal was retested at 100 and 200 cps., there was a significant drop in the threshold. The last eight determinations were all made in the frequency band where the primary and secondary curves appear to overlap, and the table shows a variability range of more than 10 decibels in this region. The 5.5-decibel threshold obtained at 350 cps. on August 26 is assumed to be on the secondary curve, while the higher value (12.6) for the same frequency nine days later is thought to represent a return to the primary curve.

Table 8 and figure 16 present all the data on threshold determinations in this species. Most of the data are based on a single subject, but two additional animals were used to check specific points. Specimen N, for example, was both trained and tested at 300 cps., and gave a value within 1 decibel of that

obtained as a primary threshold for specimen A-1.

AUDITORY THRESHOLD DETERMINATIONS
IN *Thalassoma bifasciatum*

The optimum shock levels were 10 to 15 volts. The intertrial intervals varied from two to 15 minutes because of frequent intertrial crossings. Often, after a trial, the animal continued to cross back and forth every few seconds for several minutes. The observer, then, had to wait until these crossings slowed down to fewer than one per minute before another trial could be begun. The water level had to be very low, usually 0.6 cm. or less. These fish regularly assumed a position with the nose at the barrier, and, if the water level was too high, the light beam along the top of the barrier remained cut. The interval between sound and shock was 10 seconds, and the sound level was varied in 2-decibel steps. Four animals were tested and reached the criterion of avoidance training in three to four days.

Figure 17, upper, is a representative threshold record for a specimen of *Thalassoma*. In this instance, no "warm-up" trials were required, but there was a trace of a plateau

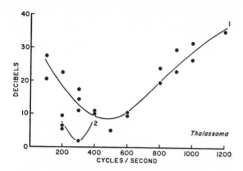

FIG. 18. Summary of threshold determinations for four specimens of the blue-head wrasse (*Thalassoma bifasciatum*). The data are given in table 9. Curve no. 1 represents the primary thresholds and curve no. 2 is the secondary low-frequency series.

effect about 10 decibels above the threshold level.

Table 9 and figure 18 summarize all the threshold determinations in this species. The secondary low-frequency curve is not so clear in this species as in *Haemulon* or *Lutjanus*. It is possible, for example, that the lower point at 100 cps. should be part of this secondary curve, but there are not sufficient data to

TABLE 10

AUDITORY THRESHOLD DETERMINATIONS IN A SINGLE SPECIMEN (NO. NS-5) OF THE BEAU-GREGORY, *Eupomacentrus leucostictus*

Date	Frequency, in Cycles per Second	Threshold, in Decibels
7/10	440	14.2
7/15	400	4.0
7/19	400	6.8
7/21	200	11.8
7/22	100	23.3
7/24	100	23.6
7/26	100	4.6[a]
7/27	200	−4.5[a]
7/29	600	21.3
7/31	600	18.9
8/3	600	−10.4
8/5	800	−2.0
8/6	1000	13.0
8/8	1100	22.7
8/10	1200	36.5
8/12	900	6.8

[a] Secondary low-frequency thresholds.

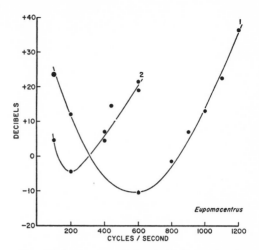

FIG. 19. Summary of threshold determinations made for a single specimen of the beau-gregory (*Eupomacentrus*, no. NS-5). The values are listed in table 10. Curve 1 is the primary threshold series, and curve 2 is the secondary low-frequency curve.

establish this 7-decibel difference as significant. Furthermore, at 200 cps., it is not clear whether the threshold point at 9.4 decibels really belongs with the secondary curve or not, but we have assumed that it does because it occurred after this animal (no. 2) had been

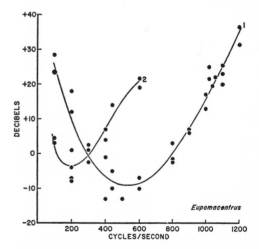

FIG. 20. Summary of threshold determinations for four specimens of the beau-gregory, *Eupomacentrus leucostictus*. The data are given in table 11. Curve 1 is the primary threshold series, and curve 2 is the secondary low-frequency curve.

TABLE 11

AUDITORY THRESHOLD DETERMINATIONS IN THE BEAU-GREGORY, *Eupomacentrus leucostictus*

Fish No.	Date	Frequency, in Cycles per Second	N[a]	T[b]	Mean, in Decibels	σ
NS-5	7/22	100	23	48	23.3	4.6
NS-5	7/24	100	17	26	23.6	2.0
NS-5	7/26	100	20	31	4.6[c]	1.7
No-3	9/10	100	22	48	23.6	3.8
No-3	9/11	100	24	53	28.2	3.5
No-1	9/9	100	20	37	3.0[c]	1.7
NS-5	7/21	200	35	73	11.8	5.2
NS-5	7/27	200	20	33	−4.5[c]	2.6
NS-6	8/17	200	11	18	19.0	1.9
NS-6	8/23	200	15	22	−7.3[c]	1.4
No-3	9/4	200	19	49	0.6[c]	5.1
No-1	8/7	200	17	24	−7.6[c]	1.7
NS-6	8/15	300	21	41	2.4	3.6
No-3	9/2	300	22	37	−2.6	1.9
No-1	9/4	300	26	43	1.1	3.2
NS-5	7/15	400	19	30	4.0	12.1
NS-5	7/19	400	33	57	6.8	2.1
NS-6	7/19	400	23	36	−1.4	2.0
No-1	8/2	400	20	37	−13.6	2.4
NS-5	7/10	440	25	41	14.2	3.7
NS-6	7/10	440	9	16	−9.9	1.3
NS-6	7/12	440	10	21	−5.2	2.0
No-1	8/31	500	25	48	−13.4	3.6
NS-5	7/19	600	19	37	21.3	3.1
NS-5	7/31	600	23	62	18.9	5.6
NS-5	8/3	600	5	13	−10.4	2.1
NS-6	7/20	600	23	35	−7.6	2.8
NS-5	8/5	800	9	34	−2.0	2.7
NS-6	7/22	800	17	37	−2.2	4.2
NS-6	8/14	800	13	24	2.8	1.5
NS-5	8/12	900	15	21	6.8	1.2
NS-6	8/12	900	10	27	6.2	2.8
NS-5	8/6	1000	17	32	13.0	2.2
NS-6	7/24	1000	30	65	16.9	3.5
NS-6	7/26	1020	11	25	21.6	3.1
NS-6	7/30	1020	19	38	24.9	1.5
NS-6	7/31	1040	19	44	19.2	4.0
NS-6	8/2	1060	19	35	22.1	3.8

[a] Number of points of inflection in the threshold determination curve.
[b] Number of trials on which the threshold determination was made.
[c] Secondary low-frequency thresholds.

TABLE 11—(*Continued*)

Fish No.	Date	Frequency, in Cycles per Second	N	T	Mean, in Decibels	σ
NS-5	8/8	1100	17	53	22.7	5.0
NS-6	8/6	1100	19	43	25.4	4.5
NS-6	8/8	1100	11	22	19.6	1.7
NS-5	8/10	1200	21	36	36.5	1.7
NS-6	8/10	1200	19	30	31.0	2.3

tested five previous times. Were it not for the strong indications of this secondary curve in other species, the lower threshold points at 200 and 300 cps. might have been overlooked as simply representing a high degree of variability.

AUDITORY THRESHOLD DETERMINATIONS IN *Eupomacentrus leucostictus*

This species was resistant to electric shock, and the optimum shock levels were varied from 10 to 35 volts. Usually the higher voltages had to be used during the threshold tests, because the animal developed a tolerance for the shock. The water level at the barrier was about 1.2 cm. Intertrial crossings were frequent, and the intertrial intervals had to be varied from two to five minutes. The positions of the animals in the test compartment before a trial were extremely variable, and, unlike the other species tested, there appeared to be no habitual position for any individual. The interval between sound and shock was 10 seconds, and the sound level was varied in steps of 2 decibels. Four animals were tested, and these reached the criterion of avoidance training in about four days.

Figure 17, lower, shows a sample threshold record for specimen NS-6 of *Eupomacentrus*. This record is an example of a long "warm-up" effect. Figure 10, upper, is an example of the plateau effect. Note that the plateau represents a temporary threshold value of about 20 decibels, i.e., more than 33 decibels above the actual threshold determination.

Above 600 cps., the threshold data for this species are consistent and show only a small degree of variability. The determinations from 600 cps. down show extreme variability. Were it not for the secondary threshold data in *Haemulon* and *Lutjanus*, these data at low frequencies might be interpreted as representing individual differences, intrinsic variability, or as the result of some inadequacy in the testing methods.

Table 10 is a list of threshold determinations, in chronological order, made on a single specimen (NS-5). Figure 19 is a graph of these same determinations. This specimen was initially trained at 440 cps., and the test frequencies were subsequently lowered to 400, 200, and 100 cps., in that order. After two determinations at 100 cps. on July 22 and 24, the threshold at the same frequency on July 26 dropped almost 20 decibels, and the next determination at 200 cps. (July 27) showed a 16-decibel drop from the previous one at that frequency. On this basis, therefore, these lower values are assumed to be secondary thresholds. The next series of determinations at 600 cps. gave high threshold values on July 29 and 31, and a 29-decibel drop on August 3. Subsequent tests at higher frequencies showed that the lower value at 600 cps. was clearly part of the primary curve. The assumption was made, therefore, that the two high points at 600 cps. were part of the secondary curve.

Specimen NS-6 was also trained at 440 cps., but subsequent testing was done at higher frequencies, and these values fell in line with those for NS-5. When NS-6 was tested at 300 and 200 cps., there was a drop of 25 decibels from the primary to the secondary curve at 200 cps. The small number of tests on the remaining two specimens did not elicit a clear difference between primary and secondary thresholds.

Plateau effects were commonly noticed when these animals were tested at frequencies below 800 cps. The record shown in figure 10, upper, is typical of the results obtained. In this example, the plateau is at a level that would place it close to curve 2 of figure 19. The high thresholds obtained at 600 cps. may actually represent such plateaus, and, had it

been possible to continue the trials, these same determinations might have shown values some 20 or 30 decibels lower.

Figure 20 and table 11 are composites of the data on all the specimens of this species that were tested. The separation of the data into the primary and secondary low-frequency threshold curves follows the distinction between determinations made early and late in the study, as described above for figure 19.

PART 3

The data on two species (*Epinephelus guttatus* and *Prionotus scitulus*) are incomplete and must be treated as preliminary. It is not possible to place these species in either of the other groups, since the data are not sufficient for the presence or absence of secondary low-frequency thresholds to be demonstrated.

AUDITORY THRESHOLD DETERMINATIONS IN *Epinephelus guttatus*

Threshold determinations were made on only a single individual, although additional animals were trained and tested.

This species was difficult to test. Training to the avoidance problem was slow. After seven days of daily training (20 trials per day), the animal began to avoid the shock sporadically, and it was not until 10 days later that the first threshold determination could be made. The critical period in a series of trials came when the threshold was approached. The fish began to cross the barrier regularly about every five to 10 seconds. The intertrial intervals were increased to 15 minutes, in some instances, before a significant trial could be run. The water level at the barrier was extremely critical. If it was increased to 10 cm., the crossings went on regularly for periods of up to 30 minutes before they slowed down sufficiently to permit the starting of a trial. At a level of 7.5 cm., the animal had great difficulty in crossing, and often both avoidances and escapes ceased. The optimum level was found to be 9 cm., and a variation of 1 cm. either permitted numerous intertrial crossings or inhibited avoidances.

The shock levels had to be varied during

the course of training and testing. In initial training, 25 volts was adequate to produce escapes and, eventually, avoidances, but as avoidances became more regular, the shock level was increased to 30 volts or the avoidances soon became irregular. When a threshold was tested for, however, shock levels had to be reduced to 15 or 20 volts, since it was found that the higher levels not only inhibited avoidances but also inhibited escapes, and the animal often attempted to escape in the wrong direction or burrow down between the layers of rubberized hair insulation.

The animal exhibited a number of irregularities in performance which became especially pronounced as the threshold was approached. The stimulus intensity was reduced in 5-decibel steps after each avoidance, and,

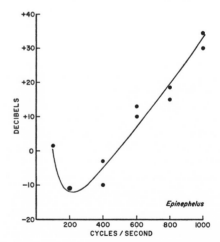

FIG. 21. Summary of threshold determinations for one specimen of the red hind, (*Epinephelus guttatus*). The data are given in table 12.

TABLE 12
AUDITORY THRESHOLD DETERMINATIONS IN THE RED HIND, *Epinephelus guttatus*

Date	Frequency, in Cycles per Second	N[a]	T[b]	Mean, in Decibels	σ
8/6	100	9	16	1.4	3.3
7/12	200	7	13	−10.7	3.5
7/14	200	8	15	−11.2	3.8
7/29	400	10	18	−10.2	4.1
7/31	400	6	20	−3.3	5.1
8/1	600	11	21	12.5	3.1
8/4	600	13	23	9.8	4.2
8/2	800	5	12	14.6	6.8
8/5	800	10	17	18.5	4.8
8/3	1000	8	15	34.4	4.7
8/6	1000	9	14	29.8	3.5

[a] Number of points of inflection in the threshold determination curve.
[b] Number of trials on which the threshold determination was made.

after the first negative response in which the animal received a shock, intertrial crossing began. As mentioned above, excessive intertrial crossings usually could be controlled by an increase in the intertrial interval, but on some occasions, the trials had to be terminated. On a number of trial sessions, the fish showed a preference for one side of the test tank, and it persisted in avoiding from one side and only escaping from the other. If this behavior remained consistent, then the trials were doubled, i.e., two trials at the same intensity. Unfortunately, after about 10 or 15 trials, the animal changed its preferred side. The initial position of the fish at the onset of the sound varied and was important to the response. If, in the initial position, the animal faced away from the central barrier, with its nose in a corner, the response was quite slow, and a full 10 seconds of the sound-shock interval elapsed before the fish turned around and crossed. Often the response was a partial one in that the fish just turned around but did not cross. Partial responses were not rewarded by termination of the trial, because it was feared that the full response would be weakened thereby. Usually, the observer waited until

the animal turned with its nose toward the barrier before beginning a trial. The threshold records that were considered valid were only those in which these irregularities were virtually absent, which meant that a number of partial records had to be discarded.

Despite the fact that the threshold curve given here is based on only a single individual, it is still considered a valid series of determinations.

Table 12 and figure 21 present the available threshold data on this specimen. No evidence of a secondary threshold curve was present.

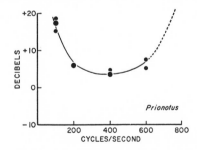

FIG. 22. Summary of threshold determinations for three specimens of the slender sea robin (*Prionotus scitulus*). The data are given in table 13.

TABLE 13

AUDITORY THRESHOLD DETERMINATIONS IN THE SEA ROBIN, *Prionotus scitulus*

Fish No.	Date	Frequency, in Cycles per Second	N^a	T^b	Mean, in Decibels	σ
A	7/9	100	27	42	15.3	2.4
B	7/9	100	30	67	18.5	3.1
B	7/10	100	26	50	17.4	3.1
B	7/11	100	23	39	17.1	2.8
B	7/12	100	24	38	17.8	2.5
A	7/7	200	17	33	6.5	1.5
B	7/8	200	19	34	5.8	2.1
B	7/13	200	24	44	5.9	2.9
A	7/6	400	10	28	4.8	2.6
B	7/7	400	16	33	3.5	2.1
C	7/9	400	28	45	3.9	2.9
C	7/10	600	30	67	5.1	3.1
A	7/11	600	28	49	7.4	2.0

[a] Number of points of inflection in the threshold determination curve.
[b] Number of trials on which the threshold determination was made.

It is not known, therefore, if this audiogram represents only a single curve or if it is a combination of the two that could be detected in other species tested.

AUDITORY THRESHOLD DETERMINATIONS IN *Prionotus scitulus*

The optimal shock voltage was 12 volts. The intertrial intervals averaged three minutes. The water level was 1 to 2 cm., and the animals crossed the barrier by almost leaping out of the water. Early in the training period, it was found that an interval of 10 seconds between the onset of the sound and the onset of the shock was insufficient for this species. The usual behavior of the animal was that it started to move toward the barrier slowly after the sound had been on for about five to eight seconds, hesitate at the barrier for as long as 10 seconds, and then abruptly hurtle across. A water level that was higher than 2 cm. enabled the animal to remain partially across the barrier. An interval of 20 seconds between the onset of the sound and the shock

was found to be optimal, and the sound level was varied in 2-decibel steps during the threshold determinations.

Crossings during the intertrial interval were virtually absent. The animals normally assumed a quiescent position against the far wall of the compartment immediately after a trial. Three specimens were used in this study, but, unfortunately, all three died before additional data could be gathered. This species is uncommon at Bimini, so that the likelihood of obtaining more animals was small, and the data, although incomplete, are presented here.

Table 13 and figure 22 present the threshold data on *Prionotus*. Despite replications at the low frequencies, there was no evidence of a secondary curve. The dotted line in figure 22 is an extrapolation of the audiogram above 600 cps. The lowest threshold values were at 400 cps. at about 4 decibels.

Some preliminary tests indicated that the thresholds for frequencies above 600 cps. rose sharply, and the extrapolation of the curve in figure 22 is based on these partial records.

DISCUSSION

FOR THE NINE SPECIES TESTED, a number of features in common can be seen from the data. The lowest thresholds were in the 300–500-cps. range, clearly so in *Eupomacentrus*, *Thalassoma*, *Lutjanus*, *Epinephelus*, and *Prionotus*, and, aside from the secondary low-frequency thresholds, also essentially true for *Haemulon*. The lowest thresholds in *Holocentrus* and *Equetus* were almost an octave higher (600–800 cps.).

The upper frequency limits were about 1000–1200 cps. in all except *Holocentrus ascensionis*, for which the upper limit was 2800 cps. It is important to qualify conclusions about upper frequency limits with a statement of the sound pressures at which the animals were tested. A pressure of 45–50 decibels (re 1 microbar) was the limit here, primarily because above this level considerable harmonic distortion and clipping of the output signal occurred. It is also a fact that these pressures are well above the sound levels normally present in the area (see below).

The equipment also limited the tests of low-frequency limits, in that 100 cps. was the lowest undistorted frequency that could be reliably achieved with the speakers. The range of thresholds for the six species was from −15 to +35 decibels. Here it becomes important to separate the data into primary and secondary low-frequency thresholds. As here defined, the primary thresholds were those determinations that were made during the early phases of training of the subjects. After replication and additional training, the threshold values dropped abruptly in four of the species. These are defined as the secondary low-frequency thresholds. In summary, the highest primary threshold at 100 cps. was that of *Lutjanus* (36 decibels). *Eupomacentrus* and *Thalassoma* were next (about 25 decibels), followed by *Holocentrus* and *Haemulon* (5 to 10 decibels) and *Epinephelus* (about 0 decibel). The secondary low-frequency thresholds in *Lutjanus*, *Eupomacentrus*, *Thalassoma*, and *Haemulon* were lower by 15 to 20 decibels. *Holocentrus* and *Equetus* did not

show a secondary curve even after extensive training, and the data on *Epinephelus* and *Prionotus* were probably insufficient for this phenomenon to be detected.

From the data presented, it was evident that the squirrelfish (*H. ascensionis*) had the broadest frequency spectrum as far as sound reception in general is concerned. The highest sensitivity was at 800 cps., with a threshold of −24 decibels, and positive responses went up to 2800 cps., at an intensity of +53 decibels. The other, smaller species of squirrel fish (*H. vexillarius*) gave threshold values 10 decibels or more above those for *H. ascensionis*.

The highest sensitivity of all species tested here was shown by the cubbyu (*Equetus*), with a threshold of almost −40 decibels at 600 cps.

The species with the poorest sensitivity was the schoolmaster (*Lutjanus apodus*), with its lowest threshold from 300 to 500 cps. at about +10 decibels. At 1000 cps., the threshold curve rose sharply to almost 40 decibels.

The highest sensitivity of the blue-head (*Thalassoma*) was at 500 cps., at a pressure level of about +5 decibels, and that of the sea robin (*Prionotus*) was at 400 cps. at about +4 decibels.

The grunt (*Haemulon*) showed a remarkably clear distinction between the primary and secondary low-frequency thresholds. Its lowest thresholds were on the secondary curve from 200 cps. down, at a pressure of about −16 decibels. The highest sensitivity on the primary curve was from 400 to 600 cps., at about −8 decibels. The threshold rose to more than +40 decibels at 1100 cps.

The threshold curves for the blue-head (*Thalassoma*) appeared to be intermediate between the curve for *Lutjanus* and that for *Haemulon* in a number of respects. The secondary low-frequency curve dipped lower at 300 cps. (to +1 decibel) than that for *Lutjanus*, but it rose at 200 cps., not like the case of *Haemulon*. The entire primary curve was generally almost 10 decibels lower than that for *Lutjanus* and about 10 decibels higher than that for *Haemulon*. The high-frequency portion of the curve for *Thalassoma* did not rise so sharply as that for the other two species. The threshold at 1200 cps. was 35 decibels.

Despite the relatively large number of determinations for the beau-gregory (*Eupomacentrus*), the data below 500 cps. are confusing. Based on the results from the other species, we can assume the existence of a secondary low-frequency curve; otherwise we would be at a loss to explain the hump in the curve at 300 to 400 cps. As it is, the curves, as drawn in figure 19, are only approximations and extrapolations. The lowest threshold was at 500 cps. (−14 decibels), and at 1200 cps. the curve rose to about +33 decibels.

The data for the red hind (*Epinephelus*) were limited to a small number of highly variable determinations based on a single specimen. Thus the threshold determinations are to be considered preliminary for this species. A secondary low-frequency curve was not detected. The range of highest sensitivity was from 200 to 400 cps. at below −10 decibels. At 1000 cps., the threshold was about 32 decibels.

The data on *Prionotus* were also incomplete in that the highest frequency tested was 600 cps. From 200 to 600 cps. the thresholds were in the order of 3.5 to 7.4 decibels, and at 100 cps. the curve rose sharply to about 3 decibels. Although no specific data are available for the higher frequencies, some preliminary tests indicated the probability of a steeply rising curve.

How do the thresholds reported here compare with those determined by other workers? In the following review, the values given in the original papers all have been converted to the reference point of 0 decibel = 1 microbar (=74 decibels above the 0.0002-microbar threshold for human hearing at 1000 cps.)

The majority of reports have been on members of the Cypriniformes (Ostariophysi), whose possession of a Weberian apparatus has apparently increased both the range and sensitivity of their hearing.

Although Stetter (1929) was one of the first to do any intensity studies, he gave no specific figures on sound levels. For the Characidae, von Boutteville (1935) reported a threshold of about −60 decibels (at 650 cps.). The same author determined a threshold of −40 to −45 decibels (at 650 cps.) for the eel (*Gymnotus*).

Phoxinus laevis, the Elritze, was widely used by European workers, and a threshold of −50 to −40 decibels at 258 cps. was reported by Diesselhorst (1938).

Among the catfishes, *Macrones* has a threshold of −60 decibels at 400–1500 cps. (Dorai Raj, 1960). The common bullhead (*Ameiurus nebulosus*) appears to have the lowest threshold of any species tested, according to Autrum and Poggendorf (1951). These authors report a threshold near the lower limit of human hearing (i.e., near −70 decibels) for all frequencies from 60 to 1500 cps. The figures were confirmed by Kleerekoper and Roggenkamp (1959), and they showed almost a straight horizontal line for the threshold values at different frequencies. The lowest thresholds were between 200 and 1800 cps. They found that if the swim bladder was damaged, the thresholds went up about 20 decibels at 750 cps., and hearing was greatly impaired at all higher frequencies. Damage to the lateral line nerve affected the sensitivity to frequencies below 400 cps. Thus the separate sensitivities of the inner ear and lateral line could be plotted, and the resultant curves show a remarkable resemblance to the double curves obtained by us for *Haemulon* and other species.

The upper frequency limits for these ostariophysines were all high: 4000 cps. for *Ameiurus* (Farkas, 1936), almost 6000 cps. for *Semotilus atromaculatus* (Kleerekoper and Chagnon, 1954), 7000 cps. for characids (von Boutteville, 1935), more then 8000 cps. for *Phoxinus* (von Frisch, 1938). Rough (1954) claimed positive responses from carp (*Cyprinus carpio*), up to 22,000 cps., but no intensity figures were given.

Although lacking a Weberian apparatus, the mormyrids and labyrinthine fishes possess air chambers directly coupled to the perilymphatic fluid and inner ear. The studies of Diesselhorst (1938), Stipetić (1939), and Schneider (1941) showed upper frequency limits of more than 3000 cps. for mormyrids, with a threshold of −50 to −40 decibels at 258 cps. (Diesselhorst, 1938). Schneider (1941) reported upper frequency limits of 4500 cps. for certain labyrinthines.

Upper frequency limits in most other non-ostaryophysine species are considerably lower. Tables 14 and 15 summarize the majority of reports.

TABLE 14

SUMMARY OF REPORTED THRESHOLD DATA IN TELEOSTS WITHOUT A WEBERIAN APPARATUS

Genus and Family	Upper Frequency Limit, in Cycles per Second	Reference
Gobius (Gobiidae)	800	Dijkgraaf, 1949
Corvina (Sciaenidae)	1000	Dijkgraaf, 1949
Corvina (Sciaenidae)	1500–2000	Maliukina, 1960
Sargus (Sparidae)	1250	Dijkgraaf, 1949
Anguilla (Anguillidae)	600	Diesselhorst, 1938
Lebistes (Poeciliidae)	435[a]	Farkas, 1935
Lebistes (Poeciliidae)	2068	Farkas, 1936
Mugil (Mugilidae)	1600–2500	Maliukina, 1960

[a] 640 in young.

Deserving special mention is the report (in abstract) that *Holocentrus ascensionis* can respond to frequencies up to 8000 to 9000 cps. (Winn and Marshall, 1960), but no indication was given as to the method of testing or the intensities used. When the data presented in the present paper are considered, the figures given by Winn and Marshall must remain in doubt, at least until further details become available.

In this connection, it might be added that no data are available on the threshold of feeling in fishes. It may well be that responses to high frequencies, as reported by Rough (1954) in the carp and Winn and Marshall (1960) for squirrelfish, actually represent integumentary tactile reception. It appears to be of little value to test organisms at stimulus intensity levels far beyond the maximal intensities encountered by the animals in their normal environment. The fact that human subjects often can detect powerful ultrasonic signals is well known, but that they can do so is obviously not a function of the auditory sense.

Sound pressure thresholds for non-ostariophysines as given by other authors are listed in tables 14 and 15.

The figure given by Griffin (1950) for the sea robin (*Prionotus evolans*) was not considered a threshold, but it appears to fall close to the determinations made here for *P. scitulus*. Griffin obtained responses at a frequency of 100 cps. and a pressure level of 17 decibels (re 1 microbar), and our figures at this frequency average 17.2 decibels.

If the figures in tables 14 and 15 are at all comparable to the ones reported by us, apparently the thresholds are distinctly below those for the species tested here. The figures for *Holocentrus* as given are of the same order of magnitude as those for *Anguilla* by Diesselhorst (1938). It is likely that the frequencies used in the reports cited are in the most

TABLE 15

SUMMARY OF REPORTED THRESHOLD DATA IN TELEOSTS WITHOUT A WEBERIAN APPARATUS

Genus and Family	Threshold (re 1 Microbar), in Decibels, at Cycles Per Second	Reference
Anguilla (Anguillidae)	−20–0, at 250	Diesselhorst, 1938
Mugil (Mugilidae)	−50, at 640	Maliukina, 1960
Corvina (Sciaenidae)	−45, at 320	Maliukina, 1960
Corvina (Sciaenidae)	−50, at 500–600	Maliukina, 1960
Mullus (Mullidae)	Below −30, at 450–900	Maliukina, 1960
Gaidropsarus (Gadidae)	−30, at 750	Maliukina, 1960

sensitive range of the hearing of the animals.

In order that the threshold figures determined here and in the earlier literature can be properly compared, it is necessary to know such details as the methods of measuring intensities, the sound insulation used (if any), the frequency response of the monitoring equipment, and the distance of the sound source from the monitoring hydrophone.

Kritzler and Wood (1961) attempted to determine a complete audiogram in a shark (*Carcharhinus leucas*). Their data, based on positive reward conditioning, range in threshold values from 10 decibels (re 1 microbar) at 100 cps. to a low level of about −15 decibels at 400 to 600 cps., to more than 10 decibels at 1400 cps. In consideration of the fact that the shark has no swim bladder and therefore receives all sounds either through direct conduction to the inner ear or by way of the lateral line system, these low thresholds are quite remarkable and may indicate that an air chamber need not function as the main transducer in sound reception, and that the acoustical difference between the water medium and the bone or cartilage of the neurocranium may be sufficient to permit low-frequency detection (i.e., below 1500 cps.). However, it should be noted that the response criterion used by Kritzler and Wood was a subjective judgment on the part of the observer, and these data would bear confirmation.

Also, in an elasmobranch, Dijkgraaf (1963) conditioned the dogfish (*Scyliorhinus canicula*) to respond to a tone of 180 cps. The method was that of classical conditioning, and the results indicated a threshold at about 30 to 40 decibels.

Despite the apparent accuracy of Maliukina's (1960) data, she gave no details as to the actual mechanics of the experiment. No information was given on the sound-measuring equipment, nor what, if any, sound insulation was used.

The method of sound measurement used by Diesselhorst (1938), Dijkgraaf (1949), and others was to compare the test signals with their own auditory thresholds. Diesselhorst used a loudspeaker outside the test aquarium, while Dijkgraaf used tuning forks in contact with the aquarium wall. Diesselhorst's signal generator was calibrated so that, once his own

threshold values were determined for the test frequencies, he was able to calculate the intensity of the actual test signal. Dijkgraaf determined his auditory thresholds by placing his ear against the wall of the aquarium. Griffin (1950) attempted to duplicate Diesselhorst's experimental conditions, but, in addition, to measure the sound pressures with a calibrated hydrophone and sound-level meter. He concluded that Diesselhorst's determinations were accurate within about 10 decibels. The main factor that must taken into account is the transmission loss through the water-glass-air interfaces. At a water-air interface, sound generated under water has a critical angle of about 13 degrees from the normal. Beyond this point all the energy is reflected. More than 99.9 per cent of sound impinging directly on the surface is reflected (Vigoureux, 1960; Horton, 1959). Griffin (1950) estimated that in Diesselhorst's (1938) and von Boutteville's (1935) experiments, only 0.012 per cent of the sound generated by the external loudspeaker reached the inside of the aquarium. None of these early investigators took into account the reflection, reverberation, and standing waves within the aquarium.

As is pointed out above, the acoustical resistance of water is much greater than that of air. With the use of the equations given by Albers (1960), the acoustical intensity in air of 1 microbar of sound pressure is about 2.3×10^{-9} watts per square centimeter, whereas at the same pressure the intensity in water would be only about 6.7×10^{-13} watts per square centimeter. At equivalent intensities, sound pressures in water are almost 60 times those in air. The sound-pressure threshold in human beings is usually taken at 0.0002 microbar, or 74 decibels below 1 microbar, with an intensity of 10^{-16} watts per square centimeter. The same intensity in water gives a sound pressure of almost 38.5 decibels below 1 microbar. If the figures given by Diesselhorst (1938), Maliukina (1960), and others are correct, then apparently the true intensity thresholds in many fishes are actually considerably lower than those for human hearing in air. A threshold of −70 decibels, as reported for *Ameiurus* by Autrum and Poggendorf (1951), would be equivalent in terms of intensity to −98.5 decibels in air! When the

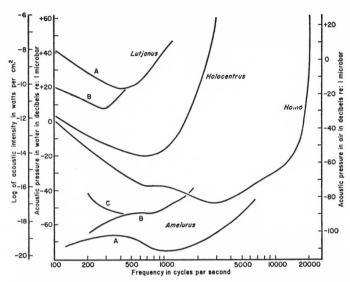

FIG. 23. Composite graph showing comparisons among auditory thresholds in the schoolmaster (*Lutjanus*) and squirrel fish (*Holocentrus ascensionis*), as described in this report; the human audiogram according to Sivian and White (1933); and the auditory thresholds of the catfish (*Ameiurus nebulosus*) as given by Autrum and Poggendorf (1951) and Kleerekoper and Roggenkamp (1959). All these curves are plotted against the extreme left-hand ordinate—acoustic intensity in watts per square centimeter. The acoustic pressures in water are on the left ordinate, and the equivalent pressures in air (against which the human thresholds are plotted) are on the right-hand ordinate. See text for discussion.

general intensity levels of ambient noise, even in calm weather, are considered, threshold levels such as these would seem to make the animals inordinately sensitive to noise of little or no informational value.

Figure 23 presents the sort of comparison made in the above paragraph. The auditory threshold curve in human beings is based on that used in most textbooks. It is the minimum acoustic field audiogram of Sivian and White (1933). It is plotted against the right-hand ordinate, with the sound pressure expressed in terms of decibels re 1 microbar. The equivalent acoustic intensity is shown on the extreme left-hand ordinate in terms of the logarithm (base 10) of the energy in watts per square centimeter. Two of the species tested here, the squirrelfish (*Holocentrus ascensionis*) and the schoolmaster (*Lutjanus apodus*), are plotted on the same graph. The thresholds of these aquatic animals are plotted against the extreme left-hand ordinate of

acoustic intensity. Parallel to this scale is the equivalent acoustic pressure in water in decibels re 1 microbar. Curves A and B for *Lutjanus* are the primary and secondary threshold values, respectively. For comparison, the data on the catfish (*Ameiurus*) are also included. Curve A is the audiogram reported by Autrum and Poggendorf (1951). Curve B is copied from the work of Kleerekoper and Roggenkamp (1959) and represents the effect on the audiogram of *Ameiurus* after damage to the swim bladder. Curve C is the result of the additional damage to the lateral line nerve.

The primitive nature of the sound generating and measuring equipment used by these earlier works, the factors presented above, and the somewhat ambiguous nature of positive responses by their experimental animals all lead us to believe that the previous reports on auditory thresholds in fishes badly need re-evaluation and confirmation. Griffin (1950) pointed out the need for acoustical controls and unequivocal responses, as well as indicating the importance of accurate, under-water sound measurements in order that threshold determinations can be made with precision and dependability.

SIGNIFICANCE OF SECONDARY LOW-FREQUENCY THRESHOLDS AND PLATEAUS

The presence of secondary low-frequency thresholds in our data is of considerable interest. In most cases, they appeared after considerable training and testing in the low-frequency range. The clearest example is that of *Haemulon*, in which the entire shape of the audiogram curve became changed when the secondary curve was detected. The absence of the secondary curve in our data on *Epinephelus* is probably not significant, since these determinations were based on a single specimen and a relatively small number of threshold determinations. The absence of a secondary curve is certainly significant in *Holocentrus* and *Equetus*, since some of the animals were retested almost daily over a period of more than two months.

What does the secondary low-frequency curve indicate? We conclude that it shows there are two mechanisms or two sensory modalities operating to receive low-frequency vibrations and that the two receivers have thresholds of about 20 decibels apart. There is, of course, the possibility that only one receptor is involved, with two separate central neural mechanisms of different levels of excitation, but such a conclusion would appear to be untenable since there is no neurophysiological evidence to support it.

Evidence exists, however, to support the possibility of multiple sound receptors in fishes. Three systems are to be considered as potentially responsive to low frequencies: the general cutaneous sense, the lateral line, and the inner ear.

Experimental work on the possible functions of the cutaneous tactile sense in low-frequency detection is sparse. Parker and van Heusen (1917) were among the earliest workers to propose a cutaneous sense in fishes capable of receiving vibrations. Manning (1924) showed an increase in responsiveness produced by strychnine. This drug, used on goldfish, presumably increased the sensitivity of the integumentary sense organs. In sound localization studies on *Phoxinus*, von Frisch and Dijkgraaf (1935) demonstrated that the animals could detect the direction of the sound source only if the distance was small and the sound intense. They voiced the suspicion that an integumentary sense was being used. Later, von Frisch (1938) was more positive in stating that frequencies from 16 to 129 cps. were received by a cutaneous sense, although he did not eliminate the possible role of the lateral line. However, Reinhardt (1935) obtained positive directional responses from both *Phoxinus* and *Ameiurus* to low frequencies despite the destruction of the inner ear and lateral line. In *Gobius paganellus*, Dijkgraaf (1949) determined the upper frequency limit as 800 cps., and he postulated that this species detected sound mainly through a cutaneous receptor. Dorai Raj (1960), studying the catfish (*Macrones gulio*), obtained positive responses to frequencies down to 15 cps. in animals the lateral line nerves of which had been severed.

The functions of the lateral line have been investigated by many workers, and functions including chemical sense, temperature sense, and sound reception have been only some of the many ascribed to this structure. Parker (1902, 1918) proposed that the lateral line was sensitive to low-frequency vibrations and, especially, to shock waves in the water. Rode (1929) claimed a sensitivity of 2 to 60 cps. for the lateral line. Dijkgraaf (1933, 1947b, 1952) demonstrated that the lateral line can detect water movements and is used in avoidance of both moving and stationary obstacles. This organ effectively extends the range of tactile sense, termed by Dijkgraaf the "Ferntastsinn." The use of action potentials from the lateral line nerve showed its response to vibrations up to 150 cps. in frequency (Schreiver, 1935, 1936), and also that it reproduces frequencies microphonically up to 180 cps. (Suckling and Suckling, 1950). This microphonic activity was studied further by Jielof, Spoor, and de Vries (1952) and by Kuiper (1956). Essentially, Kuiper confirmed most of Dijkgraaf's observations and concluded that the lateral line is a tactile receptor and that "alternating water currents produced by the object are the stimuli for the organ." Harris and van Bergeijk (1962) described the response of lateral line organs to displacement of water produced by the "near-field" effect of a nearby sound generator.

In a recent review of lateral line function, Dijkgraaf (1962) emphasized the fact that the lateral line is primarily sensitive to the "damming phenomenon" which is a local displacement effect produced by a moving object. In agreement with Harris and van Bergeijk (1962), he stated that the effective stimulus was displacement rather than pressure. Repetition or rhythmicity of the stimulus appears not to be significant, and therefore Dijkgraaf eliminated the lateral line as being a low-frequency sound detector. He cited evidence that the destruction of the lateral line and inner ear does not eliminate responses to low-frequency sound. There is, however, a considerable body of evidence that the lateral line does respond to vibrations, and Kuiper (1956) even stated that the cupula is "an ideal vibration perceptor." Furthermore, in many of the ablation experiments, only the lateral line nerve (vagus branch) was cut, and the cephalic canals were still presumably functional. The evidence on the response of lateral line cupulae to water displacements seems unequivocal, and, within the mechanical limits of the receptor, the cupulae should respond equally well to rhythmic vibrations as to non-rhythmic flow phenomena, and, indeed, Harris and van Bereijk (1962), Suckling and Suckling (1950), and many others have shown such response to be true. Dijkgraaf (1962) also eliminated the functioning of the lateral line in the detection of locomotor currents. We fail to see the difference between water displacements produced by "moving obstacles" and those produced by the hydrodynamics of fish locomotion. Certainly the extent to which integumentary receptors participate in displacement detection is not known, but, on the basis of physiology, mechanics, and behavior, the lateral line functions as a short-range subsonic receptor.

Since it has been clearly established that the lateral line detects water displacements of both a rhythmical and a non-rhythmical nature, it is evident that it must be capable of sound detection in the low frequencies. Especially in view of the sparse evidence on

general cutaneous sense, we must accept the idea that the lateral line and the integumentary tactile receptors constitute a single system as far as low-frequency sound is concerned.

Most authors agree that the portions of the teleost inner ear that are the specific sound receptors are the sacculus and lagena. Probably the earliest reports of any validity are those of Manning (1924) and von Frisch and Stetter (1932). Pearson (1936) described the central connections of nerves from the inner ear and postulated that the coarse fibers from the saccular root transmit sonic stimuli. Von Frisch (1938) described the connection of the Weberian ossicles in *Phoxinus* as transmitting vibrations from the swim bladder to the saccular otolith—the sagitta. He also stated that the lagenar otolith (asteriscus) can receive sonic stimuli by way of bone conduction. In *Lebistes*, which lacks a Weberian apparatus, Farkas (1938a, 1938b) reported that the sagitta is the otolith that receives vibrations through the fenestra sacculi. The most definitive work was that of Dijkgraaf (1949 and 1952) who demonstrated that the auditory function of the inner ear resides in the sacculus and lagena. Action potential techniques were used by Zotterman (1943) to detect the sonic reception of the macula sacculi. Similar results were obtained by Lowenstein and Roberts (1951) in elasmobranchs, but in addition they were able to detect action potentials from the utriculus as well. No one has yet been able to separate the sacculus and lagena in terms of their function in sound reception. The role of the lagena, then, has not been clarified. For the present, we assume that the inner ear constitutes a single mechanism by which the fish receives sound.

From the above discussion, it appears likely that two mechanisms are involved in the reception of low-frequency sound: the inner ear and the lateral line-integumentary system. Such a possibility is in agreement with the conclusions based on the presence of primary and secondary low-frequency thresholds as described here. The threshold curves for frequencies above 500 cps. are almost certainly representative of the sensitivity of the inner ear mechanism. The primary low-frequency curve is a logical continuation of the curve for the same mechanism. We conclude, therefore, that the secondary curve represents the sensitivity of the lateral line-integumentary receptors. It must be realized, however, that this conclusion is tentative in that it is based on only indirect evidence; considerable further investigation is required to support it.

Some support for this interpretation can be derived from the data presented by Kleere-koper and Roggenkamp (1959) on the catfish (*Ameiurus*). In this case the damage to the lateral line produced a clear increase in the thresholds for low frequencies.

As noted above, direct contact of the hydrophone with the insulating material in the experimental tanks resulted in a 2-decibel rise in the sound level that was received. Quite possibly direct integumentary reception was involved in cases in which the experimental animal was touching the rubberized hair. Suckling (1962) found that brushing the dorsal fin spines or any scales distant from the lateral line organs resulted in an increase in action potentials from the lateral line nerve. Possibly, therefore, with increased training, the animals learned that low-frequency sound detection by way of the lateral line was more efficient.

From the aspect of central nervous mechanisms, it is remarkable that, with two receptors for the same class of stimuli, the more sensitive and efficient is not used immediately. If we accept the conclusions of the above paragraphs, it appears that many of our experimental animals utilized the inner ear mechanism first and, after additional training, switched to the more sensitive low-frequency detector. Our data indicate that this switch does not occur with predictable regularity.

A roughly parallel situation exists in the combination of rod and cone receptors in the retina. Here are two distinct receptor systems for the same class of stimuli, and their thresholds overlap. The dark adaptation studies of Blough (1956, 1958) have shown that, when the thresholds are tracked by means of the staircase technique, the cone threshold is reached first. At this point there is a temporary plateau, followed by another drop to the level of the rod threshold (Blough, 1961). This phenomenon appears similar to the plateau effect that our studies have demon-

strated in auditory sensitivity of fish, and its existence strengthens our hypothesis that two sensory systems are involved at the low frequencies.

An additional observation of significance is that the sequence of frequencies used to test the animals has an effect on the threshold determinations. The effect was particularly evident in the data on the beau-gregory (*Eupomacentrus*). When the fact that the avoidance response involves not only sensory but perceptual factors is considered, it is really not surprising that length and sequence of testing should affect the threshold data.

THE FUNCTION OF THE SWIM BLADDER IN SOUND RECEPTION

According to Griffin (1950, 1955) and Pumphrey (1950), a fish is essentially transparent to water-borne sound, and its only acoustical discontinuity is the swim bladder (or other gas chamber). Sound reception under water requires the presence of a transducer constructed of material very different in acoustical properties and density from the surrounding medium. Air bubbles are known to be excellent reflectors and resonators (Horton, 1959; Meyer, 1957), and certainly the swim bladder can serve efficiently as a transducer. Marshall (1951) and Jones and Pearce (1958) have shown that fish swim bladders are effective sonic reflectors and that 50 per cent or more of impinging sound energy is returned by the bladder, while a smaller percentage is reflected by the rest of the body of the fish. However, some other portions of the fish, such as the skull, may also serve as acoustical discontinuities and thus permit sound reception by bone conduction. The swim bladder still appears to be the most obvious and efficient sonic transducer that the fish possesses. Harris and van Bergeijk (1962) consider swim bladders as aquatic middle ears which transform pressure waves into near-field displacements.

If we accept the above contention, fishes with swim bladders should have better hearing than those without. Furthermore, those species in which the swim bladder is acoustically coupled to the inner ear should have the highest auditory sensitivity and broadest range.

As reviewed above, the Cypriniformes

apparently possess the lowest auditory thresholds and highest upper frequency limits. The auditory capacities of these fishes are undoubtedly enhanced by the Weberian apparatus which couples the auditory signal received by the swim bladder to the inner ear in a manner analogous to the operation of the middle ear ossicles in mammals. Other air chambers can serve in similar fashion as, for example, the branchial cavity in the labyrinthine fishes (Schneider, 1941).

Among non-ostariophysines, in a number of forms the swim bladder has anterior extensions which are either coupled directly to the perilymphatic fluid (as in many clupeids) or attached to the occipital region of the neurocranium (Froese, 1938). Wohlfahrt (1938) described long, thin, anterior extensions of the swim bladder in herrings. These terminate in gas-filled capsules enclosed in bone and coupled to the perilymph by an elastic "fenestra."

Although satisfactory auditory thresholds have not been reported for any clupeid fishes, probably their auditory sensitivity is high.

Our data have shown that *Holocentrus ascensionis* has a low threshold and broad frequency response spectrum, probably related to the contiguity of the anterior end of the swim bladder to the skull, as described by Nelson (1955). However, *H. vexillarius*, with the same swim-bladder construction, exhibits a higher auditory threshold, and *Equetus*, with no such specialization, possesses a much lower auditory threshold.

Species with reduced swim bladders or without swim bladders should have poor hearing. The evidence is sparse. Bull (1928) was unable to condition a blenny (*Blennius*) to respond to sound. In *Gobius*, Dijkgraaf (1949) showed an upper frequency limit of only 800 cps., and he postulated that most sound reception in this species took place through lateral line or cutaneous tactile senses. Tavolga (1958) demonstrated the inability of *Bathygobius* to discriminate its mating sounds from other low-frequency noises.

Superficially, there appears to be little difference in basic structure between the swim bladder of *Haemulon*, that of *Epinephelus*, and that of *Lutjanus*, yet *Lutjanus* has a threshold at 500 cps., some 15 decibels higher

than the others. *Eupomacentrus* has a swim bladder of the thin-walled type, tightly wedged in against the dorsolateral body wall, and its auditory-threshold curve is only a few decibels higher than that of *Holocentrus*. The smallest swim bladder of the six species tested here was that of *Thalassoma*, of which the general-threshold curve falls somewhere between that of *Haemulon* and that of *Lutjanus*. To assess the exact degree of acoustical coupling between the swim bladder and the inner ear in any of these forms is difficult, and probably other factors enter into auditory sensitivity in addition to just the shape and position of the bladder. The construction of the inner ear would certainly be one such factor. What should be investigated are the general acoustical properties of swim bladders and their degree of connection with the inner ear through the musculature, vertebral column, and skull. Some correlations may be discovered which will clarify the function of the swim bladder as an under-water microphone, if, indeed, it has any such function in many species.

Furthermore, the validity of the statement that the fish is acoustically transparent is open to question. To test this statement, some direct measurements are needed as to the acoustical coupling and transmission of sound through the skin, skull, vertebral column, and swim bladder as well. If a swim bladder with good coupling to the otic region were a requirement for under-water hearing, then species such as the blue-head and sea robin should be virtually deaf, and sharks should be completely insensitive to all except low frequencies detectable by the lateral line. The data of Kritzler and Wood (1961) certainly demonstrate that hearing in sharks is as good as that of many teleosts, and Dijkgraaf (1963) showed that sectioning of the acoustic nerve in the dogfish reduced the sensitivity at 180 cps. by about 20 decibels.

CHARACTERIZATION OF THE ACOUSTIC STIMULUS

Questions arise as to the exact nature of the stimulus produced by the under-water speakers used here, the nature of the stimulus received by the sense organ, and which sense organ is stimulated. For purposes of this discussion we can assume that the sound source is a pulsating sphere. In such a case, the acoustic energy produced is measured in terms of ergs or watts per square centimeter, and the surface is taken to be a sphere surrounding the sound source. It is evident that the energy flow through this spherical surface is inversely proportional to the square of the distance from the center of the sound source, which is the commonly known inverse square law for transmission loss due to divergence or spreading (Albers, 1960). Sound energy, i.e., intensity, is directly proportional to the square of the acoustic pressure, according to the equation

$$I = p^2/\rho c,$$

in which I equals the intensity in ergs per square centimeter, p equals the pressure in dynes per square centimeter ($=$microbars), and ρc equals the acoustic radiation resistance of water (approximately 150,000 grams per square centimeter per second). Pressure, therefore, is inversely proportional to the distance from the sound source. Empirically, however, such a proportion obtains only in an infinite medium and at distances well over one wave length.

A sound field actually consists of energy that can be measured in two different ways: as pressure or as displacement. Harris and van Bergeijk (1962) have shown that both these factors must be considered in the characterizing of an under-water sound stimulus, especially at short distances and low frequencies. They showed that water displacement produced by a pulsating sphere involves two factors. One is the propagated pressure wave, i.e., the "far-field," and the other is the "near-field" displacement effect. In the far-field, the displacement amplitude and distance are linearly related, and the pressure at a given frequency is also directly proportional to the displacement according to the equation

$$p/\rho c = 2\pi f d,$$

in which p equals the pressure in dynes per square centimeter, ρc equals the acoustic resistance of water, f equals the vibration frequency in cycles per second, and d equals the displacement of water in centimeters.

The corrected formula for displacement

and pressure (Harris, personal communication) would include the near-field effect:

$$d = \frac{p}{i2\pi f\rho c}\left(1 + \frac{\lambda}{i2\pi r}\right).$$

The symbols represent the following:

$d =$ displacement amplitude in centimeters
$p =$ acoustic pressure in dynes per square centimeter ($=$microbars)
$i =$ square root of -1 (representing a 90° phase lag)
$f =$ frequency in cycles per second
$\rho =$ density of water (taken as 1 gram per cubic centimeter)
$c =$ velocity of sound in water (approximately 150,000 cm. per second for sea water; Tschiegg and Hays, 1959)
$\lambda =$ wave length of sound ($= c/f$)
$r =$ distance from the center of the pulsating sphere

The first factor in the above equation is the displacement produced by the far-field propagated wave. Note that the second factor, which is the correction for the near-field effect, is dependent on wave length and distance. At distances of less than one wave length, this factor becomes increasingly significant. Since wave length and frequency are inversely related, the near-field effect becomes of greater importance at the low frequencies.

In the near-field effect, the displacement amplitude varies approximately according to the equation (Harris and van Bergeijk, 1962)

$$d = A^2 D/r^2$$

for a pulsating sphere of radius A. The increase in the radius during pulsation is D, and the distance from the center of the sphere is r. It follows that at short distances the displacement is inversely proportional to the square of the distance (as opposed to the far-field effect, in which displacement is inversely proportional to the distance). It should be noted that the near-field displacement itself produces a pressure wave and that displacement and pressure are two representations of the same energy.

In the equipment used in the present study, the hydrophone was essentially a pressure receiving device and did not respond to water

TABLE 16

CALCULATED DISPLACEMENT AT THRESHOLD (IN ANGSTROM UNITS)

	Frequency, in Cycles per Second										
	100	100^a	200	200^a	400	600	800	1000	1200	1600	2000
Holocentrus ascensionis	21	—	1	—	3	<0.1	<0.1	<0.1	<0.1	0.2	0.8
Holocentrus vexillarius	82	—	14	—	2	0.2	0.3	0.4	1	—	—
Haemulon	33	3	7	0.6	2	0.4	3	14	—	—	—
Lutjanus	1300	130	124	14	10	8	17	22	—	—	—
Thalassoma	207	—	44	8	3	2	4	7	10	—	—
Eupomacentrus	231	21	20	2	0.6	0.5	0.3	2	8	—	—
Epinephelus	15	—	1	—	0.5	2	2	9	—	—	—
Equetus	6	—	0.2	—	<0.1	<0.1	—	<0.1	—	—	0.2
Prionotus	92	—	7	—	2	1	—	—	—	—	—

^{a} These values are for the secondary low-frequency thresholds.

displacement per se. The acoustic pressures, as measured by our hydrophone, were produced entirely by the local water displacement of the near-field effect.

It is important to determine the displacement effect of the acoustic stimulus levels at the thresholds. This would be particularly significant for the secondary low-frequency curves, since we believe that these represent lateral line thresholds and since Harris and van Bergeijk (1962) have shown this organ to be primarily sensitive to near-field displacements.

Based on the equations for displacement and pressure given above, we can calculate the theoretical displacement amplitudes. For example, at a pressure of 1 microbar and a frequency of 100 cps. and for a distance of several wave lengths from the sound source, the displacement is approximately 1 A. ($=10^{-8}$ cm.). At distances of less than one wave length (for 100 cps. one wave length is 1500 cm.), the second factor, i.e., near-field, increases in value. At a distance of 1 cm., for example the displacement is about 240 A., and at 10 cm. it is about 25 A.

The threshold values, therefore, can be converted from pressure values to displacement amplitudes. One difficulty, however, is to determine the value of r in the equation. On the basis of the behavior of most of the fish, we can assume an average distance from the sound source of 20 cm. Table 16 shows the calculated displacement amplitudes (in Angstrom units) for the average threshold values as obtained in the present study.

Jielof, Spoor, and de Vries (1952) stated that the resonant frequency of the lateral line cupular organ was about 100 cps. Kuiper (1956) found the highest microphonic output of a single cupula at about 75 to 100 cps. In a species of perch (Acerina) he determined the approximate threshold level of 25 A. as being the minimum displacement in the vicinity of the cupular hairs necessary for the production of a microphonic impulse. Harris and van Bergeijk (1962) estimated a value of 20 A. for Fundulus.

A comparison of the microphonic threshold and a response threshold is difficult to make. A large number of reacting cupulae may have some amplifying effect. There are certainly species differences in the number, distribution, canal enclosure, and sensitivity of the cupulae. The distribution of cupulae throughout the lateral line system may also act to pick up water displacements more efficiently. Lastly, the response of the animal in the avoidance apparatus involves perceptual as well as sensory factors.

What is the nature of the stimulus as received by the sense organ? In the human ear, a pressure wave impinges upon the tympanum, and it is clear that the received energy is in the form of pressure, since near-field displacement in the air medium would be negligible. Subsequently, however, this pressure wave must be translated and amplified into a displacement effect, because the sensory hair cells of the organ of Corti respond specifically to a mechanical deformation (von Békésy, 1960). The lateral line organs, according to Kuiper (1956) and Harris and van Bergeijk (1962), are directly displacement sensitive. As such, they can respond only to near-field effects when the displacement amplitude is sufficiently above noise level to be detected. The value of this noise level was calculated by Kuiper (1956). The displacement resulting from Brownian movement was given as about 3 A. (reported as 0.3 as a result of a typographical error). From table 16 it is evident that most of the displacement values below 400 cps. are significantly above the Brownian noise level. *Equetus* is a notable exception. However, only some of these values are significantly above the threshold limit of 25 A. as given by Kuiper (1956). In the higher frequencies, above 400 cps., none of the values approach Kuiper's threshold, and most give figures below his theoretical noise level.

It is certainly true that, like the human ear, the inner ear of a fish contains hair cells that respond to displacement. We are led to the conclusion, therefore, that, again as in the human ear, a pressure wave is received and converted into the endolymphatic displacements. The Weberian apparatus of the Cypriniformes can take the pulsations of the swim bladder and transmit these into the endolymph as do the middle ear bones of mammals. Harris and van Bergeijk (1962) suggested that the swim bladder can respond to pressure pulsations in the medium and convert these into a local near-field displacement effect. The studies of Dijkgraaf (1950) and Qutob (1960) indicate that the swim bladder may function as a pressure receptor. We suggest further that other structures, such as skull bones, vertebrae, and even scales, can produce significant displacements as a result of an impinging pressure wave, and, by means of lever-like or tension-spring arrangements, these displacements can be amplified or efficiently transmitted. Such displacements may then be of an order of magnitude large enough to produce a suprathreshold displacement of the endolymphatic fluid.

The data reported by Autrum and Poggendorf (1951) and Kleerekoper and Roggenkamp (1959) gave threshold values of below 0.001 microbar at 100 and 200 cps., equivalent to displacement values far below the level produced by Brownian movement. It seems hardly likely that the animals (*Ameiurus*) could detect a signal at a signal-to-noise ratio below unity. Harris and van Bergeijk (1962) provide at least one explanation for the data reported by Poggendorf (1952) and Autrum and Poggendorf (1951). The experimental tanks were very small and the area of the piston set in the floor of the tanks was large enough to produce a significant "jiggling" effect on the water and the fish. It is possible, therefore, that the fish were responding to water displacements and pressure changes produced in this way. The flat nature of the threshold curves obtained by this method shows an almost complete independence from frequency changes.

The report by Kleerekoper and Roggenkamp (1959) is not clear about the source of the control threshold data, as to whether these were derived directly from the Autrum and Poggendorf (1951) paper or were determined independently. Thus these data may be significant only in that they show a change in thesholds after lateral line and swim bladder damage.

The study of Dijkgraaf (1963) on *Scyliorhinus* used high-intensity sound at a low frequency, and the distance of the subject from the sound source was only about 5 cm. Thus the actual displacement effect may have been much greater than his sound-pressure figures indicated.

TRAINING AND TESTING METHODS

All previous auditory studies on fishes have utilized either classical conditioning or instrumental reward training techniques, as defined by Hilgard and Marquis (1940) and Kimble (1961). In classical conditioning, the unconditioned stimulus is invariably presented to the subject whether or not he makes a response to the conditioned stimulus. Both beneficial (food) and noxious (electric shock) unconditioned stimuli have been used in a variety of test situations. Studies of audition in fish have used both types. Examples using food include the report of Autrum and Poggendorf (1951) and that of Kleerekoper and Chagnon (1954), and those using electric shock include the report by Froloff (1928) and that by Maliukina (1960).

In instrumental reward training, the reward is contingent on the response, i.e., on presentation of the conditioned stimulus, the subject must make the required response prior to receiving the reward. The reward can consist of food or the escape from a noxious situation. If no response is given, then no reward is delivered or the noxious stimulus continues. Many variants of this technique have been employed for sensory threshold studies: discriminative training, single trial measures, and response rate measures (Ash, 1951; Blough, 1956, 1958; Hilgard and Marquis, 1949). An example of the use of instrumental reward training for auditory studies in fishes is the report of Kritzler and Wood (1961).

The technique used in the present study was neither of the above. We have used what Hilgard and Marquis (1940) called "instrumental avoidance training," and evidently this is the only reported use of this technique in sensory investigations of fishes. Operationally, the technique consists of the paired presentation of a neutral and a noxious stimulus (electric shock). The avoidance response is generally preceded in the training sequence by escape training, in which the appropriate response simply turns off the shock. Since the conditioned stimulus is invariably paired with the unconditioned stimulus, the subject then learns that the conditioned stimulus is a signal for forthcoming punishment. The next step is for the subject to learn that an immediate response enables him to avoid the shock altogether. In the context of threshold determinations, once the subject has learned to avoid the shock by making the appropriate response to the conditioned stimulus, then the learned response becomes an objective index of the fact that the subject has received the stimulus. If a subthreshold stimulus is presented, then the learned response will not be made and the subject will be shocked and will make the learned escape response.

The processes involved in the acquisition and retention of the avoidance response have been and are focal points of theoretical controversy in psychology, and we avoid this area as being irrelevant to the purpose of this research. A general statement as to the theoretical basis of avoidance learning is, however, pertinent. The fundamental idea was expressed most simply and directly by Maier and Schneirla (1942), who stated that the avoidance response is the result of two stages of learning. The first is contiguity learning, in which the association of the conditioned and unconditioned stimuli is established by virtue of their pairing in time, and the escape response is basically the result of autonomic patterning. The second stage is a higher nervous process in which the subject learns to anticipate the unconditioned stimulus. This phase is termed "selective learning." Most recent reports have adopted this view of two-stage learning. Miller (1951), Mowrer (1961), Solomon and Wynne (1954), and others call the first stage in avoidance training the acquisition of a "fear" which later becomes transformed into an acquired drive.

In sensory threshold studies of mammals, three general avoidance procedures have been used. Culler, Finch, Girden, and Brogden (1935) described the method that used a leg flexion response by means of which the subject avoided a shock. Brogden and Culler (1937) used this technique for auditory studies. The second procedure has been the use of a rotating cage. Brogden and Culler (1936) described this method as one in which the subject had to turn the cage a predetermined amount in order to avoid a shock. The use of this method for auditory studies was reported by Ades, Mettler, and Culler (1939), and Meyer and Woolsey (1952). The third method, which is similar to the one used by us, was the shuttle box which required the subject to cross a barrier at the onset of the conditioned stimulus in order to avoid the shock. This method has been described by Warner (1932) and Horner, Longo, and Bitterman (1961), and its use for auditory studies in cats was reported by Butler, Diamond, and Neff (1957).

The avoidance response is a useful technique in psychophysical studies for a number of reasons, both theoretical and practical. It is superior to classical conditioning in that it is more properly an overt behavioral response, rather than being purely autonomic in origin. In our studies of teleost fishes, we have found that, once the optimal parameters of shock level and water level are known, most animals reach a 90 per cent response criterion within 150 to 200 trials (i.e., six to eight days). The responses are, for the most part, clear, unambiguous, and easily replicable. The resistance to extinction of an avoidance response has a great advantage in threshold studies, because numerous trials at suprathreshold stimulus levels can be run with little or no effect on the response. It appears that the avoidance response serves as its own reënforcer. Conversely, in trials at subthreshold levels, the additional escape training also aids in reënforcing the avoidance response. Although no actual comparisons of methods have been made, the threshold values obtained by the avoidance methods may be lower than those derived from positive reward techniques. According to the signal detection theory (Swets, Tanner, and Birdsall, 1961), experimental conditions can alter the results of psychophysical studies, particularly of sensory threshold determinations. In the avoidance technique, the animal is punished only at subthreshold stimulus levels, but is free to give positive responses ("false alarms") in the absence of a stimulus (viz., intertrial crossings). The subject, therefore, would operate as though it were primarily concerned with never missing an occasion when the conditioned stimulus is presented. One result is that the number of false positive responses increases, i.e., the number of such responses when no conditioned stimulus is present. In the avoidance situation these "false alarms" would be manifested by an increase in intertrial crossings. This increase was clearly shown by the observations reported here. A second consequence is that the threshold should be lowered, as compared to situations in which the subject attempts to keep the number of false positive responses to a minimum. The threshold shifts as predicted by signal detection theory may be expected to be small, in the order of 5 decibels.

In 1948, Dixon and Mood introduced a new psychophysical method for threshold determination which has come to be known as the "staircase" or "up-and-down" method. It is a modification of the classical method of limits. Guilford (1954) termed this method very

efficient, particularly for locating threshold levels when there is no prior information as to the approximate stimulus intensities to be tested. Objections have been raised to the use of the staircase method in human studies because of the tendency in human observers to avoid repeating judgments, but it would seem that such an objection does not apply to lower vetebrates. Since the 1950's, this method has come into wide usage for animal sensory threshold determinations, particularly by psychologists influenced by B. F. Skinner. The method has been used with birds for the determination of visual acuity, dark adaptation, and color thresholds. The reports of Blough (1956, 1958) and Guttman and Kalish (1956, 1958) serve as examples of the utilization of the staircase method in sensory studies. However, we know of no comparisons between thresholds obtained by the staircase method and those obtained by the older and more standardized psychophysical methods, such as the methods of limits, average error, and constant stimuli.

RELATION OF SOUND PRODUCTION TO HEARING

Fish (1954) has shown that virtually any species of fish is capable of sound production. By her technique of electrical stimulation, sounds were elicited not only from organs specialized for sound production, but from general muscular contractions against a drum-like swim bladder. Our discussion is concerned, however, with the types of sounds for which there is evidence of some behavioral significance to the animals, whether the sound is produced by pharyngeal teeth, swim-bladder drumming muscles, or other mechanisms.

Sound production among the Cypriniformes is known in a few cases. Faint knocking sounds have been detected from minnows. Dijkgraaf (1932) described them in *Phoxinus*, and recent studies by Delco (1960), Winn and Stout (1960), and Stout (1960) have demonstrated the function of such sounds in *Notropis* as being related to species and sex discrimination. Klausewitz (1958) has described loud knocking sounds as part of aggressive behavior in a loach (*Botia*). Although the fresh-water bullhead (*Ameiurus*) is not known to produce any sounds, the marine ariid catfish (*Bagre* and *Galeichthys*) are known to be sonic (Burkenroad, 1931; Tavolga, 1960). In these forms, the sounds are produced by an "elastic spring" of bone attached to the swim bladder, and their occurrence appears to be related to nocturnal schooling (Tavolga, 1962). From what is known of the auditory sensitivity of this group of fishes, it is certain that the intensity and frequency of their sounds are within their range of hearing.

Most of the best-known sound producers have not been studied from the viewpoint of their auditory capacities. Recent reviews by Schneider (1961) and Maliukina and Protasov (1960) showed in general that few sonic species have been tested. Prominent in this category are the members of the Sciaenidae, the great choruses of which have been described by Knudsen, Alford, and Emling (1948) and by Dobrin (1947). These and other studies have established the role of sound production in sciaenids in spawning or pre-spawning behavior (Dijkgraaf, 1947a; Protasov and Aronov, 1960; Schneider and Hasler, 1960).

Nothing is known of the auditory system of the toadfishes, the powerful sound output of which has been investigated by Fish (1954), Fish and Mowbray (1959), Tavolga (1958, 1960), and Gray and Winn (1961), or of the codfish, of which the sonic capacities have been described recently by Brawn (1961). Of all the known sound-producing fishes in which the sound appears to have some behavioral significance, the only teleost in which auditory sensitivity has been tested, prior to the present report, is *Corvina* (Sciaenidae). In *Corvina*, as in most sciaenids, sound production is limited to the male and occurs during the spawning season. The sound, as described by Dijkgraaf (1947a), Shishkova (1958b), and Protasov and Aronov (1960), consists of low-pitched grunts or thumps, and occurs during feeding and in interindividual contacts as well as during breeding. As determined by Dijkgraaf (1949) the upper frequency limit of hearing in *Corvina* is about 1000 cps. Maliukina (1960) showed it to be considerably higher (1500–2000 cps.), and she also demonstrated thresholds of −45 decibels at 320 cps. and −50 decibels at 500 to 600 cps. It appears that *Corvina* rivals even the ostariophysines in its high sensitivity to sound.

Of the nine species reported upon here, *Holocentrus ascensionis* clearly has a low threshold and the broadest frequency response. This species is also one of the most vociferous sound makers in the Bimini area (Moulton, 1958). Although the sounds appear to be related to territorial activity, the exact behavioral significance of them has not yet been established (Moulton, 1958; Winn and Marshall, 1960). The sounds of the squirrelfish and of the groupers, as described by Moulton (1958), have their dominant frequencies in the range below 300 to 400 cps. Although no figures are available on the intensity of these sounds, they certainly fall in the sensitive range of hearing of most fishes in the area. The sounds of European codfish (*Gadus callarias*), as described by Brawn (1961), are apparently of high intensity and very low frequency—in the region of 50 cps. Certainly such sounds would be in the range of sensitivity of the integumentary and lateral line organs, and they may be of sufficiently high intensity to affect the inner ear as well.

In this connection, it is noteworthy that an auditory threshold has been reported for another gadid fish, *Gaidropsarus mediterraneus*, of almost −30 decibels at 740 cps., by Maliukina (1960).

Low-frequency, non-harmonic sounds are characteristic of swimming movements of fishes. These have been described as "swimming sounds" and "hydrodynamic sounds" by Moulton (1960) and Shishkova (1958a). Such noises are commonly produced by fishes, particularly during rapid changes in direction or speed. The predominant frequencies are below 100 cps. and are probably mainly subsonic. It is not likely that these sounds can be detected through the inner ear, but the lateral line and associated organs would be admirably suited for reception of such stimuli.

There is little information available on the intensities of fish sounds. Under laboratory conditions, Fish (1954) reported sound outputs of more than 30 to 40 decibels from toadfish and sea robins at distances of less than 3 feet. The sonic intensities of individual fish can rarely be accurately measured under field conditions, but it is well known that nighttime choruses of sciaenids and marine catfish produce an ambient noise level higher than 30 decibels (Knudsen, Alford, and Emling, 1948; Tavolga, 1960).

Ecological Considerations

A recent installation of under-water, sound-detecting equipment at the Lerner Marine Laboratory has brought out some data pertinent to the study of auditory sensitivity in fishes. Tavolga and Steinberg (1961) described a conference which took place in connection with this installation. A report describing the facility (Smith, 1961) has included figures on ambient noise in the Bimini area. Monitoring over a period of some months (more than 48-hour continuous time spans) has revealed that noise levels off the west shore of Bimini in 17 fathoms of water averaged 1.7 decibels (re 1 microbar) and ranged generally from 0 to 4 decibels. Occasional, infrequent, short-duration peaks were encountered up to about 16 decibels. These most intense sound pulses were presumably produced by some form of marine life, probably fishes, close to the hydrophone. Man-made noise from distant shipping increased noise levels by about 3 decibels, and vessels passing almost directly over the hydrophone produced sound pressures of over 30 decibels.

In another report on this installation, Steinberg, Kronengold, and Cummings (1962) stated that, aside from cetacean sounds, "most of the recorded sounds contain major frequencies below 1000 cps." Steinberg (personal communication) informed us that the usual ambient noise levels and spectra off Bimini do not differ significantly from those reported by Knudsen (*in* Albers, 1960), and that most of the ambient noise is produced by surface waves.

In the shallow water of Bimini Bay, Kritzler and Wood (1961) reported an ambient noise level of −14 decibels. Much of the inshore and shallow-water noise is caused by snapping shrimp and by air bubbles rising from the substrata. This is mostly high-frequency sound (over 2000 cps.).

Knudsen, Alford, and Emling (1948) gave ambient noise measurements for a number of localities. Their figures, here transposed to a reference level of 1 microbar, include Long Island Sound, where the noise level varied from −8 decibels on a calm day to +9 decibels on a rough one. Off Fort Lauderdale, Florida, the figures ranged from −1.5 to +10.5 decibels. Most sea noise was found to be in the frequency range below 1000 cps. Sound pressures from marine life, especially seasonally spawning fishes, increased ambient noise levels to about 35 decibels. A single boat-whistle blast from a toadfish went up to almost 30 decibels, but this was at close range.

Figure 24 is a graphic comparison of auditory thresholds and ambient noise spectra. Curve 1 is the audiogram for *Lutjanus*, and curve 2 represents the data on *Holocentrus ascensionis* as presented in this paper. Curve 3 is the spectrum of noise in the experimental tanks. None of the threshold values determined in this work falls below this noise spectrum. Curves 4 and 5 are taken from the data of Knudsen (as reported by Albers, 1960) and represent the ambient noise spectra for ocean waters at sea state 6 (12–20-foot waves) and sea state 0 (calm), respectively.

The significance of these data in conjunction with the available information on auditory capacities of fishes is that fishes are virtually deaf to ambient noise at frequencies higher than 1500 to 2000 cps. Possibly high-energy outputs from long-range, echo-ranging equipment may be detected, but it seems hardly likely.

Ambient noise in the 800–1500-cps. range would certainly be detected by Cypriniformes, but most other fishes would not hear this sound. Some forms, such as *Holocentrus* and *Equetus*, would be likely to receive this portion of the ambient noise spectrum.

The 300–800-cps. range of noise would probably be detected by most marine fishes, with the possible exception of forms such as *Lutjanus* or *Prionotus* which would be sensitive only to occasional high-level peaks more than 10 decibels in intensity.

Noise in the frequency range below 300 cps. is likely to fall within the range of detection of the integumentary and lateral line senses of most species. In consideration of the way in which threshold differences at these frequencies were manifested in the present study, it appears that low-frequency sound must have a very different perceptual value to the fish.

"Water noise" (produced by air bubbles, water currents, and so on), crustacean noises,

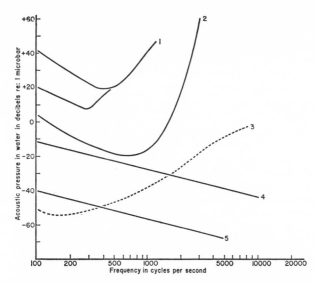

FIG. 24. Composite graph showing the auditory thresholds in *Lutjanus* (curve 1) and *Holocentrus* (curve 2) as shown in figure 23. These are compared to ambient noise levels and spectra. Curve 3 is the spectrum of noise levels in the experimental tanks used in the present report. Curves 4 and 5 are the spectra of sea noise (sea states 6 and 0, respectively) as based on the Knudsen curves given by Albers (1960).

and many stridulatory sounds of fishes are predominantly in the high-frequency range, and these would not be likely to form any part of the perceptual world of fishes. The noise produced by wave motion and the hydrodynamic shock waves from movements of fishes should fall into the range of sensitivity of fish hearing. Feeding sounds, and similar sounds produced by the gnashing or rubbing of jaw or pharyngeal teeth, are of low intensity and contain mostly high-frequency components. It is doubtful that these noises can be detected, even by ostariophysines, except in extreme high-intensity cases of fishes crushing shellfish, barnacles, or corals. Most fish sounds produced by swim bladder and associated structures are certainly within the frequency and intensity range of the highest sensitivity of most fishes tested. This fact is a remarkably good instance of the correlation of receptor and emitter organs.

The extremely high frequency, indeed the ultrasonic frequency, of the sounds of echo-ranging of cetaceans, as described by Kellogg (1961) and many other investigators, is well beyond normal detection by fishes. The echo-ranging clicks of cetaceans also contain a strong sonic component. Each click is actually a pulse of white noise. There is no published information on the exact spectrum and relative intensities of the various components of a cetacean click, but Sutherland and Dreher (1962) have reported measurements of up to 39 decibels re 1 microbar as sound pressures from echo-ranging sounds of captive porpoises. These same authors present spectrograms which indicate that the sound energy in the echo-ranging sounds at frequencies below 2000 cps. is a small percentage of the total acoustic pressure. The majority of cetacean whistles are at frequencies above 4000 cps. and at pressures below 20 decibels re 1 microbar. We conclude, therefore, that most marine fishes are probably not able to detect either the echo-ranging or the communicatory sounds of cetaceans. It is probable, however, that fishes can detect the low-pitched hooting and groaning sounds produced by some of the baleen whales (Mysticeti) (Schevill and Watkins, 1962). It is interesting to note that, in an apparently parallel situation, many nocturnal moths have evolved highly specialized ultrasonic detectors which enable them to escape the echo-ranging insectivorous bats (Roeder and Treat, 1961).

It is, of course, quite possible that fishes are capable of detecting high-frequency and high-intensity sounds through the general cutaneous sense. It is a well-established fact that the human ear can perceive frequencies far above the upper auditory limit of 17 to 20 kilocycles per second. The small difference in density between the tissues of a fish and its medium would be enough to enable a detection of even ultrasonic vibrations not only by surface neuromasts but by deeper receptor end-organs. Such a possibility would explain the results reported by Winn and Marshall (1960) of squirrel fishes that responded to signals up to 9000 cps., and by Rough (1954) of carp that reacted to frequencies of 22,000 cps. Extrapolation from the data obtained in the present experiment indicates that the acoustic pressures must be far above 50 decibels above 1 microbar for them to be sensed. Whether the reception of such high intensities constitutes "hearing" remains to be determined.

LIMITATIONS OF THE PRESENT WORK

The avoidance conditioning method as used here severely limited the number of species that could be investigated. Thus far, both this study and that of Wodinsky, Behrend, and Bitterman (1962) have shown that any species of fish that can be trained to escape the shock by crossing the barrier will eventually learn to avoid the shock. Certain species are evidently not capable of solving the initial problem of escape. The following is a list of species, in addition to the nine reported here, that were capable of both escape and avoidance conditioning:

Sergeant major (*Abudefduf saxatilis*, Pomacentridae)
Night sergeant (*Abudefduf taurus*, Pomacentridae)
Striped parrotfish (*Scarus croicensis*, Scaridae)
Rainbow parrotfish (*Scarus guacamaia*, Scaridae)

The following is a list of species at Bimini in which neither escape training nor avoidance was found possible with the apparatus used:

Slippery dick (*Halichoeres bivittatus*, Labridae)
Bucktooth parrotfish (*Sparisoma radians*, Scaridae)
Frillfin goby (*Bathygobius soporator*, Gobiidae)
Spotted scorpionfish (*Scorpaena plumeri*, Scorpaenidae)
Queen triggerfish (*Balistes vetula*, Balistidae)
Cowfish (*Lactophrys quadricornis*, Ostriciidae)
Puffer (*Sphaeroides spengleri*, Tetraodontidae)
Porcupinefish (*Diodon hystrix*, Diodontidae)
Bahamas toadfish (*Opsanus phobetron*, Batrachoididae)

It is interesting to note that some species within the same families (Scaridae and Labridae) show a diversity in their behavior within this avoidance situation. In most cases, the reason for failure to condition certain forms was that their most frequent response to shock was to "freeze" and remain in a corner. Surprisingly, it was found that the plectognaths, as a group, were extremely sensitive to electric shock. Shocks up to 10 volts were required to get any sort of swimming response from these fishes, but, after a few repetitions, the subjects went into an immobile state and often died.

It is clear that, for many species, threshold determinations cannot be obtained with the avoidance technique. However, other objective methods such as classical conditioning or reward conditioning are available. In this connection, it would be of interest to try all the methods on the same species and see if threshold differences are produced by the use of different response criteria. It must be emphasized that in all this work we have been dealing with a response threshold as opposed to a sensory threshold, a distinction that has been described and discussed by Pollack (1961). For purposes of interspecies comparisons and ecological interpretations, this behavioral approach to the study of auditory capacities seems to us more useful than a physiological investigation of the properties of the receptor organs.

Another limitation of the present work has been that only single frequencies were used, and the sound was turned on abruptly, maintained throughout the trial, and abruptly terminated. Further experiments are indicated in which sounds of various harmonic and non-harmonic complexity could be used as the conditioned stimulus. Discontinuous bursts of sound, masking background noise, and discriminatory studies are some of the various studies to which this technique could be applied.

The equipment, particularly the underwater loudspeakers, limited the range of intensities and frequencies that could be tested. The effects of high-intensity, high-frequency sound could be tested. The extreme low frequency, subsonic, end of the spectrum still needs clarification. In this connection, extirpation techniques such as those used by Dijkgraaf (1949) and by Kleerekoper and Roggenkamp (1959) should be attempted in order to separate the two modalities that the fishes use at low frequencies.

SUMMARY

SINGLE-TONE INTENSITY thresholds were obtained for nine species of marine teleosts. The following is a list of the species tested and their families:

Squirrelfish, *Holocentrus ascensionis* (Holocentridae)

Dusky squirrelfish, *Holocentrus vexillarius* (Holocentridae)

Blue-head wrasse, *Thalassoma bifasciatum* (Labridae)

Beau-gregory, *Eupomacentrus leucostictus* (Pomacentridae)

Blue-striped grunt, *Haemulon sciurus* (Pomadasyidae)

Schoolmaster, *Lutjanus apodus* (Lutjanidae)

Red hind, *Epinephelus guttatus* (Serranidae)

Slender sea robin, *Prionotus scitulus* (Triglidae)

Cubbyu, *Equetus acuminatus* (Sciaenidae)

The technique was a modified shuttle-box utilizing avoidance conditioning. The animal was trained to swim across a shallow barrier upon hearing the test sound, and in so doing avoided a mild electric shock. The interval between the onset of the sound and the onset of the shock was 10 seconds. This technique resulted in clear objective responses to the test sounds. Most species took five to seven days, at 25 trials per day, to achieve a 90 per cent criterion of avoidance.

The test sounds were single-frequency tones produced by an under-water loudspeaker. The experimental tanks were soundproofed, and the sound pressures were monitored to an accuracy of ±1 decibel.

Once training was completed, the thresholds were obtained by lowering the sound pressure of the test tone with each successive avoidance in steps of 2 or 5 decibels. When the animal ceased to avoid, the sound pressure was raised at successive trials until avoidance recurred. By such alternative increase or decrease in sound levels, the threshold for that frequency could be determined. This is the so-called "staircase method" which has recently come into wide usage in sensory psychophysics. The threshold was calculated from these data as being the point at which a positive response can be expected 50 per cent of the time. Each animal was tested at several frequencies, and each point on the audiograms was replicated at least once for the same animal or other subjects of the same species.

For the nine species tested, there were a number of features in common. The lowest thresholds were in the 300–500-cps. range in most. The lowest thresholds in *H. ascensionis* and *Equetus* were almost an octave higher (600 to 800 cps.). The upper-frequency limits were about 1000 to 1200 cps. in all except *H. ascensionis*, in which the upper limit was 2800 cps. This species had the broadest frequency spectrum, with its highest sensitivity at 800 cps. (threshold value −24 decibels), and at 100 cps. it was +4 decibels. The highest sensitivity was in *Equetus*, with a threshold of −40 decibels at 600 cps. The species with the poorest sensitivity was *Lutjanus apodus*, for which the lowest threshold was +10 decibels at 300–500 cps. Other species exhibited intermediate values, and the shapes of the audiogram curves were all very similar.

In the testing of low frequencies, i.e., below 500 cps., some species showed a clear-cut change in sensitivity after considerable training and testing. All the data, especially for *Haemulon*, *Lutjanus*, and *Eupomacentrus*, pointed strongly to the existence of two systems of sound detection. We conclude that initially the fish used the less sensitive detector and, after additional experience, switched abruptly to a receptor at least 20 decibels more sensitive than before. On various morphological and behavioral grounds, this phenomenon is interpreted as the utilization of two sensory modalities: the inner ear and the lateral line. The lateral line system is known to be a low-frequency receptor and is particularly responsive to near-field displacement effects.

The generalizations and inferences that are drawn from this study are that marine fishes are virtually deaf to frequencies of more than 2000 cps., except for the possibility that such sounds exist in intensities verging upon the thresholds of pain receptors. The highest sensitivities are below 1000 cps. In a comparison of the characteristics of ambient sea noise with the audiograms of marine fishes, it becomes evident that fish are not sensitive to most normal ambient noise levels. The detection of low frequencies appears to be quite efficient to 100 cps. and lower, which lends weight to the idea that the lateral line functions as a short-range obstacle and moving-object detector.

LITERATURE CITED

ADAMS, J. K.
1957. Laboratory studies of behavior without awareness. Psychol. Bull., vol. 54, pp. 383–405.

ADES, H. W., F. A. METTLER, AND E. A. CULLER
1939. Effect of lesions in the medial geniculate bodies upon hearing in the cat. Amer. Jour. Physiol., vol. 125, pp. 15–23.

ALBERS, V. M.
1960. Underwater acoustics handbook. University Park, Pennsylvania State University Press.

ASH, P.
1951. The sensory capacities of infrahuman mammals: vision, audition, gustation. Psychol. Bull., vol. 48, pp. 289–326.

AUTRUM, H., AND D. POGGENDORF
1951. Messung der absoluten Hörschwelle bei Fischen (Amiurus nebulosus). Naturwissenschaften, vol. 38, pp. 434–435.

BEHREND, E. R., AND M. E. BITTERMAN
1962. Avoidance-conditioning in the goldfish: exploratory studies of the CS-US interval. Amer. Jour. Psychol., vol. 75, pp. 18–34.

BÉKÉSY, G. VON
1947. A new audiometer. Acta Oto-Laryngol., vol. 35, pp. 411–422.
1960. Experiments in hearing. (Edited and translated by E. G. Wever.) New York, McGraw-Hill Book Co.

BLOUGH, D. S.
1956. Dark adaptation in the pigeon. Jour. Comp. Physiol. Psychol., vol. 49, pp. 425–430.
1958. A method of obtaining psychophysical thresholds from the pigeon. Jour. Exp. Analysis Behavior, vol. 1, pp. 31–43.
1961. Experiments in animal psychophysics. Sci. Amer., vol. 205, pp. 113–122.

BOUTTEVILLE, K. F. VON
1935. Untersuchungen über den Gehörsinne bei Characiniden und Gymnotiden und den Bau ihres Labyrinthes. Zeitschr. Vergl. Physiol., vol. 22, pp. 162–191.

BRAWN, V. M.
1961. Sound production by the cod (Gadus callarias L.). Behaviour, vol. 18, pp. 239–255.

BREDER, C. M., JR.
1950. Factors influencing the establishment of residence in shells by tropical shore fishes. Zoologica, vol. 35, pp. 153–158.
1954. Further studies on factors influencing the reactions of tropical shore fishes to shells. Ibid., vol. 39, pp. 79–84.

BROGDEN, W. J., AND E. A. CULLER
1936. Device for the motor conditioning of small animals. Science, vol. 83, pp. 269–270.
1937. Increased acoustic sensitivity in dogs following roentgen radiation of the hypophysis. Amer. Jour. Physiol., vol. 119, pp. 13–23.

BULL, H. O.
1928. Studies on conditioned responses in fishes. Part I. Jour. Marine Biol. Assoc. Plymouth, vol. 15, pp. 485–533.
1929. Studies on conditioned responses in fishes. Part II. Ibid., vol. 16, pp. 615–637.

BURKENROAD, M. D.
1930. Sound production in the Haemulidae. Copeia, pp. 17–18.
1931. Notes on the sound-producing marine fishes of Louisiana. Ibid., pp. 20–28.

BUTLER, R. A., I. T. DIAMOND, AND W. D. NEFF
1957. Role of auditory cortex in discrimination of change in frequency. Jour. Neurophysiol., vol. 20, pp. 108–120.

CORNSWEET, T. N.
1962. The staircase method in psychophysics. Amer. Jour. Psychol., vol. 75, pp. 485–491.

CULLER, E., G. FINCH, E. GIRDEN, AND W. J. BROGDEN
1935. Measurements of acuity by the conditioned-response technique. Jour. Gen. Physiol., vol. 12, pp. 223–227.

DELCO, E. A. JR.
1960. Sound discrimination by males of two cyprinid fishes. Texas Jour. Sci., vol. 12, pp. 48–54.

DIESSELHORST, G.
1938. Hörversuche an Fischen ohne Weberschen Apparat. Zeitschr. Vergl. Physiol., vol. 25, pp. 748–783.

DIJKGRAAF, S.
1932. Über Lautäusserungen der Elritze. Zeitschr. Vergl. Physiol., vol. 17, pp. 802–805.
1933. Untersuchungen über die Funktion der Seitenorgane an Fischen. Ibid., vol. 20, pp. 162–214.
1947a. Ein Töne erzeugender Fisch in Neapler Aquarium. Experientia, vol. 3, pp. 493–494.
1947b. Über die Reizung des Ferntastsinnes bei Fischen und Amphibien. Experientia, vol. 3, pp. 206–216.
1949. Untersuchungen über die Funktionen des Ohrlabyrinths bei Meeresfischen.

Physiol. Comp. Oecolog., vol. 2, pp. 81–106.

1950. Über die Auslösung des Gasspuckreflexes bei Fischen. Experientia, vol. 6, pp. 188–190.

1952. Bau und Funktionen der Seitenorgane und des Ohrlabyrinths bei Fischen. Ibid., vol. 8, pp. 205–216.

1962. The functioning and significance of the lateral-line organs. Biol. Rev., vol. 38, pp. 51–105.

1963. Sound reception in the dogfish. Nature, vol. 197, pp. 93–94.

DIXON, W. J., AND F. R. MASSEY, JR.
1951. Introduction to statistical analysis. New York, McGraw-Hill Book Co.

DIXON, W. J., AND A. M. MOOD
1948. A method for obtaining and analyzing sensitivity data. Jour. Amer. Statist. Assoc., vol. 43, pp. 109–126.

DOBRIN, M. B.
1947. Measurements of underwater noise produced by marine life. Science, vol. 105, pp. 19–23.

DORAI RAJ, B. S.
1960. The lateral line system and sound perception in catfish. Jour. Madras Univ., ser. B, vol. 30, pp. 9–19.

FARKAS, B.
1935. Untersuchugen über das Hörvermögen bei Fischen. Allatctani Közlemények, vol. 32, pp. 19–20.

1936. Zur Kenntnis des Hörvermögens und des Behörorgans der Fische. Acta Oto-Laryngol., vol. 23, pp. 499–532.

1938a. Über den schalleitenden Apparat der Knochenfische. I. Fenestra Sacculi, Protoperculum und Protocolumella bei Lebistes reticulatus Pet. Zeitschr. Morph. Ökol. Tiere, vol. 34, pp. 367–415.

1938b. Zur Kenntnis des Baues und der Funktion des Saccolithen der Knochenfische. Zool. Anz., suppl., vol. 11, pp. 193–206.

FISH, M. P.
1954. The character and significance of sound production among fishes of the western North Atlantic. Bull. Bingham Oceanogr. Coll., vol. 14, pp. 1–109.

FISH, M. P., AND W. H. MOWBRAY
1959. The production of underwater sound by Opsanus sp., a new toadfish from Bimini, Bahamas. Zoologica, vol. 44, pp. 71–76.

FRISCH, K. VON
1936. Über den Gehörsinn der Fische. Biol. Rev., vol. 11, pp. 210–246.

1938. Über die Bedeutung des Sacculus und der Lagena für den Gehörsinn der

Fische. Zeitschr. Vergl. Physiol., vol. 25, pp. 703–747.

FRISCH, K. VON, AND S. DIJKGRAAF
1935. Können Fische die Schallrichtung Wahrnehmen. Zeitschr. Vergl. Physiol., vol. 22, pp. 641–655.

FRISCH, K. VON, AND H. STETTER
1932. Untersuchungen über den Sitz des Gehörsinnes bei der Elritze. Zeitschr. Vergl. Physiol., vol. 17, pp. 686–801.

FROESE, H.
1938. Vergleichend-Anatomische Studien über das Knochenfischlabyrinth. Zeitschr. Morph. Ökol. Tiere, vol. 34, pp. 610–646.

FROLOFF, J.
1925. Bedingte Reflexe bei Fischen. I. Pflüger's Arch. Physiol., vol. 208, pp. 261–271.

1928. Bedingte Reflexe bei Fischen. II. Ibid., vol. 220, pp. 339–349.

GRAY, G., AND H. WINN
1961. Reproductive ecology and sound production of the toadfish, Opsanus tau. Ecology, vol. 42, pp. 274–282.

GRIFFIN, D. R.
1950. Underwater sounds and the orientation of marine animals, a preliminary survey. Tech. Rept. no. 3, Project NR 162-429, O.N.R. and Cornell Univ., pp. 1–26.

1955. Hearing and acoustical orientation in marine animals. Deep Sea Research, suppl., vol. 3, pp. 406–417.

GUILFORD, J. P.
1954. Psychometric methods. Second edition. New York, McGraw-Hill Book Co.

GUTTMAN, N., AND H. I. KALISH
1956. Discriminability and stimulus generalization. Jour. Exp. Psychol., vol. 51, pp. 79–88.

1958. Experiments in discrimination. Sci. Amer., vol. 198, pp. 77–82.

HARRIS, G. G., AND W. A. VAN BERGEIJK
1962. Evidence that the lateral line organ responds to near-field displacements of sound sources in water. Jour. Acoust. Soc. Amer., vol. 34, pp. 1831–1841.

HAZLETT, B., AND H. E. WINN
1962. Sound producing mechanism of the Nassau grouper, Epinephelus striatus. Copeia, pp. 447–449.

HILGARD, E. R., AND D. G. MARQUIS
1940. Conditioning and learning. New York, Appleton-Century-Crofts.

HORNER, J. L., N. LONGO, AND M. E. BITTERMAN
1961. A shuttle-box for fish and a control circuit of general applicability. Amer. Jour. Psychol., vol. 74, pp. 114–120.

HORTON, J. W.
1959. Fundamentals of sonar. Annapolis, United States Naval Institute.

JIELOF, R., A. SPOOR, AND H. DE VRIES
1952. The microphonic acitivity of the lateral line. Jour. Physiol., vol. 116, pp. 137–157.

JONES, F. R. H., AND G. PEARCE
1958. Acoustic reflexion experiments with perch (*Perca fluviatilis* Linn.) to determine the proportion of the echo returned by the swimbladder. Jour. Exp. Biol., vol. 35, pp. 437–450.

KELLOGG, W. N.
1961. Porpoises and sonar. Chicago, the University of Chicago Press.

KIMBLE, G. A.
1961. Hilgard and Marquis' Conditioning and learning. Second edition. New York, Appleton-Century-Crofts.

KLAUSEWITZ, W.
1958. Lauterseugung als Abwehrwaffe bei der hinterindischen Tigerschmerle (*Botia hymenophysa*). Natur und Volk, vol. 88, pp. 343–349.

KLEEREKOPER, H., AND E. C. CHAGNON
1954. Hearing in fish, with special reference to *Semotilus atromaculatus atromaculatus* (Mitchill). Jour. Fish. Res. Board, Canada, vol. 11, pp. 130–152.

KLEEREKOPER, H., AND P. A. ROGGENKAMP
1959. An experimental study on the effect of the swimbladder on hearing sensitivity in *Ameiurus nebulosus nebulosus* (Lesueur). Canadian Jour. Zool., vol. 37, pp. 1–8.

KNUDSEN, V. O., R. S. ALFORD, AND J. W. EMLING
1948. Underwater ambient noise. Jour. Marine Res., vol. 7, pp. 410–429.

KRITZLER, H., AND L. WOOD
1961. Provisional audiogram for the shark, *Carcharinus leucas*. Science, vol. 133, pp. 1480–1482.

KUIPER, J. W.
1956. The microphonic effect of the lateral line organ. Groningen, The Netherlands, the Biophysical Group, Natuurkundig Laboratorium.

LOWENSTEIN, O., AND T. D. M. ROBERTS
1951. The localization and analysis of the responses to vibration from the isolated elasmobranch labyrinth. A contribution to the problem of the evolution of hearing in vertebrates. Jour. Physiol., vol. 114, pp. 471–489.

MAIER, N. R. F., AND T. C. SCHNEIRLA
1942. Mechanisms in conditioning. Psychol. Rev., vol. 49, pp. 117–133.

MALIUKINA, G. A.
1960. Hearing in certain Black Sea fishes in connection with ecology and particulars in the structure of their hearing apparatus. (In Russian.) Zhurn. Obshchei Biol., vol. 21, pp. 198–205.

MALIUKINA, G. A., AND V. R. PROTASOV
1960. Hearing, "voice" and reactions of fish to sounds. (In Russian.) Ouspekhi Sovremyonoi Biol., vol. 50, pp. 229–242.

MANNING, F. B.
1924. Hearing in goldfish in relation to the structure of its ear. Jour. Exp. Zool., vol. 41, pp. 5–20.

MARSHALL, N. B.
1951. Bathypelagic fish as sound scatterers in the ocean. Jour. Marine Res., vol. 10, pp. 1–17.

MEYER, D. R., AND C. P. WOOLSEY
1952. Effects of localized cortical destruction on auditory discriminative conditioning in cat. Jour. Neurophysiol., vol. 15, pp. 149–162.

MEYER, E.
1957. Air bubbles in water. *In* Richardson, E. G. (ed.), Technical aspects of sound. Amsterdam, Elsevier Publishing Co., vol. II, pp. 222–239.

MILLER, N. E.
1951. Learnable drives and rewards. *In* Stevens, S. S. (ed.), Handbook of experimental psychology. New York, John Wiley and Sons.

MOULTON, J. M.
1956. Influencing the calling of sea robins (*Prionotus* spp.) with sound. Biol. Bull., vol. 111, pp. 393–398.
1958. The acoustical behavior of some fishes in the Bimini area. *Ibid.*, vol. 114, pp. 357–374.
1960. The acoustical anatomy of teleost fishes. (Abstract.) Anat. Rec., vol. 138, pp. 371–372.

MOWRER, O. H.
1961. Learning theory and behavior. New York, John Wiley and Sons.

NELSON, E. M.
1955. The morphology of the swim bladder and auditory bulla in Holocentridae. Fieldiana, Zool., vol. 37, pp. 121–137.

PARKER, G. H.
1902. Hearing and allied senses in fishes. Bull. U. S. Fish Comm., vol. 22, pp. 45–64.
1918. Hearing in fishes. Copeia, pp. 11–12.

PARKER, G. H., AND A. P. VAN Heusen
1917. The reception of mechanical stimuli by the skin, lateral line organs and ears of

fishes, especially in *Amiurus*. Amer. Jour. Physiol., vol. 44, pp. 463–489.

PEARSON, A. A.
1936. The acoustic-lateral nervous system in fishes. Jour. Comp. Neurol., vol. 64, pp. 235–273.

PEARSON, E. S., AND H. O. HARTLEY (EDS.)
1956. Biometrika tables for statisticians. Cambridge, Cambridge University Press.

POGGENDORF, D.
1952. Die absoluten Hörschwellen des Zwergwelses (*Amiurus nebulosus*) and Beiträge zur Physik des Weberschen Apparatus der Ostariophysen. Zeitschr. Vergl. Physiol., vol. 34, pp. 222–257.

POLLACK, I.
1961. Selected developments in psychophysics, with implications for sensory organization. *In* Rosenblith, W. A. (ed.), Sensory communication. New York, Massachusetts Institute of Technology and John Wiley and Sons, pp. 89–98.

PROTASOV, V. R., AND M. I. ARONOV
1960. On the biological significance of sounds of certain Black Sea fish. (In Russian.) Biofizika, vol. 5, pp. 750–752.

PUMPHREY, R. J.
1950. Hearing. *In* Physiological mechanisms in animal behaviour. Symposium Soc. Exp. Biol., no. 4, pp. 3–18.

QUTOB, Z.
1960. Pressure perception in Ostariophysi. Experientia, vol. 16, p. 426.

REINHARDT, F.
1935. Über Richtungswahrnehmung bei Fischen, besonders bei der Elritze (*Phoxinus laevis* L.) und beim Zwergwels (*Amiurus nebulosus* Raf.) Zeitschr. Vergl. Physiol., vol. 22, pp. 570–603.

RODE, P.
1929. Recherches sur l'organe sensorial latéral des téléostéens. Bull. Biol. de la France et de la Belgique, vol. 63, pp. 1–84.

ROEDER, K. D., AND A. E. TREAT
1961. The reception of bat cries by the tympanic organ of noctuid moths. *In* Rosenblith, W. A. (ed.), Sensory communication. New York, Massachusetts Institute of Technology and John Wiley and Sons, pp. 545–560.

ROUGH, G. E.
1954. The frequency range of mechanical vibrations perceived by three species of freshwater fish. Copeia, pp. 191–194.

SCHEVILL, W. E., AND W. A. WATKINS
1962. Whale and porpoise voices, a phonograph record. Contrib. Woods Hole Oceanogr. Inst., no. 1320.

SCHNEIDER, H.
1941. Die Bedeutung der Atemhöhle der Labyrinthfische für ihr Hörvemrögen. Zeitschr. Vergl. Physiol., vol. 29, pp. 172–194.
1961. Neuere Ergebnisse der Lautforschung bei Fischen. Naturwissenschaften, vol. 48, pp. 513–518.

SCHNEIDER, H., AND A. D. HASLER
1960. Laute und Lauterzeugung beim Susswassertrommler *Aplodinotus grunniens* Rafinesque (Sciaenidae, Pisces). Zeitschr. Vergl. Physiol., vol. 43, pp. 499–517.

SCHRIEVER, H.
1936. Über die Funktion der Seitenorgane der Fische. Verhandl. Phys.-Med. Feselsch. Würzburg, vol. 59, pp. 67–68.

SHISHKOVA, E. V.
1958a. Concerning the reactions of fish to sounds and the spectrum of trawler noise. Trudy Vsesov. Inst. Morsk. Ribn. Hosaist. Okeanograf., vol. 34, pp. 33–39.
1958b. Notes and investigations on sounds produced by fishes. (In Russian.) *Ibid.*, vol. 36, pp. 280–294.

SIVIAN, L. J., AND S. D. WHITE
1933. On minimum audible sound fields. Jour. Acoust. Soc. Amer., vol. 4, pp. 288–321.

SMITH, F. G. W.
1961. The Bimini installation. Tech. Rept., Marine Laboratory, Inst. Marine Sci., Univ. Miami, to Office of Naval Research, Contract 840 (13) and (16).

SOLOMON, R. L., AND L. C. WYNNE
1954. Traumatic avoidance learning: the principles of anxiety conservation and partial irreversibility. Psychol. Rev., vol. 61, pp. 353–385.

STEINBERG, J. C., M. KRONENGOLD, AND W. C. CUMMINGS
1962. Hydrophone installation for the study of soniferous marine animals. Jour. Acoust. Soc. Amer., vol. 34, pp. 1090–1095.

STETTER, H.
1929. Untersuchungen über den Gehörsinn der Fische, besonders von *Phoxinus laevis* L. und *Amiurus nebulosus* Raf. Zeitschr. Vergl. Physiol., vol. 9, pp. 339–477.

STIPETIĆ, E.
1939. Über das Gehörorgan der Mormyriden. Zeitschr. Vergl. Physiol., vol. 26, pp. 740–752.

STOLL, L. M.
1955. Hormonal control of the sexually dimorphic pigmentation of *Thalassoma bifasciatum*. Zoologica, vol. 40, pp. 125–132.

STOUT, J. F.
1960. The significance of sound production during the reproductive behavior of *Notropis analostanus*. (Abstract.) Anat. Rec., vol. 138, pp. 384–385.

SUCKLING, E. E.
1962. Lateral line in fish—possible mode of action. Jour. Acoust. Soc. Amer., vol. 34, p. 127.

SUCKLING, E. E., AND J. A. SUCKLING
1950. The electrical response of the lateral line system of fish to tone and other stimuli. Jour. Gen Physiol., vol. 34, pp. 1–8.

SUTHERLAND, W. W., AND J. J. DREHER
1962. Sound recordings of captive porpoises. Physiol. and Chemical Sciences Research Memorandum, LTM 50105, Lockheed-California Co.

SWETS, J. A., W. P. TANNER, JR., AND T. G. BIRDSALL
1961. Decision processes in perception. Psychol. Rev., vol. 5, pp. 301–340.

TAMM, K.
1957. Broad-band absorbers for water-borne sound. *In* Richardson, E. G. (ed.), Technical aspects of sound. Amsterdam, Elsevier Publishing Co., vol. 2, pp. 240–286.

TAVOLGA, W. N.
1958. The significance of underwater sounds produced by males of the gobiid fish, *Bathygobius soporator*. Physiol. Zool., vol. 31, pp. 259–271.
1960. Sound production and underwater communication in fishes. *In* Lanyon, W. E., and W. N. Tavolga (eds.), Animal sounds and communication. Publ. Amer. Inst. Biol. Sci., no. 7, pp. 93–136.
1962. Mechanisms of sound production in the ariid catfishes *Galeichthys* and *Bagre*. Bull. Amer. Mus. Nat. Hist., vol. 124, pp. 1–30.

TAVOLGA, W. N., AND J. C. STEINBERG
1961. Marine animal sounds (conference report). Science, vol. 134, p. 288.

TEICHNER, N. W.
1954. Recent studies of simple reaction time. Psychol. Bull., vol. 51, pp. 126–149.

TOWER, R. W.
1908. The production of sound in the drumfishes, the sea robin and the toadfish. Ann. New York Acad. Sci., vol. 18, pp. 149–180.

TSCHIEGG, C. E., AND E. E. HAYS
1959. Transistorized velocimeter for measuring the speed of sound in the sea. Jour. Acoust. Soc. Amer., vol. 31, pp. 1038–1039.

VIGOUREUX, P.
1960. Underwater sound. Proc. Roy. Soc. London, ser. B, vol. 152, pp. 49–51.

WARNER, L. H.
1932. An experimental search for the "conditioned response." Jour. Genet. Psychol., vol. 41, pp. 57–89.

WINN, H. E., AND J. MARSHALL
1960. Sound production of squirrelfishes. (Abstract.) Anat. Rec., vol. 138, p. 390.
1963. Sound-producing organ of the squirrelfish, *Holocentrus rufus*. Physiol. Zool., vol. 36, pp. 34–44.

WINN, H. E., AND J. F. STOUT
1960. Sound production by the satinfin shiner, *Notropis analostanus*, and related fishes. Science, vol. 132, pp. 222–223.

WODINSKY, J., E. R. BEHREND, AND M. E. BITTERMAN
1962. Avoidance-conditioning in two species of fish. Anim. Behaviour, vol. 10, pp. 76–78.

WOHLFAHRT, T. A.
1938. Von den Öhren der Fische. Die Bezeihungen des inneren Öhres zur Schwimmblase besonders bei heringsartigen Fischen. Aus der Natur, vol. 15, pp. 82–87.

WOODS, L. P.
1955. Review of Atlantic species of *Holocentrus*. Fieldiana, Zool., vol. 37, pp. 91–119.

ZOTTERMAN, I.
1943. The microphonic effect of teleost labyrinths and biological significance. Jour. Physiol., vol. 102, pp. 313–318.

Part V
DIRECTIONAL HEARING AND THE LATERAL LINE

Editor's Comments
on Papers 11 Through 15

11 PARKER
The Function of the Lateral-Line Organs in Fishes

12 PARKER
Sound as a Directing Influence in the Movements of Fishes

13 VON FRISCH and DIJKGRAAF
Can Fish Perceive Sound Direction?

14 DIJKGRAAF
On the Stimulation of the Distance-Touch-Sense in Fishes and Amphibians

15 HARRIS and VAN BERGEIJK
Evidence That the Lateral-Line Organ Responds to Near-Field Displacements of Sound Sources in Water

In Paper 11 G. H. Parker provided a thorough and critical review of the evidence to date (1904) on the many functions ascribed to the lateral line of fishes. With some additional data of his own, he concluded that the lateral-line organs are "not stimulated by light, heat, salinity of water, food, oxygen, carbon dioxide, foulness of water, pressure of water, currents, and sounds." Water vibrations of low frequency were concluded to be adequate stimuli, and, curiously, these were not considered as sounds. In the second article by Parker, Paper 12, he provides some of the earliest experimental evidence that fish can orient to a sound source, although the possible function of the lateral line evidently did not occur to Parker, possibly because he had already dismissed the ability of the lateral line to detect "sounds."

The collaboration of von Frisch and Dijkgraaf (Paper 13) provided one of the best-controlled field studies on sound directionalization in fish, although the results were essentially negative. Significantly, however, they found that intense sounds of low frequency did elicit directional responses, and they attributed this to the general cutaneous sense. Again, possibly because of an unnecessarily narrow definition of "sound," the function of the lateral line was not considered.

In 1947, Dijkgraaf published what has become a classic paper on the function of the lateral-line system (Paper 14). Distinguishing between "pressure waves" and "displacement effects" ("Druckwellen" and "Stauungserscheinungen"), he showed that fishes and some aquatic amphibians not only detect water turbulences but can sense the presence of nearby obstacles. The local compression or damming up ("Aufstau") that occurs between the obstacle and a fish moving toward it enables the fish to detect the obstacle. He called this sense: the distance-touch-sense ("Ferntastsinn") and attributed it to the lateral-line system. The conception of this as an acoustic phenomenon was denied because it did not fit the particular definition of "sound" that was being used.

The problem of essentially two forms of vibrational or acoustic energy was finally resolved in 1962. Willem A. van Bergeijk, a student of Dijkgraaf's and a fine comparative physiologist, teamed up with an acoustic physicist, G. G. Harris, under the then-existing basic research program of the Bell Telephone Laboratories. Although physicists evidently recognized and understood the distinctions between acoustic near- and far-fields, the biologists and psycho-acousticians did not. Paper 15 was an essential bridge as well as an important contribution to our understanding of lateral line function.

The problems of directional hearing and lateral-line function are far from solved at the present time, but we have moved a long way in the past 50 years, from arguments as to whether fish can hear at all to investigations of specific mechanisms and properties of audition in fishes (see Paper 2).

11

Reprinted from *Bull. U.S. Bur. Fisheries*, **24**, 185–207 (1904)

CONTRIBUTIONS FROM THE BIOLOGICAL LABORATORY OF THE BUREAU OF FISHERIES AT WOODS HOLE, MASSACHUSETTS.

THE FUNCTION OF THE LATERAL-LINE ORGANS IN FISHES.

By G. H. PARKER,

Assistant Professor of Zoology, Harvard University.

INTRODUCTION.

The habits of fishes, like those of most other animals, are inseparably connected with their sense organs. Thus in the matter of feeding, Bateson (1890) has pointed out that probably the majority of fishes seek their food by sight. Many such fishes when kept in confinement are known not to feed at night or even in twilight, though they may be ravenous feeders in daylight. Other fishes, including the eels, skates, sturgeons, suckers, flat-fishes, etc., many of which are bottom fishes and often nocturnal in their habits, seem not to depend upon sight in seeking their food. Their powers of sight are often deficient, and food excites them chiefly through its action on their organs of taste, smell, or touch. As Bateson observed, none of these fishes start in quest of food when it is first put into their tanks, but remain undisturbed for an interval, doubtless until the scent has been diffused through the water. Then they begin to swim vaguely about, and appear to seek the food by examining the whole area pervaded by the scent. The search is always made in this tentative way, whether the food is hidden or within sight, and it is first seized when by accident it is come upon.

Herrick (1903c) has made the interesting discovery that in the cat-fish, which seeks its food in the way just described, the organs of taste pervade the whole skin, and the fish will seize unseen food with great precision, provided only that it is brought near the skin. Thus in this fish the organs of taste largely replace the eye as a means of discovering the food.

From these examples it must be clear how close is the relation between sense organs and habits. The sense organs, in fact, are the usual means of initiating those simple acts which, when taken collectively, constitute what are popularly known as habits, for the sense organs are the avenues through which the external influences enter the animal and excite it to action. How essential, then, in studying the habits of any group of animals, must be a knowledge of their sense organs.

From this standpoint the elucidation of the habits of fish is particularly important, for their sense organs bear close comparison with those of human beings.

and their environment withal is so different that they afford a most fascinating field for investigation. It is now fairly well established that many fishes possess in a high functional state the five chief senses of man—taste, smell, touch, hearing, and sight; but it is also known that many fishes possess a sixth set of organs, the lateral-line organs, for which there is no representative in man. As these are well-developed and conspicuous structures in many cases, they may be suspected of playing an important part in the economy of these animals, and it is the purpose of this investigation to ascertain something of their rôle in the ordinary habits of some of our fishes.

HISTORICAL REVIEW.

Every one who is at all conversant with the external markings of fishes is familiar with a line which, in most instances, extends along the side from tail to head. This line, known from its position as the lateral line, consists usually of a row of small pores which lead into an underlying canal, the lateral-line canal. In the head of the fish this canal usually branches into three main stems, one of which passes forward and above the eye, another forward and immediately below the eye, and a third downward and over the lower jaw. These three canals, like the lateral-line canal, open on the surface by numerous pores, and, together with this canal, constitute the lateral-line system.

According to Leydig (1868, p. 3) the pores of these canals were recognized over two centuries ago by Stenon (1664) and by Lorenzini (1678) in elasmobranchs, and by Rivinus (1687) in fresh-water fishes. Subsequently the canals were described by many of the earlier anatomists, particularly by Monro (1785), and an excellent summarized account of them was given by Stannius (1846, p. 49) in his comparative anatomy of the vertebrates. Thus before the middle of the last century the gross anatomy of these organs had come to be fairly well recognized.

All the earlier investigators, so far as their opinions are known to me, seem to have regarded the lateral-line system as a system of glands for the production of the mucus so characteristic of the skins of many fishes. Suggestions contrary to this, however, came from two sources. First, observations on elasmobranchs had shown that this group possesses, in addition to the lateral-line system proper, a set of closely related organs, the ampullæ of Lorenzini. Jacobson (1813) studied the structures of these organs with the view of determining what their probable function was, and concluded from their extensive nerve supply that they were certainly sense organs and probably stimulated mechanically, like delicate organs of touch. Treviranus (1820, p. 146), concurred in Jacobson's opinion that the ampullæ were sense organs, and believed that they probably represented a sense quite distinct from any that we possess. Knox (1825, p. 15) in reviewing the whole subject made the interesting statement that "we can not * * * greatly err in considering these organs as organs of touch, so modified, however, as to hold an intermediate place between the sensations of touch and hearing." Finally, Savi (1841) suggested that in the torpedo they might be organs for the reception of electrical stimuli.

A second body of evidence that suggested the nonsecretory nature of the lateral-line system came from investigations on the vesicles of Savi. These are closed, sac-like organs found in clusters in the anterior part of the head of the torpedo. Like the ampullæ of Lorenzini, they are undoubtedly closely related to the lateral-line system. They were originally described by Savi (1841) as nervous organs, and a sensory function was claimed for them by Wagner (1847). This opinion was subsequently supported by Schultze's discovery (1863, p. 11) that the epithelium of these organs contained an abundance of sense cells. Thus the sensory nature of the vesicles of Savi and of the ampullæ of Lorenzini was clearly in the minds of several of the earlier investigators at a time when the nearly related lateral-line system was regarded as a purely secretory mechanism.

In April, 1850, Leydig (1850a) gave a preliminary account of certain large sense organs found by him in the lateral-line canals on the head of the ruffe (*Acerina cernua*), and later in the same year he (Leydig, 1850b) figured and described these organs in detail not only in the ruffe, but in several other species of fresh-water fishes. Since he could find no reason to suppose that the slime on the surface of these fishes was produced in the lateral-line canals, and since these canals contained large sense organs, he concluded that the lateral-line system was not a set of glands, but a system of sense organs which he believed to be peculiar to fishes (Leydig, 1850b, p. 171). Shortly after this, similar organs were found by Leydig (1851) in certain marine teleosts and by Müller (1852, p. 149) in elasmobranchs; and a few years later Leydig (1857, p. 196) gave in his text-book of histology, an excellent summary of the finer anatomy of these and other closely related structures. Here he briefly discussed the function of the lateral-line organs, and expressed the belief that if they must be placed under one of the five senses as usually defined, they certainly belonged under touch, but in his opinion they were very probably representatives of a new sense especially adapted for life in the water.

A few years later Schulze (1861) showed that on the skin of very young fishes there were sense organs essentially like those described by Leydig from the lateral-line canals of mature fishes. These were so distributed as to foreshadow the lateral-line canals, and they undoubtedly represented the organs which were later to occupy these canals. Schulze further demonstrated a similar system of superficial organs in the water-inhabiting stages of amphibians, and thus showed that these organs occurred in other vertebrates than the fishes, a conclusion subsequently confirmed by Leydig (1868), who, though still holding that the lateral-line organs were closely allied to the organs of touch, regarded them as sufficiently distinct to constitute a sixth class of sense organs. Leydig also suggested the possibility that these organs might be represented in other groups of the animal kingdom than the fishes and amphibians, and went so far as to intimate that certain glandular structures in the skin of the air-inhabiting vertebrates might have been derived from them.

In a second paper Schulze (1870, p. 83) pointed out the inaccuracy of this opinion and maintained that the lateral-line organs were strictly limited to fishes and the water-inhabiting stages of amphibians. He also called attention to the important and striking similarity between the sense cells in the lateral-line organs and those in the ear as described by Schultze and by Hasse, a comparison already made by Leydig (1850b, p. 180), and he concluded that the lateral-line organs were stimulated either by mass movements of the water, as when a fish swims through this medium or a current impinges on its body, or by water vibrations whose period is longer than that of the vibrations which stimulate the ear. Notwithstanding this supposed relation to the ear. Schulze agreed with Leydig in regarding the lateral-line organs as organs of touch, though specially modified to meet the requirements of an organism living in the water.

About ten years after the appearance of Schulze's second paper, Dercum (1880, p. 154) called attention to the fact that in many fishes the lateral-line canals were almost if not entirely closed, and that in consequence water could not flow through them, as was supposed by Schulze. Dercum, however, pointed out that since many of the canals were separated from the outer water by only a layer of thin skin applied to the membrane of the canal wall, the system might be said to possess numerous drumheads through which vibrations in the surrounding water could be transmitted to the fluid within the canal, and thus these vibrations could become effective in stimulating the lateral-line organs. Dercum also suggested that the effect of the vibrations might be the more intense the more nearly perpendicular they were to the surface of the canal on which they fell, and in this way it was conceivable that a fish might orient itself in reference to the direction of the vibrations.

These views were in large part accepted by Emery (1880, p. 48), who emphasized the comparison between the lateral-line organs and the internal ear, and thus lead to the opinion subsequently expressed by Mayser (1881, p. 311), Bodenstein (1882, p. 137), and P. and F. Sarasin (1887–1890, p. 54), that the lateral-line organs were accessory ears.

Meanwhile Merkel (1880, p. 55), without knowledge of the contributions made by Dercum and by Emery, showed that it was unlikely that water could be said ever to stream through the canals, and yet he gave very good reasons for supposing that the lateral-line organs were adapted to a mechanical stimulus. From his standpoint there was insufficient ground to consider the lateral-line organs as constituting a sixth group of sense organs, and he was convinced that they were merely tactile organs somewhat modified for aquatic life.

The opinions thus far presented as to the functions of the lateral-line organs are in no instance based upon experimentation, but upon such indirect evidence as that afforded by the structure of the sense organs and of their surrounding parts.

Previous to the appearance of Fuchs's paper in 1894 very few investigators had made experiments on the lateral-line organs, and such experiments as had been undertaken were of a very simple and tentative character. The earliest of these was the work of Bugnion (1873, p. 302), who showed that a living *Proteus* was not especially sensitive to solutions of alum, salt, or weak acid applied to the lateral-line organs, but that it reacted vigorously when these organs were touched with a needle. Later de Sède (1884, p. 469) reported that fishes in which the lateral line had been cut were less successful in guiding themselves in an aquarium containing numerous obstacles than were normal fish, and he stated that in his opinion the lateral-line organs did not represent a sixth sense but were organs of touch especially concerned with directing the animals. Bateson, some years later (1890, p. 237), stated that he had been unable to get responses from fishes when food substances were tried as stimuli for the lateral-line organs, and lastly, Nagel (1894, p. 191) found no evidence that the lateral-line organs of fishes and amphibians were stimulated chemically; when the lateral-line nerves in *Barbus fluviatilis* were cut on both sides the fish apparently remained normal, but when in certain fish (Schuppfisch) the nerve of only one side was cut, a slight lack of orientation and of muscle coördination could sometimes be observed. These seem to be the only noteworthy experiments on the lateral-line organs that were carried out before the time of Fuchs's work.

Fuchs (1894, p. 467) experimented chiefly on the torpedo, a fish which possesses, in addition to the lateral-line organs proper, the vesicles of Savi and the ampullæ of Lorenzini. Fuchs cut the nerves connected with these two special sets of organs, but without being able to detect any significant change in the subsequent movements of the fish. He then exposed the nerve supplying the vesicles of Savi, and, having placed it in connection with an appropriate electrical apparatus, he found that by pressing lightly on the vesicles a reduction in the current from the nerve could be demonstrated. As this reduction is believed to indicate the transmitting activity of nerves, it follows that the pressure applied to the vesicles was probably a stimulus to them and thereby brought the nerve into action. No such results were obtained from similar experiments on the ampullæ of Lorenzini, but the nerves from the lateral-line system in *Raja clavata* and *R. asterias* also gave evidence of transmission when their terminal organs were pressed. Dilute acids and heat did not stimulate the terminal organs tested, and Fuchs (1894, p. 474) concluded that pressure was the normal stimulus in the skate for the lateral-line organs and in the torpedo for the vesicles of Savi, but not for the ampullæ of Lorenzini.

Apparently without knowledge of the work done by Fuchs, Richard (1896, p. 131) performed some experiments on the gold-fish, consisting of the removal of the scales from the lateral line and the destruction of the sense organs under these scales by cauterizing with heat, or potassic hydrate. After this operation some of the fishes were unable to keep below the surface of the water, and though they soon died, Richard (1896, p. 133) believed that he had evidence enough to show that the lateral-line organs were connected with the production of gas in the air bladder.

Richard's conclusions were called in question by Bonnier (1896, p. 917), who pointed out the severity of the operations employed and intimated that the results were more probably dependent upon the excessive amount of tissue removed than upon the destruction of the lateral line. Bonnier (1896, p. 918) further recorded experiments of his own in which the lateral-line organs were destroyed by electro-cautery. Fishes thus operated upon showed two characteristics: They could easily be approached with the hand and even seized; and they failed to orient themselves in reference to disturbances caused by bodies thrown into the water. Bonnier concluded from his experiments that the lateral line, in addition to other functions, had to do with the orientation of fishes in reference to centers in the water from which shock-like vibrations might proceed.

Lee (1898, p. 139), whose experimental methods were much the same as those used by Bonnier, obtained some significant results, particularly with the toad-fish, *Opsanus tau*. When the pectoral and pelvic fins of this fish were removed, so that it might be said to be without its usual mechanical support, and the lateral-line organs were destroyed by thermo-cautery, the animal would lie quietly for some time, on either its side or back, and act as though it had lost its "sense of equilibrium." That its condition was not due to excessive injury was seen from the fact that a finless fish in which an equal amount of skin had been cauterized, but in which the lateral-line organs were intact, showed no lack of equilibrium, and in its general behavior closely resembled a normal fish. Moreover, Lee found that the stimulation of the central end of the lateral-line nerve of a dog-fish resulted in perfectly coordinated fin movements, and he therefore concluded that the organs of the lateral line are equilibration organs. How these are stimulated Lee did not attempt to decide, though he suggested (1898, p. 143) that pressure changes in the surrounding medium may be the means of stimulation.

Five years later, in experimenting on the sense of hearing in fishes, I made some observations on the lateral-line organs of *Fundulus* (Parker, 1903a, p. 59; 1903b, p. 197). These led to the conclusion that the lateral-line organs in this fish were stimulated by a very slight mass movement of the water, and they have afforded the point of departure for the present investigation.

In summarizing this historical review, it is clear that no one has ever brought forward the least reason to suspect that the lateral-line organs are ever normally stimulated by light, heat, or other ether disturbances. It is also very improbable that they are stimulated chemically, for in many instances the covered situation of the organs is not favorable for this form of stimulation, and the direct experiments of Bugnion (1873) on *Proteus*, of Bateson (1890), and of Nagel (1894) on several kinds of fish, and of Fuchs (1894) on *Torpedo* and *Raja* have always given negative results. On the other hand, it is almost universally admitted that the normal stimulus for these organs must be of a mechanical kind, either simple contact, as in touch, or vibratory contact, somewhat as in hearing. It is on this point that the majority of investigations disagree, some maintaining that the lateral-line organs are simply organs of touch (Merkel, de Sède), or of pressure (Fuchs), others that they are organs belonging to an independent class, probably intermediate between touch and hearing (Leydig, Schulze, Dercum, Parker), and, lastly, those that believe them to be accessory auditory organs (Emery, Mayser, Bodenstein, P. and F. Sarasin). That the lateral-line organs were necessary to successful locomotion as organs of equilibration, etc., was first suggested, I believe, by de Sède; and this opinion has received the support of Nagel, Bonnier, and especially of Lee. In attempting to decide between these various views, the first question that arises is: What is the normal stimulus for the lateral-line organs? It is the object of this investigation to find an answer to this question.

MATERIALS AND METHODS.

The experiments about to be described were carried out chiefly on the common mummichog, *Fundulus heteroclitus*, a fish of convenient size, great hardiness, and everywhere abundant in the neighborhood of the biological laboratory of the United States Bureau of Fisheries at Woods Hole, Mass., where the experiments were made. Besides this species seven others were also tested, though not with a full range of stimuli. These additional species were the smooth dog-fish, *Mustelus canis;* the common skate, *Raja erinacea;* the killi-fish, *Fundulus majalis;* the scup, *Stenotomus chrysops;* the toad-fish, *Opsanus tau;* the common flat-fish, *Pseudopleuronectes americanus;* and the swell-fish, *Chilomycterus schœpfi.*

The general method of experimenting was to cut the nerves connected with the lateral-line organs of a number of individuals of a given species, and, after the fish had recovered from the operation, to test them in comparison with normal individuals by subjecting both to a particular stimulus. In this way I expected to ascertain whether with the loss of the lateral-line organs the ability to respond to certain stimuli would disappear. To eliminate the effects of the operation as far as possible I usually tested a third series of fishes in which incisions had been made to reach the nerves, but in which the nerves themselves had not been severed.

In all the fishes, except the dog-fish and the skate, the nerves were cut by the method described in my previous paper (Parker, 1903a, p. 59), i. e., the fishes were etherized by being put for a few minutes in sea water containing a little ether, and the fifth and seventh nerves were then cut by an incision behind the eye, and the lateral-line nerve by an incision just behind the head; the few lateral-line organs between these two incisions were then extirpated. In the dog-fish and the skate the operation was similar, except that the fifth and the seventh nerves were more conveniently cut from the roof of the mouth than from the exterior.

The chief objection to this method of operating lies in the fact that in cutting the root of the seventh nerve it is necessary also to cut that of the fifth, so that the tactile sensibility of much of the head, as well as the innervation of the muscles of the jaws, are almost always lost. Notwithstanding the apparent severity of the operations the fishes usually recovered, and even a few hours after the operation began feeding and acted in most respects normally. The majority lived for several weeks, and some of them for over a month. Care was exercised, however, to see that they were properly fed, for the paralyzed state of the muscles of the jaws, though not interfering much with respiration, did make it difficult for the fish to grasp food.

Normal and, as I shall call them, cut fishes were then subjected to the following range of stimuli and their reactions noted: Light, heat, salinity of water, food, oxygen, carbon dioxide, foulness of water, pressure of water, currents, stimuli to equilibrium, vibrations of high frequency (sound), and vibrations of low frequency.

EXPERIMENTS.

Light.—To ascertain whether light was a stimulus for the lateral-line organs the following device was used: An oblong glass aquarium, measuring about 60 cm. in length, 25 cm. in breadth, and 25 cm. in height, was half-covered with opaque cloth, so that one end and the adjacent halves of the top and of the sides were impervious to light. The apparatus was set up in a dark room and illuminated by a 16-candle incandescent electric light, so placed that the light fell across the uncovered half of the aquarium, but without entering the darkened half. The aquarium was filled with sea water and specimens of *Fundulus heteroclitus* were introduced to see if they would assemble in the light or in the dark. It was soon found that these fishes followed one another by sight, and the records finally taken came from experiments in which single fishes were put in the aquarium and their reactions observed. After a fish had become accustomed to its new surrounding, which happened usually in about ten or fifteen minutes, and which was indicated by the fish leaving the bottom of the aquarium and beginning to sport about near the surface of the water, observations were made at intervals of one minute as to whether the fish was in the dark

254

or in the light. It soon appeared that a number of individuals were almost indifferent to the light, being found as commonly in one place as in the other. Others were more generally in the light, and fishes were tested until fifteen such were obtained. These fifteen were tested accurately by being placed individually in the aquarium and by having their positions determined at minute intervals for ten minutes. In 150 observations these fishes were 93 times (62 per cent) in the light.

They were then all operated upon by having the nerves to the lateral-line organs cut. Twelve recovered and were tested as in the first experiment. In 120 observations these fishes were 79 times (66 per cent) in the light. It is therefore highly improbable that the slight tendency to assemble in the light shown by some individuals of this species is in anyway dependent upon the lateral-line organs; in other words, light is not a stimulus for these organs.

Heat.—The stimulation of the lateral-line organs by heat was tested also on *Fundulus heteroclitus*. Five individuals with the nerves to the lateral-line organs cut were compared with five normal individuals by subjecting them to water of different temperatures in cylindrical glass jars 35 cm. high and 23 cm. in diameter.

The temperature of the outside water in which the fishes had been caught was at this time of year (August) about 19.5° C. When the five normal fishes were put in the glass jar filled with water at this temperature, they at once swam to the bottom, and, as is usual with them when first introduced into an aquarium, remained swimming about in the deeper water for some time. Finally, they rose to the surface and sported about in the upper water, remaining there unless frightened by some movement or other disturbance about them, whereupon they would again make a temporary descent. Cut fish acted in all respects like normal ones except, perhaps, that they were not so agile in their movements, but this slight reduction in their quickness of response was not due to the cutting of the nerves of the latteral-line system, for it was observable in fish in which the skin, but not the nerves, had been cut.

In water at 14° C., the reactions of normal and of cut fishes were indistinguishable from those in water at 19.5° C.

At 9° C., much the same was observed as at 14° C., but there was a slight though noticeably greater tendency here to keep in the deeper water than at 19.5° C. This tendency, however, was not pronounced enough to allow one to say that the fish had deserted the top; after having been frightened away from the top they returned less freely than at 14° C. or 19.5° C. In this respect, however, the normal and cut fishes agreed.

Two temperatures higher than 19.5° C. were tried. At 25.5° C. both normal and cut fishes swam down, and for the most part stayed in the deeper water. Now and then an individual would swim to the top, but it almost always quickly returned to the bottom. In these respects normal and cut fishes were indistinguishable.

At 30.5° C., both normal and cut fishes swam to the bottom of the vessel and stayed there persistently. In the course of fifteen minutes not a single fish came to the surface, whereas at 19.5° C. all fishes returned to the surface usually in three to four minutes. Moreover, the fishes continually nosed about on the bottom of the jar as though they were seeking still deeper water.

Since in all these temperature experiments the normal fish and the cut ones reacted in essentially the same way, I conclude that heat is not a stimulus for the lateral-line organs.   This is in agreement with Fuchs's results (1894, p. 473) on the vesicles of Savi which were stimulated by pressure but not by heat.

The reactions of *Fundulus* to heat, though of negative value so far as the purposes of this paper are concerned, have an interesting biological bearing.   It appears from the experiments given that at a temperature of 19.5° C. (corresponding to that of the outside water from which the animals had been taken), or at lower temperatures down to 9° C., the fish remain, when otherwise undisturbed, near the top of the water; but at temperatures above 19.5° C., particularly about 30° C., they seek the deeper water and remain there.   In other words, they are negatively geotropic in the cooler water (9° to 19.5° C.), and become positively geotropic in the warmer water (25.5° C. to 30.5° C.), the increase of temperature causing a reversal of the sense of geotropism.   This change is just the opposite of that recently pointed out by Torelle (1903, p. 475) for the frog.   This animal remains near the surface of the water at high temperatures, and goes to the bottom at low temperatures, the turning point being at about 10° C.   Probably these reactions, though reversed in the two instances, are not without significance for these two species.   The frog may be thus protected from severe cold and the mummichog from overheated surface water.

Salinity.—Near the shore, and particularly near the mouths of rivers, the salinity of the sea water is subject to much variation, and it is not impossible that differences in this respect might be responded to by fishes through their lateral-line organs. Tests in this direction were made upon *Fundulus heteroclitus* by subjecting normal and cut individuals to the action of sea water variously diluted or concentrated. The sea water at the end of the government wharf at the Woods Hole laboratory is well mixed by the tides, and has the usual specific gravity of about 1.025.   Water taken from this source was diluted with tap water to decrease the salinity, or concentrated by boiling to increase it.   Care was taken after the boiled water had been cooled to aerate it thoroughly before it was used in experiments.

Normal and cut fishes were placed first in glass jars containing ordinary sea water and then in jars containing the diluted sea water.   The fishes showed no characteristic reactions to mixtures containing 90 per cent, 80 per cent, 70 per cent, or 60 per cent of sea water.   In the mixture containing half sea water and half fresh water a decided reaction was obtained in that the fishes swam about in an excited way, often with darting movements, and were as frequently found in the deeper water as near the top.   Very slight evidence of this condition could at times be detected in the 60 per cent and 70 per cent mixtures, but the reactions were most decided in the 50 per cent mixture.   Since the normal and the cut individuals were indistinguishable in respect to these reactions, there was no reason to suppose that the diminished salinity of the water was a stimulus for the lateral-line organs.

Both classes of fishes were put into sea water concentrated by boiling to three-fourths its original volume (the specific gravity was something over 1.030).   In this water the fishes swam and respired normally, though it was evident that they were buoyed up by the greater density.   Normal and cut fishes were again indistinguishable, and there was therefore no reason to suppose that the increased density had any stimulating effects on the lateral-line organs. In this respect my results agreed with those of Bugnion (1873, p. 302), who experimented with salt solutions upon the lateral-line organs of *Proteus*.

Food.—The normal stimulus for taste in animals, as in the human being, is the dissolved material in their food. Judging from the aquarium habits of some fishes, they seek their food chiefly by the eye, but it is also possible that the juices of the food may excite them. To ascertain whether the lateral-line organs are thus stimulated, I placed a single individual of *Fundulus heteroclitus* in a small vessel of sea water and, after it had become quiet, endeavored to discharge from a capillary tube some mussel juice on the lateral line of the body, the substance of *Mytilus edulis* being a favorite food of this fish. The extreme activity of the fish made such an experiment rather difficult, but after frequent trials on several individuals I got no results that could be said to indicate that the lateral-line organs were stimulated.

In a second set of experiments I etherized the fishes and cut the spinal cord just behind the head. After recovery, such fishes act as though the trunk muscles were paralyzed and swim about slowly by the pectoral fins. If properly fed they live for a week or more. They often rested on the bottom of the vessel in which they were kept, and when quiet afforded an excellent opportunity for testing the lateral-line organs. But even under these circumstances I never obtained reactions from these fishes that led me to conclude that the sea water decoction of mussel discharged on their lateral lines ever stimulated these organs. In this respect my results agreed with those of Bateson (1890, p. 237), and I conclude that the lateral-line organs are not stimulated by food.

Oxygen.—The oxygen dissolved in sea water is essential for the life of marine fishes, and as the amount varies in different parts of the sea, it is possible that this substance may serve as a stimulus to the lateral-line organs. To test this possibility, specimens of *Fundulus heteroclitus*, normal and cut, were introduced into sea water that had been boiled to expel the dissolved gases and then cooled with as little exposure to air as possible. When the fish were introduced they swam rapidly throughout the whole vessel, and their respiration was characterized by rapid and deep swallowing movements. These features disappeared very quickly on transferring the fish to ordinary sea water. Since normal and cut fishes acted alike in this experiment, there was no reason to suppose that lack of oxygen was in any way a stimulus for the lateral-line organs.

Carbon dioxide.—As carbon dioxide is one of the most extensive waste products from animals' bodies, it might be regarded as a possible means of polluting water, and the lateral-line organs might serve to detect this pollution. To ascertain whether carbon dioxide was a stimulus for these organs, normal and cut individuals of *Fundulus heteroclitus* were introduced into sea water through which carbon dioxide gas had been bubbling in minute streams for over half an hour. Both classes of fishes acted as though they were in ordinary sea water, and there was no reason to conclude that carbon dioxide had any effect upon the lateral-line organs.

Foulness of water.—A quantity of foul water taken from a vessel in which marine animals and plants were decaying was mixed with sea water and cut and normal individuals were introduced into it and their reactions observed. Although this mixture had a most offensive odor to the experimenter, the two sets of fishes behaved as though they were in ordinary sea water, and hence the general condition of foul water could not be said to afford a stimulus for the lateral-line organs.

Salts, food substances, oxygen, carbon dioxide, and the materials in foul water would probably all act as chemical stimuli on the lateral-line organs, if they acted at all, but since none of them appear to be stimuli for these organs, the observations of Bugnion (1873), Fuchs (1894), and Nagel (1894) to the effect that the lateral-line organs are not stimulated chemically, were confirmed. This view of the nonchemical reactiveness of the lateral-line organs has been clearly maintained from a morphological standpoint in two recent papers by Herrick (1903a, 1903b.)

Pressure of water.—Fuchs (1894, p. 474) suggested that changes in the hydrostatic pressure might be the means of stimulating the lateral-line organs. In testing this proposition normal and cut individuals of *Fundulus heteroclitus* were subjected to diminished hydrostatic pressure in a cylindrical glass museum jar three-fourths full of water. The jar was about 80 cm. high and 25 cm. in diameter, and was provided with an air-tight top. By means of a small hand pump air contained after the jar was closed was removed until the pressure was reduced from the usual 15 pounds per square inch to about 5 pounds.

When the fish were first put into the jar they all descended, as is usual, to the bottom, but after the removal of air had continued for some time they came to the top of the water, and when the pressure had fallen to about 5 pounds, it was evident that they were unable to keep below the surface of the water without vigorous and continuous swimming. Since they possess air-bladders, it seemed likely that the reduced pressure had caused such an enlargement of these organs that the fish were carried to the top of the water by their own buoyancy, and this explanation was tested by inserting capillary glass tubes into the sides of several, so that as the pressure was reduced the air could escape from the bladder. When the fish were subjected to diminished pressure under these conditions, air was seen to escape from them, and they remained quietly swimming at the bottom of the jar. Evidently the first set of fish were kept near the top of the water through their altered specific gravity. Normal and cut fishes reacted in essentially the same way in these experiments, hence there was no reason to suppose that a diminished hydrostatic pressure was a stimulus to the lateral-line organs.

In a similar way normal and cut fishes were put in a water-tight jar in which the pressure could be raised from 15 to 22 pounds on the square inch. When first introduced the fishes went to the bottom, and after the pressure was put on they remained there with the exception of short intervals, when by vigorous swimming they could get into the upper part of the jar. From such situations, however, they would often almost drop to the bottom. As in the experiments with reduced pressure, so here the air-bladder doubtless played a controlling part; for when it was punctured so that with increased pressure water could enter it, the fish swam much more freely. The increased pressure, nevertheless, stimulated the fishes, for they never seemed to come into a restful state in the fifteen minutes or so during which they were under pressure. Since the reactions of the normal and cut fishes were indistinguishable, however, there was no reason to suppose that increased hydrostatic pressure is a stimulus for the lateral-line organs.

258

These observations make it appear improbable that changes in hydrostatic pressure, as suggested by Fuchs (1894, p. 474), are stimuli for the lateral-line organs. Nor in fact do the observations made by Fuchs really lend much support to this hypothesis. He found that when he pressed on the lateral-line organs of *Raja*, the electrical changes in the nerves connected with them indicated that the organs had been stimulated. But the pressure thus exerted was without doubt of a very different kind from increased or decreased hydrostatic pressure; it was very probably a *deforming* pressure and not one that exerts its influence in all directions equally. It is well known that for the stimulations of the tactile organs of the human skin a deforming pressure is vastly more effective than such a pressure as is obtained by putting the hand deep in water. Under such circumstances the tactile sensations are not strongest from the parts under greatest pressure but from the region of greatest deformation, i. e., where water and air meet. It seems to me, therefore, that Fuchs's experiments demonstrate that the lateral-line organs can be stimulated by a deforming mechanical influence, but since hydrostatic pressure does not deform to any great extent, there is no reason to suppose that it stimulates these organs. Hence I do not think that my observations are at variance with those of Fuchs, but that he drew a wrong inference from what he observed.

Currents.—From the time of Schulze's second paper on the lateral-line organs (1870), water currents have been regarded with more or less favor as stimuli for the lateral-line organs. To ascertain whether currents do stimulate these organs, I have experimented on *Fundulus heteroclitus, F. majalis, Stenotomus chrysops, Pseudopleuronectes americanus, Mustelus canis,* and *Raja erinacea.* All these fishes when introduced into running water swim against the current, i. e., they are strongly rheotropic.

I tested the smaller species (*Fundulus heteroclitus, F. majalis, Stenotomus chrysops,* and *Pseudopleuronectes americanus*) by exposing them in a large open trough to a gentle flow of water. The trough, which was about 50 cm. wide, always contained a depth of at least 10 cm. of water and was about 3 meters in length. An inlet was established at one end and an outlet at the other, and a gentle current of water was kept flowing through the trough. A normal *Fundulus heteroclitus* when put in this trough immediately turned its head against the current and swam toward the source, often making its way actually into the open end of the inlet tube. If in its progress the fish was swept into the adjacent and more quiet water near the side of the trough, it would often sport about there for a while, but on returning to the current it would take up again its course toward the inlet. At times when the current was strong there would form on the sides of the trough small backset currents, and it was instructive to observe how quickly the fish reversed its direction when by any accident it was carried from the main current into a backset. In all the many fishes tested, irrespective of illumination, etc., they swam against the current.

Individuals in which the nerves to the lateral-line organs had been cut proved to be absolutely indistinguishable from normal fishes under these conditions. In agility and certainty of response there was no difference between the two sets. Hence I was led to conclude that the lateral-line organs were not essential to the fish in swimming against a current, and that therefore a current was probably not a stimulus for these organs.

Similar experiments were made with *Fundulus majalis* and *Stenotomus chrysops*, both of which gave results identical with those obtained from *Fundulus heteroclitus*. *Pseudopleuronectes americanus*, normal and cut, also swims against the current, but often takes hold of the bottom of the trough by a sucker-like action of the whole body. This temporary anchoring, however, was as characteristic of the cut fishes as it was of the normal ones, and there is no reason to suppose that the lateral-line organs were involved.

The larger fishes, *Mustelus canis* and *Raja erinacea*, were tested not in the trough but at one of the tide openings on the wharf outside the laboratory. Here at certain tides a steady broad current maintains itself, and in this it was comparatively easy to experiment with these fishes. Normal and cut individuals were put into a simple harness made of twine and to which a cord was attached so that they could be conveniently restrained. By this means they could be placed in the current where desired and their reactions noted. Both the dog-fishes and the skates swam vigorously against the current, and this happened irrespective of the condition of the lateral line. In fact it was impossible to tell from the reactions of the fish in the water whether the nerves to the lateral-line organs had been cut or not. My own experiments, therefore, confirm the opinion of Tullberg (1903, pp. 13, 15) that the lateral-line organs are not concerned with swimming against a current.

Stimulus to equilibrium.—The ability of a fish to keep its equilibrium at rest or in motion has, from time to time, been stated to be dependent at least in part on the lateral-line organs. So far as I am aware, the first investigator to make suggestions in this direction was Richard (1896, p. 131), who supposed that the lateral-line organs were at least indirectly connected with the equilibrium of a fish in that they influenced the amount of gas in the air bladder. Lee (1898, p. 144), however, first clearly expressed the belief, based upon extended observations on the toad-fish and the dog-fish, that the lateral-line organs were primarily organs of equilibration. Because of the growing favor in which this view has been held, I felt that it was desirable not only to make new observations in this direction, but also to repeat carefully the experiments of those who had already advocated this theory, with the view of gaining a critical insight into the present standing of the question. For these reasons I have carried out experiments on the equilibration function of the lateral-line organs in *Fundulus heteroclitus*, *Stenotomus chrysops*, *Opsanus tau*, and *Mustelus canis*.

When the nerves to the lateral-line organs in the species of fishes just mentioned were cut by the methods already described, and the fishes were allowed to recover from the shock of the operation, it was remarkable how little changed they seemed to be. So far as their ordinary movements were concerned they were often indistinguishable from normal fishes. They swam with agility and kept their equilibrium perfectly. My own observations entirely support Lee's statement (1898, p. 140) that the destruction of all the lateral-line organs "does not seem to interfere much, if any, with the animal's equilibrium." I usually found it impossible to bring a cut fish to rest on its side or back, for when displaced from its usual upright position it reacted as a normal fish by struggling to return to that position.

Those fishes that possess air bladders, such as *Fundulus* and *Stenotomus*, had no difficulty after the operation in keeping below the surface, and I found no reason to suppose that the lateral-line organs had any influence on the amount of gas contained in the air bladder, as conjectured by Richard (1896). In fact, all my observations supported Bonnier's opinion that Richard's results were due to the severity of his operations and not to the loss of the lateral-line organs, and since many fishes with well-developed lateral-line systems have no air bladders, it seems to me highly improbable that these sense organs are directly concerned with the state of the bladder.

I next repeated Lee's experiments on the toad-fish, *Opsanus tau*, and the dog-fish, *Mustelus canis*. Lee (1898, p. 140) states that after the removal of the pectoral and pelvic fins from the toad-fish, the natural means for support for the resting animal, and the destruction of the lateral line organs, there were "decided evidences of a lack of the sense of equilibrium." The fishes were unsteady in their movements and would lie quietly upon the side or back, in this respect being in strong contrast with individuals whose fins and skin had been cut to an equal extent, but whose lateral-line systems were still intact. These, according to Lee, were active and certain in their movements, showed no lack of equilibrium, and in general closely resembled normal individuals.

My own observations on *Opsanus* do not support those of Lee. I prepared six toad-fish by cutting off the four fins as Lee did and then severing the nerves to the lateral-line organs. This operation was easily carried out by following the careful topographical account of the lateral-line system given for this species by Clapp (1898). Of the six fishes operated upon one died shortly after the operation but the remaining five all lived over five days and one over a week. These I carefully compared with five other fishes from which the four fins had been removed and the skin, but not the nerves to the lateral-line organs, had been cut. So far as the retention of equilibrium was concerned, I found it impossible to distinguish one set from the other. Both, though rather irregular in their locomotion, retained fairly upright positions, and none ever showed the characteristic disturbances seen in the locomotion of many fishes from which the ears have been removed. Occasionally individuals could be found that would lie quietly often for some time on the side or back, as described by Lee, but these always proved to be moribund and usually died within a day or so after this symptom appeared. Since cases of this kind occurred among those fishes in which the lateral-line organs were intact, as well as among those in which the nerves had been cut, I concluded that the loss of equilibrium seen in these instances was not due to the exclusion of the lateral-line system, but to general weakness preceding death. I therefore do not believe, as Lee does, that the loss of the lateral-line organs in *Opsanus* is accompanied with any special disturbance in equilibrium.

Lee (1898, p. 142) also experimented upon the dog-fish by exposing the lateral-line nerve and stimulating its central end, whereupon he obtained well coordinated muscular movements like those seen on stimulating the ampullar organs of the internal ear. I have repeated this experiment on *Mustelus canis* and can confirm Lee's statements even to detail. I have worked with care only on the pectoral-fin reactions, but these will suffice to give a clear insight into the nature of the response. When, as Lee states (1898, p. 142), the left lateral-line nerve is stimulated centrally, the left pectoral fin is elevated and the right depressed. Since this reaction, which is always very marked and clear, is of a kind to restore equilibrium, one might conclude with Lee that the lateral-line organs are organs of equilibration, but exactly the same reaction can be called forth by touching the skin with the electrodes. If the lateral-line nerve is cut on one side of the body and the electrodes are applied on that side and at a point posterior to the cut, the pectoral-fin reactions that occur are the same as those seen when the lateral-line nerve is stimulated centrally. Since the pectoral-fin reactions thus obtained disappear when the spinal cord anterior to the region of stimulation is cut, there can be no doubt that the general cutaneous terminations of the spinal nerves are the recipients of the stimulus. Hence Lee's conclusion that the lateral-line organs are organs of equilibration must be qualified by the statement that there is no reason to suppose that these organs are more concerned with this function than is the integument. This opinion is supported by certain observations made by Lyon (1900, p. 79) to the effect that when the tail of a dog-fish is turned laterally, compensating movements of the eyes can be observed even though the second and eighth nerves are cut. Since these movements disappear on cutting the spinal cord, Lyon concludes that the afferent path is from the sensory nerves of the skin or muscle.

So far as equilibration is concerned, the lateral-line organs are certainly much inferior to the ear and even the eye. Thus if the nerves to the lateral-line organs of a dog-fish are cut, the animal will continue to swim as a normal individual does. If the eyes are covered, normal swimming still continues. But if the eighth nerve of a dog-fish is cut, and the animal is made to swim rapidly, it will usually lose its equilibrium even with the whole lateral-line system intact, and if the eyes are covered it invariably does so. Thus while the eye may in part supplement the ear in orientation, the lateral-line organs seem to be of no significance in this respect, and our only reason for supposing that they are of value in equilibrium is the fact that on stimulating the lateral-line nerve, fin movements, etc., occur such as are produced by stimulating the ampullar organs of the ear; but this does not raise them as organs of equilibration to an order higher than that of the skin. Since in this respect they are much inferior to the internal ear, it is misleading to designate them as special equilibration organs.

Vibrations of high frequency (sound).—The suggestion made by Emery (1880), Mayser (1881), Bodenstein (1882), and others, that the lateral-line organs may be accessory ears, calls for a test of these organs by sounds. To carry out this I used the same apparatus that I had formerly employed to test the sense of hearing in fishes (cf. Parker, 1903a, 1903b). This consisted of a marine aquarium, one end of which was made of wood and in which was hung a smaller glass aquarium closed at one end (that next the wooden end of the large aquarium) by a silk net of coarse mesh. Thus the fish could be restrained in the smaller aquarium and yet be subjected to sound from the sounding-board at the end of the larger one. As a source of sound I used a tuning fork driven by electricity and giving out 100 vibrations per second. It was placed on an isolated base so near the sounding-board that a very slight movement was sufficient to bring it into contact with the board, and thus the sound could be conveyed to the water. Experiments were made on *Fundulus heteroclitus, F. majalis, Stenotomus chrysops,* and *Mustelus canis.*

My experiments on *Fundulus heteroclitus* confirm my results of a year ago (Parker, 1903a, p. 56; 1903b, p. 199). When normal individuals of this species were stimulated by sound they often responded by pectoral fin movements and almost invariably by an increase in their respiratory rate. This continued to be true even after the nerves to the lateral-line organs had been cut, and I therefore concluded that the lateral-line organs were not essential to these responses. Since the pectoral fin and the respiratory reactions disappeared in individuals whose eighth nerves had been cut, but whose lateral-line organs were intact, it was evident that while in this species these sounds were effective stimuli for the ear they were not so for the lateral-line organs.

Fundulus majalis reacts in many respects like *F. heteroclitus*. Its movements, however, are often more sudden and darting than in the other species. To vibrations of the tuning fork the animals usually spread the fins and often gave a short dart forward. This continued after the nerves to the lateral-line organs had been cut, and ceased only with the cutting of the eighth nerve; hence I conclude that also in *F. majalis* sound is a stimulus for the ear but not for the lateral-line organs.

Although I tested a considerable number of *Stenotomus chrysops* and *Mustelus canis*, both in normal condition and with their lateral-line nerves cut, I was unable to elicit from them any unquestionable reactions to the sound from the tuning fork. This stimulus certainly did not act on the lateral-line organs of these two fishes, and from the experiments on the two species of *Fundulus*, I conclude that there is no reason to suppose that a sound of 100 vibrations per second is a stimulus for the lateral-line organs, though it may be for the ear.

Vibrations of low frequency.—When a slow but noiseless vibration was given to the aquarium containing *Fundulus heteroclitus*, the fishes, as I have elsewhere stated (Parker, 1903a, 1903b), were vigorously stimulated. The stimulus that affects them seemed to proceed from a movement of the body of water in the aquarium as a whole, for the most convenient way to produce this stimulus was to make the aquarium and the supporting table vibrate slightly by drawing the aquarium a little to one side, thus straining the table slightly, and then letting it go. The motion thus produced, when written off on a moving surface, was found to consist of a series of vibrations very close to six per second, and each time the aquarium was made to vibrate, about forty such vibrations were accomplished before the apparatus came to rest again.

I have nothing to add to my former statements (Parker, 1903a, p, 59; 1903b, p. 199) about the reactions of *Fundulus heteroclitus* to this stimulus. When normal individuals are first introduced into an aquarium they swim at once to the bottom, and only after some time and numerous cautious attempts do they come to swim at the surface. As I have already noted, any slight disturbance, such as a quick movement of the observer or a slight jar given to the aquarium, is sufficient to cause them to descend at once. If, by means invisible to the fishes, the slow vibration already described is given to the aquarium, they dart at once to the bottom and remain there some time before returning to the surface. When the fish again begin to swim upward toward the surface, their progress may at any moment be stopped by causing the aquarium to vibrate, for they will again descend. Under no circumstances will the normal fishes rise and stay at the surface while the aquarium is in vibration. These reactions are in my experience practically invariable.

When individuals with the nerves to the lateral-line organs cut are subjected to similar tests, the contrast with normal fishes is striking. Cut fishes will continue to sport about near the surface, or even swim upward from below, while the aquarium is in vibration.   In fact the vibration seems to have no effect upon them except in that it produces ripples on the top of the water, and when they come under the influence of these they usually descend a few inches into water which, so far as one can judge from the particles of silt contained in it, is not in motion. from the surface ripples. Here they will remain and sport about during the vibrations, though this region would be immediately deserted by a normal fish.   Hence I conclude that a body of water vibrating at a relatively slow rate, six per second, is a stimulus for the lateral-line organs in *Fundulus heteroclitus*..

The reactions of *Fundulus majalis* to vibrations of low frequency, except for the darting movements already mentioned, were almost identical with those of *F. heteroclitus*.   Normal individuals reacted to the vibrations usually at once by descending; cut ones gave no evidence of being stimulated.   In one set of the normal fishes that were being tested preparatory to operations two were found that could not be said to respond to the vibrations.   Such conditions were never met with in *F. heteroclitus*, and they were so rare in *F. majalis* that they constitute an unimportant exception to the statement that the two species in their lateral-line reactions are essentially alike.

Stenotomus chrysops when put in the aquarium usually swam down to the bottom and remained in the deeper water, sometimes with the lower fins in contact with the floor of the aquarium, sometimes a few inches above this.   In all tests of vibrations made with these fishes, care was taken that the stimulus should be applied only when the fishes were not in contact with any solid body, i. e., when they were suspended somewhat above the bottom of the aquarium.   Under such circumstances a noiseless vibration almost invariably called forth a very characteristic reaction. When quietly suspended in the water the fish usually rests with its head pointed obliquely downward and its tail up.   On stimulating it with a vibration it almost invariably sets its fins and changes the direction of its axis so that its head points obliquely upward.   This was observed clearly in six out of seven normal fishes. These six were then operated upon by cutting the nerves to the lateral-line organs. Five recovered, and none of these reacted to the vibrations of low frequency unless the aquarium was made to vibrate very considerably.   Under such circumstances occasional, but unquestionable, reactions, precisely like those just described, were observed.   Since these reactions are not interfered with by cutting the eighth nerves, and occur when the literal-line organs are excluded, it is probable that they result from a stimulation of the general cutaneous nerves.   Thus in *Stenotomus chrysops* one form of stimulus is probably effective for two sets of sense organs, those of the skin and those of the lateral-line system.

In testing the smooth dog-fish, *Mustelus canis*, for reactions to vibrations of low frequency, I found the ordinary individuals too large for work in the aquarium, and I therefore experimented on young animals not over a foot and a half in length.   As already noted, none of the specimens I tested gave any response to the tuning fork at 100 vibrations per second.   To the slower vibrations, six per second, all fishes tested were very responsive and reacted usually in a very uniform way.   In seven young fishes that were tested all raised the tail when the aquarium was made to vibrate, and if the fishes were high in the water they usually swam to the deeper situations. These reactions, particularly the elevation of the tail, were unusually regular.   I noticed no change in the respiratory rate. It was with difficulty that even these young fishes were tested, for, since they were relatively large, it was only now and then that they were not in contact with solid parts of the acquarium, and consequently in position for satisfactory stimulation. Notwithstanding this difficulty, however, enough unquestionable reactions were obtained to place beyond doubt the statements made above.

After the nerves to the lateral-line organs were cut, both the elevation of the tail and the downward swimming ceased. To ascertain how much of the loss of response was due to the cutting of the skin, etc., I made the necessary skin apertures for cutting the nerves in one individual, but did not sever the nerves, and then tested the animal. It still elevated the tail with great regularity on stimulation. On cutting the nerves this reaction entirely disappeared. Hence I believe the loss of reactiveness is due to the elimination of the lateral line organs and not to the shock of the operation. Six of the seven dog-fishes operated upon recovered, and most of them lived for two or three weeks after the operations. When tested toward the end of this period they were as characteristic as they were a short time after recovery.

I attempted similar experiments with small skates, *Raja erinacea*, and succeeded in getting on stimulation excellent tail reactions like those described for the dog-fish, but since these fishes were always in contact with the solid bottom of the aquarium it was impossible to say with certainty that they were not directly stimulated through their tactile organs. On cutting the nerves to the lateral-line organs, however, these tail reactions disappeared. Although I believe it would be hazardous to draw any conclusion from the experiments on the skate just recorded, the records on the four other species of fishes tested show beyond a doubt that the lateral-line organs are stimulated by water vibrations at the rate of 6 per second, though they are not stimulated when the rate reaches 100 per second.

DISCUSSION OF RESULTS.

From the foregoing experiments I conclude that the lateral-line organs of the species of fishes experimented upon are not stimulated by light, heat, salinity of water, food, oxygen, carbon dioxide, foulness of water, pressure of water, currents, and sounds. They are stimulated by vibrations of low frequency, as surmised by Schulze (1870), and these may be of service to the fishes in their orientation and equilibration reflexes, as suggested by de Sède (1884), Bonnier (1896), and especially by Lee (1898). There is, however, no reason so far as I can discover, for designating these organs as special organs of equilibration such as the ear, for in this respect they are of no higher value than the skin, and they are certainly inferior to the eye.

The stimulus for the lateral-line organs (a water vibration of low frequency) is a physical stimulus intermediate in character between that effective for the skin (deforming pressure of solids, currents, etc.) and that for the ear (vibrations of high frequency), and indicates that these organs hold an intermediate place between the two sets of sense organs named. This opinion, even from an actual genetic standpoint, has already been urged by many observers. Leydig (1850 b, p. 180) long ago pointed out the histological similarity between the sense organs of the internal ear and those of the lateral-line system; and Schulze (1870) emphasized this relation and brought into strong contrast the histological differences between the organs of the ear and the lateral-line system and those of the sense of taste, a contrast strengthened by the recent work of Herrick (1903 a, 1903 b, 1903 c).

The innervation of the lateral-line organs and of the ear also supports the belief in the genetic relations of these parts. Mayser (1881, p. 311) first pointed out the interesting fact that the nerves from the lateral-line organs and from the ear all terminate in one central structure, the so-called tuberculum acusticum, and this observation has been confirmed and its significance admitted by almost all subsequent investigators.

The development of the ear and of the lateral-line organs has led to still more important results, however, for in this way it has been shown that both sets of organs are derived from the skin, and that the relations of the ear to the lateral-line organs are such that, as Beard (1884, p. 143) declared, the ear may be regarded as a modified part of the lateral-line system. This opinion was accepted by Ayers (1892, p. 306) in his interpretation of the work of Allis (1889), and has been maintained recently by Cole (1898, p. 197) as now fully established, notwithstanding the fact that in some fishes, like *Amia*, the ear and lateral-line organs develop separately (Beckwith, 1902).

Finally, the physiological evidence shows that these organs are intermediate in character between the skin and the ear, and support the conclusion elsewhere expressed (Parker, 1903 b, p. 198), that together these sense organs represent what may be figuratively spoken of as three generations, in that the skin represents the first generation, which gave rise to the lateral-line organs, from which in turn came the ear. Thus the organs of touch, of the lateral-line system, and of the ear form a natural group, genetically connected as just indicated.

It may well be asked what disturbances in the water under natural conditions give rise to stimuli for the lateral-line organs. To determine this I tried some experiments with normal and cut *Fundulus heteroclitus*. It seemed to me probable, since the vibratory stimulus for the lateral-line organs was usually accompanied by ripples on the surface of the water, that by blowing on the water and producing strong ripples a movement might be induced in the deeper water sufficient to stimulate the lateral-line organs. This was tested by putting normal fish one at a time in an aquarium about a foot deep and blowing on the surface of the water till strong ripples were produced. All the fishes invariably went to the bottom and stayed there while the water remained agitated. These fishes were then cut, and after recovery again tested. While none of them would stay in the superficial water obviously in motion, as, in fact, was to be expected, none sought the bottom as they formerly had done, and there was no doubt left in my mind that when wind blows upon the surface of water it causes a motion of the deeper water, which stimulates the lateral-line organs. If this be true it follows that the more active fishes should have better developed lateral-line organs than the more sluggish bottom ones, and, at least so far as sharks and rays are concerned, this has been claimed to be so by Garman (1888, p. 65) and by Ewart (1892, p. 81).

I also tried the effects on normal and cut *Fundulus heteroclitus* of dropping unseen objects into the water. This was done with as little noise as possible, and almost always was followed by a sudden spring on the part of a normal fish generally away from the center of disturbance, so that I am led to conclude that the disturbances set up by such an object as a stone falling into the water stimulate the lateral line organs and with more or less directive effect, as surmised by Bonnier (1896).

That the movements generated in the water by the male *Polyacanthus* when mating are stimuli for the lateral line organs of the female, as suggested by Stahr (1897), may be true, but is unsupported by any proof.

So far as these observations go they show that surface wave movements, whether produced by moving air on the water or solid bodies falling into the water, are accompanied by disturbances which are stimuli for the lateral-line organs. This doubtless is the most usual form of stimulus for these organs in surface fishes, for I have shown that currents and direct wave action are probably not effective in this respect.

SUMMARY.

1. The lateral-line organs are not stimulated by light, heat, salinity of water, food, oxygen, carbon dioxide, foulness of water, water pressure, water currents, and sound.

2. The lateral-line organs are stimulated by water vibrations of low frequency—six per second.

3. The lateral-line organs may be of service to the fish in orientation, but they are of no more significance in equilibration than the skin, and are inferior in this respect to the eye and the ear.

4. Waves on the surface of the water produced by air currents and the disturbances made by bodies falling into the water produce vibrations in the deeper water that stimulate the lateral-line organs.

5. The skin, the lateral-line organs, and the ear form a natural group of sense organs whose genetic relations are such that the skin (organs of touch) may be said to be the first generation from which the lateral-line system has been derived, and this in turn has given rise to the ear.

LIST OF REFERENCES.

ALLIS, E. P.
   1889. The anatomy and development of the lateral-line system in Amia calva. Journal of Morphology, vol. 2, no. 3, pp. 463–566, pls. 30–42.

AYERS, H.
   1892. Vertebrate Cephalogenesis. II. A contribution to the morphology of the vertebrate ear, with a reconsideration of its functions. Journal of Morphology, vol. 6, no. 1, pp. 1–360, pls. 1–12.

BATESON, W.
   1890. The sense organs and perceptions of fishes; with remarks on the supply of bait. Journal of the Marine Biological Association, new series, vol. 1, pp. 225–256, pl. 20.

BEARD, J.
   1884. On the segmental sense organs of the lateral line, and on the morphology of the vertebrate auditory organ. Zoologischer Anzeiger, Jahrg. 7, no. 161, pp. 123–126; no. 162, pp. 140–143.

BECKWITH, C. J.
   1902. The early history of the lateral line and auditory anlages in Amia. Science, new series, vol. 15, p. 575.

BODENSTEIN, E.
1882. Der Seiterkanal von Cottus gobio. Zeitschrift für wissenschaftliche Zoologie, Bd. 37, Heft 1, pp. 121–145, Taf. 10.

BONNIER, P.
1896. Sur le sens latéral. Comptes rendus des Séances et Mémoires de la Société de Biologie, série 10, tome 3, pp. 917–919.

BUGNION, E.
1873. Recherches sur les organes sensitifs qui se trouvent dans l'epiderme du protée et de l'axolotl. Bulletin de la Société Vaudoise des Sciences Naturelles, série 2, vol. 12, no. 70, pp. 259–316, pls. 11–16.

CLAPP, C. M.
1898. The lateral-line system of Batrachus tau. Journal of Morphology, vol. 15, no. 2, pp. 221–264, pls. 19–20.

COLE, F. J.
1898. Observations on the structure and morphology of the cranial nerves and lateral sense organs of fishes; with special reference to the genus Gadus. Transactions of the Linnean Society of London, series 2, zoology, vol. 7, pt. 5, pp. 115–221, pls. 21–22.

DERCUM, F.
1880. The lateral sensory apparatus of fishes. Proceedings of the Academy of Natural Sciences of Philadelphia, 1879, pp. 152–154.

EMERY, C.
1880. Le Specie del Genere Fierasfer nel Golfo di Napoli e Regioni limitrofe. Fauna und Flora des Golfes von Neapel, 2 Monographie, 76 pp., 9 tav.

EWART, J. C.
1892. The lateral sense organs of Elasmobranchs. I. The sensory canals of Laemargus. Transactions of the Royal Society of Edinburgh, vol. 37, pt. 1, nos. 5–6, pp. 59–85, pls. 1–2.

FUCHS, S.
1894. Ueber die Function der unter der Haut liegenden Canalsysteme bei den Selachiern. Archiv für die gesammte Physiologie, Bd. 59, pp. 454–478, Taf. 6.

GARMAN, S.
1888. On the lateral canal system of the Selachia and Holocephala. Bulletin of the Museum of Comparative Zoology, Harvard College, Cambridge, vol. 17, no. 2, pp. 57–119, 53 pls.

HERRICK, C. J.
1903a. On the phylogeny and morphological position of the terminal buds of fishes. Journal of Comparative Neurology, vol. 13, no. 2, pp. 121–156.

1903b. On the morphology and physiological classification of the cutaneous sense organs of fishes. American Naturalist, vol. 37, no. 437, pp. 313–318.

1903c. The organ and sense of taste in fishes. Bulletin of the United States Fish Commission for 1902, pp. 237–272.

JACOBSON, L.
1813. Extrait d'un Memoire sur une organe particulière de sens dans les raies et les squales. Nouveau Bulletin des Sciences, par la Société philomatique de Paris, tome 3, no. 72, pp. 332–337.

KNOX, R.
1825. On the theory of the existence of a sixth sense in fishes; supposed to reside in certain peculiar tubular organs, found immediately under the integuments of the head in sharks and rays. The Edinburgh Journal of Science, vol. 2, pp. 12–16, pl. 2, figs. 18–19.

LEE, F. S.
1898. The functions of the ear and the lateral line in fishes. American Journal of Physiology, vol. 1, no. 1, pp. 128–144.

LEYDIG, F.

1850a. Vorläufige Notiz über ein eigenthümliches Verhalten der Nerven in den Schleimcanälen des Kaulbarsches. Tagesberichte über die Fortschritte der Natur- und Heilkunde (R. Froriep), Abtheilung Zoologie und Paläontologie, Bd. 1, no. 79, pp. 121–122.

1850b. Ueber die Schleimkanäle der Knochenfische. Archiv für Anatomie, Physiologie, und wissenschaftliche Medicin, Jahrg. 1850, pp. 170–181, Taf. 4, fig. 1–3.

1851. Ueber die Nervenknöpfe in den Schleimkanälen von Lepidoleprus, Umbrina und Corvina. Archiv für Anatomie, Physiologie, und wissenschaftliche Medicin, Jahrg. 1851, pp. 235–240, Taf. 9, fig. 1–2.

1857. Lehrbuch der Histologie des Menschen und der Thiere. Frankfurt a. M., 8vo, xii–551 pp.

1868. Ueber Organe eines sechsten Sinnes. Verhandlungen der Kaiserlich Leopodinisch-Carolinischen Deutschen Akademie der Naturforscher, Bd. 34, no. 5, 108 pp., 5 Taf.

LORENZINI, S.

1678. Osservazioni intorno alle Torpedini. In Firenze per l' Onofri, 1678. (Cited from Leydig, 1868, p. 3.)

LYON, E. P.

1900. Compensatory motions in fishes. American Journal of Physiology, vol. 4, no. 2, pp. 77–82.

MAYSER. P.

1881. Vergleichend anatomische Studien über das Gehirn der Knochenfische mit besonderer Berücksichtigung der Cyprinoiden. Zeitschrift für wissenschaftliche Zoologie, Bd. 36, Heft 2, pp. 259–364, Taf. 14–23.

MERKEL, F.

1880. Ueber die Endigungen der sensiblen Nerven in der Haut der Wirbelthiere. Rostock, 4to, 214 pp., 15 Taf.

MONRO, A.

1785. The structure and physiology of fishes explained and compared with those of man and other animals. Edinburgh, fo., 128 pp., 44 pls.

MÜLLER, H.

1852. Die nervösen Follikel-Apparat der Zitterrochen und die sogenannten Schleimkanäle der Knorpel-Fische. Verhandlungen der physikalisch-medicinischen Gesellschaft in Würzburg, Bd. 2, pp. 134–149.

NAGEL, W. A.

1894. Vergleichend physiologische und anatomische Untersuchungen über den Geruchs- und Geschmackssinn. Bibliotheca Zoologica, Heft 18, xiii+207 pp., 7 Taf.

PARKER, G. H.

1903a. Hearing and allied senses in fishes. Bulletin of the United States Fish Commission for 1902, pp. 45–64, pl. 9.

1903b. The sense of hearing in fishes. American Naturalist, vol. 37, no. 435, pp. 185–204.

RICHARD, J.

1896. Sur les fonctions de la ligne latérale du Cyprin doré. Comptes rendus des séances et Mémoires de la Société de biologie, série 10, tome 3, pp. 131–133.

RIVINUS, A. Q.

1687. Observatio anatomica circa poros in piscium cute notandos. Acta eruditor, Lipsiæ, 1687, pp. 160–162. (Cited from Leydig, 1868, p. 3.)

SARASIN, P., and F.

1887–1890. Zur Entwicklungsgeschichte und Anatomie der ceylonesischen Blindwühle Ichthyophis glutinosus, L. Ergebnisse naturwissenschaftlicher Forschungen auf Ceylon, Bd. 2, 263 pp., 3 Taf.

SAVI, P.

1841. Osservazioni sul sistema nervoso dell' organo elettrico della Torpedine. Atti della terza Reunione degli Scienziati italiani, tenuta in Firenze, 1841, pp. 328–329, 334–337.

SCHULTZE, M.

1863. Untersuchungen über den Bau der Nasenschleimhaut. Abhandlungen der naturforschenden Gesellschaft zu Halle, Bd. 7, pp. 1-100, Taf. 1-5.

SCHULZE, F. E.

1861. Ueber die Nervenendigung in den sogenannten Schleimkanälen der Fische und über entsprechende Organe der durch Kiemen athmenden Amphibien. Archiv für Anatomie, Physiologie, und wissenschaftliche Medicin, Jahr. 1861, pp. 759-769, Taf. 20.

1870. Ueber die Sinnesorgane der Seitenlinie bei Fischen und Amphibien. Archiv für mikroskopische Anatomie, Bd. 6, pp. 62-88, Taf. 4-6.

DE SÈDE, P.

1884. La ligne latérale des poissons osseux. Revue scientifique, série 3, tome 7, no. 15, pp. 467-470.

STAHR, H.

1897. Zur Funktion der Seitenorgane. Biologisches Centralblatt, Bd. 17, no. 7, pp. 273-282.

STANNIUS, H.

1846. Lehrbuch der vergleichenden Anatomie der Wirbelthiere. Berlin, 8vo, xii+482 pp.

STENON, N.

1664. De musculis et glandulis observationum specimen cum epistolis duabus anatomicis. Amstelodami, 1664. (Cited from Leydig, 1868, p. 3.)

TORELLE, E.

1903. The response of the frog to light. American Journal of Physiology, vol. 9, no. 6, pp. 466-488.

TREVIRANUS, G. R.

1820. Ueber die Nerven des fünften Paars als Sinnesnerven. In Vermischte Schriften anatomischen und physiologischen Inhalts. Von G. R. Treviranus und L. C. Treviranus. Bd. 3, pp. 135-146.

TULLBERG, T.

1903. Das Labyrinth der Fische, ein Organ zur Empfindung der Wasserbewegungen. Bihang till Kungliga Svenska Vetenskaps-Akademiens Handlingar, Bd. 28, Afd. 4, no. 15, 25 pp.

WAGNER, R.

1847. Ueber den feineren Bau des electrischen Organs im Zitterrochen. Abhandlungen von der Königlichen Gesellschaft der Wissenschaften zu Göttingen, Bd. 3, pp. 141-166.

12

Reprinted from *Bull. U.S. Bur. Fisheries,* **30,** 99–104 (1910)

SOUND AS A DIRECTING INFLUENCE IN THE MOVEMENTS OF FISHES.

❧

By G. H. PARKER, S. D.,
Professor of Zoology, Harvard University.

❧

The detection of the direction of a sound by the human ear is not generally accomplished with great accuracy, especially when the source of the sound is placed symmetrically in reference to the two ears. In man the one sense organ concerned in these operations is the ear. In fishes there are at least three sets of organs that may be involved in like operations, the skin, the lateral-line organs, and the ear, for though the function of hearing has been denied to fishes by some recent workers, there seems to be sufficient evidence to warrant the conclusion that at least certain fishes hear. Whether, however, fishes respond to sounds in a directive way or not is a matter that, so far as I am aware, has never been subjected to experimental test. It is the purpose of this paper to discuss the directive influence of sounds on the movements of fishes, and it is believed that work such as this will throw light on the question of the temporary distribution of fishes in reference to such centers of sound production as are afforded by naval gun practice, etc.

In attempting to test the question of the directive influence of sounds upon the movements of fishes, experiments were first tried in a large floating cage anchored in open sea water, but it was soon found that the disturbances produced by the wind and the sunlight were too great to admit of conclusive work, and recourse was finally had to experiments conducted in running sea water indoors. These experiments were carried out in the Biological Laboratory at the Woods Hole Station of the United States Bureau of Fisheries.

The fishes were tested in a tank about 50 cm. wide, 60 cm. deep, and 100 cm. long. The tank was made of wood 3.5 cm. thick; on the inside its walls were painted black, its bottom white. At one end of the tank there was a controllable inlet of sea water and at the other end an outlet. When the water in the tank was high enough to flow out at the outlet it was within a few centimeters of the top. The tank stood on a strong table and its upper edge was provided with a low black curtain so that persons moving about the laboratory could not be seen by the fishes. The tank was illuminated by an incandescent electric light hung directly over its center and some feet above the level of the water, or by diffusely reflected daylight from a white ceiling above. At each end of the tank a cord was attached to the ceiling and from a hook on the end of the cord an iron ball was suspended, the whole device being so adjusted that when at rest the ball just touched the middle of the end of the tank. The ball, like the bob of a long pendulum, could be withdrawn from the end of the tank, and when released it would strike the end a blow that could be kept reasonably constant by a gauge to mark the point at which the ball was liberated. The ball weighed about 4,300 grams and was ordinarily released at such a point that it struck the end of the tank with a calculated velocity of 84 cm. per second; in other words, at the moment of impact with the end of the tank the ball had a momentum of about 361,200 C. G. S. units. This blow produced in the tank a low booming noise which was used as the stimulus for the fish. It probably affected the nerve endings of the skin, of the lateral-line organs, and of the ears of the fishes that were tested.

In experimenting with a given species of fish, five individuals were placed in the tank and allowed to remain there till they were thoroughly accustomed to their surroundings, often a matter of half a day or so. Then the current of water was shut off, and shortly afterwards the stimulus was applied by allowing the ball to fall once every 10 seconds against the end of the tank. This was continued for 50 blows, and between blows the interior of the tank was cautiously inspected from the middle of one side, and a record was made of the distribution of the five fishes by noting the number in the half of the tank at whose end the blow had been struck. This form of observation was facilitated by marking on the white bottom of the tank a transverse line that divided the area in halves and that could be used as a line of reference in deciding on the distribution of the fishes. After 50 trials had been made with blows delivered at one end of the tank, the ball was shifted to the cord at the other end of the tank and an equal number of blows was delivered at that end; the combination of the two sets of records thus obtained showed whether the fishes tended to approach the sound center or retreat from it. The whole operation was then repeated on five new individuals, and this process was kept up until reasonably constant results were obtained. In all, eight species of fishes were tested, and these fell more or less naturally into three classes.

The first consisted of those fishes that on stimulation tended to retreat from the region of sound production. They are well illustrated by the tautog (*Tautoga onitis*), whose reactions are summarized in the following table:

TABLE I.—DIRECTIVE RESPONSES OF TAUTOGA ONITIS TO SOUND.

Lot numbers.	Number of occurrences in a possible 250 in half of tank nearer sound.		Totals.
	West half.	East half.	
1–5	83	80	163
6–10	85	87	172
11–15	79	86	165
16–20	90	84	174
21–25	82	86	168
Grand total	......	......	842

The grand total of occurrences in a possible 2,500 in the half of the tank nearer the sound was 842, or 34 per cent.

In this table are recorded the reactions of 25 fishes in lots of 5 each.   Each lot was subjected to 50 individual stimuli from the concussion of the iron ball against the end of the tank, and after each blow the number of individuals in the half of the tank next the sound center was recorded.   The addition of these 50 records in the first lot of fishes (1–5) when the blows were delivered at what may be called the west end of the tank was 83; when the blows were delivered at the east end it was 80.   Had all the fishes remained all the time in the half of the tank next the sound center, these records would have been 250 each.   It is, therefore, quite clear that in both instances the fishes avoided to a considerable degree the half of the tank next the sound center, and this same feature, of course, appears when these records are added together.   The same is true for the other four lots of fishes (6–10, 11–15, 16–20, and 21–25), and the grand total shows that out of a possible 2,500 records only 842, or rather less than 34 per cent, were from the half of the tank next the sound center.   Had the fishes been indifferent to the direction of the sound, we should have expected 50 per cent of the records to have been from the half of the tank next the sound center and the same proportion from the other half; had they been attracted by the sound, the record would have been something over 50 per cent for the region next the sound center; as it was, they have shown themselves as distinctly repelled by the sound, in that in only about 34 per cent of the total number of possible records were they in the half of the tank nearer the sound center.   It is quite clear from these records, then, that *Tautoga onitis* tends to swim away from a sound center.

The same condition as that seen in *Tautoga*, though a little less pronounced, is to be observed in the scup (*Stenotomus chrysops*), as table II shows.

TABLE II.—DIRECTIVE RESPONSES OF STENOTOMUS CHRYSOPS TO SOUND.

Lot numbers.	Number of occurrences in a possible 250 in half of tank nearer sound.		Totals.
	West half.	East half.	
1–5	87	81	168
6–10	93	85	178
11–15	89	92	181
16–20	88	89	177
21–25	96	90	186
Grand total	......	......	890

The grand total of occurrences in a possible 2,500 in the half of the tank nearer the sound was 890, or 36 per cent.   In *Stenotomus*, though the individuals avoided the sound center in a well-marked way, they were found somewhat more frequently (36 per cent) near the center than were the tautogs (34 per cent).

Young kingfishes (*Menticirrhus saxatilis*), as table III shows, also avoided the region of the sound center, though they were found there somewhat more frequently (39 per cent) than *Stenotomus* (36 per cent).

TABLE III.—DIRECTIVE RESPONSES OF MENTICIRRHUS SAXATILIS TO SOUND.

Lot numbers.	Number of occurrences in a possible 250 in half of tank nearer sound.		Totals.
	West half.	East half.	
1–5	85	109	194
6–10	98	110	208
11–15	102	90	192
16–20	89	86	175
21–25	103	96	199
Grand total	....	....	968

The grand total of occurrences in a possible 2,500 in the half of the tank nearer the sound was 968, or 39 per cent.

Young swellfish (*Spheroides maculatus*), as can be seen from table IV, show much the same condition as the kingfish, though they were found rather more frequently (42 per cent) in the region of the sound center than the kingfish (39 per cent).

TABLE IV.—DIRECTIVE RESPONSES OF SPHEROIDES MACULATUS TO SOUND.

Lot numbers.	Number of occurrences in a possible 250 in half of tank nearer sound.		Totals.
	West half.	East half.	
1–5	101	107	208
6–10	112	103	215
11–15	106	98	204
16–20	101	110	211
21–25	96	105	201
Grand total	....	....	1,039

The grand total of occurrences in a possible 2,500 in the half of the tank nearer the sound was 1,039, or 42 per cent.

The butterfish (*Poronotus triacanthus*) is by no means easily kept in confinement and records were obtained from only one lot of five such fishes. These records show that the occurrences of this fish in the half of the tank next the sound center were 47 per cent of the total; in other words, this fish had apparently a slight tendency to keep away from the sound center. This tendency, however, was so slight and the records were based upon such a small number of individuals that not much confidence can be placed in these results.

Of the five fishes thus far discussed, four (*Tautoga, Stenotomus, Menticirrhus,* and *Spheroides*) showed unmistakable evidence of the avoidance of a sound center and are in strong contrast with a second class of fishes which we found to approach such a center.

The second class of fishes is well represented by the sea robins (*Prionotus carolinus and Prionotus strigatus*).

TABLE V.—DIRECTIVE RESPONSES OF PRIONOTUS CAROLINUS AND PRIONOTUS STRIGATUS TO SOUND.

Lot numbers.	Number of oc-currences in a possible 250 in half of tank nearer sound.		Totals.
	West half.	East half.	
1–5	129	143	272
6–10	152	137	289
11–15	124	162	286
16–20	131	148	279
21–25	139	136	275
Grand total	....	....	1,401

The grand total of occurrences in a possible 2,500 in the half of the tank nearer sound was 1,401, or 56 per cent.

As table V shows, young specimens of *Prionotus carolinus* and *Prionotus strigatus* exhibited unmistakable tendencies to gather near the sound center. In each of the five groups tested the total numbers of occurrences on the side of the sound center were well above 250, the point of indifference. These species, therefore, afford a good example of fishes that move toward a sounding body in contrast to the four species mentioned as forming the first group. It is a matter of some interest to note that sea robins make a grunting noise themselves, and it may be that they hold together in schools by following this noise, in which case their movements toward a sound center such as was used in these experiments would be entirely natural.

The third class of fishes consist of those which move neither toward a sound center nor away from it. This class includes fishes that are much disturbed by sounds, but instead of being directed by these disturbances cease locomotion after a moment or so of swimming and remain quiescent till the sounding has come to an end. The best illustrations of this class are the killifishes, *Fundulus heteroclitus* and *Fundulus majalis*. After they had become accustomed to their surroundings they swam about freely near the surface of the water but when the sounding began they went at once to the bottom of the tank and remained quietly in seclusion in any nook or corner that they could find till the sounding had ceased. The cunner, *Tautogolabrus adspersus*, probably also belongs to this class, though when under the influence of sound it often moves about and its distribution indicates at times some tendency to move toward the sound center.

From all these records collectively it is quite clear that some fishes move away from sound centers, others move toward them, and still others, though much disturbed by sounds, move neither toward nor away from the sources. Throughout these experiments it was generally noticed that after the sounding ceased the fish very quickly returned to a state of normal locomotion and equal distribution. This condition is well illustrated by records taken from *Stenotomus*. Five of these fishes were placed in the tank, and after they had become quiet their distribution was recorded in the usual way; they were then subjected to sound till they assumed a characteristic distribution for this condition; and finally they were allowed to come to rest again. The time occupied in these operations is recorded in the following table:

TABLE VI.—NUMBERS OF INDIVIDUAL STENOTOMUS, OUT OF 5, OCCURRING IN THE HALF OF THE TANK NEXT THE SOUNDING APPARATUS BEFORE THE FISHES WERE SUBJECTED TO SOUND, DURING SOUNDING, AND AFTER THE SOUND HAD CEASED.

Number of the stimulus.	No sound.			Sound.			No sound.					
	7.35	7.40	7.45	7.50	7.55	8	8.05	8.10	8.15	8.20	8.25	8.30
1	2	4	3	0	1	0	0	0	2	3	2	3
2	3	3	2	1	1	0	0	0	2	4	2	4
3	3	4	2	3	1	0	0	1	3	2	2	2
4	3	0	1	3	1	0	0	1	2	3	4	4
5	4	1	2	2	1	1	0	0	1	4	0	3
6	0	3	4	4	1	1	0	1	3	0	2	3
7	3	2	4	3	2	1	0	1	2	4	2	2
8	2	3	4	1	3	1	0	1	0	2	1	3
9	4	5	1	3	2	2	0	1	1	2	3	4
10	5	5	0	1	2	2	0	2	0	3	2	3
Totals	29	30	23	21	15	8	0	8	16	27	20	31

An inspection of this table shows that during the period preceding the application of the sound (7.35 a. m. to 7.45 a. m.) the distribution of the fishes was fairly uniform, that during the application of the sound (7.50 a. m. to 8 a. m.) the fishes gradually withdrew from the sound center, and that within 15 to 20 minutes after the sound ceased a condition of distribution was attained fairly comparable with that seen at the beginning of the test (7.35 a. m. to 7.45 a. m.). The conclusion to be drawn from these observations is that, though the direction of the locomotion of a fish can be very considerably influenced by sound, this influence ceases very shortly after the sound ceases.

In attempting to apply these conclusions to the problems presented in the handling of fishes, several considerations must be kept clearly in mind. It is quite obvious that in one way or another many fishes are stimulated by sound. But most of the sounds that we deal with are generated in the air, and these sounds either fail to enter water or enter it to so slight a degree that they are of little or no significance for the fishes. The surface between water and air is an extremely difficult one for sound to penetrate in either direction, so that most sounds that are generated in the water or in the air stay in the medium of their origin. Hence many of the sounds that are produced by the discharge of guns, etc., in the air enter the water to so slight a degree (as can be ascertained by immersing oneself in the water at the time the sound is produced) as to be unstimulating to the fishes, though they may be deafening to the observer in the air. Such sounds as reach the fishes, however, not only stimulate them to move, but, as these observations show, influence the direction of their movements. But this directive influence is almost as short in duration as the stimulus. It is, therefore, improbable that sounds of brief duration can have much effect on the temporary distribution of fishes within their reach. That fishes should be attracted over any considerable area or repelled from that area by sound would seem to demand some more or less *continuous* source of sound production.

13

CAN FISH PERCEIVE SOUND DIRECTION?

Karl von Frisch and Sven Dijkgraaf

This article was translated expressly for this Benchmark volume by the Department of Animal Behavior, American Museum of Natural History, from "Können Fische die Schallrichtung wahrnehmen?" in Zeitschr. Vergleich. Physiol., 22, 641–655 (1935), with the permission of Springer-Verlag, Berlin, Heidelberg, New York

The title poses a question of special interest for two reasons. According to the "time theory", which is most popular, recognition of the direction of a sound source depends, in humans, primarily upon the small difference in time with which the sound arrives at the two ears. In fish, the external ear is lacking, and the internal auditory organs are close together; furthermore, in water, sound travels more than four times faster than in air. Under these circumstances, it is hardly imaginable that sound direction is perceived in fish by a mechanism similar to the human one. To this one must add that the auditory acuity of most freshwater fishes (Ostariophysi) depends on the swim bladder, which receives the sound waves and transmits them to the labyrinth via the Weberian apparatus. But the swim bladder is an unpaired organ, so that a sound passing through it always reaches both labyrinths simultaneously. From the point of view of the physiologists and of the followers of the "time theory", therefore, fish should not be able to recognize the direction of a sound.

Such a negative result may satisfy the physiologists, but it displeases the biologists - and this brings us to the second reason for our lively interest: Of what use is the great auditory acuity to a fish if it cannot recognize the direction of a sound source? The biologist expects a more positive answer.

F. Reinhardt concludes (p. 570, this vol.) that Phoxinus laevis and Amiurus nebulosus are not capable of telling the direction of a sound. He made his experiments in tanks as large as possible - some had a width and length of several meters each - and tried to prevent interfering echoes with special sound absorbers at the sides of the vessel. But we know how much directional hearing in man is affected by a closed space! And because, in general, we lack confidence in negative results, a re-check under the most advantageous conditions seems desirable: In open water and in the fish's own habitat. A welcome occasion presented itself this summer at our country place: Brunnwinkl.

As a site for the experiments we selected an untouched part of the Northern shore of Lake Wolfgang, which is shown in Figs. 1 and 2. The gravelly bottom, without plants, declines, first slowly, then more rapidly. In the shallow shore zone, one regularly sees schools of minnows. One prerequisite for the projected training experiments was that each school remain for prolonged periods in the same general vicinity. The expectation was fulfilled. One minnow, distinguishable by its plumpness, was seen every day for two weeks; we saw another, recognizable by a pigmentary anomaly, regularly for 11 days in the same group, until a sudden change in weather disturbed the fish. In addition, the behavior of the fish after just a few trials clearly indicated that our guests at the feeding station were always the same individuals.[1]

---

[1] Apparently other fishes are also quite "sessile". On the first day of trial several perch (Perca fluviatilis) were annoyingly in evidence, as they chased the minnows. In the first hour, we caught 6 perch with rod and reel. Though they were common in neighboring parts of the lake line, none was seen for weeks thereafter at our station. Apparently we had removed all the indigenous perch, and new ones did not migrate in until much later, and then in very small numbers.

As a source of sound, we used a "Boschhorn" [an automobile horn, made by the Bosch Electric Works - tr.] without a sound cone, as is usual in automobile claxons. It was sealed for use under water. The tone (approx. e^1), could be heard loudly above the water. The oscillations of the membrane were so strong that small objects immediately above it vibrated violently and the horn's vibrations could be clearly felt by a hand in the water at a distance of about 30 cm.

Blinding the fish in the open was out of the question, so we had to eliminate optic sources of error in some other way. After some preliminary trials, we devised the following system:

One of the local flatboats (a "Traundl"), about 9 m long, was moored parallel to the shore. Just beyond its lakeward gunwale, at a depth of about 40 cm, we set up on the lake bottom two feeding trays, 2.5 m apart (Fig. 3). Each tray consisted of a brass wire stand, covered with green cloth, about 14 cm across. Under it, the claxon was mounted so that the feeding tray hooded it completely, hiding it (Fig. 4). The horn was connected by a rubber-insulated cable to a 6v battery in the boat, where it could be actuated by means of a key. A similar cable extended to the second feeding station, which looked exactly like the first one. Above each feeding station, stood a tripod, with a pipe of galvanized sheet iron so set up that it ended just barely above the tray.

The claxon was sounded intermittently, while at the same time, finely chopped earthworms were emptied into the pipe, the end of which opened into the tray; the food sank slowly down the pipe, and spreads over the feeding tray, if it is not first caught by the fish.

This feeding with accompanying sound lasted about 2 minutes, and was then followed by a 10-minute pause, after which another feeding session began, either at the same station, or, after changing the horn, at the other one. In this way, the fish were supposed to learn that food was obtained only at the source of sound.[2]

At the first sound of the claxon, the fish, which had congregated in curiosity, shot apart startled. But the appetizing fare made them quickly confident. After a few days this was the situation: As soon as we came along with our boat and made preparations, the swarm of about 30 minnows (the number remained fairly steady) came along, and congregated about the green feeding trays. Sometimes at one station, sometimes at another; sometimes moving back and forth between the two, or even separated into two groups, one about each station. Occasionally, the fish merely stood about, isolated and waiting, in the vicinity.

When the claxon sounded, it was as if "assembly" had been blown. The fish immediately congregated with lively agitation at the feeding stations (Fig. 5). In other words, auditory training per se had been successful. But even after 55 trial feedings no definite orientation toward the sound was apparent.[3]

If the fish were evenly distributed throughout the vicinity when the horn sounded, each went to the station closest to it; if the fish happened to be in the vicinity of the sounding station they usually congregated correctly, but if the majority were assembled about the silent one, then they often went to it instead,

---

[2] In the beginning we also performed a pseudo-feeding with am empty feeding pipe, so as not to give the fish any optical cues, but this was later shown to be unnecessary.

[3] With the first sound of the claxon, we began our observations, avoiding any movements that might have provided an optic clue. Then the fish were fed at the place where the sound originated, so that each experiment reinforced the training. As a rule we could undertake 5 feeding-training cycles per day, after which the fish were satiated, and their interest flagged.

only to wander indecisively back and forth between the two. Their marked school-ing instinct only served to underline this mass reaction, and brought out even more clearly their indecision. Of course in some cases we did have the impres-sion that the fish oriented themselves toward the sound, and a summary of all pertinent observations does indeed show a slight preponderance of correct choices.

In 50 trials with the claxon (7/27 to 8/6/1935) the choice between the source of the sound, and the soundless station was: 12 times correct, 12 times mostly correct, 14 times indeterminate, 8 times mostly wrong, 4 times wrong.

But this may have been caused by the fact that the minnows that happened to be in the immediate vicinity of the claxon became visibly excited by its loud sound, thus attracting the others by their behavior.

To overcome this objection, we set up several wire contraptions exactly like the green feeding trays, but covered with white material - to the right and left of the feeding stations and also some 2 meters further out. The minnows were never fed at these stations. Consequently, they paid no attention to the white hoods. Now we intercalated among the above-described experiments, during which feeding was on the green tables, some control experiments in which the claxon was placed under one of the white hoods away from its usual place. No food was given there, so as not to cause future spontaneous aggregations at the white stations. The first two of these experiments were convincing: Though there were no minnows in the vicinity of the white station under which the claxon was, at the first blasts a number of fish swam with good orientation from one of the green tables toward the 2 meter distant sound source. Without congregating or even remaining there, they turned back again. Repetitions of the experiment on subsequent days were never more convincing. We were not able to decide whether the first result was a chance event, or whether the fish had been trained so well to their green feed-ing stations that the sound could not lure them away to the white trays, where there never was anything to be had.

We consequently changed out dispositions and increased the number of green feeding stations to four. Over each tray stood a tripod with the feeding tube. Under one was the claxon, under the others unconnected cables. Recognition of the sound's direction would be more convincing if it required a single correct choice out of four equivalent possibilities. It was further expected that, as minnows like to school, they would not often remain evenly distributed at all four stations simultaneously; if we gave the tone signal at the right time, we could eliminate optic signals from the fish closest to the source of sound.

The four feeding stations constituted the corners of a square about two meters along each side. To make them easily accessible to us we serviced the feeding stations from two boats (Figs. 6 and 7).

As these experiments immediately followed the previous series, a new train-ing period was unnecessary. The minnows quickly adapted to the new conditions. The effect of increasing the number of feeding stations was to loosen up the school; fish often patrolled the stations in small groups, or stood about dis-persed; at other times the reunited school swam from one station to the next. The location of the claxon was altered at each experiment. In the first few minutes after a feeding, the fish tended to visit the last place at which they had been fed more often than other places, but this was not a continuing, dis-turbing, influence.

In these 27 experiments, choice of the place of congregation was 4 times correct, 18 times mostly correct, 2 times indeterminate, 1 time mostly wrong, 2 times wrong.

Among these 27 experiments are 12 in which, at the start of the noise, not a single fish happened to be near the site of origin of the sound. Here, too, the result was positive (3 correct, 5 mostly correct, 1 doubtful, 1 mostly wrong, 2 wrong).

In spite of the favorable statistics, observation revealed that a directed approach to the sound source occurred but rarely (according to our protocols, in 6 of 27 trials). Very often, as a matter of fact, one had the impression that at the sound of the claxon, the minnows aimlessly searched the various feeding stations, but that they noticed it when they were in the close proximity of the sound, i.e., at the correct feeding station; they remained there and searched with more vigor, and thereby soon attracted the others.

To determine behavior as objectively as possible, 12 of the 27 trials were "numerical trials". Using a stopwatch, we estimated every ten seconds how many minnows were in the vicinity of each station. The numbers, which were called out, were noted by an assistant. Estimates could hardly be exact, but as the same person always estimated at the same station, while the claxon position was changed, individual differences must have been minimized.

The results of these counts are represented graphically in Fig. 8. The abscissa represents time, in 10 second intervals; the ordinate, the number of fish at the four feeding stations. (The sounding station is drawn with a heavy line, the one where feeding took place during the previous run by a broken line).

We always started counting some minutes before the signal. This part of the curve shows an irregular up and down, corresponding to the aimless searching about of the fish, often with considerable aggregations here and there, as their schooling drive dictated, but without preference for any particular locus. After the start of the signal, (heavy vertical bar) there is invariably a congregation at one or more loci, and, with 2 exceptions, within 30 seconds, a preferential aggregation at the source of the sound. But one also notices that in only two of the 12 trials the source of the sound was chosen at once and unmistakably (trials 101 and 110), 7 times the fish congregated first at one or several other places and found the correct spot by "trial and error" ("mostly correct" choice; trials 97, 98, 99, 102, 103, 111, 113), once they selected mostly wrong (trial 104), and twice completely wrong (trials 100 and 112). As soon as there was an unmistakable aggregation at one station, counting was interrupted, and feeding started, to continue training.

Training to a sound was thus accomplished. For the future, this was valuable proof that a problem of this sort does not present too great a psychological stress for the fish, and that the general assumption, that one can train fish successfully in the feral state, was validated. That there was recognition of the direction of the sound, however, is supported by only a few observations. And as the source of the sound was very intense, and the distance to the fish small, the suspicion arose that the minnows did not orient themselves by ear but by their integumental sense organs, through which they recognized the directions whence the vibrations came.

To test this, we set up the sound source at a greater distance. Seven trials with the claxon at five to twenty meters from the stand of the minnows were negative; the fish did not swim toward the sound. This confirmed our suspicion. However, as it was possible that a strong attachment of the fish to their normal feeding grounds was interfering with their reactions and as, furthermore, the servicing of the distant feeding stations presented difficulties, so we selected the other approach: We used a quieter sound source.

II

The disposition of the feeding trays remained, for the time being, as before (Figs. 6 and 7). But instead of the claxon we used underwater loudspeakers, driven by an electronic buzzer and amplifier (see wiring diagram Fig. 9). Pitch and intensity were variable within limits.

Three loudspeakers were made by the firm E. Th. Edelmann (Munich) (Fig. 10a); the fourth was a radio speaker (Fig. 10b) which produced the same tone, and had nearly the same timbre.

Whereas we had had to move the claxon at each experiment, now there was a speaker under each feeding station, connected by a cable to a switch box in the boat, from where it could be activated at will. Pitch was about e^2, intensity so low that the sound could be heard but softly above water; the hand felt no vibrations, even in the speaker's immediate vicinity.

As the interval between these experiments and the previous series was only two days, a retraining period was not necessary. After the first 6 feedings, the minnows responded well to the soft tones by congregating at one or several feeding stations. But now there was not a single indication that they recognized the direction of the sound. Between 18 and 28 August, in 40 trials (16 "counting" trials) they clearly swam toward the sound 6 times, and just as definitely to the wrong station 30 times; 4 trials were inconclusive (these results refer to the reaction of the fish at the onset of the sound signal). Had selections been made only by chance, the ratio of correct:wrong selections would have been 6:18. The excess of wrong choices can be explained by the fact that in the majority of instances we gave the signal at a station at which there were few or no fish, and that the fish, upon perceiving the signal would congregate at the nearest station, after which they would rush aimlessly from one to the other until they were successful. If they happened to be near the sound at the signal, they nearly always congregated there.

From 28 August to 9 September, bad weather interrupted the work. Constant southerly winds were particularly disturbing because they caused large waves on shore. When we resumed the trials, the 3 Edelmann speakers would not function properly, so that only the radio speaker (Fig. 10b) remained usable, and we had to return to our original, somewhat clumsy, method of placing the speaker under a different station after each trial.

III

The test series with the soft tones seemed to strengthen the assumption that the positive responses to the claxon should be attributed to an integumental sense, rather than to audition. However, with the negative results, the suspicion that there might be an interfering factor reawakened. One such might be an echo from the sides of the boats on either side of the experimental area (Fig. 7). Therefore we again changed our dispositions, and placed a wooden stool with thin legs and without a backrest into the shallow water, connecting it to shore by a 4 m long wooden runway. Lakeward, 3 feeding stations, 1.5 m apart, were placed on the bottom (Fig. 11). In this way, sound reflecting surfaces were eliminated as much as possible. To allow feeding even at the furthest station, the feeding wire was attached to a stick (Fig. 11). As long as we had only one speaker, someone had to climb into the water after each trial to change the position, which however did not bother the minnows. The buzzer was on shore, and blind cables led to the two silent stations; the tone was set at a^1.

After the prolonged pause that had occurred, 12 training feedings were necesary until the minnows again responded unequivocally with excitation and congregation to the signal. In 28 trials (16 "counting" trials), they were, correct at once 4 times, wrong at once 4 times, and 9 times undetermined. In spite of the better disposition, there was no evidence that they recognized the direction of the sound. It did occasionally seem, especially on the fourth day, as if the fish, once they had reached the source of sound, remained there longer, but on the very next day, their behavior was quite indeterminate in this respect. By diving, we determined that the strength of the sound increased considerably with approach to the source over the distances involved here. Thus, if the positive congregations are to be considered as the result of training, and not due to chance, it is possible that the fish recognized the feeding station by the intensity of the sound. Under no circumstances had they learned a directional search.

Meanwhile 3 new speakers arrived, and from now on again one sound source lay under each station, and could be activated as needed from the shore. Their tones (a^1) were somewhat louder than with the previous speakers, but not nearly as droning as those of the claxon. They were, clearly audible out of the water, but vibrations could not be felt by the hand, even in closest proximity.

The new sound sources were magnetic loudspeakers of the free-swinging type, in which the usual paper cone was replaced, for submerged use, with a metal membrane, and which were hermetically sealed (Fig. 10c). They were built in our shop by Mr. J. Bräu.

Retraining was not necessary, as the trials immediately followed the previous ones, the arrangement of the stations was the same, and the fish reacted to the tones per se very well. In 33 trials (20 "counting" trials), they swam correctly at the first time to the right station 11 times, to the wrong one 21 times, and indefinitely once. As they had to choose between one correct and two wrong locations, their selections were evidently due to chance. To record this objectively, and to exclude any bias on our part, we made 20 "counting" trials on the last 3 days, and we predetermined the place where the sound would originate in advnace, and began counting exactly 2 minutes before the first signal. Consequently it was no more our doing, but only chance which determined the positions of the fish immediately before the signal. They made 6 correct and 14 wrong choices. This quantitative result corresponds exactly to the immediate impressions: that the school congregates, at the first signal, at that station which is closest, or toward which the fish happen to be swimming. In Fig. 13 the results of the 9 trials of the final day are, graphed as an example. Three correct choices (trials 252, 254, 257) are opposed to 6 wrong ones. As on that day we had reached the 74 training feeding since 10 September, no success was to be expected from further training.

We see therefore from this series of experiments that minnows cannot determine the direction whence a sound comes. They swim, when the signals start, toward any station, usually toward the nearest one. But it was not even possible to determine with certainty whether the fish, once they had located the source of the sound accidentally, remained there (as they did with the claxon). Compare Fig. 8 with Fig. 13. Whereas in the former the fish definitely preferred to remain at the source of the sound, in the latter, the school often swims toward a silent station after having approached the sounding one (see Fig. 13). It is true that some indications of an attempt to remain near the source of the sound can be read into these and some other, not shown, curves. But even in this respect, the behavior of the fish remained largely undetermined.

We have thus been able to confirm with our experiments in open water, in the natural habitat of the fish, the results of Reinhardt. Minnows are clearly not able to tell the direction when a sound comes through their auditory organ. If this realization may satisfy the theoretician-physiologist, it will leave the biologist that much the less. But he must make do. The highly developed auditory sense of the Ostariophysi may have importance as an alarm mechanism, can draw the fish's attention to a source of sound, but to orient it to, or away from, the source is the function of other sense organs.

Summary

Even under favorable conditions, in open water and in their native environment, minnows are not able to determine the direction of a sound (training experiments).

When extremely intense sound sources are used, which produce noticeable vibrations in the water, some orientation toward the source is indicated, when the fish are close to the source of sound. As there is no orientation when the sound is further away or less intense, orientation must be ascribed to a skin sense, not to hearing. The minnows learn more or less to find very loud sound sources by trial and error. With less intense sound sources, they do not succeed even in this, or at least succeed very poorly. We assume that in those experiments that turned out positively the animals were led to the source of sound by the increasing intensity of the sound, whether through the ear or the skin sense remains undetermined.

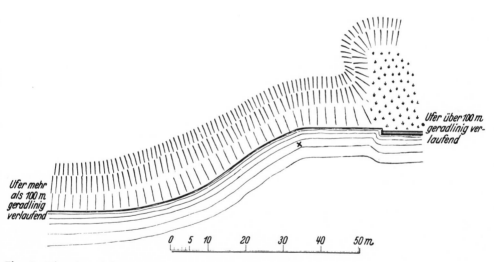

Fig. 1   The site of the experiment (x) and its surroundings: *left,* shore in a straight line for more than 100 m; *right,* shore in a straight line for more than 100 m. Reprinted from *Zeitschr. Vergleich. Physiol.,* **22,** 641–655 (1935); copyright © 1935 by Springer-Verlag, Berlin, Heidelberg, New York

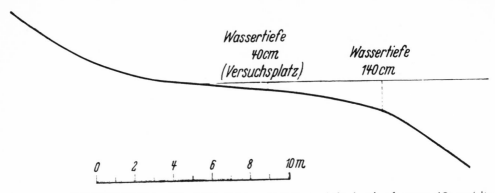

Fig. 2 Section of shoreline at the site of the experiments: *left*, depth of water, 40 cm (site of the experiment); *right*, depth of water, 140 cm. Reprinted from *Zeitschr. Vergleich. Physiol.*, **22**, 641–655 (1935); copyright © 1935 by Springer-Verlag, Berlin, Heidelberg, New York

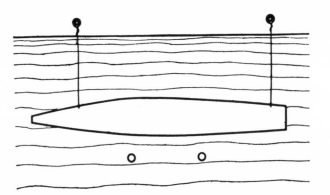

Fig. 3 Disposition for trials I: boat parallel to shore, lakeward two feeding stations. Reprinted from *Zeitschr. Vergleich. Physiol.*, **22**, 641–655 (1935); copyright © 1935 by Springer-Verlag, Berlin, Heidelberg, New York

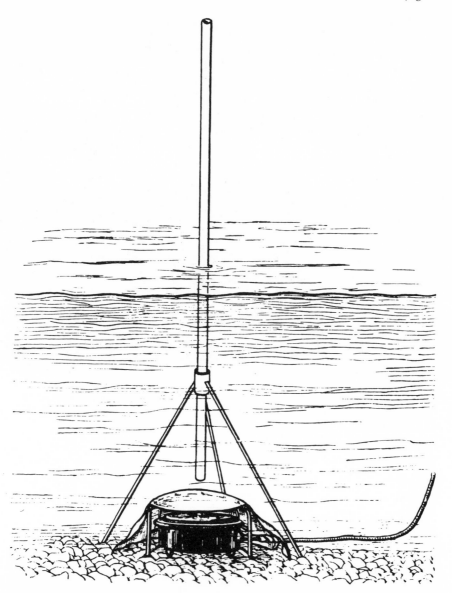

Fig. 4 Wire stand covered with material serves as a feeding station, under it the claxon, over it the feeding tube from which during a training run chopped-up earthworms fall on the feeding tray. Reprinted from *Zeitschr. Vergleich. Physiol.*, **22,** 641–655 (1935); copyright © 1935 by Springer-Verlag, Berlin, Heidelberg, New York

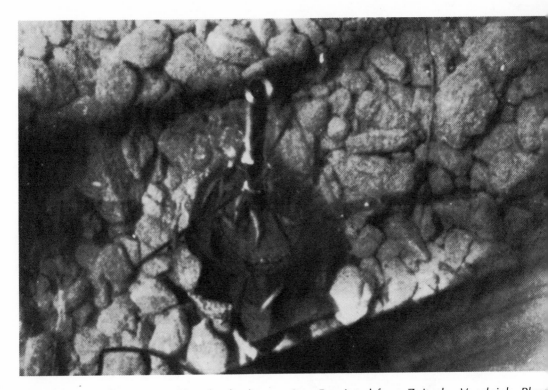

Fig. 5 Minnows congregate at the feeding station. Reprinted from *Zeitschr. Vergleich. Phys.* **22,** 641–655 (1935); copyright © 1935 by Springer-Verlag, Berlin, Heidelberg, New York

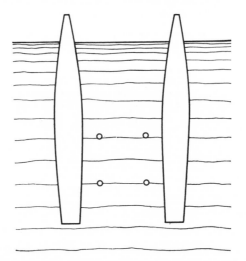

Fig. 6 Four feeding stations between two boats moored at right angles to the shore. Reprinted from *Zeitschr. Vergleich. Physiol.,* **22,** 641–655 (1935); copyright © 1935 by Springer-Verlag, Berlin, Heidelberg, New York

Fig. 7   The disposition (Fig. 6) seen from the lake. The feeding stations are visible as dark spots; over them, the feeding tubes. Reprinted from *Zeitschr. Vergleich. Physiol.*, **22,** 641–655 (1935); copyright © 1935 by Springer-Verlag, Berlin, Heidelberg, New York

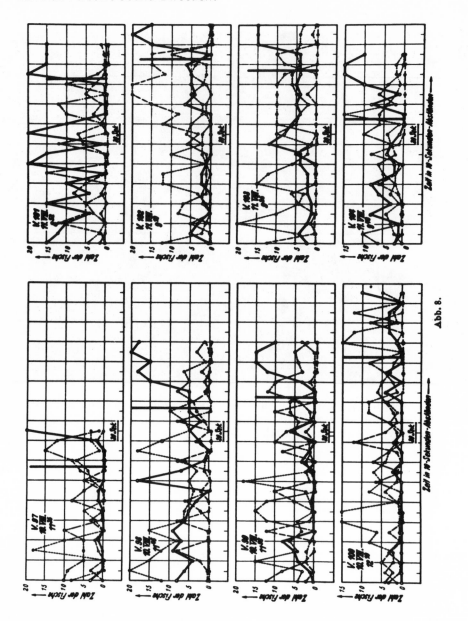

Abb. 8.

288

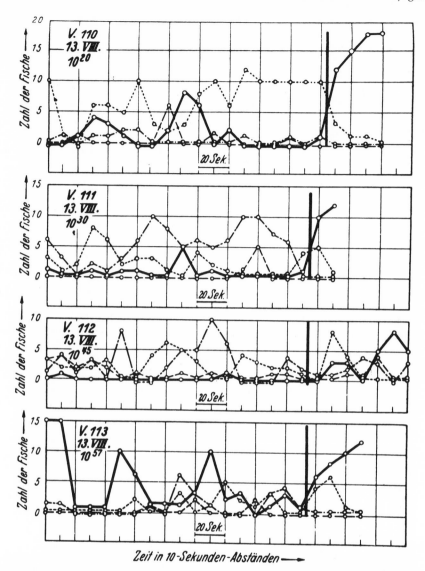

Fig. 8 Results of 12 "counting trials" with the claxon. Number of fish at the four feeding stations at 10-sec intervals. *Heavy line,* station with the claxon; *dotted line,* silent station where the feeding had occurred at the previous trial; *dashed-and-dotted lines,* the other two feeding stations; heavy vertical bar, start of the tone signal. In experiment 101, the sound source was at the table where (the day before) the previous feeding had taken place. Ordinate, number of fish; abscissa, time, sec. Reprinted from *Zeitschr. Vergleich. Physiol.,* **22,** 641–655 (1935); copyright © 1935 by Springer-Verlag, Berlin, Heidelberg, New York

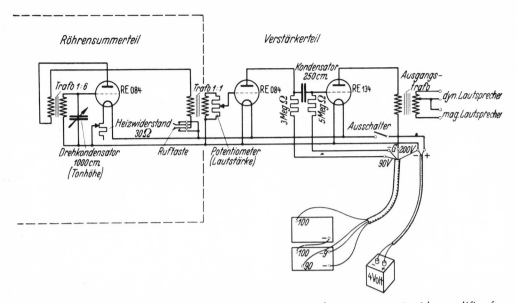

Fig. 9 Wiring diagram of the tone generator (electronic humapparatus) with amplifier for activation of the loudspeaker. Labels (approximately top to botton left to right): tone (hum) generator; transformer 1:6; variable condensor, 1000 cm (pitch); variable resistor to filament heating current; contact key; transformer 1:1 variable potentiometer (intensity); amplifier; condensor 250 cm; interruptor; output transformer; (leads to) electrodynamic loudspeaker; (leads to) magnetic loudspeaker. Reprinted from *Zeitschr. Vergleich. Physiol.*, **22**, 641–655 (1935); copyright © 1935 by Springer-Verlag, Berlin, Heidelberg, New York

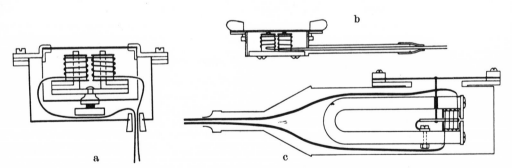

Fig. 10 Magnetic loudspeakers used: (a) cone loudspeaker (Edelmann); (b) radio earphone by Siemens; (c) free-swinging system (modified for use under water). Reprinted from *Zeitschr. Vergleich. Physiol.*, **22**, 641–655 (1935); copyright © 1935 by Springer-Verlag, Berlin, Heidelberg, New York

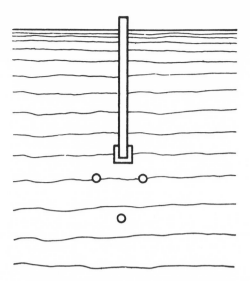

Fig. 11 Disposition for trials III. Three feeding stations and the dock. Reprinted from *Zeitschr. Vergleich. Physiol.*, **22,** 641–655 (1935); copyright © 1935 by Springer-Verlag, Berlin, Heidelberg, New York

Fig. 12 Lakeward view (from land) overlooking disposition III. Under the tubes the feeding stations are seen as light spots. The feeding wire is attached to a stick; the little dish at the end of the wire is just being filled with chopped rainworms. Reprinted from *Zeitschr. Vergleich. Physiol.*, **22,** 641–655 (1935); copyright © 1935 by Springer-Verlag, Berlin, Heidelberg, New York

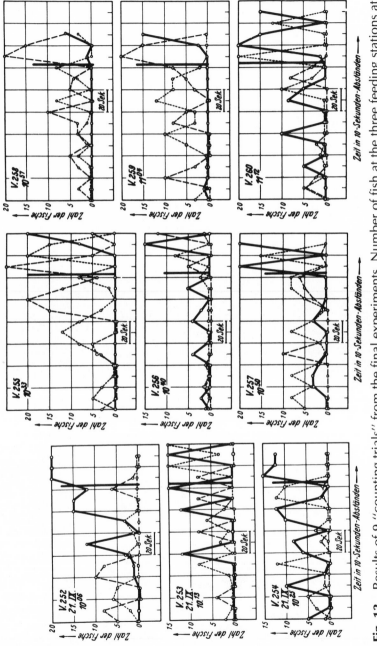

Fig. 13 Results of 9 "counting trials" from the final experiments. Number of fish at the three feeding stations at 10-sec intervals. *Heavy line*, station with loudspeaker; *dotted line*, silent station where feeding had occurred at the previous trial; *dashed line*, the other silent station; *heavy vertical bar*, start of tone signal. Reprinted from *Zeitschr. Vergleich. Physiol.*, **22**, 641–655 (1935); copyright © 1935 by Springer-Verlag, Berlin, Heidelberg, New York

14

ON THE STIMULATION OF THE
DISTANCE-TOUCH-SENSE IN FISHES AND
AMPHIBIANS

Sven Dijkgraaf

*This article was translated expressly for this Benchmark
volume by Brigitte Cappelli, from "Uber die Reizung des
Ferntastsinnes bei Fischen und Amphibien," in* Experientia, **3**,
*206–208 (1947), with the permission of Birkhauser Verlag,
Basel*

It is well known that moving objects, and even motionless bodies, can be,
to some extent, "felt-at-a-distance" by fish,[1] and by aquatic amphibians.[2] In
both cases, this ability is located in the sense organs of the lateral line.
It is generally agreed that stimulation of these organs must depend in some way
on movements or pressure changes in the water, caused by the moving object. Details, however, are neither clear, nor universally agreed upon. First, therefore, we shall briefly describe the physical events that accompany the movement
of a submerged body.

Following in the wake of a moving object is a turbulence which can be sensed
by the lateral line organs as soon as it reaches the fish's body. Usually, however, the object is detected before the turbulence reaches the fish, and reception must therefore depend on events that occur in the space in front of the
moving object. To understand what happens, we must differentiate between pressure waves and displacement effects.

Pressure waves, which propagate in all directions at the speed of sound
(about 1450 m/sec) are generated only by sudden velocity changes of the moving
body. Their intensity depends upon the body's acceleration; at constant velocity there are no pressure waves.

Displacement effects, on the other hand, are always present about a moving
object; they are felt as "resistance of the water", and their intensity depends
on the size and shape of the object, and increases with increasing speed. Displacement effects are localized phenomena, closely related to the moving object
spatially. One differentiates between: (1) a local increase in pressure, the
displacement pressure,[3] e.g., the rise of water under the keel of a ship, or at
an abutment in a flowing river (Fig. 1); (2) a local displacement of the water
particles, which flow apart to make room for the moving object, and are simultaneously propelled forward (a "dam-up" [Aufstau]; this phenomenon can be made
visible by particles suspended in the water).

In reviewing the subject, Kramer[4] mentions turbulent flow and pressure
waves, referring to them, because of their nature, as "sound phenomena", but
overlooks the displacement effect. As he, too, had discovered that a test animal senses an approaching object before its turbulence can reach the body's sense
organs, he understandably attributes great importance to pressure waves as stimuli for the lateral line organs.

Some time ago, I already voiced doubts about this interpretation,[5] and cited
facts that seemed inconsistent with it. According to von Frisch and Stetter,[6]
the minnow does not perceive low-frequency sounds through the lateral line which
is sensitive, however, to very slight currents in the water, and therefore presumably also to the displacement effect (which is equivalent to a local current).
New experiments in fish, as well as observations on Xenopus laevis, Kramer's experimental animal, have led me to conclude that perception at a distance of approaching objects depends primarily on displacement phenomena, and that there
are no valid reasons for assuming that sound effects are involved.

The two phenomena can be investigated separately because a body that moves through the water at a constant velocity produces only displacement effects, but no pressure waves. If under such circumstances perception at a distance does occur, it must have been mediated by the displacement effect. (Here, and in all that is to follow, the turbulence originating in the wake of a moving object is disregarded, though it, too, may be implicated in distance perception; nothing is known for sure about this). In this connection one must mention that a blind Corvina nigra, gliding quietly and smoothly along, sensed the aquarium wall (at right angles to its line of progress) at a distance of 1 - 2 cm. (Swimming slowly, Corvina moves by supple rowing of its pectorals; the fish is 20 - 25 cm long). Pressure waves were essentially of no practical importance in this case. I should like to interpret the events in this way: as the fish swims, its nose is subject to various displacement effects (pressure, flow) which change as the fish's movements are altered. Presumably, the fish does not perceive these "autogenous" processes as special stimuli. But when the fish approaches the aquarium wall, the water particles driven forward by the nose can no longer escape unimpeded, and produce an "unexpected" change in the displacement conditions (a feeling of "increased water resistance") which alerts the fish to the obstacle.

One can also make the opposite experiment, and stimulate a motionless fish with a moving object. For this I selected Nemachilus barbatulus, a species which normally spends much of its time lying at the bottom of the aquarium. A blind specimen was first trained to flee an approaching plate, 8 x 8 mm, from which it received a slight shock. In order to be certain to avoid sudden accelerations, the plate was attached to a heavy, lead-filled tube, suspended from four thin, and long metal wires (Fig. 2). To produce a stimulus, the leaded tube was pulled back about 4 cm, then released to swing, pendulum-like, toward the fish, which perceived the approaching plate at a distance of 2 - 4 cm (flight response). Before each trial the tube was aimed so as to swing normal to the fish's side, passing through its "rest position" 2 - 3 cm from the body wall. Though the velocity of the plate is not quite constant, changes are smooth, and minimal just at the instant of perception.

Furthermore, slight hammer taps at the distal end of the tube, which propelled the disk with a strongly damped motion about 1 cm toward the fish, never elicited a response up to a fish-plate distance of 5 cm, though they produced an intense pressure wave (sound effect).

I believe that these, and other, observations permit me to conclude that perception at a distance is, in fish, dependent upon displacement phenomena, and not upon pressure waves.

Now consider Xenopus laevis. This African frog spends all its life in the water, and even the adult has a well developed lateral line system (Fig. 3), which consists, as in all amphibia, exclusively of sensory buds. Kramer investigated the function of the lateral line with spheres of modeling clay (7.5 cm diameter), kept submerged, and attached to a single metal wire so that they vibrated slightly. He found as the limit of performance in a single, blind animal, that it swam vigorously toward the clay ball when it was at a distance of 15 cm. The container was an earthen vessel, 87 cm across. Kramer specifically mentions that the limit of performance is not reached in smaller basins, of more usual dimensions. He attributes this, because he conceives the stimulus as a sound phenomenon, to interfering "echo effects" from the basin wall.

In rechecking these experiments, I noticed in my clawed frogs,[7] seeing ones as well as blinded ones, first of all the extremely lively reaction which took place in animals at the surface as soon as a wave was produced by touching the water-surface reached the frog. It immediately orients itself very precisely toward the center of the disturbance, often leaping in its direction. The slightest touch of the surface, e.g., a single touch with a needle, elicits the reaction, even when the frog is more than 30 cm away. When one places a living mealbug on the surface, the frog can find his prey rapidly, and over the shortest route, clearly guided by the waves which the struggling insect makes on the surface. The biologic significance of this reaction is thus clear.

Kramer, too, noted and described the directed capture-reaction elicited by surface waves.[8] He considered the "up and down motion of the taut skin at the end of the nose and on the digits" as the eliciting stimulus, and mentions further that the reaction occurs even where only the nose, or the anterior digits extend out of the water. Elimination of the lateral line organs, (cautery of the sense buds) did not, under these conditions, eliminate the response. Some participation of the lateral line organs, however, seems probable, especially because of the following observations.

I was surprised to discover that an oriented reaction also took place when no part of the animal was above the surface, when, in fact, the entire animal was several centimeters below the surface, an observation I repeated over and over again, with several frogs, both before and after blinding (enucleation under ether). In general, when the nose of the frog extended above the surface, the reactions were more lively, but frogs submerged 3 - 5 cm still reacted nicely. If one touches the surface some 7 - 10 cm to the left or right of the animal, it turns to the stimulated side. If one touches the surface behind the frog, it backs up, or turns. This reaction does not take place immediately, but only after a certain latent period, during which the traveling waves have reached and may have passed beyond, the animal. What sense organs are involved here? Probably not the sense of touch, as no perceptible local deformations of the skin occur. The lateral line organs are probably stimulated by depth-effects of the surface waves. As with displacement phenomena, so, here too, there are localized pressure changes and movements of water particles.

To determine the limit of sensitivity of these stimuli, I made the following quantitative observations. In a square, all-glass aquarium (20 x 29 cm, water depth 6.5 cm) a blinded frog reacted, by turning to the stimulated side, to the second or third touch of a 1 mm thick glass needle to the surface. The most elevated portions of the animal (upper part of the posterior fins = web of foot, see Fig. 3) were about 4 cm below the surface. With a depth of water of 16.5 cm, I obtained the following limiting values: an upward slanting frog, the nose and finger tips of which were about 8 cm below the surface, still reacted (though not rapidly, and with poor orientation) to a slight touch of the surface with the fire-polished tip of a 6 mm glass rod. Even 11 cm below, careful touching of the surface, still elicited a search reaction, albeit a non-directed one. At a depth of 14 cm no reaction was elicited. Another blinded frog reacted in a vessel 25 x 34 cm and 10 cm deep water in a nicely oriented fashion when lying flat at the bottom, i.e., at a depth of 6 to 7 cm.

If one wishes to make valid determinations concerning the limits of sensitivity of the lateral line organs, it becomes necessary to eliminate the influence of the surface waves by using a sufficient water depth. In an all-glass aquarium 20 x 29 cm, and at a water depth of 16.5 cm, a blind bullfrog, resting on the bottom, reacted to the involuntary trembling of a 6 mm thick glass rod held vertically in the water, at a distance of up to 15 cm by turning toward the stimulated side. It reacted to a slight voluntary movement of the rod 1 - 2 cm in its direction at a distance of 20 cm. Most remarkable was the fact that sometimes reaction to the involuntarily trembling rod occurred when its tips were but 6 - 7 cm deep in the water, even though the animal was 14 - 15 cm below the surface and laterad to the point of immersion. With the rod immersed for 2 cm I saw no clear-cut reaction; mere motion of the water surface was completely not responded to.

Thus, the sensitivity of the distance-touch-sense, which I found, agrees well with that found by Kramer. Contrary to his report, however, the determinations could be made without difficulty in a basin of normal size. The difference he observed in the response in small as compared to large basins, is therefore, presumably not, as he considered, to be interpreted as an echo of a "sound phenomenon". Possibly, surface waves contributed to the effect, as in the experiments on the lateral line organs such waves must have been produced by the wires that dipped into the water. That reflection of these waves should be more disturbing in a small aquarium than in a large one is obvious.[9]

Concerning the question brought up at the outset, in regard to the physical nature of the distant touch stimulus the following experiment must be mentioned. A glass sphere of 7 - 8 mm was suspended from a 30 cm long cotton thread and, at a depth of 5 - 8 cm, was dragged to the side of the body of a blind Xenopus, with as constant a speed as possible (about 10 cm/sec). Always the approaching sphere was perceived at a distance of 2 - 3 cm distance (rapid, target-oriented turn). Even in this experiment there can be no pressure waves, so that in Xenopus, as in fishes, it seems ascertained that displacement phenomena play a part in distant touch.

Summarizing, we conclude that in fish as in amphibians distance-touch-sense depends primarily upon damming phenomenon which develops in front of every body moving through water. In the case of perception at a distance of a resting body, it is the change in the displacement produced by the fish itself, i.e., the increase in water resistance, which is perceived. It is not correct to speak of "reflection" of water waves in this case, as is often done in the literature. Because flowing water is not reflected by collision with an object, but it is deflected along its surface.

Under water, Xenopus laevis reacts to minor surface waves, and that approximately to a depth of 10 cm.

[*Editor's Note:* In the original, an English summary follows the German article.]

Footnotes:

[1] S. Dijkgraaf, Z. vergl. Physiol. 20, 162-214 (1933).

[2] G. Kramer, Zool. Jb. Abt. Zool. Physiol. 52, 629-676 (1933).

[3] L. Prandtl, Abriss der Stromungslehre. Braunschweig 1931 (Abb. 50).

[4] G. Kramer, l.c., 645 (1933).

[5] S. Dijkgraaf, l.c., 174 (1933).

[6] K. von Frisch und H. Stetter, Z. vergl. Physiol. 17, 686-801 (1932).

[7] The animals were kindly given to me by Prof. Raven, and were raised at the Utrecht Zoological Institute.

[8] Surprisingly, Kramer nevertheless considers surface waves as "changes in the environment, which have little objectively in common with prey stimuli". (l.c., 632, 1933).

[9] However, Kramer's experiments must have been performed in relatively shallow water. At one point he speaks of a "shallowly filled basin;" further details are lacking.

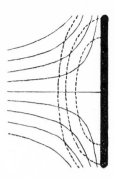

Fig. 1 Displacement-pressure lines (*dashed*) from a disc-shaped obstacle in a steady flow of water; in the converse case (*solid lines*), lines of equal ratio from a vibrating disc in standing water. (After Prandt 1.) Reprinted from *Experientia,* **3,** 206–208 (1947); copyright © 1947 by Birkhauser Verlag, Basel

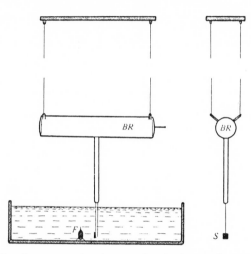

Fig. 2 Apparatus for the mechanical stimulation at a distance of *Nemachilus barbatulus* with a vibration-free moving plate. *Left,* side view; *right,* front view. BR, lead-filled tube (17 × 3 cm, 1250 g); F, fish; S, disc. Length of suspension wire, 125 cm; water depth, 5 cm. Reprinted from *Experientia,* **3,** 206–208 (1947); copyright © 1947 by Birkhauser Verlag, Basel

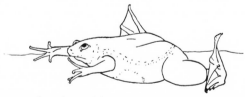

Fig. 3 The clawed frog, *Xenopus laevis,* resting on the bottom. Lateral line organs indicated (simplified around head). (After Kramer.) Reprinted from *Experientia,* **3,** 206–208 (1947); copryight © 1947 by Birkhauser Verlag, Basel

15

Reprinted from *J. Acoust. Soc. Amer.*, **34**(12), 1831–1841 (1962)

Evidence that the Lateral-Line Organ Responds to Near-Field Displacements of Sound Sources in Water

Gerard G. Harris and Willem A. van Bergeijk

Bell Telephone Laboratories, Inc., Murray Hill, New Jersey

The lateral-line organ of killifish is shown to be sensitive to a linear function of water displacements associated with the near-field of sound sources, with the displacement probably being the most important factor rather than velocity or acceleration. The near-field effect is discussed and is shown to be important not only for the lateral-line organs but also for the acoustical and vestibular organs. It is emphasized that the near-field effect introduces considerable complications into the study of the acoustico-lateralis system, and is of conceptual importance for the theory of hearing and the study of schooling in fish.

THE lateral line is a collection of sensory organs distributed over the skin of the lower aquatic vertebrates. Its name derives from the usually very prominent pigmented streak which runs along the flanks of most fishes. In this streak a great number of sensory organs is found. The lateral-line system is not confined to this "side-line," however, and is usually most elaborately developed on the head of the fish. Amphibian larvae, as well as adults of those species that spend most or all of their lives in water (e.g., *Xenopus* sp.), also have well-developed lateral-line systems. Since embryologically the lateral-line system and the inner ear derive from a common anlage, and since the innervation and morphology of the two organ systems are very similar, they are usually considered together in the textbooks as the *acoustico-lateralis system*. Although the morphological and developmental kinship of ear and lateral line is straightforward and well-established, their physiological and functional relationship has been a matter of dispute almost since the discovery of the lateral-line system, over a century ago.[1] The disagreement has centered on the question of what constitutes the proper stimulus for the lateral line. Reasoning by analogy would make one expect that the lateral line may be sensitive to sounds (like the auditory portions of the inner ear), to fluid motions (like the semicircular canals), or to some gravitational acceleration (like the otolith organs). Of course, the lateral line may have a wholly unique function, unlike any of the inner ear organs. The evidence available in the literature is almost equally divided in support of the first two hypotheses. Well-documented evidence[2–5] shows the lateral line sensitive to "low-frequency vibrations." The work of Jielof, Spoor, and de Vries[3] and the work of Kuiper[4]

are particularly compelling in this respect. Equally compelling evidence supports the view that the lateral line is sensitive to water currents only[6–8]; the experiments of Sand[8] and the beautiful work of Dijkgraaf[6] are the outstanding contributions here.

We wish to develop a case in favor of the notion that the lateral-line organ is predominantly sensitive to water displacements. We also wish to point out that the two views expressed above are both partially correct and that great care must be taken in the study of the acoustico-lateralis system to separate both physical stimuli and sense modalities. To do this it is useful to discuss some general effects of moving objects in water and the acoustic *near-field effect* in particular.[9] This is done in Sec. I. Section II then deals with some experiments with the lateral-line organ on the head of killifish (*Fundulus heteroclitus*) which show that the lateral-line canal organ is sensitive to water displacements. Finally, in Sec. III general comments are presented concerning some of the complications which may arise when measuring hearing and related sense modalities in aquatic animals.

I. EFFECTS OF THE ACOUSTIC NEAR-FIELD

When people make measurements on the hearing of fish, they usually consider pressure variation as the important physical stimulus. The pressure variations are considered to be produced by sounds (i.e., compressional waves) which propagate at a velocity of about 1440 m/sec in water. The situation is in reality much more complex. In the first place, it is easy to produce pressure changes in water by varying water depth and by changing water currents, as well as by

[1] G. H. Parker, "The Function of the Lateral-Line Organs in Fishes," Bull. Bur. Fisheries **24**, 185–207 (1904) gives an early historical review of the subject.

[2] G. H. Parker and A. P. Van Heusen, "The Reception of Mechanical Stimuli by the Skin, Lateral-Line Organs and Ears in Fishes, especially Amiurus," Am. J. Physiol. **44**, 463–489 (1917).

[3] R. Jielof, A. Spoor, and Hl. de Vries, "The Microphonic Activity of the Lateral Line," J. Physiol. **116**, 137–157 (1952).

[4] J. W. Kuiper, "The Microphonic Effect of the Lateral-Line Organ," Publication of the Biophysical Group of the "Natuurkundig Laboratorium," Groningen, Netherlands.

[5] E. E. Suckling and J. A. Suckling, "The Electrical Response of the Lateral-Line System of Fish to Tone and other Stimuli," J. Gen. Physiol. **34**, 1–8 (1950).

[6] S. Dijkgraaf, "Untersuchungen über die Function der Seitenorgane an Fischen," Z. vergl. Physiol. **20**, 162–214 (1934).

[7] O. Lowenstein, "The Acoustico–Lateralis System" in *The Physiology of Fishes*, edited by Margaret E. Brown (Academic Press Inc., New York, 1957), Vol. II, pp. 155–186.

[8] A. Sand, "The Mechanism of the Lateral Sense Organs of Fishes," Proc. Roy. Soc. (London) **B123**, 472–495 (1937).

[9] R. J. Pumphrey, "Hearing," Soc. Experimental Biology Symposium No. 4, 3–18 (1950) gives a discussion of the near-field effect. It is surprising that his understanding of the lateral-line organ did not reach a wider audience. Also, in 1934, Dijkgraaf gave an essentially correct, though nonquantitative, description of the near-field effects (see reference 6, pp. 173–174), but he failed to see the relationship between local-water motions and other acoustic phenomena.

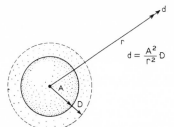

$$d = \frac{A^2}{r^2} D$$

FIG. 1. Symbols used to describe the near field of a pulsating sphere.

generating compressional waves. In the second place, one can generate water displacements which are not related to compressional waves, but can also stimulate the ear. In order to understand these matters better we consider pressure changes, water displacements, and their relation to each other in more detail.

Consider a compressional plane wave. Because of the low compressibility of water, the particle velocity for water-borne sound waves is much smaller than the particle velocity in air produced by the same pressure variations. The relationship between the magnitude of the particle velocity u and the pressure p in a plane wave is given by the equation

$$u = p/\rho c, \qquad (1)$$

where ρ is the density of the medium and c is the velocity of sound in the medium. In cgs units ρc in water is 144 000 g cm^{-2} sec^{-1}. Thus, if the pressure variation is 1 μbar (this is 74 dB re 0.0002 dyn cm^{-2}), the particle velocity is 7×10^{-6} cm sec^{-1}.

Particle velocity is independent of frequency, but the particle displacement is a decreasing function of frequency. The relationship between the velocity amplitude u and displacement amplitude d is given by the equation $u = 2\pi f d$, where f is the frequency of the sinusoidal sound wave. If we assume a frequency of 100 cps and a pressure amplitude of 1 μbar, the particle–displacement amplitude will be 10^{-8} cm or 1 Å for water.[10] Water displacement is seen to be very small even though a pressure amplitude of 1 μbar is considerable. A compressional wave by itself is a poor way of producing water displacements.

For sound waves in air the situation is quite different, due to the large compressibility of gases. In this case $\rho c = 44$ g cm^{-2} sec^{-1} and for a pressure amplitude of 1 μbar the particle–velocity amplitude is 2.2×10^{-2} cm sec^{-1}, or 70 dB larger than that for water. The factor of 70 dB also holds for displacement amplitude,

[10] This amplitude may be compared to the expected amplitude of the cupula due to Brownian motion. If we consider the cupula to be a simple harmonic oscillator, then the rms Brownian noise amplitude A is given by

$$A = (2kT/\omega^2 m)^{\frac{1}{2}},$$

where k is Boltzmann's constant, T is the absolute temperature, ω is the resonant frequency of the cupula, and m is its mass. With values appropriate to *Fundulus* A is about 20 Å.

so for 100 cps a 1-μbar pressure amplitude produces a 3×10^{-5}-cm or 3000-Å displacement amplitude.

There are, of course, many other causes of water displacement besides compressional waves. We do not consider water displacement caused by gravity, temperature differences, or rotational motion, but only those caused by moving objects. A solid object has to displace the water through which it moves. Motion is greatest near the object, but the pattern of motion máy extend out some distance. This may easily be seen in the case of a pulsating sphere (Fig. 1). If a sphere of radius A increases in size by an amount D, then, by the principle of conservation of volume and by considerations of symmetry, the water at a distance r from the sphere moves radially away from the sphere a distance d, where

$$d = (A^2/r^2)D. \qquad (2)$$

Displacement falls off as $1/r^2$.

When something moves but does not change volume, water displacements are more localized, for the water tends to move around the object and into the region just vacated. To be more specific, when a sphere moves a distance small compared to its size, the water displacement at a distant point is inversely proportional to the cube of the distance from the point to the center of the sphere. This result can be obtained from the velocity pattern around a sphere moving with a velocity U in a liquid at rest at infinity. For the velocity potential Φ in this particular case, Milne–Thompson[11] gives the expression

$$\Phi = \tfrac{1}{2} U A^3 (\cos\theta/r^3), \qquad (3)$$

where θ is the angle between the direction of motion of the sphere and the radius vector joining the center of the sphere and the point in question, r is the distance from the point to the center of the sphere, U is the velocity of the sphere, and A is its radius. Let $\theta = 0°$ be the direction parallel to the velocity of the sphere. Then $u_r = \partial\Phi/\partial r$ and $u_\theta = r^{-1}(\partial\Phi/\partial\theta)$, where u_r is the particle velocity of the liquid in the direction of the radius vector and u_θ is the particle velocity perpendicular to the radius vector, in the plane formed by the radius vector and the velocity of the sphere (see Fig. 2). Thus we have

$$u_r = U A^3 \cos\theta/r^3 \quad \text{and} \quad u_\theta = \tfrac{1}{2}(U A^3 \sin\theta/r^3).$$

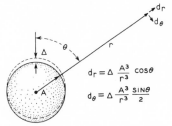

$$d_r = \Delta \frac{A^3}{r^3} \cos\theta$$

$$d_\theta = \Delta \frac{A^3}{r^3} \frac{\sin\theta}{2}$$

FIG. 2. Symbols used to describe the near field of a vibrating sphere.

[11] L. M. Milne–Thompson, *Theoretical Hydrodynamics* (The Macmillian Company, New York, 1955), 3rd ed., p. 445.

It must be noted that this is the velocity in the reference frame of the fluid but that r and θ are measured from the moving sphere. We can obtain an expression for the distance moved in the case where it is so small that r and θ are considered as constants throughout the motion. Then

$$d_r = \Delta(A^3/r^3)\cos\theta,$$

$$d_\theta = \Delta(A^3/r^3)(\sin/2)\theta. \tag{4}$$

In these equations Δ is the displacement of the sphere. The actual displacement at a given point is the vector sum of the angular and radial displacements.

It is seen that the largest displacements occur when $\theta = 0$. When $\theta = 90°$ the water displacements are parallel, but in directions opposite to the sphere displacement.

The above derivations for the water movements around a pulsating sphere and a displaced sphere are true only for an incompressible fluid. When the fluid is compressible a propagated wave is produced and, though the situation is more complicated, it is remarkably similar. This may be illustrated for the case of the pulsating sphere.[12] In a real fluid the pressure distribution obeys a wave equation. Since for a pulsating sphere there is spherical symmetry, the outgoing pressure wave p obeys the radial-wave equation

$$\frac{1}{r^2}\frac{\partial}{\partial r}\left(r^2\frac{\partial p}{\partial r}\right) = \frac{1}{c^2}\frac{\partial^2 p}{\partial t^2}, \tag{5}$$

and so p has the form

$$p = (P/r)\exp\{i\omega[t - (r/c)]\}, \tag{6}$$

where P is a constant to be determined from the displacement of the sphere, c is the velocity of sound, and ω is the angular frequency. The particle velocity u is related to the pressure via Newton's equation, which for spherically symmetric waves has the form

$$\rho(\partial u_r/\partial t) = -\partial p/\partial r. \tag{7}$$

In this equation ρ is the density of the fluid. Since u_r is an exponential function of time, $u_r = u_{0r}e^{i\omega t}$, we can solve for u_r from Eq. (7),

$$u_r = \frac{P}{\rho c r}\exp\left[i\omega\left(t - \frac{r}{c}\right)\right]\left(1 + \frac{c}{i\omega r}\right). \tag{8}$$

We assume that the radius of the sphere is much smaller than a wavelength λ; then $c/\omega r = \lambda/2\pi$ and $\lambda/2\pi A \gg 1$. If $U = U_0 e^{i\omega t}$ is the radial particle velocity at the surface of the sphere, P can be found to be

$$P = i\omega\rho A^2 U_0 e^{i\omega(A/c)}. \tag{9}$$

Substituting this value of P into Eq. (8) we find that u_r

is the sum of two terms,

$$u_r = \frac{A^2 U_0}{r^2}\exp\left[i\omega\left(t - \frac{r}{c} + \frac{A}{c}\right)\right]$$
$$+ \frac{i\omega A^2 U_0}{cr}\exp\left[i\omega\left(t - \frac{r}{c} + \frac{A}{c}\right)\right]. \tag{10}$$

The same equation holds for the particle displacement d_r if the particle displacement at the sphere D_0 is used instead of U_0, thus,

$$d_r = \frac{A^2 D_0}{r^2}\exp\left[i\omega\left(t - \frac{r}{c} + \frac{A}{c}\right)\right]$$
$$+ \frac{i\omega A^2 D_0}{cr}\exp\left[i\omega\left(t - \frac{r}{c} + \frac{A}{c}\right)\right]. \tag{11}$$

The first term in Eq. (11) is dominant for distances less than a wavelength and is called the near-field effect. We see that it is the same as Eq. (2) obtained for an incompressible fluid, except for the propagation–phase delay $\exp\{-i\omega[(r-A)/c]\}$. The second term is dominant at distances much greater than a wavelength and is the usual *far-field* wave. Note that the far field is dependent on the first power of the frequency, while the near field is independent of frequency except for its phase.

The case for an oscillating sphere is similar but more complicated, due to the angular dependence of the

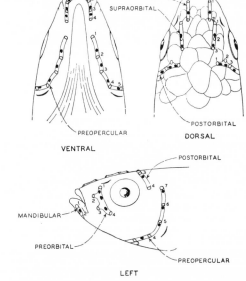

FIG. 3. Location of lateral-line canals on the head of the killifish. The numbered open circles represent pores of the canals opening to the outside. The black dots represent the sensory maculae inside the canals (from van Bergeijk and Alexander[13]). Most experiments were done by inserting an electrode in pore 2 of the nasal canal.

---

[12] See, for instance, P. M. Morse, *Vibration and Sound* (McGraw-Hill Book Company, Inc., New York, 1948), pp. 311–319.

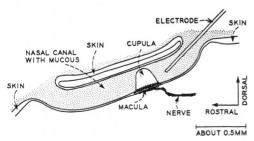

ELECTRODE→   SKIN

SKIN   CUPULA

NASAL CANAL
WITH MUCOUS

SKIN

MACULA   NERVE   ROSTRAL

DORSAL

ABOUT 0.5MM

FIG. 4. Schematic of a longitudinal section of the nasal canal with electrode in position for recording.

wave.[12] In the near field the radial component of the displacement magnitude is approximated by

$$d_r = (A^3/r^3)\Delta\cos\theta. \tag{12a}$$

In the far field the displacement magnitude is approximated by

$$d_r = \tfrac{1}{2}(\omega^2 A^3/c^2 r)\Delta\cos\theta. \tag{12b}$$

Note that the near field is again independent of frequency, while the far field increases as the square of the frequency.

More complicated motions of the source produce more complicated displacements which are not considered here. The important points to remember are the existence of the near-field effect in real fluids and the relative magnitudes of the near-field and far-field displacements. One can readily show from Eq. (12) that, for a frequency of 100 cps and a distance of $r \approx 4$ cm from a vibrating sphere of radius 1 cm, the ratio of near-field to far-field displacement is about 10^4.

Equations (11) and (12) are derived for an infinite medium. In experiments such as those to be reported here the finite size of the tank must be taken into account. The size of the tank affects the far-field considerably if it is small compared to a wavelength, but fortunately it has little effect on the near field if it is large compared to the size of the source. The tank used in our experiments was designed with this in mind. Both a vibrating ball and a vibrating plunger were used. The water movement around a ball is well represented by Eq. (4), since the phase delay is negligible. The field around a plunger is more complicated, but, as will be seen, the plunger is used for its directional properties only.

II. EXPERIMENTS ON KILLIFISH (FUNDULUS HETEROCLITUS)

Killifish were used in these experiments because they are a small, hardy, easily available fish with a well-developed system of head lateral-line canals. Figure 3 shows the system of head lateral-line organs as described by van Bergeijk and Alexander.[13] A brief resume

[13] W. A. van Bergeijk and S. Alexander, "Lateral Line Canal Organs on the Head of *Fundulus heteroclitus*," J. Morph. **110**, 333–346 (1962).

of the pertinent anatomy is given here, but reference should be made to their paper for more detail. Most of the experiments to be described were performed on the nasal canal organ. It consists of a sensory macula (represented in Fig. 3 by a black dot) at the bottom of a covered canal which is open to the water at each end (represented by open circles), and which runs close under the surface of the skin. The other canal organs are more complicated in arrangement, but can be visualized as strings of simple canals which share the same surface openings. There is always only one sensory macula between every two-canal opening. Figure 4 shows a longitudinal section of the nasal canal. In *Fundulus* the sensory macula sits near the posterior opening of the canal. In the middle of the macula a strip of about 80 sensory cells runs the length of the macula in the direction of the canal axis. Hair filaments protrude from these cells into a jelly-like cupula which rests upon the macula. The remaining part of the canal is filled with mucous.

Microphonics from the lateral-line organ were discovered by Jielof et al.[3] and were extensively studied by Kuiper.[4] These authors established, among other things, the striking fact that the frequency of the microphonic is double the stimulus frequency and that the lateral-line organ behaves as a mechanical system with a simple resonant frequency around 100 cps. Both water currents and an ingenious magnetic coupling to the cupula were used as stimuli. It was not clear from their work, however, what stimulates the lateral-line organ in the natural situation. Most of their work was done on *Acerina cernua*. We have found that the same qualitative features hold for *Fundulus*.

The experimental equipment is shown in Figs. 5 and 6. The fish was anesthetized in a 0.01% solution of MS–222–Sandoz (tricaine methanesulphonate). Care was taken to find the strength of solution which will

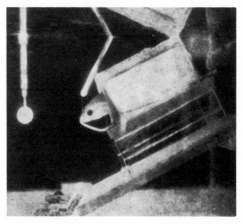

FIG. 5. Essentials of the experimental setup: Fish in foam-rubber clamp with grounding plate in the mouth, electrode in nasal canal, and 1-cm-diam vibrating ball about 3.5 cm in front of the nasal canal. Electrode slightly retouched to ensure good reproduction.

keep the fish immobile, but also alive. The fish was put into a double-strength solution for immobilization and then transferred to the regular-strength solution for experimentation. The fish would easily recover upon replacement in fresh water after an hour's experimentation. Recovery was not so certain after longer times. The water volume was approximately $30\times30\times10$ cm which was calculated to be large enough to minimize boundary effects. The fish was clamped by its body between two shaped pieces of sponge rubber, while the fish's head was held still by a nickel-silver biting piece which also served as an electrical ground. The source of water movement was a 5-mm radius ball or a 2-mm-diam piston, driven by a modified loudspeaker coil, and positioned by a mechanical arm adapted from a radial saw.

The electrode was a 50-μ Nichrome wire, insulated except for the tip. It was mechanically attached to a micropositioner and electrically attached to a type 122 Tektronix preamplifier. A schematic of the electronic equipment is shown in Fig. 7. The noise level at the input was about 10 μV in the band between 8–1000 cps. Since we wished to pick up signals which ranged from above 50 μV to below 1 μV, it was necessary to use an averaging technique in order to increase the signal-to-noise ratio. This is most conveniently and accurately done by digital sampling and computing techniques.[14] The sine waves used to drive the vibrating ball were generated by dividing the frequency of a square wave by 24 and low-pass filtering. Simultaneously, sampling pulses were generated at the frequency of the original square wave. Thus, each period of the stimulating sine wave is associated with 24 sampling pulses. The output of the lateral-line organ in response to the sine wave was

FIG. 6. General view of experimental setup showing tank, micropositioner for electrode, ball driver with strobe light attached, radial-saw positioner, and operating microscope.

sampled at these 24 pulse times per period; 500 periods were averaged by an IBM 7090 computer. Because of the fixed relationship between the signal driving the ball and the sampling pulses, the data could be produced with known phase relations. The equipment proved to be quite adaptable and signals of 1 μV could be reliably measured. Since we sampled at 24 samples per period, the maximum stimulating frequency we could generate was about 400 cps; at this point the sampling *rate* reached 10 kc, which was the maximum rate of which the analog-to-digital equipment was capable.

The electrode does not need to touch the cupula in order to detect microphonics. Figure 4 shows the electrode ready for recording in the nasal canal. As the

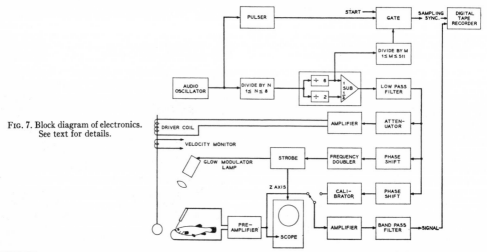

FIG. 7. Block diagram of electronics. See text for details.

[14] For a discussion of the principles underlying this statement and an introduction to the major techniques, see "Processing Neuroelectric Data," Technical Report 351, Research Laboratory of Electronics, Massachusetts Institute of Technology; also H. S. McDonald, "Techniques of Processing Signals in Biomedicine," North East Electronic Research and Engineering Meeting Record 1961, pp. 110–111.

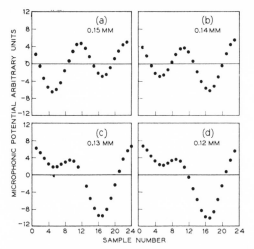

FIG. 8. Averaged microphonic potentials from a nasal canal in response to single periods of a sinusoidal stimulus. Each dot is the average of the samples from 500 consecutive periods. Plots (a)–(d) are recorded at different electrode distances from the cupula. In plot (a) the electrode is separated from the cupula, while in plot (d) the electrode is touching and pushing on the cupula. Note that as the electrode makes contact with the cupula, one of the negative peaks is reduced. The numerical values of the distances refer to an arbitrary zero point.

electrode is removed from the cupula, the microphonic diminishes. Half-maximum is about 0.2–0.3 mm from the cupula. Once the electrode is out of the canal, the microphonic diminishes rapidly, though there may be a residual tail which extends out a few millimeters. If the electrode touches the cupula, the microphonic shows bias effects.[3,4] Figure 8 shows a series of averaged microphonic potentials as a function of electrode distance from the cupula. The potentials are shown as a series of 24 discrete sample points, each of which is the average of 500 samples. In Fig. 8(a) the electrode is near but not touching the cupula. The most obvious characteristic is that there are two negative excursions of the microphonic for each cycle of the stimulus. In successive plots (b), (c), and (d) the electrode touches and pushes on the cupula. One of the negative pulses is reduced. We think that this is due to the fact that the electrode prohibits movement of the cupula in the direction toward the electrode. Each direction of swing of the cupula produces a negative swing of the potential, and when the swing in one direction is blocked, the corresponding microphonic peak belonging to a particular direction of swing can be ascertained, and so the phase can be determined.

The magnitude of the microphonic varies from fish to fish. For constant stimulus magnitude the potential magnitude can easily vary by a factor of 10 depending on the position of the electrode, conductivity of the water, condition of the particular organ, and condition of the animal as a whole.

The magnitude of the microphonic potential was measured in the following way: four points, the two positive and two negative extremes, were selected. Half the difference between the sum of the positive extremes and the sum of the negative extremes was selected as the microphonic potential magnitude. For moderate magnitudes of microphonic potential these four samples are usually 90° apart. When the microphonic is large enough to be in a region of saturation, often the positive valleys are not midway between the negative peaks. At low microphonic amplitudes, noise or some spurious first harmonic sometimes obscures the extremal values. Since for a constant frequency the phase does not change with amplitude, the points of extremes were established from microphonics of moderate amplitude and extrapolated to the low-amplitude plots. Points at 90° separation were selected in the low-amplitude plots to insure cancellation of any first harmonic. The magnitude of the microphonic was compared to the magnitude of a calibration voltage which was put through the same sampling and averaging procedure.

From these preliminary considerations let us proceed to the experimental evidence that the lateral-line organ is sensitive to water displacements. It is convenient to express this evidence in three conclusions. The first is the most general and, at the same time, in the opinion of the authors, the most firmly established. The second and third conclusions are more particular and somewhat less firmly established.

1. The lateral line is sensitive to the near field. With a vertically vibrating sphere as a source of water motion, the microphonic potential was measured both as a function of the distance of the source to the lateral-line

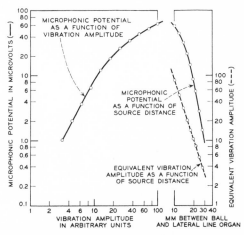

FIG. 9. Plots of the microphonic potential amplitude. The left-hand plot was taken with the ball at a constant distance from the fish. The upper right-hand plot, for which the same vertical scale is used, was taken with constant vibration amplitude. Both were taken at a vibration rate of 100 cps. Eliminating the microphonic potential from both these curves results in the lower right-hand plot, which refers to the right vertical scale. See text for details.

organ and as a function of the amplitude of vibration. Figure 9 shows, for one fish, a plot of these two functions, which demonstrates characteristic features of the data. The left-hand curve is the microphonic potential, plotted in log-log coordinates as a function of vibration amplitude of the ball with the ball held at a fixed distance and fixed frequency. In this particular case the ball was centered 21 mm from the anterior pore of the nasal canal and the frequency was 100 cps. The vibration amplitude is expressed in arbitrary units. An amplitude of 100 corresponds to an actual peak-to-peak ball displacement of 340 μ. Since the radius of the ball is 5 mm, the displacement at the nasal canal, if there were no fish present, is reduced by a factor $\frac{1}{2}(5/21)^3$ and so is approximately 2 μ. This value will certainly be altered by the body of the fish, but it is useful as an order of magnitude.

It is seen that the microphonic potential as a function of amplitude varies as the square of the displacement for potentials near 1 μV. For larger potentials the curve shows considerable saturation effects. Higher potentials than those shown in Fig. 9 can sometimes be recorded; they show even more saturation.

The upper right-hand curve shows the microphonic potential as a function of distance. The abscissa represents on a log scale the distance between the ball center and lateral-line organ in mm. The frequency and amplitude of vibration are kept constant—in this case 100 cps and an amplitude of 10 on the arbitrary scale. From this curve one can see that the microphonic potential falls off rapidly with distance, though it does not show a simple power-law dependence.

It is interesting to combine both curves by eliminating the microphonic potential. That is, for each distance the vibration amplitude of the ball is plotted which produced the same microphonic potential at the reference distance. The curve is one of equivalent amplitude as a function of distance and is a representative of the way the displacement amplitude at the lateral-line canal varies as the source is moved. Such a plot is shown in the lower right-hand part of Fig. 9. The points lie in a straight line on a log–log plot, indicating a power-law dependence. The slope of the curve for this

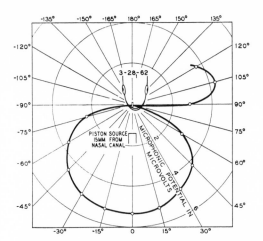

FIG. 10. Angular response of the nasal canal organ indicating its directional sensitivity. The fish is labeled by the date the experiment was done.

particular case is -3.0 ± 0.3, which is in good agreement with a slope of -3.0 expected from the near-field effect of a vibrating ball. Other killifish give similar results. Table I shows a list of fish and the slopes calculated from the curves of equivalent amplitude vs distance. The average of 9 different runs is -3.1 ± 0.1. The errors expressed here are estimates from the reproducibility of the curves. Since this slope is the same, within the experimental error, as one would expect from the near-field effect, we conclude that the lateral line is sensitive to the near-field effect. From these data alone it is difficult to say more than this, for the exact way the microphonic varies with amplitude has been eliminated from the curves. For instance, one might suppose that the lateral-line organ is sensitive to velocity squared and thus to inertial pressure. To be more definite in our conclusions we must proceed to further experiments.

2. *The lateral line is sensitive to a linear function of water displacement.* Measurements of the microphonic potential for changing directions of displacement support the above conclusion. The apparatus was modified to take a piston driver whose displacement vector was in the horizontal plane. The source could rotate at a variable radius around a vertical axis. The source was oriented so that the water displacement was directed toward the axis of rotation. The net result is that at the axis of rotation the magnitude of the displacement was kept constant, but its direction could be rotated in the horizontal plane. The nasal lateral-line organ was placed at the axis of rotation. The head and body of the fish destroy the symmetry of the apparatus, but not too much in the arc extending between the 90° points on either side of the forward axis of the nasal canal. Figure 10 shows the microphonic potential as a function of displacement direction. The curve appears to be a fair representation of a cosine curve in polar coordinates

TABLE I. Slopes of equivalent near-field amplitude vs distance obtained from experiments described in text.

Fish	Slope from log–log plot of equivalent amplitude *vs* distance
January 22, 1962	-3.0 ± 0.3
February 2, 1962	-3.6 ± 0.3
	-3.2 ± 0.3
March 20, 1962	-2.8 ± 0.3
	-3.0 ± 0.3
March 28, 1962	-3.9 ± 0.3
	-3.2 ± 0.3
April 17, 1962	-2.5 ± 0.3
	-3.0 ± 0.3
Average	-3.1 ± 0.1

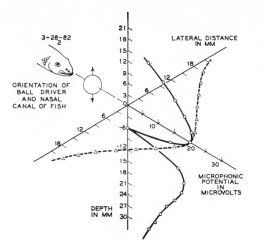

FIG. 11. Response of the nasal canal to lateral and vertical motions
of the vibrating sphere.

which would result if the component of a vector along the axis of the canal were the source of the microphonic potential.

Figure 11 shows the results of another experiment which also supports this conclusion. Here the ball source, vibrating at 100 cps with constant amplitude, is moved both *horizontally* and *vertically* in front of the fish. Both movements take place in a plane perpendicular to the fish's axis, a few milimeters in front of the animal. The vibration of the ball is vertical and, thus, in a horizontal plane passing through the center of the ball, the water displacements are also vertical, but 180° out of phase with the ball motion. When the ball is moved horizontally from left to right in front of the fish, the displacement *direction* at the nasal canal remains constant, but the displacement *magnitude* changes because the distance from the ball to the nasal canal changes. Thus, as shown in Fig. 11, the maximum microphonic potential is obtained with the ball directly in front of the fish, while the potential decreases as lateral distance is increased.

When the ball is moved *vertically*, the situation is more complicated. Not only is there a change in magnitude of water displacement, but also in direction. When this direction becomes 90° with respect to the axis of the canal, there is a null in the microphonic potential. The depth plot in Fig. 11 shows this null at 6 mm below the nasal canal.

The simplest interpretation of these data is to say that the microphonic potential is produced by a linear vector in the same direction as the canal axis. A linear function is certainly favored over a square or higher integral function. The choice of what linear function best represents the forcing term depends on additional experiments.

3. The lateral-line canal organ is probably most sensitive to water displacements rather than to velocity or acceleration. To make this conclusion, it is necessary to examine how the microphonic potential varies as a function of the *frequency* of vibration of the stimulus. Figure 12 shows a plot of the microphonic potential as a function of stimulus frequency for three different amplitudes of vibration. The curves show a simple resonance around 140 cps for the highest intensity, increasing to about 180 cps for the lowest intensity. The change in resonance frequency must be due to a nonlinear effect. This effect is present in most of the "tuning" curves which we have taken and is always in the same direction—higher resonant frequency for lower amplitude stimulation. The effect is not large enough, however, to change the phase pattern significantly.

To measure phase difference between the microphonic potential and the driver amplitude accurately, it is necessary to locate the extremal points of the microphonic potentials.

The microphonic potential is recorded at the rate of 24 samples per stimulus period. There is thus 15° between sample points and, if the extremal *sample* point were selected for phase measurements, there would be an uncertainty of ±8°. It is possible to obtain greater accuracy by simple interpolation procedures; we used the extremal of a parabola fitted to the extremal sample point and its two nearest neighbors.

The phase of the driver displacement was also recorded. As explained, it was necessary to put a calibration signal through the recording apparatus and IBM 7090 processing in order to determine the magnitude of the microphonic potential. The phase of the calibrating voltage was set to match the phase of the driver displacement. Phase measurements could then be

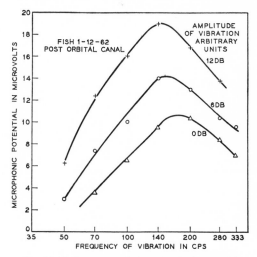

FIG. 12. Tuning curves of the microphonic potential
from a post-orbital canal.

305

made comparing the phase of the microphonic with the phase of the calibrating voltage. Figure 13 shows a plot of the phase measurements on four canal organs. The points of maximum microphonic amplitude are shown by the arrows. Except for the post-orbital canal, the phase of the microphonic at resonance occurs at about 120° behind displacement.

It is well known in mechanical systems that, at resonance, the response phase lags 90° behind the driving force. If displacement is the driving force, there is a 30° discrepancy to explain. It is difficult to explain this discrepancy by having part of the driving force proportional to velocity since velocity phase is ahead of displacement by 90°, and any addition of velocity should make the phase lag smaller than 90°, not larger. Viscous effects would also make the phase lag smaller than 90°. They represent a phase lead and were calculated to be on the order of 15° for a plane surface, but may be more inside a tube such as the lateral-line canal.

Kuiper[4] suggests that there is a delay between the physical displacement of the cupula and the microphonic potential. From his data, obtained by driving the cupula *directly* by means of a small magnet attached to it, he calculates that there is a delay of about 0.8 msec. A delay of this magnitude would also help to explain our data, for when such a correction is applied, the phases at resonance group around 90° lag with respect to water displacement. Thus, we could conclude that the driving force is proportional to the displacement. The data lack the precision to make this a compelling argument (there

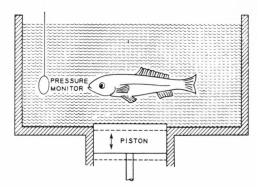

FIG. 14. Typical experimental setup for the study of fish hearing, as discussed in the text.

may be additional phase effects due to the plasticity of the fish body); nevertheless, the evidence is strongly suggestive that the water displacement in the vicinity of the canal supplies the principal driving force.

III. GENERAL CONSIDERATIONS

There is difficulty in separating the operation of the lateral-line organs, the auditory apparatus, and the vestibular apparatus in aquatic animals. The difficulty arises from the fact that there is not a distinct physical stimulus for each of these sense modalities. For instance, we have shown that water displacements excite the lateral-line organ, but under suitable conditions they may also excite the auditory and vestibular apparatus. On the other hand, pressure variations which are usually thought to be the stimulus for the auditory apparatus may also stimulate the lateral-line organ under some particular conditions.

Let us see how such confusion might occur in experiments on fish by considering a hypothetical experiment setup as shown in Fig. 14. A piston source is placed at the bottom of a small tank. The fish to be studied is placed approximately in the middle of the tank.[15] For high frequencies, when the dimensions of the tank are large relative to a wavelength, the piston is an efficient source of pressure waves. For low frequencies, however, it is not. The whole mass of water is accelerated rather than compressed, producing various types of near-field effects. When a pressure monitoring device is put into the tank, however, pressure variations are recorded nevertheless. The pressure at a point in the tank may change due to at least two factors. Suppose the area of the piston is $1/A$ times the area of the tank. Then, by conservation of volume, if the displacement of the piston is D, the surface displacement (neglecting surface waves) is D/A. At any position in the tank there is a

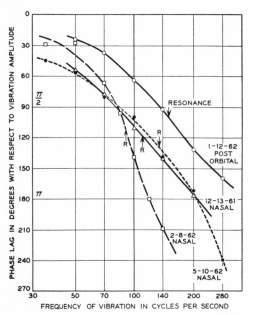

FIG. 13. Phase curves from four lateral-line canals. The resonant points, indicated by arrows R, are the frequencies of maximum response of tuning curves such as those shown in Fig. 12.

[15] This arrangement is very similar to one described by D. Poggendorf, "Die absolution Hörschwellen des Zwergwelses (*Amiurus nebulosus*) und Beiträge zur Physik des Weberschen Apparates der Ostariophysen.," Z. vergl. Physiol. 34, 222–257 (1952), though the essential parts are found in many experiments.

pressure variation, $\Delta p = \rho g \Delta h$, where g is the acceleration due to gravity, 980 cm sec^{-2}, ρ is the density of the water, 1 g cm^{-3}, and Δh is the change in height of the water, which is D/A.

Another source of pressure change will be the changing current patterns. Bernouilli's equation says that in the steady state, the pressure, depth, and velocity of a liquid are related by the equation $p - \rho g h + \rho v^2 =$ constant. If the frequency of change is low enough (i.e., dimensions of the tank are small compared to a wavelength), then this equation is approximately valid for time-varying water currents. Thus, the pressure can change due to varying currents. For the tank in Fig. 14 the pressure change due to the ρv^2 term would be a function of position, and the pressure change would be a factor $1/A^2$ less near the surface than near the piston. The water *motion* acts upon the lateral-line organ, and the *pressure changes* act upon the auditory apparatus. However, if the fish has a swimbladder connected to the ear, it may be stimulated in a complicated manner by the water displacements which deform the tissues and thus indirectly play upon the bladder.[16] Moreover, because of the large water displacements, the whole fish is moved and the vestibular apparatus may also be stimulated. Unfortunately, while all these organs are being stimulated, it is very difficult to monitor the stimulus. For instance, a pressure monitor may respond to water currents in a manner very different from the swimbladder's response.

The above is an example of how the near-field effect can stimulate the acoustical and vestibular apparatus as well as the lateral line. The situation can also be somewhat reversed. Suppose that by some device (such as eliminating the free surface) a pressure variation without a large near-field type of displacement is produced. Then it is still not safe to say that only the acoustical apparatus is stimulated since the fish may itself be a source of local near-field motion. If the fish has a swimbladder, pressure changes change the volume of the bladder, producing a local near-field effect which could stimulate the lateral-line organ. The buoyancy of the fish will also be changed and the subsequent oscillations in depth, in the fashion of a Cartesian diver, may stimulate the vestibular apparatus.

From this discussion it is clear that considerable care must be taken in investigating the acoustico-lateralis system of fishes and other aquatic animals if one wishes to separate the functions of the lateral-line organ, auditory apparatus, and vestibular apparatus.

It is also quite clear that the separate functions of the acoustico-lateralis system are intimately interrelated and that it may be worthwhile to consider the acoustico-lateralis system as a whole. It is certainly true that the parts of this system are related both embryologically and phylogenetically. In the embryo a primitive

placode develops, part of which remains on the surface and develops into the lateral-line system, and part of which invaginates and develops into the acoustical and vestibular systems. All three systems have hair cells of similar form and all three systems may perhaps be looked upon as volume-displacement detectors. The lateral line has remained a primitive water-displacement detector sensitive primarily to the near-field displacement. The acoustical system has receded into the head, which minimizes the effect of local water displacements, and, in the course of evolution, a middle ear has been added to convert pressure waves to volume displacements. In the human cochlea it is a fluid displacement which produces motions of the basilar membrane, thus generating a shear between the tectorial membrane and the hair cells.

Middle ears do, of course, have many different forms, and the conventional mammalian middle ear is only one example. The swimbladders and Weberian apparatus of *Ostariophysi*, the swimbladders with blindsacs connecting to the ear in the *Clupeids*, and the lungs of amphibian larvae connecting to the round windows of the ears[17] are other examples. A direct connection to the ear may not even be necessary; the spinal column or even the soft tissue may be sufficient to transmit the near-field effect of the vibrating bladder or lung. Aquatic middle ears apparently make use of trapped gas bubbles, while terrestrial middle ears rely on drum membranes for the interception of propagated sound energy.

The vestibular apparatus has such devices as aragonite crystals in the otolith organs which make them more sensitive to gravitational accelerations, and inertial fluid columns in the semicircular canals which make them sensitive to angular accelerations.

All of these systems make use of hair cells in one form or another. The evidence in Sec. II indicates that the hair cells in the head lateral-line organ of killifish are sensitive to displacement. It may be that all hair cells are displacement detectors. Such an hypothesis provides a useful point of view to investigate the function of hair cells in the vestibular and auditory apparatus of different species. At the same time it would be surprising if there were not some differences between hair-cell operation as found in different species. Indeed, there is the striking difference that the cochlear microphonic closely follows the sound–pressure variation, while the microphonic from the lateral-line organ is second harmonic and shows other nonlinearities.

The present paper concentrates on the stimulus for the lateral-line canal organs. Nothing has been said about the very interesting questions as to the origin of the microphonic potential and the subsequent neural responses. Much further investigation needs to be done along these lines. Nothing has been said about the use the fish makes of the lateral-line organ. A few brief comments may be appropriate here. The killifish's eyes

---

[16] An analogous case in the human ear would be the sounds one hears when his ears are syringed to free them from wax. These sounds have little relationship to the local air-pressure variations.

[17] E. Witschi, "The Bronchial Columella of the Ear of Larval Ranidae," J. Morph. **96**, 497–512 (1955).

are located on the side of the head so that there is a "blind cone" in front of the head and mouth. The fish could use the lateral-line system to detect and zero in on food in this cone. The lateral line may be very important in the schooling of fish since with it a fish would be aware of the motion of nearby fish. Pumphrey[9] has noted that deep-water fish which live in the absence of light must use their lateral line extensively. He also points out an interesting property of the near-field effect, namely, that the effect is proportional to the volume of the moving object. Consequently, a fish can detect a large predator at a large distance, while his own motion would only be detectable to the predator at a much shorter distance. This also implies that a fish has to be close to his own food in order to detect it.

For schooling behavior of fishes this notion of Pumphrey's also has an interesting implication. All schooling fishes appear to have a very extensive lateral-line system.[18] If one accepts as axiomatic the notion that all fish in a school would tend to keep as far apart as possible, but not so far as to lose lateral-line "contact," then it would follow that, as the size of the individual fish increases through growth, the interfish spacing should increase approximately proportionally with body length. As length doubles, the amplitude of water motion at some point increases with a factor 8; when distance is doubled, a decrease of water motion at the point by a factor 1/8 results again, all according to Eq. (12a). Thus, in first approximation, one would predict that the *density* of a school of fish, expressed as cm^3 *of fish/* cm^3 *of water*, would remain constant. This is, of course, valid only if the sensitivity of the lateral line remains at the same level irrespective of the size of the fish.

As fish increase in size, their volume is not the only thing of importance that increases; the amplitude of body motion during swimming increases also. Since, again according to Eq. (12a), the water motion is proportional to this amplitude, the fish could be spaced farther than predicted from the length/distance relation. However, larger fish move their bodies at a lower frequency than smaller fish, and since these frequencies most certainly fall on the ascending slopes of Fig. 12, the effect on a lateral-line organ of the larger but less frequent motions of the big fish may well be of the same magnitude as the effects of the smaller but higher frequency motions of the little fish. Depending on the sensitivity of the lateral-line organs and the precise swimming dynamics of different species of fish, school density, if proven to be indeed a constant, may turn out to be species-specific. These speculations are, of course, only first-order approximations; many other factors, such as temperature and food density, to name a few, have their influence.

Breder[19] describes four distinct stable groupings of fish: *Pods*, in which the fish are in actual physical contact; *schools*, in which the fish do not touch, but remain at a certain distance and are lined up parallel; *aggregations*, in which the fish are more loosely assembled with random orientations; and finally, the *solitary* fish, who is in no way identifiable as a group member. Breder notes that these four states are *stable*; fish can apparently remain in them indefinitely, and the transitions from one state to another are sharp, with no apparent intermediate groupings existing. We believe that it is possible to suggest at least the upper bounds for stability in the first three of these groupings. The pod is apparently held together by actual physical contact of the fish bodies, the school is held together by lateral-line "contact," and the aggregation is stable as long as visual contact is maintained. The latter supposition suggests that aggregation density is strongly dependent on turbidity of the water. Finally, the solitary state would result when all sensory contact between individuals is lost.

ACKNOWLEDGMENTS

We would like to thank Professor S. Dijkgraaf for his stimulating correspondence, H. S. McDonald for his help with the design of the electronic apparatus, and J. L. Flanagan for discussions on the near-field effect.

[18] R. L. Edwards, U. S. Fisheries Biological Laboratory, Woods Hole, Massachusetts (personal communication).

[19] C. M. Breder, Jr., "Studies on Social Groupings in Fishes," Bull. Am. Museum Nat. Hist. **117**, 393–482 (1959).

AUTHOR CITATION INDEX

SUBJECT INDEX

About the Editor

WILLIAM N. TAVOLGA is Professor in the Departments of Biology and Psychology at the City University of New York, and he has been teaching biology at the City College since 1946. He has been Research Associate in the Department of Animal Behavior at the American Museum of Natural History since 1954, and is also currently Senior Research Associate at the Mote Marine Laboratory, Sarasota, Florida. After completing his undergraduate work at the City College, he received his Ph.D. at New York University in 1949, where he worked under Professors Charles M. Breder, Jr., and Roberts Rugh.

He was awarded a Public Health Research Fellowship in 1954–1955 and a Guggenheim Fellowship in 1967–1968. In 1974, he was awarded an Erskine Fellowship by the University of Canterbury, Christchurch, New Zealand, where he gave a series of lectures in animal behavior and animal communication. In addition, he has been principal investigator for grants and contracts from the National Science Foundation and the Office of Naval Research. He is a member of several scientific societies, including the Animal Behavior Society, of which he is a Fellow.

His primary research interests are in animal communication, bioacoustics, and behavior in marine organisms. He has over fifty scientific publications in these areas, as well as in the fields of embryology, parasitology, ecology, and ichthyology. He is author of a textbook in animal behavior and editor of two volumes on marine bioacoustics.

Dr. Tavolga has traveled widely throughout the world, and lectured in most of the areas he has visited. In addition to his scientific pursuits, he has many outside interests, comprising such disparate subjects as enology and amateur radio.